Date Due

AMERICAN CLASSICS
RECONSIDERED

BOOKS BY THE REVEREND HAROLD C. GARDINER, S. J.

MYSTERIES' END
NORMS FOR THE NOVEL
EDMUND CAMPION
CATHOLIC VIEWPOINT ON CENSORSHIP

FATHER GARDINER IS ALSO THE EDITOR OF:

FIFTY YEARS OF THE AMERICAN NOVEL: *A Christian Appraisal*
THE GREAT BOOKS: *A Christian Appraisal*
THOMAS à KEMPIS: *Imitation of Christ*

AMERICAN CLASSICS RECONSIDERED

A Christian Appraisal

EDITED BY

HAROLD C. GARDINER, S.J.

New York

CHARLES SCRIBNER'S SONS

Acknowledgement is made to the following publishers and other sources for permission to quote briefly from the books indicated.

J. M. Dent & Sons Ltd. (London)	*Notes on Life and Letters* by Joseph Conrad (1925)
The Dial Press, Inc.	*The Catholic Spirit in America* by George N. Shuster
Harvard University Press	*Emerson's Angle of Vision: Man and Nature in American Experience* by Sherman Paul (1952) *Spires of Form: A Study of Emerson's Aesthetic Theory* by Vivian C. Hopkins (1951) *The Transcendentalists: An Anthology* by Perry G. E. Miller (1950) Copyright 1950, 1951, 1952 by The President and Fellows of Harvard College
Harcourt Brace & Co., Inc.	*Main Currents in American Thought* by Vernon L. Parrington (1927-1930) *Selected Essays, 1917-1932* by T. S. Eliot (1932)
B. Herder Book Co.	*A Preface to Newman's Theology* by Edmond D. Bernard (1945) *Theology of the Mystical Body* by Emile Mersch (1952)
Hodder & Stoughton, Ltd. and A. P. Watt & Son (London)	*Some Aspects of Modern Poetry* by Alfred Noyes (for British edition)
Alfred A. Knopf, Inc.	*Hieroglyphics* by Arthur Machen (1913)
J. B. Lippincott Co.	*Some Aspects of Modern Poetry* by Alfred Noyes (1924) (for American edition)
Longmans Green & Co., Inc.	*Church and State* by Luigi Sturzo, Copyright 1939
Macmillan Company, The	*The Literary History of the United States* by Robert E. Spiller et al. Copyright 1953 The Macmillan Company
Meynell, Sir Francis	*The Works of Francis Thompson* (1913)
New Directions	*In the American Grain* by William Carlos Williams (1925). Copyright 1933 by William Carlos Williams
New England Quarterly, The	"Brownson and Emerson" by A. Robert Caponigri, September 1945 issue
Oxford University Press	*Kierkegaard: The Point of View*, translated by Walter Lowrie (1939)
Princeton University Press	*Either/Or* by Sören Kierkegaard (1944), translated by Walter Lowrie
Reynolds & Son, Paul R.	*The Art of Fiction* by Henry James (1948). Reprinted by permission of Paul R. Reynolds & Son, 599 Fifth Avenue, New York 17, N. Y.
Scribner's Sons, Charles	*Modern Poetry and the Christian Tradition* by Amos N. Wilder (1952)
Sheed & Ward Limited (London)	*Freedom in the Modern World* by Jacques Maritain (1935) *What Is Literature* by Charles Du Bos (1940)
University of Chicago Press	*Symbolism and American Literature* by Charles Feidelson (1953)
University of Pennsylvania Press	*Freedom and Fate* by Steven E. Whicher (1953)

When half-gods go
The gods arrive.

EMERSON: *Give All to Love*

PREFACE

THE authors under consideration in this symposium are most probably our greatest collective claim to literary pre-eminence. They are also controversial figures. The controversy on some of them revolves around their literary stature: is Cooper, for instance, to be estimated merely in the terms applied to him by Mark Twain ("there have been daring people in the world who claimed that Cooper could write English, but they are all dead now") or in those accorded him by Wilkie Collins ("Cooper is the greatest artist in the domain of romantic fiction yet produced by America")? Or shall we be content merely to state with Vernon Parrington that "no other major writer, unless it be Whitman, has been so misunderstood, and no other offers a knottier problem to the student of American letters"? Again, did Poe have what James Russell Lowell called "that indescribable something which men have agreed to call *genius*"? or does Poe, as Dr. Durick states in his study, "tend to diminish in stature as we grow older"? —or is "genius" compatible with such diminution?

More puzzling, however, than the controversies which have arisen over the literary stature of these authors is the cloud of debate that has blown up about their philosophies and theologies, about their fundamental attitudes toward God, man, and nature, and the degree in which those attitudes have shaped or colored their work.

Was Emerson, to take him as perhaps the cardinal figure about whom the storms of debate have centered, the Pelagian such a critic as Yvor Winter would have us believe he was, and did his doctrine of self-reliance grow to its logical and awful climax in the suicide of Hart Crane? This is the position startlingly defended in Mr. Winters' chapter, "The Significance of *The Bridge* by Hart Crane," in *In Defense of Reason* (University of Denver, 1947, pp. 577-603). Or was there, as John Jay Chapman thinks, such "radiance" about his writings as about his personality that "while he lived his figure could be seen from Europe towering like Atlas over the culture of the United States." If that was his true stature, how could his influence have been as sinister as Winters estimates it was?

Or consider the various evaluations of the thought and influence of Walt Whitman. Even if we refuse to take seriously the public protests vociferated recently in New Jersey when the proposal was made to name a bridge in his honor—protests on the grounds that he was neither a great poet (he couldn't "see beyond his eyelids," it was claimed) nor a citizen of respectable moral life—it still remains true that many a popular estimate of the "good gray poet" relegates him to the role of a hairy-chested and uncouth chanter of incantations to a democracy he understood but little. On the other hand, D. H. Lawrence considers him "the greatest and the first and the only American teacher," though the teaching Lawrence attributes to Whitman may be considered a thing of very dubious worth indeed.

vi

And so the debates have gone. It may be, of course, that critical appraisal of these American writers is bound still to be slightly astigmatic, because even a hundred years or so do not afford quite enough distance for proper perspective. However that may be, the studies collected here make another valiant attempt at assessment, and I believe it is not too much to claim that this assessment is unique. This is the first time, to my knowledge, that a group of Catholic scholars has ever engaged in a corporate appraisal of our nineteenth-century American literary heritage. Back in 1950 a similar group of critics engaged, under the editorship of the present writer, to assess the more prominent modern American novelists in a symposium called *Fifty Years of the American Novel* (Scribner), and it may as well be frankly admitted that the warm accord extended to that joint work emboldened the editor to project, plan, and bring to completion this present volume.

What is unique about this corporate labor of literary scholars—beyond the mere fact of their collaboration? The uniqueness consists in this: here is a body of opinion which is explicitly based on Christian suppositions. Hawthorne's views, or Emerson's or Melville's, on free will, on God and man's relations to Him, on progress, on destiny or democracy, let us say, are here submitted to analysis by critics who not only weigh their subjects as artists, but who must inevitably evaluate those artists within an intellectual framework of accurately defined philosophical and theological beliefs.

This observation is not to be taken as implying that the contributors of the following chapters necessarily agree among themselves on the stature or ideologies of a particular author. It will become evident, for example, that Geoffrey Stone's asides on Hawthorne reveal that he does not consider him in the same light that Joseph Schwartz does—and so on. In other words, the editor did not give the critics any prior instructions or hints that they were to mold their appraisals to any rigid, restrictive Christian appraisal. But it still remains true that, writing as his individual reaction to his subject dictates, each author nevertheless bases his final judgment, where the great fundamentals of Christian thought and culture indicate such a foundation, on "pieties" that are older and more solid than the Puritan ones that will be referred to in the following pages.

I have referred above to the "golden age" of American letters. The phrase and the reality for which it stands may, of course, be debated. But certainly some of the authors here studied are the very greatest in our American literary pantheon. If not every one is of such stature, they all belong to a period in which there was a homogeneity in American letters that has never since been approached. And that homogeneity can be summed up best, I think, in the one word "God-ridden." Never since has a group of American writers been so explicitly concerned with the eternal problem of destiny, of man's place in the universe, of the agonies and glories of the soul. They were also, to be sure, concerned with more earthbound social problems—with the spirit of democracy, with the encroachments or the threat of a rising industrialization, with the vanishing frontier and the spawning city, with nationalism; but beneath all these concerns the burden of their pondering was "what is man, what is God?"

For those who wonder at the norm controlling the selection of these particular authors for study, I can only say that this is, I trust, an initial volume devoted to the nineteenth-century American greats. If the exclusion of Irving, Lowell, Bryant, Emily Dickinson, Henry Adams, and others seems strange or shortsighted, let me indicate that the chronological span here represented is, roughly, from the War of 1812 to the Civil War: that is, the bulk of the work here evaluated appeared within those years. These were, by and large, the years during which a distinctively American literature was burgeoning, and it is surely of great import that a distinctively American literature was at the same time so profoundly concerned with both the city of man that was the New America and the city of God that constantly, through the ages, beckons the "outsiders" and bids them come in.

Acknowledgments are inevitably the duty and the pleasure of all prefaces. Many who helped in this symposium by suggestions or by patient listening to the working out of half-formed ideas have been thanked in the way that matters most. I would like, however, to single out Rev. Joseph E. O'Neill, S.J., of Fordham University, who has not only contributed the chapter on Longfellow, but has also been most generous in sharing his wide knowledge of American literature. Professor John T. Frederick of Notre Dame University and Rev. Edward J. Drummond, S.J., of Marquette University, were particularly helpful in the initial stages of assembling contributors. Finally, my secretary, Miss Gloria M. Weingart, gave invaluable help not only in hours of typing but also in work on the bibliographies. To all—and to many more—my sincerest thanks and a heartfelt "God bless you."

HAROLD C. GARDINER, S.J.

CAMPION HOUSE
NEW YORK
February 22, 1957

CONTENTS

ix

AMERICAN CLASSICS
RECONSIDERED

THE ERA OF THE HALF-GODS
IN AMERICAN LITERATURE

HAROLD C. GARDINER, S. J.

As this volume was going through the final stages of preparation, the first book of a young English critic was receiving widespread attention on both sides of the Atlantic. Colin Wilson, at the age of twenty-four, had written a study, alternately praised for its insights and blamed for its youthful brashness, which had at least succeeded in introducing a new word into the vocabulary of criticism. The title of the book is *The Outsider*,[1] and if Mr. Wilson's concept of just exactly what an "outsider" is remains throughout the work considerably vague and confusing, it is also somewhat paradoxically true that his treatment of his ill-defined subject comes to a conclusion that has considerable bearing on an understanding of the American authors to be evaluated in this symposium.

Mr. Wilson's "outsider" is, to simplify, one who stands to some extent aloof from society and looks in or down upon it and, in the scrutiny, sees little that indicates society's awareness of or care for any goal or purpose. In this minimal sense, most of the authors who will be studied in these subsequent chapters can be called "outsiders." If, however, we come to differentiating "outsiders" as Mr. Wilson does roughly in his book, we shall have to contend that our American nineteenth-century authors were definitely *not* one class of "outsider." For the touchstone that Mr. Wilson seems to apply is the touchstone of futility. If an "outsider" looks on the world and its activities and, in his effort to discern some purpose in it all, comes to the conclusion that there *is* and *can be* no ultimate purpose, that there are no ultimate values and consequently no ultimate Yes or No, then, logically there would be no such thing as a literary "outsider," for what would be the purpose of writing a book that had no purpose save to say that nothing has any purpose? But such men have written books, and Mr. Wilson spends a great deal of his time and

I

wit in a discussion of extreme Existentialism. This class of "outsider" need not delay us in our introduction to the nineteenth-century American classics. Melville may have approached most closely the type of "outsider" who denies ultimate purpose to life and human activity, but even he came to discern a pattern of purpose toward the close of his life and, prior to that development, was driven far too passionately by the urge to *do* something toward finding a purpose in life to acquiesce in the intellectual Nirvana of a nineteenth-century Existentialism.

It is rather the second class of Mr. Wilson's "outsider" to which our nineteenth-century American writers can be assimilated. These are the men who look on society and, seeing the purposelessness with which most men live out their "once-born" lives, nevertheless conceive that there *ought* to be a purpose, and set out on its quest. Parenthetically, of course, it might be remarked that Mr. Wilson's glaring assumption is that "most" men never ask themselves if there is actually any ultimate Yes or No. If we believe, as indeed a study of human nature will force us to believe, that men are rational (though perhaps less acutely attuned than the creative geniuses to the problem of ultimates) and hence concerned at least for flashes in their humdrum lives with goals and ultimates, then all men are actually "outsiders." Certainly the authors to be considered in these studies were "outsiders" in this second sense, and of them—as of the ordinary man—it is safe to say, as Mr. Wilson somewhat cloudily contends, following the lead of T. E. Hulme,[2] that a sense of purpose can be realized only if there is a realization of the doctrine of Original Sin. For not only the geniuses, but society at large, is literally, since the Fall, "outside." It is the struggle to get "inside" which makes human life significant and purposeful and literature great. As Mr. Wilson rather neatly puts it: "Men are born like smashed radio sets, and before they can function properly, they must repair themselves." It might have been more accurately said: "they must be repaired." Mr. Wilson's contribution, then, to the understanding and appreciation of literary climates and trends is in his suggestion that perhaps modern criticism would do well to minimize somewhat its preoccupation with techniques and return to more theological approaches.

One of the techniques that has long engaged the attention of critics has been, of course, the technique of symbolism. A new impulse and direction has been given to such studies, it seems, by a recent book, *Symbolism and American Literature*, by Charles Feidelson,[3] which has special relevance to this present symposium, since the American literature Mr. Feidelson considers is mainly that of the nineteenth century. It is Mr. Feidelson's contention that symbolism, "in the central work of Hawthorne, Whitman, Melville and Poe, is at once a technique and a theme. It is a governing principle; not a stylistic device but a point of view; not a casual subject, but a pervasive presence in the intellectual landscape." It is "the coloration taken on by the American literary mind under the pressure of American intellectual history." And what was the "American literary mind"? It was one in which there lingered what Lionel Trilling calls the "residual pieties" of Puritan theocracy. And what was the "pressure of American intellectual history"? It was largely, as a review of Mr. Feidelson's book remarks: "the Puritan idea of useful work" which "combined with the raw nature of American society" to force "the American writer into an *acute awareness of his relation to society and the universe.*"[4]

If we take a "recall" to Original Sin, as adumbrated by Messrs. Wilson and Hulme, and study it in connection with this newly suggested approach to American symbolism in the nineteenth century, I believe that we will be struck by a suspicion that "residual Puritan pieties" are not enough to picture adequately the "mental coloration" that characterized the literature of the century. Other "pieties" were residual, too—pieties that had their roots in traditional Christianity, in dogmas that were pre-Puritan and pre-Reformation, and in the verities of scholastic philosophy. This is not to say by any means that Poe or Melville or Hawthorne or any of the other authors under consideration were conscious of deeper roots—they may or may not have been—or would not, indeed, have repudiated any such cultural affinity if it had been pointed out to them; it is to suggest, however, that their work can be adequately appreciated only if it is considered against an older theological and philosophical background. Such an approach has indeed been hinted at in such an appraisal as this of Emerson: "Many volumes have been written to prove that Emerson's final position was based on Neo-Platonism, German idealism, or Oriental mysticism; but a study of his sermons and of his early reading indicates that he had never departed from his loyalty to the faith of his fathers, the Christian tradition as developed by Christ, Paul, Thomas Aquinas, and Calvin,"[5] but the suggestion has, to my knowledge, never been systematically followed up. The studies that follow can most fruitfully be read, I suggest, if they are considered as illuminations of what I may call the common denominator running through all, namely that our nineteenth-century classics still betray, in their awareness of man and the universe, more concern with a "faith" of pre-Puritan ancestry than has been generally conceded or adequately investigated.

Let's try an experiment by way of illustration. Here is a long quotation from a very specialized work dealing with one of the more recently developed aspects of Catholic theology. The author is laying the philosophical groundwork for the magnificent treatise that will follow on the doctrine of the Mystical Body. The essence and the ramifications of that doctrine may or may not be familiar to readers of this symposium, but the philosophical aspects of it will, I trust, not sound so disagreeably "Roman" as to prejudice the reader from exploring with me the parallel I think emerges between the following passage and much of the thought of our nineteenth-century authors. The passage runs:

> We may say that absolute human perfection, if by a miracle it were to become possible, so that a man would be humanly perfect, would require a man to be deeply and completely himself, capable to express himself entirely by being true to his nature. Thus it would require that he should be interior to every man and that every man should be interior to him, by the very plenitude each would possess, and not in virtue of any advantage each would receive from their contact. Hence it would require that a man, in living his full interior life, should be able to share in all human life, to experience all human suffering, to think all human thought. It would further require that this human universality should not in any way destroy man's inwardness, but should find complete expression by deeply participating in it without at the same time violating it by undergoing disintegration. Lastly, such perfection would require that this plenitude should not encroach on the minor plenitudes of other men, but that on the contrary it should be full of respect and tenderness for them, so as to welcome them graciously and refrain from anything that might injure what a man ought to possess.

Such plenitude in the possession of human nature and universality in its operation is, even in the case of those geniuses who have been most universally human, an ever-unrealized but still ever-beckoning goal, and so the passage continues—and underlines again the cry of all "outsiders": the cry of insufficiency in the face of the staggering potentialities of the human mind, heart, and soul:

> Human nature has no means of realizing this absolute unity and transcendent universality. But we may say that, so far as our

reflections on human nature and its activity give us some knowledge of it, there is nothing in it to rule out the possibility of such perfections. How these marvels may be realized and how we may show that they are capable of going together, is another question. But that they represent man's absolute and superhuman perfection, cannot be called in question. The moment we recognize that man has a soul, that is, that the human form really existing in an individual has its own act and hence the act proper to the human form, we have no difficulty in perceiving that, to be a man in a perfect way, a man must be what he is immensely and universally, and this merely by being himself.[6]

Now it is remarkable how similar this analysis of human potentiality is to literally dozens of statements that can be found in the writings of Emerson. Dr. Pollock's study in the present volume will furnish the reader with an array of such similar sentiments. Here, perhaps it will be enough to cite but a few.[7] Such is the burden of phrases like: "The true Christianity—a faith like Christ's in the infinitude of man—is lost. None believeth in the soul of man, but only in some man or person old or departed. Ah me! no man goeth alone. All men go in flocks to this saint or that poet, avoiding the God who seeth in secret. They cannot see in secret; they love to be blind in public. They think society wiser than their soul, and know not that one soul, and their soul, is wiser than the whole world." Again: "The great god Pan of old, who was clothed in a leopard skin to signify the beautiful variety of things and the firmament, his coat of stars—was but the representative of thee, O rich and various man! thou palace of sight and sound, carrying in thy senses the morning and the night and the unfathomable galaxy; in thy brain, the geometry of the City of God; in thy heart, the bower of love and the realms of right and wrong." In the same vein: "The universe does not attract us till it is housed in an individual," for "every star in heaven is discontent and insatiable. Gravity and Chemistry cannot contain them. Ever they woo and court the eye of the beholder. Every man who comes into the world they seek to fascinate and possess, to pass into his mind, for they desire to republish themselves in a more delicate world than that they occupy."

These are but a few passages which betray one of the great concerns of Emerson. In his passionate consecration to the task of casting out "the devils of the mechanistic outlook which had alienated men from their own deeper experiences," Emerson "applied himself to the business of restoring to human life a whole range of experience from which it had arbitrarily detached itself." Man's cardinal task, Emerson maintained, "had to be to recall what in truth he is, a being who holds together within himself the 'poles of the Universe,' and who is the very meeting place of spirit and nature. He must thus widen to infinity his conception of himself, since he embraces 'on the one side elemental order, sandstone and granite, rock-ledge, peat-bog, forest, sea and shore; and on the other part, thought.' "[8]

This seminal concept in the work of Emerson was, to be sure, never embodied in any strict philosophical system; it is a discursive meditation that runs through all his thinking, and since it is stated at times in terms that can be interpreted, if one sets out so to interpret them, as "pantheistic," it has been too long the fashion to dismiss Emerson as merely a muddy and cloudy thinker, tainted with the confused metaphysics of Germanic romantic philosophy, and further dazzled by infiltrations from Eastern mysticism. But the further one examines Emerson's thought in the light of the classic Christian philosophy of man of which the above long quotation is but another, if very striking, expression, the more the realization is borne home that there is a great residue of the *philosophia perennis* in the basic Emersonian postulates.

If Emerson was no systematic philosopher, it is still true that he was the most philosophic of the authors under consideration in this volume, with the sole exception of Brownson, who, whatever his own excellent merits, did not have an influence on American letters comparable to that of any of the others here studied. Accordingly, as we turn from Emerson in these introductory remarks and ask ourselves whether the Christian philosophy of human nature finds in the other authors parallels as obvious as those that can be gleaned from Emerson, we are faced with a task that is not quite so easy nor so initially satisfying. The impression will not easily be suppressed, however, that if the quoted manifesto on man and his nature could have been read by Melville, Hawthorne, Thoreau, and Whitman, they would have been at one in saying "why, of course, that is what I have felt all along, without having the skill to be able to phrase it like that." Brownson, at least in his latter years, would not only have agreed wholeheartedly, but very probably have thought that he might have expressed it better. Cooper and the "literary historians" would probably have granted a somewhat grumpy assent but at the same time have claimed that it was a little "beyond their depth." Longfellow might have winced at the "metaphysics" of the concept, and Poe—well, perhaps Poe alone might have thought that it was but another example of "crazyite" ratiocination; though one can never be sure of Poe's seriousness when he scorns philosophizing. He himself, for instance, was constantly fascinated and perplexed by the problem of the "oneness" of man and the universe.

This is a series of conjectures, but there is evidence to support it. Most of this evidence will have to be left to appear obliquely, as it were, in the studies that follow, but perhaps it may be the place here to single out some of the fundamental philosophical questions the authors treat and the extent to which classic Christian solutions have colored their approach. There have been studies enough, in all conscience, of these nineteenth-century writers, but most of the critical work seems to rest unquestionably on the assumption or the assertion that there was a steady decline in the impact of traditional Christian thinking (especially in theology) on these authors. From Calvinism through Unitarianism to Transcendentalism and from there on, the argument seems to run, there was a constant watering-down of the teaching of the churches, in the sense that the "dogmas" of Protestant Christianity, reeling under the attacks of rationalism and the new spirits of scientific inquiry and industrial democracy, finally crumbled before the "intellectual freedom" which the Unitarian movement had inaugurated and which the Transcendentalists explored to the full.[9]

But one aspect of the philosophical and theological movements of the times has, it would appear, been largely overlooked by the critics who insist, one after another, on this "decline of dogma." There is no doubt of the fact that dogma did indeed lose its hold more and more as the century ran its course.[10] But the hold that loosened was mainly the Calvinistic creed first and then the tenets of rationalistic Unitarianism. A phenomenon which has not been fully explained, it seems, is that each emancipation from a preceding "dogma" actually, though probably all unconsciously, brought the "emancipated" thinker to some degree and for a time into the sunlight, so to speak, where the age-old and orthodox dogma of the Christian tradition did actually illumine the still lingering shadows, or flicker for a space until other approaching shadows engulfed it.

We are told, for example, that the Unitarian movement, in shaking off the grim Calvinistic dogma of the inherent corruption of human nature through Original Sin, "recovered the original principle of Protestantism, the principle of individual responsibility."[11] Whether or not this is the "original principle" of Protestantism may certainly be doubted, but the point is that Unitarianism, in restoring the concept of individual responsibility, was, in so far, not wandering farther away from Christian dogma, but actually clearing away a crucial misconception, and thus opening the door to a just estimate of the doctrine of Original Sin, and consequently of the dignity of man, not only as a rational being, but as one endowed with competence of thought to rise to a consideration of divine matters. It is undoubtedly true that, together with this liberalizing influence, as we may call this perhaps unconscious partial return to Christian tradition, the Unitarians immediately ran to the extreme of "avowing the absolute freedom of the human mind as their characteristic,"[12] thus denying the possibility of religious truth known through revelation.

In like manner, when the Transcendentalists, having eagerly seized on the "excellence" of human nature asserted by the Unitarians, went on enthusiastically to "proclaim it divine," they were actually giving expression to a profound truth which has been a commonplace, as it were, in Christian thought ever since the day St. Peter told the Church in his second Epistle that we are made, through Christ, *consortes divinae naturae* (partakers of the divine nature).[13] It is true, of course, that this profound truth was approached by Emerson and others in terms that are so romantic, so tinctured with a mixture of Platonism, Germanic romanticism, and Oriental mysticism that their face value seems to prove that the new Transcendental faith eventuated in "the creation of a mystical egocentric universe wherein the children of God might luxuriate in their divinity,"[14] and betrayed its "fundamental falsehood—the theory of the self-sufficiency of each individual."[15] But could not the divinity the Transcendentalists affimed to be in man have had clinging to it some vestiges of what Christian tradition would affirm to be the divinization of man through grace or the participation of man, through his reason, in the Eternal Law of God? John Jay Chapman, in his essay quoted above, labors at length the thought that Emerson attributes such a prime role to the "Moral Law" as to make it identical with Absolute Truth. Chapman quotes the famous passage:

> We affirm that in all men is this majestic perception and command; that it is the presence of the eternal in each perishing man; that it distances and degrades all statements of whatever saints, heroes, poets, as obscure and confused stammerings before its silent revelation. *They* report the truth. *It* is the truth.[16]

From this and similar statements which are myriad in Emerson, Chapman concludes that Emerson had in reality fallen back into the Calvinistic error, since he elevates the Moral Law to the rigid status of a "dogma"—and "dogmatic crucifixion of the natural instincts had been in progress [in New England] for two hundred years."[17] But could it be that, in the "flowering of New England," the crucifixion was followed by a fleeting resurrection occasioned by the breathing space given for an older tradition to stir for a time?[18]

That New England's flowering may have had roots in a tradition older than "Puritan pieties" does not seem to have engaged the attention of scholars hitherto in any comprehensive way. We are told, for example, that many of the early seventeenth-century Puritan leaders in Massachusetts were "well-read" in St. Thomas Aquinas, and that "Pauline and Thomistic conceptions of the rich man as the steward of possessions to be used for the benefit of the needy" was one of the elements of the Christian heritage which played so large a part in the growth of American thought.[19] It seems reasonable to suppose that in his wide perusal of contemporary European philosophical and theological thought, Emerson must have had at least a nodding acquaintance with scholastic philosophy. But there has been, to my knowledge, no specific and exhaustive examination of Emerson's reading with reference to scholastic sources.

The tenor of these present studies, however, does not depend for its validity and suggestiveness on any direct contact being proved between the authors studied and the traditional expressions of Christian dogma. What does emerge is rather a cultural continuity which the authors themselves probably would not have clearly realized to have been rooted in the Christian past. In a sense, it can be said that what these studies focus on is the *anima naturaliter Christiana*—though it is to be admitted that this phrase is so frequently invoked in a loose sense that its valid meaning is lost.

Nor is it to be anticipated that the subsequent studies will discover that the nineteenth-century American authors reached, through such continuity, any systematic or satisfying "solutions" for the moral and social problems touched on or overtly treated in their works. Often enough, they have no solutions—they are the "outsiders" groping toward an ultimate Yes or No. This is perhaps most evident in Melville. All of his works reflect the "conflict between head and heart" and his "loyalty to the heart" was characterized by "rage and defiance." It is true that he came to a "final renunciation of rage which might well have shown more joy . . . had [he] known another God than the one he found in the pyramids," but even the uneasy peace he finally won can be considered no more than a temporary respite in his battle with the eternal human problems. Again, Hawthorne had no clear answers to the problem—the basic problem of the nature and scope of free will. Melville himself believed that Hawthorne was great because of the "great power of blackness in him," which "derives its force from its appeal to that Calvinistic sense of Innate Depravity and Original Sin, from whose visitations, in some shape or other, no deeply thinking mind is always and wholly free." But other critics from Melville's day on have maintained that "Hawthorne turned his back on the conceptions of his Puritan ancestors," and that, if he was "too profound a rationalist to comprehend the mysticism that lurked at the heart of the Transcendentalist faith,"[20] he at least did not subscribe to the doctrine of human nature's innate depravity. He could not have entertained that doctrine, the following study will maintain, because of his "insistence on the cause and cure of sin in the individual heart." Thoreau, to cite another instance, has no clear solutions to the problem of the relationship of man to nature and to society. But in his questing, over and above the Greek spirit that has been discerned in his work,[21] there are unmistakable echoes of the age-old doctrine of Christian asceticism, of detachment from earthly possessions, couched in terms that would have sounded familiar to St. Francis of Assisi or to the Fathers of the Desert.

What were the basic problems these authors faced? Enough has been written, perhaps, about the cultural and economic milieu in which they created and against which they protested or for which they held out hope and inspiration. But in the philosophical and theological aspects of their work and thought, the problems always came back to revolve around some of the classical foci of Christian thought. Such problems are: the question of the "oneness" of the universe and of man's place in it as the lord and summation of creation; the particular oneness of men as brothers; the indwelling of God in the soul and in the sweep of material creation; the nature of sin and responsibility and the role of free-will in responsibility; the relationship of the individual to society. These and other central themes will be examined in the subsequent studies, but it is striking how often these great battlegrounds of human thought and experience are ventured onto by our authors in terms that are vibrant with accents an Augustine or an Aquinas

—or a Mersch—would immediately have recognized. It can be said with little fear of overstating the case that the nineteenth-century authors were speaking more than once, very likely without too clear a consciousness of the direction of their thought, about such bedrock doctrines as the immanence of God, His providence and salvific will, the freedom of the human will, detachment from created goods, the communion of saints, the ultimate triumph of good, the real and proper "divinity of man."

A pioneer though tentative work in tracing this persistence of pre-Reformation and pre-Puritan tradition in the achievements of the nineteenth-century writers was George N. Shuster's *The Catholic Spirit in America*.[22] There, particularly in Chapter 2, "The Journey of the American Mind," Dr. Shuster pays particular attention to Hawthorne and Emerson. Remarking that "inevitably the Romantic adventure led to the confines, sometimes to the interior, of the Catholic Church," Dr. Shuster considers that the "emphasis that Emerson puts on life—life that, if a man will but sense it coursing through his veins and not impair the instinct to aspire Divinely placed in it, 'will exist with God today,'" is actually "several leagues nearer to Catholic Christianity than it is to Puritanism." More than this, "these Emersonian statements coalesce into a first principle of Catholic Christianity"—one of the "primary characteristics of our Saviour's doctrine," the stress which it lays upon life, the life He came to give us more abundantly. Dr. Shuster acknowledges that as a thinker "Emerson sturdily opposed dogma and did not assent to the reality of Revelation," but makes the point suggested above, namely that the "dogma" from which Emerson—and others of his time—escaped, or refused to be confined within, was a "dogma" which was a parody of traditional Christian teaching. Often enough, in refusing to bow to such "dogma," he was seeking to "complete the narrow creed of New England in the same way, though with far less reliable means, as Catholicism completes it."

Dr. Shuster's essay in tracing the still-persistent influence of such intellectual completion in the cultural development of America was a modest attempt which has not to date stimulated others to follow up the very suggestive lead.[23] I believe that the studies that follow in this volume will be seen to take up, in a sense, where Dr. Shuster left off. Though there is no persistent reference by the various contributors to similarities with or discrepancies from the perduring Christian position, the total framework of reference from which they write is such as to throw each one's estimate of the achievements of his subject against the background of that tradition. This whole volume is a suggestion that much light is thrown on the really towering achievements of the nineteenth-century authors by an examination of how far they agree with Christian tradition—more light, perhaps, than is afforded by an insistence, as has been too long the trend, on how far they fell short.

This is by no means to maintain that Melville, Thoreau, Emerson, Cooper, and all the rest would have been better writers and more eminent craftsmen had they returned completely to the riches of, say, Tridentine doctrine. The "would-have-been-if" theory is too much the fruit of wishful—and wistful—thinking to serve as a valid critical tool. In fact, it is the very tension evident in these authors that makes for the profundity with which they scrutinize the human situation; if Melville had not wrestled with the agony of the conflict of his heart and mind, the poignance of his cry would not have been so moving—the cry of every human heart, the cry of the divine restlessness which yearns for, even when it is not sure where to turn to find, the Eternal Beauty. But tension can be appreciated only when we properly gauge the contending forces. Those forces were, of course, all the elements that other critics have been so at pains to enumerate—economic, nationalistic, political, and so on; but beneath them all, the fundamental tension was set up because the eternal and root problems of the human soul were seeking solutions—and not finding them in terms that could lead to rest, to "inside," where alone solutions *can* be found.

This approach to American literature of the nineteenth century is bound to recall the famous dictum of Arthur Machen:

> You ask me for a new test—or rather a new expression of the one test—that separates literature from the mass of stuff which is not literature. I will give you a test that will startle you; literature is the expression, through the esthetic medium of words, of the dogmas of the Catholic Church, and that which is in any way out of harmony with those dogmas is not literature.

But neither Mr. Machen nor these studies intend to state the case that baldly. It is generally forgotten by those who quote Machen that he went on to define that rather startling statement:

> Yes; it is really so, but not exactly in the sense which you suppose. No literal compliance with Christianity is needed; no, nor

even an acquaintance with the doctrines of Christianity. . . . The conscious opinions of a writer are simply not worth twopence in the court of literature. . . .[24] Think of it and you will see, that from the literary standpoint, Catholic dogma is merely the witness, under a special symbolism, of the enduring facts of human nature and the universe; it is merely the voice which tells us distinctly that man is *not* the creature of the drawingroom and the Stock Exchange, but a lonely aweful soul confronted by the Source of all souls, and you will realize that to make literature it is necessary to be, at all events subconsciously, Catholic.[25]

In somewhat the same vein, though with a theological inaccuracy that is surprising in so well-informed an author, Rebecca West, in the concluding lecture of the Dwight H. Terry series delivered at Yale University in the fall of 1956, declared that "the effort of art is directed toward restating what religion claims to know by revelation." Acknowledging that, in a sense, "religion has no need of art," Miss West nevertheless contends that "it is impossible to imagine serious art which does not treat of the same subject-matter as religion." But Miss West involves herself in difficulty when she endeavors to develop this central thought. In a strange throwback to the Calvinism that such men as Emerson long ago abandoned, Miss West puts the dilemma thus: "Man must act; God has made him want to act. But God has made man's will corrupt, so that he cannot act in a way pleasing to God." The artist, contends Miss West, is constantly striving to reconcile two irreconcilable propositions: "the world is full of many things, and some of them are beautiful, and we should be thankful for this beneficent creation"; and "the world is full of many things, and some of them are foul and shameful, yet they are all the work of the Creator. How can this be so?"

Such is not actually the dilemma the creative artist faces; it cannot legitimately be, for no such dilemma exists in the whole realm of reality. The real dilemma is the one stated in the quotation from Mersch earlier in this chapter. It is the tension set up in the inner life of every human soul and vividly realized and struggling for expression in the achievements of the creative artist—the tension, namely, between the limited possibilities of a particular human nature and the realization that a man, "in living his full interior life, should be able to share in all human life, to experience all human suffering, to think all human thought." Each one of the authors considered in these studies, each in his own way, one with keener philosophic perception than another, one with a greater wealth of symbol, is struggling with the rooted drive of the human soul "to be a man in a perfect way . . . a man immensely and universally, and this merely by being himself."

It is for this reason that these authors are, in this introduction's title, the "half-gods" of American literature. Never, in our literary history, has a comparable body of authors struggled so passionately to assess the truly human and the properly-estimated divine in human nature. The rule is perhaps proved by the exception: of all the authors here studied, only Longfellow seems to have been temperamentally unable to wrestle with the angel, and it would seem, as the assessment of him points out, that that was the very reason why his work was fated to remain in the category of "minor classicism." There need be little cause for lament that the others fell short of a completely satisfying literary statement or embodiment of the amazing truth of what human nature is in itself and in its relationship to fellow men, to nature, and to God. Vague "Over-Souls" and "Love Divine," formless "Destiny," and beckoning "Democracy" may too often be the deities tendered obeisance, but the ground and base of them all is firmer and truer than even the authors themselves realized. Since their day, American literature has had no such center. The onset of realism, the concern of literature with sociology and lately with psychiatry, have little by little shifted the center of interest from a profound, if often misdirected, concern with the towering ethical, moral, and philosophical crises of the human situation to a worried interest in environment, a too-photographic recording of social stresses and adaptability. Perhaps today we have only in Faulkner an imagination rich and wide enough to grasp what almost infinite riches lie at the disposal of an artist who can vibrate to the challenge set before human nature when it is conceived as the age-old and still-enduring Christian tradition conceived and conceives it.

Alas! the second line of Emerson's verse has not proved true— at least in American letters. The "half-gods" of the nineteenth century were not followed by "arriving gods." But we can be grateful that at one period in our cultural and literary history we did have men of a stature and a will to wrestle with the Angel. The extent of their failure and success, the measure of their daring and their vision can be appreciated truly only when they are gauged against the full glory of the message about man and God that complete Christianity gave and gives.

RALPH WALDO EMERSON
1803 - 1882

The Single Vision

ROBERT C. POLLOCK

AN interpretation of Emerson which would claim to do him justice is by no means a light undertaking. For, contrary to what seems to be a widely held opinion, he was a very complex person who thought deeply and subtly about serious matters. Indeed, the closer we come to the man himself the better we can estimate the difficulty of making a just appraisal of his essential genius.

Today, thanks to the painstaking efforts of scholars, it is possible to gain a rounded appreciation of Emerson's achievements. At the very least, we can now see that Emerson resists easy classification, and that, moreover, there is little excuse for certain misconceptions regarding him which owe their currency to the habit of pouncing upon certain words of his taken in isolation and with little regard for his basic motivations, spiritual, intellectual, and esthetic.

A contemporary scholar sums up extremely well what any serious reading of Emerson should teach us, when he says: "We are wrong to think of him as an Olympian seer, playing in solitude with Platonic abstractions. The power of his writing rests not simply on his craftsman's skill, though that was great, but on the compulsions and conflicts, the revelations and the doubts, the glories and the fears which struck fire in his imagination and compelled him to bring them to definition. Genius is the daughter of such necessity. Because he has this kind of power he will continue to be read."[1] While we might find fault with any statement which would seem to identify Platonism with abstractions in the pejorative sense, we must still agree with the main idea expressed by this author, especially when he goes on to say of Emerson that "his life of thought was not, as it has generally been represented, an eventless and static thing, to be defined and assessed, like mer-

15

chandise, by a process of random sampling," and when he says, further, "In following it we are watching a process that is always absorbing wherever it is encountered—the action of a superior imagination taking possession of its world."[2]

However, if we are to make this general assessment of the living quality of Emerson's work complete, we should stress not only the dynamism of his life and thought and the great power of his imagination, but also his capacity for highly disciplined thinking. And here again a contemporary author sums up the matter for us when she says (in reference to Emerson's ideas of literature and art) that "at no point was he soaring into a vague empyrean of irresponsible speculation, but was always sustained by the support of other thinkers, however disparate these thinkers may be from each other,"[3] and when, in addition, she tells us that his esthetic theory "is a better rationalized esthetic than his critics have generally suspected."[4]

But while Emerson was primarily a literary figure, he found himself in the situation where he had to function constructively on a theoretical level, and not merely with respect to poetry and literature, but in relation to reality as a whole. And the burdens imposed by such a diversity of interests were bound to have unhappy results. As a literary figure he had to concern himself with esthetic theory, inasmuch as he wanted to show that esthetic sensibility has an indispensable function within the whole structure of knowledge. His avowed aim was to demonstrate the objective status of esthetic experience, while justifying a symbolistic method in literature. Moreover, the need for a reappraisal of human existence in its entirety was keenly felt by him, especially since he could see that the problems confronting him as a writer and poet waited for their solution on the answer to questions of a philosophical nature.

From first to last an artist, Emerson paid the price of his diverse efforts, even laying himself open to the charge that his "failing was a lack of literary purposefulness."[5] Still, we may well question whether "a lack of literary purposefulness" exactly states the case, for it remains true that he played no small part in fortifying and expanding esthetic sensibility, as the author just quoted has himself shown.

Although Emerson spent much time brooding over philosophical matters, he never for a moment fancied himself a philosopher in any purely formal or technical sense of the terms. Far from it, for he made no bones about his deficiency in the sort of thinking that produced the works of a Hume or a Butler.[6] Yet, if we read his *Journals* along with his *Essays,* we surely cannot avoid seeing that he was capable of a high and sustained philosophical seriousness which puts the stamp of significance on much of what he says. Indeed, as it has been rightly said, "the height and depth of his thought" is one of his "distinguishing excellencies."[7]

Emerson was first and last "an artist in the medium of theory."[8] And, as an artist he brought something of value to his philosophical reflections, namely, an esthetic sensibility which held him fast to a concrete and experiential method. This method in no way implied a derogatory view of philosophical speculation, although it did fasten his attention on the strange and complex process by which experience is converted into thought. Others might disparage knowing and the contemplative life, but, as one who had imbibed copiously of Plato's wisdom, he grasped the importance and even the sublimity of soaring speculative thought. However, the sustaining purpose of his philosophical efforts was simply to extend consciousness through direct insight, and to enlarge man's vision of the world.

Emerson was quite content to translate his philosophical ideas into the broadest human terms, without trying to work them into a strictly philosophical form. Systematic thinking of a sort there would be, of course, but he would mainly content himself with the kind of system which consists in "dotting a fragmentary curve, recording only what facts he has observed, without attempting to arrange them within one outline. . . ."[9] Thus, all things considered, Emerson's approach was characterized by good sense and modesty, and if his thought may at times seem to defy abstract logic, it possesses, notwithstanding, a logic of its own, a logic of life, which is validated in the depth of personal experience.

At every step of the way, Emerson worked on two levels at once, that of principles and that of experience, for he saw with far more than ordinary clarity that men were suffering from an impoverishment of both principles and experience. But it was especially with the level of experience that he concerned himself, since he knew that while principles were absolutely essential, they would hardly manifest their truth to men who had already imposed artificial limits on experience. How could they possibly pay heed to his religious, ethical, and esthetic teachings, if they regarded the religious, ethical, and esthetic components of experience itself as strictly out of bounds? He accordingly applied himself to the business of restoring to human life a whole range of experience from which it had arbitrarily detached itself. Having himself in mind, as well as others, he noted the extraordinary facility with which we insulate ourselves from our own experiences, even from those that we might ordinarily regard as overpowering. In fact, it would seem that, more often than not, nothing really touches us and "the dearest events are summer-rain, and we the Para coats that shed every drop."[10] Clearly, then, "the Indian who was laid under a curse that the wind should not blow on him nor water flow to him, nor fire burn him is a type of us all."[11]

But Emerson knew that if men shunned what was most valuable in their experience, it was because they had accepted the fiction of a split universe, that is, a universe in which the life of the spirit is insulated from man's life in nature. What had once been regarded as inseparable had been cleft asunder, with the unhappy result that a devoutly religious attitude to life, the contemplative spirit, and poetry itself were thought to be quite foreign to man's growing preoccupation with his earthly habitation. And mechanistic philosophy had provided this separatism with an aura of intellectual respectability which lay like a black cloud over human consciousness. Hence, it would be necessary to overcome this deadly separatism by liberating man from the mechanistic nightmare, while showing that we cannot even begin to relate ourselves properly to our natural environment unless we bring to it the inner world of the spirit.[12]

In other words, Emerson was determined to cast out the devils of the mechanistic outlook which had alienated men from their own deeper experiences. He had no intention of stifling interest in the world of nature. On the contrary it was his purpose to bind men more closely to that world by effecting a thoroughgoing transformation in their perception of it. He would make them see that they had been living at second hand and had become so dulled to a cosmos teeming with surprising relationships, that they had failed to note the most revealing relationship of all, that between the world of visible things and the world of spirit accessible to man. They would thus discover that every contact with the material environment involved them in a mysterious contact with a higher world. And once this was seen, the split universe would be banished as a pernicious delusion, for men would know that their true habitat is the one all-inclusive environment which embraces spirit as well as the world of nature. No longer would these planes of reality be regarded as merely juxtaposed to each other, nor would material nature be looked upon as man's sole environment.

Men would, therefore, set about the business of refashioning their lives within the all-inclusive universe of an older tradition; and within this universe they would recover an experiential wholeness.

When Emerson asserts that "we are so much strangers in nature as we are aliens from God,"[13] he is not merely upholding the primacy of the spiritual world, but he is also implying that, together, the spiritual world and the world of nature form one single reality, one universe in which man lives his life. And he is implying, further, that man cannot even naturalize himself, cannot really plant his being within the natural world until he has gained some sense of the higher world of spirit which is half-revealed and half-hidden by material nature. Even the naturalist, in the Emersonian view, cannot strictly be called one "until he satisfies all the demands of the spirit,"[14] for "the best read naturalist who lends an entire and devout attention to truth will see that there remains much to learn of his relation to the world, and that it is not to be learned by any addition or subtraction or other comparison of known quantities, but is arrived at by untaught sallies of the spirit, by a continual self-recovery, and by entire humility."[15] Man is but a dwarf until he accepts his own elemental power to view nature in such wise that even the landscape, "every glimpse of which hath a grandeur,"[16] is perceived as a face of divinity. Let man grasp the exalted truth that "the noblest ministry of nature is to stand as an apparition of God"[17] and science itself will be kindled "with the fire of the holiest affections" and "God will go forth anew into the creation."[18]

Emerson's every line takes on new meaning once we see what he is driving at. Unwearyingly he strove to free men from the delusion of a split universe, which, as he knew, had reduced human life to a fragmented state. On one side, religion was losing a certain cosmic and natural quality and, on the other, man's life in nature was being stripped of its spiritual dimension. Religious life was fast becoming a lopsided and even freakish affair, and man's contact with nature had lost a certain spiritual rapport essential to it. Faith in God had become detached from a lived awareness of nature as that which "brings tidings from spiritual realms,"[19] while faith in science and machinery subsisted apart from any faith in divine causes. Having lost their bearings in the universe whose source and foundation is the eternal One, men had become strangers to their own experience. Man, therefore, had to recall what in truth he is, a being who holds together within himself the "poles of the Universe," and who is the very meeting place of

spirit and nature. He must thus widen to infinity his conception
of himself, since he embraces "on one side elemental order, sandstone and granite, rock-ledge, peat-bog, forest, sea and shore; and
on the other part, thought. . . ."[20]

Alfred Noyes touches on this fundamental Emersonian standpoint in declaring that "Emerson was the first writer in American
literature to begin that great work of the future—the finding and
maintaining of that central position which has been temporarily
lost in an age of specialists, that central position from which we
shall again see 'all things in one,' as Thomas à Kempis could
see them."[21] And there can be no doubt that Noyes has correctly
singled out that in Emerson which more than anything else should
enable us to enter more sympathetically into his thoughts and
attitudes.

As we have said, Emerson had no intention of loosening man's
vital connection with the material environment. He fully appreciated the positive aspects of the naturalism that had made its
appearance in modern times. For example, he saw it as a real
triumph of the human spirit that man had put away his small
measure in viewing nature, in gaining a sense of her "large style."[22]
Thus what others regarded as but a moment in the development
of a scientific attitude, he saw as a significant stage in man's spiritual ascent. The spiritual significance of the new naturalism did
not escape him, and for that reason he could rejoice because man
had expanded to infinity his conception of nature while acquiring
an ineradicable conviction that he and nature proceed from one
identical root.

To Emerson the whole modern sense of nature was illumined
by his own outlook rather than by that of mechanistic philosophy.
Especially when we consider the cluster of feelings which well up
so spontaneously within us at the mere sight of natural objects, as,
for example, when we "anticipate a supersensual utility in the sun
and stars, earth and water."[23] True, the impressions of nature may
fall so feebly on us that we fail to sense this "supersensual
utility." But, in that case, it is the function of the poet to remedy
this defect, in helping us traverse the whole scale of experience.[24]
Yet if the poet is indispensable, so too are the philosopher and
the seer, for these latter can supply the vision which will make
men more sensitive to nature's promptings regarding the realm of
the "supersensual." And through this vision men will easily understand why their contact with nature is able to arouse in them a
spirit of reverence. Moreover, they will become more responsive

to the necessary lessons in which nature exercises the mind of man, the "lessons of difference, of likeness, of order, of being and seem- ing, of progressive arrangement; of ascent from particular to general; of combination to one end of manifold forces."[25] Finally, they will be the grateful recipients of one of nature's fairest gifts, namely, an "integrity of impression made by manifold objects," and through which, for example, the stick of timber is distin- guished from the tree of the poet.[26]

Working on two levels at once, that of principles and that of experience, Emerson set out to remove the blinkers from men's eyes, so that they might perceive the indescribable wonders of a world which so loudly proclaims the hollowness of the mechanistic hypothesis. Above all, he wanted men to evaluate properly the mysterious congruity which subsists between them and the natural world. For he felt certain that when the full implications of this congruity are grasped, inward spiritual life and life in nature would be joined together, and the ancient precept "know thyself" and the modern precept "study nature" would at last be fused into one maxim.[27] To spiritually-minded men who had discovered their ties with nature, nothing, surely, could be more liberating than the knowledge that soul-searching and a searching of earth and sky are not alien to each other, and that if the eyes of the soul "wander incessantly to the unfathomable abyss,"[28] the eyes of the body should be endlessly engaged in a closer scrutiny of nature.

People were awed by this rather strange man who could marvel before the spectacle of his own inward life and yet feel the marrow of the world in his bones. They heard him proclaim that "when a man lives with God his voice shall be as sweet as the murmer of the brook and the rustle of the corn,"[29] and that "as a plant upon the earth, so a man rests upon the bosom of God . . ."[30] But they also heard him say of man that "so much of nature as he is ignor- ant of, so much of his own mind does he not yet possess."[31]

As they listened they felt he was really before them and standing solidly behind his words, and that he was speaking *"from within, or from experience,"* and not *"from without,* as spectators merely." But apart from the authentic note in his message, he himself had declared that "if a man do not speak from within the veil, where the word is one with that it tells of, let him lowly confess it."[32] Still at times, they must have been somewhat puzzled to hear one and the same person speak so earnestly of spiritual matters and yet so vividly of the ordinary things of life. There before them stood a man whose spiritual gravity and power of inward absorption brought forcibly to mind an image of the Puritan mystic, and from whose lips yet poured forth a profusion of magical phrases affirming his belief that nature, as "the city of God,"[33] was no vain show. And when he offered them his own version of what it means to accept nature as "the city of God," they were more certain than ever that he was speaking "from within the veil."

II

AN AUTHENTIC NATURALISM

It might be said by way of objection that Emerson's concern to join together religious life and life in nature is, in the final analysis, meaningless, inasmuch as he seems to equate religion with pantheism. And here an objector might cite a contemporary scholar who asserts that although at times Emerson "sounds very much as if he believed in God," the "higher will" he acknowledges "can be described only in pantheistic terms. . . ." But a closer study of Emerson will most certainly lay bare the inadequacy of such a view. Indeed it would seem that the more balanced interpretation is offered by another writer who denies that Emerson's position can be classified under the term "pantheism," or, for that matter, under such terms as "emanationism," or "evolutionism." For, as he says, none of these terms "precisely and exhaustively characterizes his solution of the problem of contingency." In this writer's view, we may perhaps summarize it best in "saying that the entire force of the first and absolute cause is directed to the actuality of the individual, to every individual, and that every individual exists by the full influx of the first cause." "This conception," he tells us further, "does not in any way raise the question of the identity of the individual with the absolute cause, for the reply is apparent before the question takes form: the individual, by its individuality, cannot be equated with the Absolute; the Absolute by its infinity, cannot be exhausted, either by a single individual or by an infinity of individuals."[2]

Emerson's thought on the Absolute and the finite is characterized by his desire to take account of both unity and duality. If the Absolute is indeed the cause and ground of all things, it nevertheless does not reduce them to nullity through its all-enveloping reality. As a matter of fact, Emerson was congenitally unable to view any question one-sidedly and statically, for his mind was, one might say, spontaneously dialectical, and it was just this natural disposition which made Plato's dialectical procedure so congenial to him. Emerson's characteristic way of approaching questions is also seen in his treatment of the problem of experience itself, for he views it sometimes monistically and sometimes dualistically. But his attitude was, as he said, "somewhat better than whim at last," for, as has been well said, for Emerson "each extreme was tacitly conditioned by a third view in which both became partial."[3] Clearly, then, his attitude to the fundamental question of the relation between the world of nature and the Absolute was anything but capricious. He did not deliberately seek out inconsistency. But neither did he shy away from it when he found it staring him in the face from the very center of his own thinking and his own experience. Quite the contrary, for inconsistency prodded him into an inescapable awareness of a wider standpoint in which opposites would find their reconciliation.

Emerson wished to bring to focus a certain truth, namely, that nature, as "the city of God," is the indispensable medium of intellectual and spiritual discernment. As the product, not of manifold power, "but of one will, of one mind,"[4] of the Supreme Being, or "the eternal ONE,"[5] whose attribute is self-existence,[6] nature is an ever novel effect descending from above and in an unbroken obedience.[7] Thus, as the descending manifestation of spirit, nature is no stranger to man. In truth, it is bound to the human spirit by ties whose occult and mysterious character account for the intimations and suggestions which permeate man's experiences of the natural world.

Parenthetically, let us note here that in holding to this doctrine of nature as a manifestation of a supra-material realm, Emerson attributed so much independence to the human spirit in its power to apprehend nature's deeper meanings, that at times he sounds like a subjective idealist. But his real intent is merely to stress the profound interiority of the human spirit. The spirit of man in its inwardness is, as it were, the terminus of a spiritual utterance whose source, while beyond time and space, yet reaches man through the instrumentality of nature. Idealism appealed to him only as a means of upsetting the complacency of the materialist, and throwing into relief the reality of mind, not only "as a part of the nature of things,"[8] but as a part which yet occupies a highly unique position in its relation to spiritual reality. He saw idealism as "a hypothesis to account for nature by other principles than those of carpentry and chemistry."[9] But in denying the existence of matter, idealism fails to satisfy the demands of spirit, and "leaves me in the splendid labyrinth of my perceptions, to wander

without end."[10] How he felt regarding this denial of the reality of
matter can also be seen in a later essay, when, in speaking of our
contact with things in nature, he says, "These enchantments are
medicinal, they sober and heal us. These are plain pleasures, kindly
and native to us. We come to our own, and make friends with
matter, which the ambitious chatter of the schools would persuade
us to despise."[11]

Emerson particularly wanted to show that there is something
transpersonal in human personality which explains the connection
between human knowledge and the abyss of being, as well as man's
ability to perceive the spiritual dimension in things. This transpersonal something is, of course, the divine presence itself. As he
says, "Into every intelligence there is a door which is never closed,
through which the creator passes."[12] Hence, if deep calls unto
deep, if the spirit of man can be so profoundly perceptive of the
whole scale of being, it is because ". . . the Maker of all things and
all persons stands behind and casts his dread omniscience through
us over things."[13] All thinking is, at bottom, a "pious reception,"[14]
for, "when we discern justice, when we discern truth, we do nothing
of ourselves, but allow a passage to its beams."[15] Therefore it can
be rightly said that "the intellect, seeker of absolute truth, or the
heart, lover of absolute good, intervenes for our succor . . ."[16]

Emerson attempted to "pluck the strings of tension" in men by
contrasting their habitual state of consciousness with a truly
human state. In place of that original relation to the universe to
which every man is called, there was a blind and ignorant following of custom, and a "squalid contentment with conventions," and
"satire at the names of philosophy and religion . . ."[17] Men were
living at second hand and had accepted penny-wisdom substitutes
for what was authentic. Even when men yearned to drink deeply
of life, they were enslaved by the grotesque notion that living one's
life had to be postponed from day to day.

No mere generalizer or a propounder of formulas, Emerson
merely wished to resuscitate a primal state of consciousness in
which man feels his continuity with the great world around him,
experiencing a sense of participation and of barriers swept away,
and in addition, a sense of contact with a spiritual source of things.
Subtle links of continuity on the one hand and, on the other, a
vivifying relation to the realm of spirit in the depth of the soul—
together these constitute the basis of a rounded human experience.
But how was he to make others aware of his? Would he not have
to penetrate to "the aboriginal Self"[18] in man, in order that the

primordial experiences might stand revealed? Would he not also have to contend with the blight of sophistication—an "impudent knowingness"[19]—and a spurious "second thought"[20] which kills primal conviction?

In the light of Emerson's desire to create a new fusion of religious life and life in nature, we can see why he would envision morality itself in cosmic terms. Mere moralism would have been repugnant to him, for he found it necessary to view everything, morality included, within the setting of a real universe (i.e., Nature in the large sense, which includes spirit). "But speak the truth," he says, "and all nature and all spirits help you with unexpected furtherance. Speak the truth, and all things alive or brute are vouchers, and the very roots of the grass underground there do seem to stir and move to bear you witness."[21] Only when men feel that as men they are strong "by the whole strength of nature"[22] will they have the power to withstand "the maxims of a low prudence" which declares the "first duty is to get land and money, place and name."[23]

For Emerson it was never a question of a spiritual versus a naturalistic outlook, since, as we have seen, he steadfastly refused to recognize any split between the higher and lower worlds. We would say that for him the real opposition lay between a genuinely spiritual outlook and a spiritual outlook which was denatured. It seemed to him that everything was conspiring to make religion something artificial in the universal scheme, something apart from man's life in the world of nature. While rationalism and mechanistic philosophy had done their part in promoting this death-dealing separatism, religion itself, at least the religion of his own forbears, had prepared the ground in its lack of a cosmic root. When he complained that the miracle was no longer "one with the blowing clover and the falling rain,"[24] he was merely reminding men of the delusion of the split universe. Indeed, so completely had this separatism dulled their senses, that they no longer regarded the marvelous interlacing of processes in nature as "the endless circulations of the divine charity [which] nourish man."[25]

As the enemy of a denatured outlook, Emerson strove to make men more sensitive to their natural environment. Man's sense of wonder and his instinct for the mystery in things were enfeebled and it was necessary to restore them to full vigor. The curtain had to be raised from the most ordinary facts, to discover their secret and enthralling wonders. Man had to be taught to marvel again at the miracle of being, so that "the light of rising and of setting suns, . . . the flying cloud, the singing bird, and the breath of flowers"[26] will not seem alien to the deeper promptings of the spirit. Man had to be free from a prison of his own making, if he was to repossess a primal wisdom which includes a vision of nature, and even more fundamentally, spiritual understanding, or knowledge of God, which Emerson identified with *"matutina cognitio,"* the morning knowledge of the Schoolmen, as against *"vespertina cognitio,"* or evening knowledge, which is the knowledge of man.[27]

Man is imprisoned in man. Therefore, he, Emerson, would dedicate himself to the business of freeing him. Men were by no means content with their condition. They naturally wanted to live their own lives, they were thirsting for real existence and loved "to be caught up into the vision of principles."[28] They would therefore know how to respond to one who understands that "The imaginative faculty of the soul must be fed with objects immense and eternal."[29] Men yearned to do something worthwhile, something truly in keeping with human nature and which would make its absolute demands upon them and which they could do with all their heart. Yet the essential appeal capable of stirring men to their roots was lacking, the appeal which would base itself on a true understanding of man's desire for an all-embracing unity of life. Scholars, thinkers, and writers were making no vital communication to society, and the public disregarded them. Accordingly, in speaking the words which would reanimate man with a consciousness of his true dignity and the unity proper to human life, Emerson felt he was doing something that was in its own way as necessary as the labors of the Abolitionists. Apparently conscience-stricken for a spell by what he deemed his remissness is not aiding the anti-slavery fight, he regains perspective in reflecting that he had quite other slaves to free, the "imprisoned spirit" and "imprisoned thought."[30]

III

AN ANCIENT TRADITION

In ancient classical philosophy Emerson found that very fusion of spirituality and a cosmic sense which he knew to be coeval with the human spirit. And in his quick response to this ancient outlook, which was as manna to his soul, he was experiencing what Catholic thinkers down the years had experienced before him. No matter how deficient the ancient thinkers were in terms of the more comprehensive vision of things vouchsafed to the believing mind of the Christian, they had, nonetheless, a magically evocative power which could be found nowhere else and which had a transforming effect on all who came in contact with them. But what was especially entrancing to Catholics was just that vision to which Emerson was groping, and whose essential feature was a great structured universe in which man has his place as a true cosmos within a cosmos.

Given such a vision, so congenial to the Catholic spirit, how else could Catholic culture develop save by remaining true to it? That is why we find medieval Catholic culture so completely dominated by the notion of an all-inclusive universe in which the whole spiritual order has its place. It was natural, therefore, for the medieval man to regard the world of the spirit as an actual part of his environment and as capable of acting on him and influencing him as things in time and space. When we consider that in modern times the very notion of "universe" has been stripped by physical science of its larger connotation, and that the essential vision has paled even for many religious people, we can more readily appreciate Emerson's efforts to recapture it.

Let us dwell for a moment on this great scheme envisioned by the ancients and to which several schools of thought contributed. For our purpose it will be enough to consider the contribution of Platonists and Stoics. On one hand, the Platonists had taught a doctrine of a transcendent spiritual reality, while yet offering to men's minds the spectacle of a structured scheme in which the world of man had its fixed place. The Stoics, on the other hand, believed in the dynamic immanence of a rational principle which permeates the universe to its innermost core, leaving nothing untouched. Despite the shortcomings of the Platonist view, it has remained a tower of strength to Christians; and as for Stoicism, it, too, while even more glaringly defective, has yet given new shape to human consciousness. Both aspects of that ancient vision found new scope in Catholic Christianity—Platonic transcendence and that outlook which found magnificent expression in *The Hymn of Cleanthes* or in Marcus Aurelius' "O dear city of Zeus."

There is significance in the fact that Emerson himself exhibited in some degree these two strains, the Platonic and the Stoic. His Platonism is evident in his doctrine of a spiritual reality beyond the world of the senses, a spiritual reality which is directly accessible to us. It is also revealed in his cherished view that every fact can be given its widest horizon by being raised from one level to another. To him Plato "represents the privilege of the intellect,

the power, namely, of carrying up every fact to successive platforms and so disclosing in every fact a germ of expansion."[1] This
expansion from one level to another of every fact is organic and
has, moreover, an objective import, since "the mind does not
create what it perceives, any more than the eye creates the rose."[2]
The objects in our physical environment thus represent more than
themselves, since they constitute the germ of an infinite meaningfulness.

As for Emerson's Stoicism, one can say that no ancient Stoic
was more overcome than he before the great spectacle of a universe
whose humblest forms bespoke divinity. Nor did any Stoic feel
more deeply than he the divine immanence which manifested itself
to him in the opulence of natural forms and the power and magnifi-
cence of nature's processes.

We know, of course, that Emerson was also influenced by
Asiatic writings.[3] Hence we can sum up the various influences by
saying with Santayana that "he felt his affinity to the Hindoos and
the Persians, to the Platonists and the Stoics."[4] But these Asiatic
traces by no means separate him from the great tradition of
thought stemming from Classicism and Christianity, since this
tradition is also heavily indebted to the East. We might, indeed,
characterize this tradition as essentially an effort to reconcile the
notion of limit and measure, in which the Greeks excelled, with
the sense of the measureless and boundless, which was more congenial to the Eastern mind. Emerson himself turned toward the
East because its mode of thinking appealed to his own sense of
an all-pervasive Infinite. Yet he loved Western ways of thinking,
for in them he found what he also regarded as indispensable,
namely, the Classical respect for form and measure. Thus, in full
approval of both Eastern and Western orientations, he can say,
"if the East loved infinity the West delighted in boundaries."[5]

In his attempt to recapture the single vision of the older tradition, Emerson was severely handicapped by a lack of knowledge
of the way in which that vision took shape down through the
centuries. Still, it must be acknowledged that, despite grave defects, and considering his practical aim, something great emerges
in his conception.

If we bear in mind his desire to view moral and spiritual life
within the framework of a great cosmic order, we can deal more
justly with his failure to confront the problem and mystery of evil
more adequately than he did. Undoubtedly he was hard-pressed
by the fact of evil. If his placid outward demeanor often conveyed
an easy optimism, we should not be deceived, since this was in

some measure the result of a severe inner discipline. Besides, his own personal tragedies, which had been shattering experiences, were quite enough to shock him out of a self-complacent optimism.

Yet, if Emerson felt the reality of evil, how was he to accept it without jeopardizing his notion of a great ordered scheme which was ruled by intelligence and not by brute force? If evil was real, so was the order of the universe and its rational principle. How, therefore, deal with evil while yet showing that the universal order always holds sway, and with it the goodness which is bound up with the unity of things? As we know, he apparently solved the problem to his own satisfaction by having recourse to the view that "against all appearance, the nature of things works for truth and right forever,"[6] thereby making evil fade away as a result of the beneficent action of Goodness itself. Thus a "Beautiful Necessity"[7] reigns over things, always assuring the triumph of the good. If this is indeed Emerson's view, then it would appear that evil has been banished as illusory, so eager is he to safeguard the cosmic order in which truth and justice are seen as operating with a certain impersonal force. And nature itself, which, in other contexts, is presented by him as a living presence manifesting divinity, is turned into a convenient abstraction.

If Emerson had made a serious study of Catholic thought, he would have been struck by the masterful way in which the problem of evil is handled, in full awareness of the ultimate mystery and yet with no essential violation of the cosmic outlook of the ancients. If anything, that cosmic outlook is deepened and broadened. For to these Christian thinkers, no matter how grave the disorder introduced into the world, the power of an omnipotent and creative God always stands above it, making evil serve the Divine Plan for the whole universe. Evil itself is, therefore, never a total disorder, for it, too, is ordered. What we have, then, in the Catholic conception is a magnificent optimism which, nevertheless, does not diminish by one iota the factuality of evil or its gravity. In the framework of Catholic doctrine, evil does not fade away under the magic wand of a beneficent necessity or through a more or less automatic process of universal compensation, nor can it be disregarded through an easy confidence in Goodness itself. On the contrary, evil becomes all the more terrible as the violation on the part of free rational beings of an order which has been freely and lovingly instituted by God Himself.

Clearly, Emerson's optimism lacked a proper metaphysical foundation. However, when we set out to criticize it we should at least keep in mind its basic motivations. We can, if we wish, link it in part with Emerson's desire to fortify human initiative. But we should also remember his effort to restore to religious life a profound sense of cosmos, so that spirituality would illumine and transfigure man's life as a cosmic being. Nor should we overlook his stubborn belief that at the heart of things there is that which makes untenable the tragic view of life, such as we find it in classical civilization with its conception of an overruling Fate. Obviously, his optimism has its roots, not in the ancient pagan world, but in a world which is under the sign of Christianity; and if, in upholding it, he was forced into evasions in handling the problem of evil, the answer, strangely enough, is to be found in his yearning for a reconciliation of inward spirituality with the cosmic sense—a reconciliation which is certainly one of the glories of the Catholic tradition.

Emerson's approach to the problem of evil is particularly regrettable in view of the fact that he had dedicated himself to the task of reattaching men to their own experience. His ruling passion was fidelity to the data of experience, yet he was driven to violate the data in dealing only obliquely with that which bites so deeply into our lives, namely, evil itself. Today, we are painfully aware of what has been called "the gods and devils of the human soul." Emerson, it would seem, resolutely averted his gaze from the devils. Yet, he felt impelled to do so in order to restore to life a certain massive and cosmic grandeur which had formerly been associated with religion, and which in modern times had been diverted from it. Perhaps he also felt an overwhelming need to shut out the devils with whom the religion of his own forebears had made him all too familiar, in order to win back his own dignity and freedom as a human being and to regain a proper view of the universe and man's spiritual ties with it. Undoubtedly, too, he was reacting against a religious conception which had become all too personal in excluding ideas like "universal justice" and "universal truth" which had once aroused deep religious emotion. To one like himself who was profoundly affected by Plato's doctrine of archetypal Ideas, universal justice and universal truth were living realities and never mere abstractions. Considering, then, all aspects of Emerson's optimism, we can appreciate the fact that despite its shortcomings, it represents in some degree a real effort to restore an older conception of things.

It has in fact been said that Emerson "was trying to describe an ancient way of seeing by means of a modern vocabulary which had been designed to repress it."[8] Specifically, what the author, here quoted, has in mind is Emerson's concern with an organic apprehension of things in contrast to "intellectual perception," which, according to Emerson, "severs once for all the man from the things with which he converses."[9] As he shows, Emerson set himself against the modern reduction of the thinking ego to a destructive abstraction, in seeing clearly that "an interest in the *how* more than the *what* of knowing would eventually be 'punished by loss of faculty.' "[10] But Emerson's fidelity to the *"what* of knowing" was tied in with his effort to rehabilitate human experience and with it man's relations to a spiritual and cosmic order. Thus he was indeed trying to restore an ancient way of seeing and to an extent which should command our respect. Most certainly, he was offering men a glimpse of the true dimensions of human existence, despite the resistance offered him by the very vocabulary at his disposal and by ingrained habits of thought which could only be dissolved by a kind of violence on his part which also had the effect of throwing him off center.

We have emphasized the empirical character of Emerson's approach. Granting that he violated this empiricism in his handling of the problem of evil, although for reasons which were by no means petty, it is still true that he believed with all his heart in an experiential method. The strength of his belief can be measured by the fact that his search for the single vision in no way caused him to turn his back on the world of multiplicity. "A faithful reporter of multiplicity,"[11] he was unfailingly sensitive to the boundless diversity of things. And like the great thinkers of the Greek world, he had no intention of obliterating boundaries and limit, for, as he says, "the very definition of the intellect is Aristotle's: 'that by which we know terms or boundaries.' "[12] How he felt in the matter is also evident from his educational advice: "Give a boy accurate perceptions. Teach him the difference between the similar and the same. Make him call things by their right names."[13]

Emerson knew only too well that reality resists every attempt to reduce it to an undifferentiated whole, such as is to be found in a materialistic or a spiritualistic monism. "Recognize the inextinguishable dualism," he writes in his *Journal,* ". . . But also show that to seek the Unity is a necessity of the mind . . ."[14] But apparently this conviction of Unity is not only rational but also a matter of belief, for he writes, "A believer in Unity, a seer of Unity, I yet behold two."[15] More likely then, this search for unity arose not only out of "a necessity of the mind," but out of what he elsewhere describes as *the universal impulse to believe,* that is the material circumstances and is the principle fact in the history of the globe."[16]

As to nature itself, what he beheld was a wondrously diversified world, exhibiting everywhere amazing contrasts and a polarity of opposites. "Nature is upheld by antagonism,"[17] he says, and when he looks upon God as the very resolution of all such antagonism, he is merely pointing up his acceptance of its cosmic and fruitful character. But Emerson's keen awareness of diversity and antagonism was not without its painful side, as we may gather from his words, "Cannot I conceive the Universe without a contradiction?"[18]

True enough, as it has been noted, his attempt to view the endless variety of things in relation to "the absolute End"[19] often led him to a too rapid ascent from diversity to unity. But it would be wrong to interpret such an ascent as mere flight from the complexity of the world. On the contrary, Emerson sought multiplicity out, experiencing real exultation in perceiving nature's inexhaustible opulence. But, nonetheless, he believed with every fiber of his being in the essential relatedness of all things; and the unity he envisaged was fully concrete—"the inexplicable continuity of this web of God,"[20] in which "contrary and remote things cohere."[21] Things are strictly related, and no matter how small or large the range of our perception, we find, not merely "surprises and contrasts," but a "guiding identity" running through them."[22]

There can be no doubt that Emerson had a lived awareness of this wholeness, and that it was activized by contact with the simplest objects in nature. But if he was capable of total absorption in ordinary things, his heart fairly danced with joy before the variety of nature's forms and "the majestic beauties which daily wrap us in their bosom."[23] And even the single glimpse became a moving experience when it was caught up in the panoramic view and when in his imagination he projected it against the background of the world and the universe, and when finally he saw it in relation to the all-fair, "the ever-blessed ONE,"[24] whose infinity encircles the humblest of objects.

Nothing so plainly demonstrates Emerson's sensitivity to the complexities of the real world as his grasp, not merely of a universal relatedness, but of its dynamic character. The astonishing interplay of the most divergent things and the ceaseless tension of opposites fascinated him. Spellbound before so enthralling a spectacle, he wished that others might perceive it as vividly as he

did, for he knew how effectually it could arouse the intellect from
a state of torpor and lethargy.

But Emerson saw much more than a world teeming with opposition and tension, for he was too keenly perceptive of life and
motion to miss the universal rhythm which nothing escapes. Thus
he writes: "That great principle of Undulation in nature, that
shows itself in the inspiring and expiring of the breath; in desire
and satiety; in the ebb and flow of the sea; in day and night; in
heat and cold; and, as yet more deeply ingrained in every atom
and every fluid, is known to us under the name of Polarity,—these
'fits of easy transmission and reflection,' as Newton called them,
are the law of nature because they are the law of spirit."[25] And
with the "solar eye" of his spirit he beheld how rhythm pervades
man's life as an individual and his life in relation to all that lies
around and beyond him. In one sovereign moment he is face to
face with his own baffling uniqueness; but, in the inescapable flow
of life, this experience gives way to one in which the individual is
drawn out of himself and into the embrace of the universe. Always
there is this rhythmic movement, this universal Undulation, an
ebb and flow, an oscillation of states.

The intellect itself is not immune, for its daily history is characterized by a ceaseless alternation between expansion and con-
traction. Thus, no matter where he looks, Emerson finds unfailing
manifestations of a universal rhythm, which governs spiritual as
well as cosmic processes: ". . . the chemical and ethereal agents
are undulatory and alternate; and the mind goes antagonizing
on . . ."[26] And this rhythm also shows itself in the relation between
the spiritual and material sides of human life, and between thought
and action, perception and expression, struggle and repose, breadth
of life and intensity of life, society and solitude, culture and
originality, history and character. To flout this universal rhythm
is to do violence to the simplest facts of experience, while exposing
oneself to the crudest errors through a static conception of things.
But when we grasp the true proportions of rhythm, we gain a new
insight into the wonderfully dynamic unity of the universe and
its awesome necessities.

Clearly, then, no interpretation of Emerson has any claim to
adequacy which does not do full justice to that which inspired his
every thought and word—his synoptic vision. Such a vision forbids
any discrediting of the world of nature which lies expanded before
us. It also rules out every fragmenting conception in making
manifest what has so often been overlooked by good philosophers,

namely, the extreme importance of the category of relation.
Hence, Emerson's unfailing concern with unity was justified, for
he knew that nothing can be viewed in isolation in a universe
which is truly a universe, and whose unity, moreover, is dynamic.
"Nature is intricate, overlapped, interweaved and endless,"[27] and
the single vision does not permit the weaving of "a spotted life of
shreds and patches."[28] The togetherness of all things was thus for
Emerson the primal truth, and in his fidelity to it he was the
worthy heir of a great tradition in which we find some of the
greatest of the Christian mystics. And like these mystics he knew
that one cannot seek God with the whole of one's being without
attempting at the same time to view Him and all things in one
great vision.

IV

AN AUTHENTIC INDIVIDUALISM

Emerson's habit of seeing things in the widest context, that is,
in relation to the Universe and finally to the eternal ONE, governs
his conception of human individuality. Accordingly, we should
think twice before applying to his view the term "individualism"
in its derogatory sense. The implacable foe of fragmentation, he
could never rest satisfied with any conception of individuality
which would make of it a spiritually self-sufficient entity, and
one devoid of all ties to the universe. Everywhere in his works we
find statements of the essential Emersonian doctrine. Nothing can
escape from the "magic circle of relations,"[1] for "relation and connection are not somewhere and sometimes, but everywhere and
always."[2] And it is this insistence on the fact of a universal inter-
relation and interpenetration of things which is behind his statement that "to the young mind every thing is individual, stands
by itself."[3] He is not denying individuality, he is merely pointing
to the fact that, with the growth of understanding and knowledge,
we discover how separate things are yet bound together by common roots which run underground.

The Emersonian viewpoint is also clearly stated in a variety of
ways. Thus he tells us that "nothing is quite beautiful alone; nothing but is beautiful in the whole. A single object is only so far
beautiful as it suggests this universal grace."[4] Again he asserts
that in order to be beautiful a thing must have "a certain cosmical
quality, or a power to suggest relation to the whole world, and so
lift the object out of a pitiful individuality."[5] "The fable of

Proteus has a cordial truth," he writes. "A leaf, a drop, a crystal, a moment of time is related to the whole, and partakes of the perfection of the whole. Each particle is a microcosm, and faithfully renders the likeness of the world."[6]

As for man himself, he, too, must be viewed in his relatedness, for he, above all, is "a bundle of relations," whose "power consists in the multitude of his affinities, in the fact that his life is intertwined with the whole chain of organic and inorganic being."[7] "Our life," he says, "is consentaneous and far-related. This knot of nature is so well tied that nobody was ever cunning enough to find the two ends."[8]

We may expect, then, that his view of human individuality is far more intricate and subtle than is ordinarily supposed. In general, it may be said that his conception took shape within a framework of ideas fashioned out of his determination to uphold both the diversity of things and that Blessed Unity which "compels every atom to serve an universal end."[9] Thus, while he lays stress on the originality and uniqueness of each individual person, he can yet speak of the unity of all men in a way which sounds like a fullfledged monism. No one has insisted more than Emerson on the need for individual self-culture, and no one in his day so completely exemplified a certain aloofness from society, which was dubbed "scholastic asceticism."[10] Still, it was Emerson who said that "man is explicable by nothing less than all his history,"[11] and that "our knowledge is the amassed thought and experience of innumerable minds. . . ."[12] It was he also who declared that "so massive is our debt to tradition that in a large sense, one would say that there is no pure originality."[13]

However, although Emerson regards the unity of mankind as real, this unity seems to have but an ideal status, inasmuch as it operates largely in and through each individual consciousness, taken in isolation, rather than through the actual expansion of communal life. Apparently, in his view the single individual, as such, develops a social consciousness, thereby bringing unity down to earth as a recognized value. It would appear, therefore, that Emerson failed to see the way in which the growing unification of mankind finds its actual embodiment in and through the evolution of concrete society as a whole. He could, indeed, envisage a gradual improvement of society, but the relation between the development of society and its structures on one hand and expanding social consciousness on the other seems to have escaped him. Hence he can rejoice because "the world is awakening to the idea of union,"[14] and still fall back into an isolationism which is content with a merely ideal rather than an actual concrete union.

Nevertheless, by way of compensation, Emerson's doctrine not only puts a much-needed stress on social consciousness as it expands within the depth of personal life, but it also gives to the unity of mankind a transcendent status which is no abstraction, having behind it all the splendor and reality of the Platonic Idea, which, in the Emersonian framework, seems to have a creative energy. As we see, then, Emerson's conception upholds the unity of mankind as an absolute value, and he really apprehended this value in its objectivity. Emerson's sense of value was very great, and it manifests itself here as clearly as in so many other things with which he concerned himself. Nevertheless, although he upholds the unity of mankind as a value, while throwing into focus the role of the individual person in bringing that value down to earth, he still failed to grasp that side of the process of unification which has to do with social and institutional development. However, he was certainly not alone in an age which was just beginning to discover the reality of society *qua* society. Besides, the circumstances of his day were such as to make imperative his stress on the inward and personal consciousness of mankind's unity, in grounding that consciousness, not in a purely evolutionary process, regarded materialistically, but in each individual's vital relation to a spiritual and transcendent sphere.

Unity was so intensely real to Emerson that for him the real opposition lay, not between individuality and sociality, but rather between a genuine form of individuality, which maintains its anchorage in the eternal and absolute value of unity, and the spurious form, which has sundered itself from that value. Emerson's quarrel with the society of his day was, therefore, not the expression of a rank individualism. It was simply the outgrowth of his conviction that this society promoted not the true form of individuality, but mere particularism, or the spurious form. To him it seemed that society had reduced what should have been a unity, consciously experienced, to a hodgepodge of individuals, who having in the depth of their spirit suffered amputation from the trunk, "strut about so many walking monsters . . ."[15] Men fear to express what they are, as though they "are ashamed of that divine idea which each of us represents,"[16] and in forgetting their eternal moorings, are so reduced to a fragmentary status that they are hardly to be reckoned as individual characters. In this degenerate state, they are unable to resist the process of aggregation which rides roughshod over them, and, instead of having truly personal fates, are "reckoned in the gross" and are called the "mass" and the "herd."[17]

In thus appearing to make the actualization of mankind's unity in time purely a matter of individual consciousness and self-culture, Emerson was not able to view history in a way which would bring it to life. For history, after all, is essentially the process of man's unfolding within the developing forms of associated life. Nevertheless, Emerson's conception was not without value, even in regard to history, since it enabled him to show that, as the fruit of a living relation of the human soul to a world beyond space and time, the very aspiration toward unity must ultimately be explained from above rather than from below.

At a time when evolutionism was in the air, and when men were beginning to regard things *sub specie temporis,* Emerson's insistence in viewing history *sub specie aeternitatis,* that is, in terms of a reality transcending the temporal order, is not to be scoffed at. In his own way, Emerson was offering resistance to an absolute immanence, especially of the materialistic type. For not only could he proclaim the sacredness of history,[18] but he could also affirm the absolute originality of the individual person, as well as the openness of the human soul to a spiritual world beyond the world of matter. He was therefore helping substantially to form an atmosphere in which a historically minded man like Orestes Brownson could arrive at a more realistic view of society and history, without ceasing to stress the transcendent dimension and the individual's vital relation to it.

Emerson's affirmation of the vertical or spiritual as against the horizontal or temporal axis in history served a practical purpose, for it lent a certain metaphysical support to his appeal to men to rid themselves of a deadly fixation on the past which made them its slavish imitators. If history is in some real sense sacred, if its relation to the Eternal One runs right through it as a primary fact, then that relation is just as real in the living present as it was in the past. Men had to be brought to a realization that a divine force is operative here and now, and in a town meeting as well as in the great centers of culture. He would make them see that the world is "plastic and fluid in the hands of God,"[19] and that each moment breathes its own immortal breath. The world has felt God's impulse in the past and would feel it again, and men must have the courage to respond to it. Men must recognize a "trans-

cendent destiny," in viewing themselves as "redeemers and bene-
factors, obeying the Almighty effort and advancing on Chaos and
the Dark."[20] Clearly, then, "it is the office of a true teacher to
show that God is, not was; that He speaketh, not spake."[21] If
man fears to implant himself firmly in the present, and "with
reverted eye laments the past, or heedless of the riches that surround him, stands on tiptoe to foresee the future,"[22] it is a sign
he lacks faith not only in the God of history, but in the human
soul itself through which God makes Himself heard.

Manifestly, Emerson was not acclaiming the value of individuality in a merely emotional or irresponsible way. For he knew
that men would remain impervious to any doctrine of salvation
which was directed only to the soul in general, rather than to
the individual soul. In an age as socially and politically ebullient
as the nineteenth century, a sense of individual human dignity and
freedom was not wanting. But the modern dichotomy between
religious life and life in the world showed itself once again, and
the new feeling for the dignity of each individual was being severed
from its spiritual roots. Emerson, of course, saw this and expounded a doctrine which aimed at a deepening of consciousness
in order that the new élan toward the realization of individual
dignity and freedom might be transformed into a passionately
held religious conviction. His appeal, therefore, was strictly to
the individual soul and not to the mass of men, and he sought to
make the individual soul aware of its true proportions in relation
to the universe and divinity.

We have made the point that Emerson's true purpose was to
differentiate between a genuine and a spurious individuality, and
not to introduce antagonism between individual self-culture and
community-mindedness. The dominant theme of unity, so profusely expressed in his works, forbade any doctrine of the individual which would controvert it. We can see this still better
when we realize that he was trying to show that true individuality
is to be measured by one's power to live, each in his own way, the
universal life. Thomas Mann expresses exactly what we think
was Emerson's true doctrine: "The world hath many centres, one
for each created being, and about each one it lieth in its own
circle."[23] Individuality and universality are, therefore, not opposed,
since the individual is no mere fragment of the universe, being
rather a focal point, or point of concentration. Emerson's view of
the individual thus seems to be a reflection of a doctrine which
from its presentation by Leibniz has had a notable career in

European thought. For in Emerson we have the constant refrain of an individually wrought wholeness of human life, which is intrinsically bound up with the larger scheme of things.

Emerson's cosmic conception certainly suggests this doctrine of the individual as representative of the whole, as, for example, in the following assertions: "The entire system of things gets represented in every particle";[24] "The world globes itself in a drop of dew";[25] "The value of the universe contrives to throw itself into every point."[26] His essential teaching is also suggested by his statement that "The true doctrine of omnipresence is that God reappears with all his parts in every moss and cobweb."[27]

As for man, Emerson observes that "every mind is different; and the more it is unfolded, the more pronounced is that difference." But he takes care to add that the elements entering in the individual "tend always to form, not a partisan, but a possessor of truth."[28] The unfolding of individuality is hence necessarily tied in with a growth in universality; and even when we aim at a petty end, "our act arranges itself by irresistible magnetism in a line with the poles of the world."[29] Willy-nilly, the individual is enclosed in a real universe and serves its purpose, consciously or unconsciously. And when "the particular man aims to be somebody; to set up for himself; to truck and higgle for a private good . . ." he will learn that "pleasure is taken out of pleasant things, profit out of profitable things, power out of strong things, as soon as we seek to separate them from the whole."[30]

In showing the true role of individuality as against mere particularity, Emerson cannot emphasize enough the truth that "A man is a method, a progressive arrangement; a selecting principle . . ."[31] For it is through one's inborn capacity and traits, one's peculiar temperament and talents that a true position in the scheme of things is established. Each individual is thus called to live the life of the whole by following the line of his own essential bias and by holding to his own vantage point. Away from this vantage point, the world becomes merely external and alien, and history itself loses its meaning. That is why Emerson can say in regard to history, "every mind must know the whole lesson for itself—must go over the whole ground,"[32] and also that "the hours should be instructed by the ages and the ages explained by the hours."[33] History too has its centers, one for each individual, and it concentrates its force, not on human nature in the abstract, but on a living being who, as an individual, occupies one of these centers.[34]

If we examine a volume published in 1826, Sampson Reed's

Observations on the Growth of the Mind (7th ed., Chicago, 1867, p. 95), a book which impressed Emerson at the time, we find statements which bring out the idea of true individuality as constituting the very gateway to a larger life. Reed is endeavoring to show that the mind must grow from an internal principle, and that even from infancy it is endowed with a principle of freedom which should be respected, and with propensities peculiar to itself which will govern its power of absorbing what is peculiarly adapted to it. But what is particularly worth noting is the following (p. 95): "It becomes us then to seek and cherish this *peculium* of our own minds, as the patrimony which is left us by our Father in heaven—*as that by which the branch is united to the vine* (emphasis added)—as the forming power within us, which gives to our persons that by which they are distinguished from others . . ."

Emerson likewise regards true individuality as that by which each is rooted in a common ground of being and life. In recognizing that "Each mind has its own method,"[35] he was not adopting a crass individualism. He was merely accepting a fact and tracking down the implications in terms of his spiritual-cosmic doctrine. And the primary implication, that which blazoned across his consciousness, was the individual's absolute importance as an original way of expressing the whole, as one of an infinite number of variations on the same theme. Hence, when a new mind is sent into the world, we should wait and see what this new creation is, and "of what new organ the great Spirit had need. . . ." For indeed "The charm of life is this variety of genius, these contrasts and flavors by which Heaven has modulated the identity of truth, and there is a perpetual hankering to violate this individuality . . ."[36]

The irreplaceable uniqueness of every human person is at the very forefront of Emerson's thought, and he regards the coming of a person as a veritable irruption into the world, and through which universality is given a new and diversified expression. As a singular spiritual subject each individual is called to occupy his own position in the scheme of things, and in doing so discovers his mysterious contact with the spiritual foundation of things as well as with nature itself. Later, William James would express the same sort of thing in saying, "Knowledge about life is one thing; effective occupation of a place in life, with its dynamic currents passing through your being, is another."[37]

Emerson wished to emphasize the validity of experience, even of the most personal sort, when one lives his life truly, that is, as an authentic individual. As he says: "The poet, in utter solitude remembering his spontaneous thoughts and recording them, is found to have recorded that which men in crowded cities find true for them also. The orator distrusts at first the fitness of his frank confessions, his want of knowledge of the persons he addresses, until he finds that he is the complement of his hearers;—that they drink his words because he fulfills for them their own nature; the deeper he dives into his own privatest, secretest presentiment, to his wonder he finds this is the most acceptable, most public, and universally true. The people delight in it; the better part of every man feels, This is my music; this is myself."[38]

In the light of Emerson's doctrine we can sense the intensity of his feeling when he says: "Is it not the chief disgrace in the world not to be an unit; not to be reckoned one character—not to yield that peculiar fruit which each man was created to bear. . . ."[39] Indeed it was this penetration into the deeper meaning of individuality which made him sensitive to that inner push in each individual by which he seeks actualization, and which so often produces an extravagance of movement, even eccentricity. Thus he says, "to every creature nature added a little violence of direction in its proper path, a shove to put it on its way; in every instance a slight generosity, a drop too much." And so it happens that nature makes men "a little wrong-headed in that direction in which they are rightest. . . ."[40]

There is one thing that remains to be said regarding Emerson's doctrine of the individual. For while this doctrine has a perdurable value, it has nonetheless a certain bourgeois tinge which recommended it to those who were concerned only with mere self-affirmation and self-esteem. Emerson, we cannot forget, was a child of bourgeois culture, a thriving bourgeois culture, and his thought is quite understandably colored by it. Incontestably, bourgeois culture advanced personal values, but it also contributed to their deformation. Considering that his doctrine was given a certain shaping by the age in which he lived, it is not surprising to find lines in his works which conjure up the bourgeois image rather than the deeper reality he was vitally concerned with. Besides, the wider significance attributed to the individual in his authentic doctrine had to be disentangled from his own natural egoism, of which he had his fair share. We would expect, therefore, inevitable confusions, which only a lifetime of personal growth could eliminate, at least in part.

V

SYMBOLIC VISION

We have yet to consider that which lies at the heart of the Emersonian approach, namely, the desire to reconstitute and validate the symbolic consciousness, since it is in and through this consciousness that man experiences the power of material things to convey something beyond themselves. As a being who lies open to God, man is able to sense the supersensual value of things. For nature, as a descending manifestation of spirit, as the very apparition of God, is primarily a living symbol of that which lies above it.

As a symbol of spirit, the most prosaic fact or dull, heavy, despised thing can become, to the aroused intellect, a gift of precious gems, "an Epiphany of God."[1] Hence it can be said that "We learn nothing rightly until we learn the symbolical character of life."[2] Knowing this, "the highest minds of the world have never ceased to explore the double meaning, or shall I say the quadruple or the centuple or much more manifold meaning, of every sensuous fact. . . . For we are not pans and barrows, nor even porters of the fire and torchbearers, but children of the fire. . . ."[3] As "children of the fire," it is natural, therefore, for men to revere nature, the symbol, even "with coarse but sincere rites,"[4] and for the poet to resign himself "to the divine *aura* which breathes through forms."[5]

Since nature is a symbol, it can be used as a symbol. And it is here that language performs its highest and truest function. Words, of course, "cannot cover the dimensions of what is in truth,"[6] yet symbolic language can suggest in a forceful way what is finally inexpressible. And Emerson himself amply demonstrated in his discourses this power of the living word to convey the truth of what was ultimately beyond the grasp of the mind—an elusive yet shining realm of knowledge. For, as Santayana rightly says, in referring to those who venerated Emerson: "More than the truth his teachings might express, they valued the sense it gave them of a truth that was inexpressible."[7]

If nature is indeed the symbol of spirit, "in the whole, and in every part,"[8] then the highest function of language is to convey the larger meaning of things. For through the living metaphor, natural objects, as the emblem of spirit, bring forth answering echoes in the psyche, hinting at realities which escape the grasp of mere concepts and generalizations taken by themselves. It is this fact which leads Emerson to declare as follows: "The use of symbols has a certain power of emancipation and exhilaration for all men. . . . We are like persons who come out of a cave or cellar into the open air. This is the effect on us of tropes, fables, oracles and all poetic forms. . . ."[9] It follows, therefore, that a language which has gone stale, having lost its quality of living metaphor, its symbolic depth, is one which has become, in fact, a barrier to experience and to the normal ascent of the mind from the world of things to the realities of spirit. Having declined into abstractions which are no more than ostensive signs and practical instruments, such a language is no longer one with the living fact, and is thereby rendered incapable of performing its highest function. And when language loses its evocative power, its power to stir up energies and mysterious sympathies and to suggest truths far beyond what is given in the visible world, "wise men pierce this rotten diction and fasten words again to visible things."[10]

In its growth, language exhibits the non-arbitrary character of all natural development. As Emerson says, ". . . each word is like a work of Nature, determined a thousand years ago, and not alterable. We confer and dispute, and settle the meaning so or so, but it remains what it was on spite of us. The word beats all the speakers and definers of it, and stands to their children what it stood to their father."[11] "Language," he says again, "is a city to the building of which every human being brought a stone; yet he is no more to be credited with the grand result than the acaleph which adds a cell to the coral reef which is the basis of the continent."[12]

In line with his view of a certain inevitability in the growth of language, Emerson believed that the symbol, despite its poetic origin, is something found rather than made. Thus he asserts that "this expression or naming is not art, but a second nature, grown out of the first, as a leaf out of a tree."[13] But, nevertheless, he still insists on the transitory character of the symbol, "for all symbols are fluxional; all language is vehicular and transitory. . . ."[14] While reaching depths of the psyche inaccessible to mere abstract statement, a true symbol is yet never more than a temporary vehicle, and having performed its function, it leaves the spirit independent of the visible object which originally awakened inner perception.

The contact with things of nature is indispensable, inasmuch as man's spirit is interwoven in the fabric of nature, and the roots of thinking reach farther into the natural world than is commonly supposed. But in leaping beyond the boundaries of time and space, the human spirit always manifests its privileged position with respect to the outer world. Hence symbolic experience is a flowing thing which stimulates the ascending life of intuitive thought, an experience which implies an organic union of spirit and nature, but of a type which permits thought to leave the things of material nature far behind.

We should overlook neither the Stoic aspect of Emerson's outlook nor the Platonic. It is the Stoic aspect which is in evidence when he plays up the organic relation which binds the human spirit of the universal scheme. But it is the Platonic aspect which show itself in his view that man is the closest point of contact with a transcendent order which surrounds and envelopes nature. By virtue of his spiritual nature man is receptive to the influence of Absolute Spirit, or, if we wish, the Logos, which is also the archetypal principle behind nature. Man possesses, therefore, an intuitive power, which, while prompted by nature and the knowledge of nature gathered by the sciences, is endowed, nonetheless, with a certain intrinsic independence. Thought's function is not merely to provide us with transcripts of the outer world, for it occupies an original position in the universe by virtue of its power to rise infinitely beyond the world of visible things. Enjoying as it does a vital contact with the Infinite, thought has an implicit content which is inexhaustible; hence the widening scope of consciousness, as thought soars upwards in an ascending spiral, always seeking an exodus from every closed circle which would stifle the impulse to infinitude.[15]

How well Emerson's very presentation of an idea conformed to his conception of thought as an expanding life is attested in the following characterization by Francis Thompson: "In some of these essays he is like a great eagle, sailing in noble and ample gyres, with deliberate beat of the strong wing, round the eyrie where his thought is nested."[16] Emerson, he tells us further,

> has his own mode of progression. The gyres are widening gyres, each sweep of the unflagging wing is in an ampler circuit. Each return of the idea reveals it in a deeper and fuller aspect; with each mental cycle we look down upon the first conception in an expanded prospect. It is the progression of a circle in stricken water. . . . And thus the thought of this lofty and solitary mind is cyclic, not like a wheel, but like the thought of mankind at large; where ideas are always returning on themselves, yet their round is steadily "widened with the process of the suns."[17]

But, as we have said, Emerson regards symbolic sight as essential to the very process by which an organic expansion of meaning takes place. That is, in his view the intuitive operation of the mind is sustained and nurtured by poetic imagery, and through such imagery the implicit, latent, and mysterious content of thought becomes a luminous presence. Consequently, thinking at its very deepest is one with the symbolizing process. Nevertheless, for Emerson, the human psyche, in all its profound interiority, plays a highly autonomous role in relation to the outer world.

The poetic image is therefore all-important in that interiorizing process by which the whole of nature is taken into thought. Stimulated by such a viewpoint, Emerson spared no effort to find the appropriate image which would bring the inner world of the spirit to life. And how well he succeeded can be gathered from the following lines by the aforementioned poet:

> No prose-writer of his time had such resources of imagery essentially poetic in nature as Emerson—not even Ruskin. His prose is more fecund in imagery, and happier in imagery, than his poetry—one of the proofs (we think) that he was not primarily a poet, undeniable though some of his poetry is. With such figurative range, such easy and inexhaustible plasticity of expression, so nimble a perception, this iterative style was all but inevitable. That opulent mouth could not pause at a single utterance. His understanding played about a thought like lightning about a vane. It suggested numberless analogies, an endless sequence of associated ideas, countless aspects, shifting facets of expression; and it were much as if he should not set down a poor three or four of them. We, hard-pushed for our one pauper phrase, may call it excess in him: to Emerson, doubtless, it was austerity.[18]

It is interesting to note that Emerson was enthralled, not only by Plato's power to achieve "transcendental distinctions," but also by his method of appealing to ordinary things in building up his thought, for "he fortified himself by drawing all his illustrations from sources disdained by orators and polite conversers; from mares and puppies; from pitchers and soup-ladles; from cooks and criers; the shops of potters, horse-doctors, butchers and fishmongers."[19]

Clearly, in Emerson's view the perceptual experience which underlies the élan of thought and its sense of vanishing limits has esthetic sensibility as an indispensable dimension. "The images," he writes, "the sweet immortal images, are within us—born there,

our native right, and sometimes one kind of sounding word or
syllable awakens the instrument of our souls and sometimes another. . . ."[20] And if the power is in the image, that is because the
power is in nature itself, which, as symbol of spirit, is congenial
to our faculties. "Our music, our poetry, our language itself are
not satisfactions, but suggestions,"[21] which yet have the power
to pierce the wall of insensibility which screens us from a whole
realm of meaning which mere abstract generalization is powerless
to reach. Referring to the kind of metaphor or analogy which
relates "inner" experience to "outer" experience, he writes, "there
is nothing lucky or capricious in these analogies, but they are
constant and pervade nature. These are not the dreams of a few
poets, here and there, but man is an analogist, and studies relations in all objects. He is placed in the center of beings, and a
ray of relation passes from every other being to him."[22]

Obviously then, an organic language is indispensable to the
normal functioning of spirit and mind, and is the necessary vehicle
in that whole process by which man takes the universe into himself. Originally each word was a stroke of genius in providing the
imaginative medium in and through which thought itself could
expand toward infinity, like inspired eloquence which compels the
listener to enter immediately into truth. It was the work of an
intellect which took its direction from its celestial life, while
abandoning itself to the nature of things and allowing itself to be
caught up into the life of the Universe. Today as yesterday, the
restoration of language to its organic character depends on men
who understand that besides the privacy of the power of the individual man "there is a great public power on which he can draw,
by unlocking, at all risks, his human doors, and suffering the
ethereal tides to roll and circulate through him. . . ."[23]

Considering the role of Platonism in Emerson's attempt to rehabilitate symbolical consciousness, we can see why there is in
him a tendency to make the relation of symbol to its visible object
transitory and even somewhat tenuous. As it has been said,
Emerson flees from "the material aspect of the symbol to the idea
represented and from that idea to others,"[24] thereby achieving a
type of symbolism which is "ideal rather than structural."[25] However, as this author points out, there is compensation in the
Emersonian attitude, for "the symbol represents the result of that
creative process by which the poet participates in the flowing
action of nature; if it is well wrought, it will produce the same
immediate effect of spiritual elation which objects of nature in-

spire. It is thus the point of contact between men and the material world."[26] Yet to do Emerson strict justice, it was not so much a matter of flight from matter as an attempt to give full scope to man's openness to a transcendent world of spirit, while rooting him at the same time in the world of nature. Emerson wished to show that inner perception or symbolic sight has an organic and non-arbitrary character which results not only from man's participation in "the flowing action of nature," but from his reception of an in-streaming light from a higher world. The whole creative process of the poet, who comes closer to things than others, is, therefore, one in which an intuitive element is fused with a sensuous element. That is why, in Emerson's view, it is "not metres, but a metre-making argument that makes a poem—a thought so passionate and alive that like the spirit of a planet or an animal it has an architecture of its own, and adorns nature with a new thing."[27]

In a theory like Emerson's which tries to fuse into one single experience suprasensuous and sensuous elements, there is apt to be a certain undue weighting on the side of the "ideal," as against empirical fact. In history a balance between the inner world of the spirit and the outer world of the senses has been seldom achieved, and the historical moment with its need to accentuate one position as against another has resulted in a kind of zigzagging through which man has gradually perceived the possibilities of each. We might also add here that if men have felt impelled to envisage a balance, it is because they were steeped in Christianity, gaining from it the strength to cleave to the given facts and even to penetrate more deeply into them, while yet soaring upward to a realm of infinite truth.

Emerson combed the literature of East and West in his quest for symbols which had been fashioned by the genius of a people, and to which we must return if we would recapture an experience once vividly possessed. These symbols are indeed indispensable; but so, too, are the symbols which have sprung to life in our own age, and of which we must make full use. For, like every age, ours has made its contribution to human experience, and also to the imaginative process without which experience cannot be intellectually and spiritually assimilated. And what is true of our age in general is most certainly true of the New World itself. Therefore, it behooved Emerson to remind his generation that it still awaited its poet, and that it lacked the genius to recognize the values of its incomparable materials. As he says, "Our log-rolling,

our stumps and their politics, our fisheries, our Negroes and
Indians, our boasts and our repudiations, the wrath of rogues and
the pusillanimity of honest men, the northern trade, the southern
planting, the western clearing, Oregon and Texas, are yet unsung.
Yet America is a poem in our eyes: its ample geography dazzles
the imagination, and it will not wait long for metres."[28]

VI

A PURITAN, A ROMANTIC, AND AN AMERICAN

Once we gain the proper standpoint in interpreting Emerson, we
can see why the sweeping generalizations that have been mustered
against him are rather unsatisfactory. Most certainly the attempt
to dispose of him by classifying him as a devotee of the so-called
Romantic religion of self-deification is futile. Even if we do find
in him a strain of Romanticism, this does not constitute by itself
an indictment, for the interpretation of Romanticism is very much
an open question, and will surely be recognized as such when we
gain a better perspective of history and its underlying exigencies.
Like all great movements in history, Romanticism represents a
crucial moment in the very unfolding of human life, and it was
inevitable that there would be a tension between the new and
the old and a confusion of aims, resulting from the failure to grasp
the true implications of what was being freshly perceived. Therefore, we must avoid the simplistic interpretation which would
discern in Romanticism nothing but a religion of self-deification.

Moreover, we should shun the temptation to conjure up easy
generalizations concerning modern history, as, for example, the
view that the leading motif from the Renaissance on is this deify-
ing self-assertiveness, which, it has been argued, was also the
great motivating force behind Romanticism.

This oversimplified approach is untenable, for it confuses the
issue by identifying the unfolding of personal life in history with
a "titanic assertion"[1] of human self-sufficiency. Surely it is somewhat inaccurate to lump together the very emergence of human
personality in a historical process with the deviations and excesses
to which it has invariably given rise.

In his many works Don Luigi Sturzo, the eminent sociologist
and historian, has effectively demolished any view of things which
takes no account of a real historical process, which, as he has
abundantly shown, is bound up with the very unfolding of human
personality. In his *Church and State* he writes, discussing Dante,

"The personality of man and Christian as sung by Dante has continued its unceasing evolution up to our time, and will develop still further."[2] Regarding Romanticism itself, he asserts that despite the literary and artistic excesses of Romanticism, "the underlying exigencies of the Romantic movement were sound: a return to historical, traditional, ethnical, religious and popular values. . . . Such a balance between past and present could be achieved only through a violent eruption, which in its impetus would overthrow established and crystallised positions."[3]

Another author has come forward in defense of romantic and post-romantic literature. According to him, vitalities came to expression in this literature which, despite the fact that they "may not be couched in recognizable Christian forms, are not *ipso facto* to be defined as un-Christian or idolatrous."[4] Indeed he believes them to be defensible expressions of something inherent in Christian faith. And expressly mentioning both Emerson and Wordsworth, he insists that "a powerful latent Christian tradition is to be found in their work."[5]

History is far too complex an affair to permit of our disposing of a man's lifework with a few pigeonhole generalities. Emerson is a case in point, for in him great historical forces came to expression, forces which, as we have intimated, have a core of rightness, even if he himself was not able to express them with an ideal perfection. And this essential core of rightness is all the more important because it has to do with a certain primordial pattern of human experience rather than with abstract theories as such.

There is no doubt that Emerson absorbed much from Romanticism, for he found in it elements that were congenial to his own point of view, not the least of which was an expression of the newly emerging esthetic sensibility to whose further liberation he had dedicated himself. But if the Romantic strain was strong in him, so was the Puritan, which, moreover, served as a powerful disciplining factor. Nor should we forget that he was also an American, wonderfully sensitive to the possibilities that lay concealed in the New World, and aware also of the fecundating effects of America upon the imagination itself.

Let us dwell briefly on Emerson's relation to his own Puritan lineage. The aforementioned writer who finds in Emerson "a latent Christian tradition" declares that Stuart Sherman "rightly identifies the Puritan lineage in Emerson, however obscured." And Sherman's "chief theme," he tells us, "is that Emerson transmits in new and revitalized form 'the vital forces of the great moral traditions, while at the same time he emancipates them from the dead hand of the past.' "[6] But, curiously enough, in listing the elements in Emerson which reflect this lineage, this author makes no mention of that which surely lies at the heart of Puritanism, at least in its primary expression, namely, a transcendent and religious direction of life.[7]

It is important to stress the fact that Emerson was protesting against any view of reality which ignores its spiritual dimension. In other words, any humanistic doctrine of the flat, horizontal type would be unpalatable to him. In fact it was just this religious orientation of his thought which accounts for his nostalgia when he looked back at his Puritan ancestors. "There was in the last century," he says, "a serious habitual reference to the spiritual world, running through diaries, letters and conversation . . . compared with which our liberation looks a little foppish and dapper."[8] And in his *Journal* he writes, "I thought yesterday morning of the sweetness of that fragrant piety which is almost departed out of the world. . . ."[9] Musing over this lost piety, his nostalgia must have become especially sharp when he recalled that "An old lady who remembered these pious people said of them that 'they had to hold on hard to the huckleberry bushes to hinder themselves from being translated.' "[10]

Emerson's preoccupation with the spiritual problem boiled down to the essential question, how "to replace for us the piety of that race [the Puritans]?"[11] For, although Puritan piety had its attractive side, it yet sprang from a theological outlook against which he was revolting. Emerson's beloved and redoubtable Aunt Mary may have hit home in her jibe that he knew only a few bugbear words of Calvinism, but, for all that, he was too immersed in that tradition not to have grasped something of its essential character and spirit.

Even if there was a lingering trace of the "Puritan mystic" in him, he knew that Calvinism went counter to his own understanding of things, especially his conception of man and the world of nature and of the relation between them. As regards human nature, Calvinism narrowed its power and scope in a way that was entirely repugnant to him. For, in Emerson's view, human nature is the very bedrock of religious life in its intrinsic competence to reach a knowledge of moral and spiritual truths, and in its receptivity to a continuous influx of light. Thus his affirmation: "We lie open on one side to the deeps of spiritual nature, to the attributes of God. Justice we see and know, Love, Freedom, Power. . . ."[12]

The alien character of Calvinism in relation to the Emersonian doctrine is easily seen when we consider that its great emphasis on the absolute and creative Will of God, made at the expense of the Divine Intelligence, was not likely to bring to the forefront the notion of nature as reflecting its Maker in its very meaningfulness as well as in its organic unity. Nor could the Calvinist view of the universe effectively resist the mechanistic philosophy which reduced poetry to the status of an ornament, with no claim to any validity in terms of an organic experience. Yet, as we know, the early Puritans made use of a vital symbolism, but they were still burdened by a certain opposition between their basic theological outlook and the human exigency to symbolize. Hence as it has been said, the more a religious writer adhered to this Protestant tradition, "the farther he left behind him the Catholic theory that it was permissible to make frank use of sensuous material and to appeal to the senses in worship and religious art. Also the more difficult his task as an artist."[13]

True enough, Calvinism had an appreciable effect on man's creative activity, but that activity was shorn of much of its human value. Man is plunged into a creative activity which, in making manifest a conformity to the Divine Will, likewise makes manifest the elect of God. But even when surrounded by a mystical aura, such activity was of an external conquering character, entirely alien to the kind of relationship envisioned in Emerson's conception. Thus, human nature, "girt in the poison robes of depravity," to recall a phrase familiar to Transcendentalists, confronts a universe whose significance as a manifestation of divinity has been effectively nullified—a universe which would hardly answer to Emerson's claims on behalf of symbolic consciousness.

The Calvinist doctrine may have proved useful up to a point, in putting iron into the blood of men engaged in the grim work of subduing the wilderness. For a fatalistic spirit held them to their task. Indeed, Emerson perceived a certain grandeur in their granitelike attitude, especially when contrasted with the state of affairs in his own day. "Our America," he says, "has a bad name for superficialness. Great men, great nations, have not been boasters and buffoons, but perceivers of the terror of life, and have manned themselves to face it."[14] And if all great nations and great literatures had this sense of "something which cannot be talked or voted away," the Calvinists must be given their due, for, he avers,

"Our Calvinists in the last generation had something of the same dignity. They felt that the weight of the Universe held them down to their place. What could *they* do?"[15]

But whatever might be said in defense of Calvinist doctrine as it affected human activity, it is a fact, nonetheless, that it introduced grave distortions of elemental truths. And when in the natural course of events human experience once again expanded spontaneously to the full circle of normalcy, the Calvinist doctrine clearly betrayed its inadequacy. Certainly this inadequacy was made manifest in man's creative enterprise itself. For man cannot pursue his creative task without taking the universe into himself, as something meaningful and lovable. Everything in the outer world must be, so to speak, interiorized by him, even the very landscape, for as Emerson said, nothing should be left unrepresented, and "yonder mountain must migrate into his mind."[16] In a hundred ways, through the arts and by means of knowledge, what was merely external thus becomes a potent force in the very depth of man's being.

In America, the need to build up a meaningful relation to the environment assumed mammoth proportions, thereby accentuating the "divided consciousness" already so manifest among the Puritans. For in America a new tension developed between a spiritual orientation and life in time and space, since, along with their religious orientation, men were inevitably taken up with a world whose raw incompleteness was an irresistible challenge to human achievement. But instead of making this tension fruitful, Calvinism turned it into a bitter inner conflict, so that men alternated between a religious longing surcharged with mystical feeling and a materialistic urge to dominate and possess. The split between religion and life in the world seemed complete, and it was to overcome this very split that Emerson offered his conception, designed primarily to illumine human experience itself and its unitary pattern.

We must credit Emerson with exceptional acumen in perceiving that the essential solution lay in the direction of a thoroughgoing transformation of outlook, so that men might once again possess an ancient wisdom regarding the organic unity of things, while grasping the full scope of their relation to the universe. As we have said, Emerson was functioning on the experiential level, aiming at a restoration of experience in its organic unity, so that the inseparability of sensuous and suprasensuous elements might be made manifest. In fact, as we have suggested, he was trying

to restore an older way of viewing things which we would broadly
identify with a tradition at once Classical and Catholic. While he
fell short of an adequate comprehension of that tradition, still,
he was aiming at something close to it, and this despite the fact
that he permitted his rejection of Puritan Christianity to cloud
his mind in regard to Catholic Christianity itself. But even here
the entire story remains to be told, since there are indications in
his *Journals* that he was by no means insensitive to the majesty
and sublimity of Catholic Christianity.

If only he had had a better acquaintance with the Classical-
Christian tradition, he would have been entranced by its marvelous
fusion of elements so dear to him: a sense of an all-embracing
Universe which infinitely surpasses the physical universe of modern science (hence the medieval notion of *Natura* as an all-contain-
ing reality) ; a profound attachment to material nature regarded
as, in some real sense, sacramental, and as manifesting, therefore,
in its every atom, the divine presence; and, following from this,
a high regard for the value of symbolic consciousness, which, despite the Catholic passion for logic, always held its own; an awareness of the structural unity of experience, embracing sensuous,
intellectual, and mystical elements; an unshakable conviction of
man's power to transcend in the very act of knowing a "vicious
dualism" of subject and object; and an equally unshakable conviction of man's natural aptitude for transcendent truth; and
lastly, a superb mastery of the Classical sense of limit and measure
along with an exalted awareness of Infinity and the immeasurable.

VII

AMERICANS AND AN ANCIENT TRADITION

The vital comprehensiveness of the Emersonian standpoint
cannot be missed if we but study it seriously, and with historical
understanding. And what will emerge from such a study, as of
special importance, is the fact that Emerson belongs in a wider
tradition than that of the American humanists. As it has been said:

> . . . Emerson could not remain the exclusive property of the
> American humanists. He has done much to enrich their tradition,
> but the "leaping lightning" of his spirit sprang from their grasp
> when they sought to confine him within the sharply-defined bound-
> aries of their critical world. The bad effect of neohumanist criticism
> upon readers of Emerson has been to close their eyes to the
> existence of that element of mysticism in Emersonian thought,

which, embarrassing though it may be, is the highest rationale
Emerson has offered of art's value in the world of man. In the
event of a new upsurge of faith, this element in Emerson's aesthetic
may again take on the fresh colors which it wore for nineteenth-
century seekers. . . .[1]

We have already pointed to the ancient tradition against which
we must project Emerson's thought if we are to bring all its meaning and value to the surface. However, the importance of his
thought is still further augmented by the fact that he was no
isolated figure in American life, for he belongs in the company of
those Americans who have sought for an integral conception of
things which would be adequate to a full human experience. Without dwelling on Brownson (whose debt to Emerson and Transcendentalism in general is far greater than is usually realized), there
was, significantly, at the beginning of our philosophical development, Jonathan Edwards, and in recent times, Charles S. Peirce,
the most brilliant figure in our own golden age of philosophy. Both
thinkers stood for an all-inclusive viewpoint which would not only
take account of a transcendent realm of spirit and idea, but would
also give an absolute significance to man's life in time and space.
Edwards, it is true, grounded himself in the theology of Calvin,
but, nevertheless, he broke through its confines in his doctrine
of a God, who, in joy, has created a world which is indescribably
lovely and utterly lovable. And in his view of the visible world
as a disclosure of that which lies above and beyond it, he was
upholding the very doctrine which was to find such ample expression in Emerson.[2] Here certainly was a thinker who was rediscover-
ing for himself elements of an ancient tradition, and so effectively
that he has been favorably compared with great medieval Catholic
figures. And as for Peirce, considering his many-sided doctrine,
nothing could seem more natural than that he should acknowledge,
as he does, his close ties with medieval Catholic thought.[3]

In the light of all that we have presented, there can be no doubt
that Emerson is indeed representative of a very significant trend
in American life, a trend which will be more thoroughly explored
once it is perceived. No one has more consistently stressed human
dignity and human possibilities within the framework of a real
world than Emerson, and yet he was profoundly concerned with
the need to emphasize the primacy of man's spiritual orientation.
Like those others we have mentioned, he saw that a spiritual direction of life does not uproot man from his own temporal world but

rather fastens him to it more integrally and more securely and in a way which furthers his innate dignity as a rational and spiritual being. This spiritual emphasis is brought out by a writer who tells us that for Emerson "morality in human life looks not from man to man, but directly from the individual to the absolute spiritual forces whose theatre he is."[4] And another contemporary scholar has this to say: "However much Emerson may have altered the idea of self-reliance to fit the drama of his life, the self and its experience of dependence on a higher source of spiritual power became the ground of his vision."[5] And he also states that Emerson's "daily problem was to maintain a living connection between the horizontal-worldly and the vertical-otherworldly, to live on as many of the platforms of experience that intervened as he could."[6]

Emerson, therefore, was no alien figure when he spoke out to the American people, for he was a living reminder of truths which American experience itself rendered inescapable. We can even say that his whole effort to achieve a meaningful relation between the world of matter and the world of spirit was profoundly American, for, certainly, Americans would never be brought to an effective awareness of things spiritual through mere disparagement of things material.

It is usually supposed that Emerson was appealing to a people whose souls had become subject to the dollar, and who were bartering away their human birthright for petty gain. This is an oversimplification, for Emerson was keenly aware of the positive forces that were stirring the souls of men, and it was to these that he appealed in helping men overcome that in them which was ignoble and degrading. He estimated correctly the power of acquisitiveness in a world of such boundless physical resources as America, but he also knew that men would never gain the strength to withstand the maelstrom of acquisitiveness unless their living contact with so promising an environment were radically transformed. Above all, he saw that materialism must be fought not simply by affirming the higher universe of the spirit but by helping men rid themselves of the "divided consciousness" and therefore of the "split universe" which was ravaging American life and rendering a great people spiritually impotent.

Emerson had a universal appeal in his day, because he had something valuable to offer. Communities everywhere, even the more simple communities of the West, were impressed by his message and felt the "high voltage" in his discourses. If he did

not always succeed in fusing idea and symbol in his poetry, he
demonstrated his power with the symbol in his spoken essays, and
often with dazzling effect.

He was a born phrasemaker, and what he had to say hit home.
This man whose visage had something of the American Indian
about it, and who, like the Indian, was keenly alert to his surroundings, even when he seemed most Olympian in his air of detachment, spoke a language which stirred men deeply. And he
spoke with a directness and simplicity which went straight to
the heart of his listeners. In this respect we can hardly do better
than cite these words of the French critic Charles Du Bos:

> The natural elevation, the directness, the sanity of Emerson: in
> him always the terseness of the spoken word, of a word spoken by a
> man who has never had to achieve simplicity, in whom it is as
> inborn as the sound of his voice: those are the qualities that, when
> I was a youth of seventeen and knew nothing of America, led me
> to think of Emerson as the greatest American, and, leaving all
> question of genius aside, those are the qualities that today make
> America lovable to me. . . .[7]

Emerson, as we have said, never spoke to men in the mass, but
always directly to each individual soul to whose primordial experience he could make his appeal, and with a simple dignity
which excluded the slightest suggestion of condescension. Moreover, he never remained long on the heights, for he was soon back
on familiar ground, conversing in terms of everyday experience,
and demonstrating anew the sincerity of his words: ". . . I embrace
the common, I explore and sit at the feet of the familiar, the low."[8]

He did not merely call on men to throw off the shackles of conformity, and resist circumstances. He did not merely hurl denuncia-
tions, although he knew how to make people wince when he be-
moaned the fact that man had become "the treadle of a wheel,"
"a tassel at the apron-string of society," "a money-chest."[9] Nor
was he content to declare that man "skulks and sneaks through
the world,"[10] that he has ". . . foreclosed his freedom, tied his
hands, locked himself up and given the key to another to keep."[11]
True to the Transcendentalist creed of always affirming the positive, he sought to communicate the need for a total reorientation
of the mind and spirit by opening men's eyes to the reality, not
merely of ideas, but of their perceptual experience of truth. And
in calling attention to such experience of the immediately given,
he insisted that it was not a matter of mere choice, for such per-

ception "is not whimsical, but fatal."[12] Furthermore, he challenged the crude notion that spiritual truths can be evaluated by those who ignore the spiritual data themselves, as when he says: ". . . the definition of *spiritual* should be, *that which is its own evidence.*"[13]

He succeeded in bringing sublime truths into an immediate and even matter-of-fact relation to everyday concerns, and indeed so effectively that he broke the spell of one's routine, whether of the mechanic, the cooper, the miller, or the lawyer, relating one's being and even one's very craft and skill to the universal scheme, so that each one felt that his life was truly intertwined in it. To men keenly aware of new-found rights, he spoke of the basic right which must be cherished above all else, the right "to traverse the star-lit deserts of truth."[14] He made the dedication to truth something as elemental and attractive as the right to appropriate space in the wilderness, and as exciting. He asked his audiences why they should renounce their right to seek truth "for the premature comforts of an acre, house and barn."[15] And in unforgettable phrases he dwelt on the primacy and necessity of speculative thought, while taking care never to violate the American instinct for action and practicality. Indeed he elevated action to a higher dignity by insisting that without it "thought can never ripen into truth,"[16] inasmuch as action in its higher meaning has to do with the way in which a man conducts his life. Action was thus all-important, because, as he also affirmed, man's very "health and erectness consist in the fidelity with which he transmits influences from the vast and universal to the point on which his genius can act."[17] "Of what use is genius," he asked, "if the organ is too convex or too concave and cannot find a focal distance within the actual horizon of human life?"[18]

He touched off something in the souls of men, not by drawing a veil over the things they knew so well and loved, or by underrating perceptual experience, but rather by revealing the poignant beauty of the near at hand, which speaks of a still higher beauty apprehended only by the inner eye of the mind. And as he discoursed, the ordinary objects one met along the way became alive with mysterious meanings, and one suddenly realized that his hundred acres of plowed land were located not simply in America, or on the terrestrial globe, or even in the physical universe, but within the widest reaches of infinity itself. But when he spoke of religion as the very basis of an all-inclusive and organic consciousness, men found themselves restored to a primal experience in which religion is seen to have the same organic and functional position

in the universal scheme as nature's processes, and, indeed, as all
true art, whether of St. Peter's at Rome or of an American clipper
ship.

Henry James, the younger, in his essay on Emerson is endeavoring to explain Emerson's power. He recalls that Matthew Arnold
had contested Emerson's complete right to the title of man of
letters. "Yet," says James, "letters surely were the very texture
of his history."[19] But James himself feels constrained to acknowledge a germ of truth in Arnold's view, for, as he says, Emerson
"is a striking exception to the general rule that writings live in the
last resort by their form; that they owe a large part of their fortune to the art with which they have been composed." In fact he
declares that "it is hardly too much, or too little, to say of Emerson's writings in general that they were not composed at all."[20]
Indeed Emerson, in James's view, "differs from most men of
letters of the same degree of credit in failing to strike us as having
achieved a style."

But of Emerson's "importance and continuance," he seemingly
has no doubt, believing that in this he "shall probably not be gain-
said by those who read him." As for those who do not, they "will
hardly rub him out."[21] And he then comes to the nub of the matter,
for, according to him, Emerson "did something better than any
one else; he had a particular faculty, which has not been surpassed,
for speaking to the soul in a voice of direction and authority. . . .
It penetrates further, it seems to go back to the roots of our feelings, to where conduct and manhood begin; and moreover, to us
to-day, there is something in it that says that it is connected
somehow with the virtue of the world, has wrought and achieved,
lived in thousands of minds, produced a mass of character and
life."[22]

In the light of all that has been said, these words of Henry
James are surely loaded with meaning. And the more we ponder
them the more we must acknowledge that whatever we may think
of Emerson's style, we must yet concede that he had the literary
power to communicate something of prime importance—what we
have called the single vision—and by means of a symbolical consciousness which he possessed to a superlative degree. Valiantly
and unremittingly he dwelt on the absolute importance of this
vision, while showing how man's "continual self-recovery" is
bound up with the deepening to infinity of his self-knowledge, since
he is in truth a being who holds within himself the "poles of the
Universe."

JAMES FENIMORE COOPER
1789 - 1851

Myth-maker and Christian Romancer

CHARLES A. BRADY

A FEW days after James Fenimore Cooper's death, which took place on September 14, 1851, a meeting was held in New York, with Washington Irving in the chair. The great American city had grown away from what it had been in Irving's *Knickerbocker History* and *Salamagundi Papers;* it was even further removed from the Theocritean city of Cooper's *Satanstoe* and *The Water Witch*. In the last decades of Cooper's life, the old corsair "with the blue surtout buttoned up to his throat and his hat over his eyes," as Nathaniel Willis once described him, had come to look on New York as Carlyle would later look on London. But the members of the literary community, at least, were loyal to their first lion. They formed a committee to set up in New York a colossal statue of the dead writer. After years of fruitless effort, the Cooper Monument Association turned over its inadequate funds to a group in Cooperstown where, in the end, a slender shaft, with a statue of Leather-Stocking on it, was reared in Lakewood Cemetery.

The situation is allegorical in more ways than one. Cooper's original high critical estate has, over the intervening years, dwindled into something less than a slender shaft which, as it happens, is still crowned by Leather-Stocking, though contemporary criticism is now willing to set those sullen pioneers, the Bush family and the family of Aaron Thousandacres, at the base of the pediment.

The present study intends to suggest that the whole Cooper question be reopened, and that Cooper be revalued as something much more than a pioneer novelist who is extrinsically important because he happens to have been first in certain fields. This study agrees with Marius Bewley, in *The Complex Fate*,[1] that Cooper

belongs to a line of novelists who represent America's "greatest
achievement in art," and that he "is seriously underestimated at
present." It accepts George Macaulay Trevelyan's humane caution
that "any author who was, for a number of years together, considered to be a great writer by a large number of the elect spirits
of any former age, must have some great merit." Among those
"elect spirits," incidentally, was this not inconsiderable company:
Honoré de Balzac, Franz Schubert, William Makepeace Thackeray, Herman Melville, William Cullen Bryant, Francis Parkman,
Walt Whitman, Ivan Turgenev, and Anton Chekhov.

One of the main difficulties with the chorus of praise accorded
Cooper by these "elect spirits" was that it was so indiscriminate.
Like the first stage of Cooper criticism, which now begins to appear
to have been right in its main outlines, they admired without
giving reasons. The second, deprecatory phase relegated his novels
of the sea and forest to the lowly and mistaken state of children's
classics—a singularly unfortunate lot for Cooper since, in so
many respects, those same masterpieces are about as suitable for
juvenile readers as the works of Faulkner or Hemingway.

The third phase of Cooper criticism, from which we are just
now emerging, established him as a sociological novelist and a
critic of society. It seems to me that he has been overpraised on
this plane. He is a shrewd observer and a crotchety conservative
philosopher who never manages to integrate his observations into
fiction or subdue them to the purposes of the novel. *Homeward
Bound* and *Home As Found*, for example, anticipate Dickens'
strictures on American provincialism in *Martin Chuzzlewit*. But
Martin Chuzzlewit is a great novel; they are not. On the whole,
the intuitions of the first school—and of such more recent critics as
Carl Van Doren, D. H. Lawrence, and Yvor Winters—are more
nearly correct. It is time now to assign ordered reasons for those
intuitions.

On the biographical plane, Cooper has not fared ill. In fact,
after the more or less false start of Lounsbury's bland and condescending generalizations, one is tempted to conclude that, in
Spiller's and Grossman's very good books, he has just about received his biographical due. A swift montage, an impressionistic
collage, of Cooper's life reveals paradox and ambivalence constantly trisecting the speciously simple planes of his exterior
existence. He lived through a great socio-political shift during
which the United States passed from a Federal republic, with a
landed aristocracy in the ascendent, to a turbulent democracy out

of which a capitalistic plutocracy began to emerge. Cooper's sympathies and pocketbook lay on the side of the old squirearchy and the even older patroons; nevertheless certain of his deepest intuitions were sometimes at variance with these exterior convictions. The hard clarity of his political theory warred against the hardly admitted intimations of his best fiction.

In a sense, *The Prairie's* Natty Bumppo and Ishmael Bush, for all that they seem to be so diametrically opposed, are both different aspects of the same fundamental revulsion from the dialectics of property. So are the Chainbearer and his adversary, Aaron Thousandacres, in the second volume of the Littlepage trilogy. And there were still other aspects of this Cooper flight from the awkward necessities of the unromantic present. Susan Cooper's fragrant memoir of her father recalls a significant tableau—"my father and Dr. Bailey with white powdered heads," playing at being pre-Revolutionary aristocrats in a kind of private Twelfth Night revel. By birth and temperament Cooper, the self-styled American Democrat, remained an aristocrat who never lost a nostalgia for minuet and powder.

Like so many other men, Cooper, in his public and private faces, revealed two quite different personalities. To take his public face first, his prefaces, his editorial asides, his bristling demeanor in court and toward the press make him out a stiff precisian as irritated by America as young Martin Chuzzlewit, yet, testy as an Irishman in London or a Gascon in Paris, eager and willing to fight a duel against any European traducer of the young republic. It was this tinder-dry irascibility of his which Sydney Smith struck off when he warned Tom Moore who said that he was going to visit Cooper in London: "Then call him out the first thing you do, for, as it must come to a duel sooner or later, you may as well begin with it."

Smith's witty thrust was well deserved. In Europe Cooper was the choleric man of the medieval manuals. Deciding of Paris that it is "the centre of so much that is excellent, and of so much that cannot be named," a prim judgment that is echoed deliciously, years later, by daughter Susan, when she remembers "that enchanting, wicked, dreadful city, containing many excellent people, and many fiendlike spirits." Comparing the beauties of the Rhine, "so far as native partiality might permit, with the claims of our own Hudson." Condescending to the Alps with the written comment that "a fairer morning never dawned upon the Alleghenies than that which illumed the Alps." Setting, years after-

ward in *The Oak Openings,* the cap on this fierce jingoism with
the brag: "Thus it is that one American mocking-bird can outsing
all the birds of Europe united."

Yet there was another side of the shield, too. Even in Europe,
the American lion, while one would never term him precisely
amiable, knew how to roar softly on occasion. One could wish
that Walter Savage Landor might have been passing on the Paris
staircase where Cooper and Scott first met.

"Est-ce Monsieur Cooper, que j'ai l'honneur de voir?" asked
the Scottish lion in his Doric burr.

"Monsieur, je m'appelle Cooper."

"Eh, bien, donc—je suis Walter Scott."

Monsieur, je m'appelle Cooper. What a title for one of Landor's
Imaginary Conversations!

Then there was the affable Parisian Cooper who was the friend
of Adam Mickiewicz, greatest of Polish poets and one of the
greatest of Polish patriots. The Cooper who bowed to General
Kellerman in the streets; who escorted one of his daughters to
waltz at a *salon* where Chopin and Liszt were to play for dancing;
who employed "a fine old cuirassier of Napoleon's wars for posti-
lion"; who received letters addressed *À Monsieur Cooper à Paris,*
and signed *Most affectionately yours Lafayette;* who wrote letters
to his little son beginning: *Adieu, petit gamin. Je vous aime de
tout mon coeur.*

Once, at a Paris dinner for George Canning, Cooper naively
wondered about the Papal Nuncio's observance of a fast day. "It
was a fast day in the church and I watched his lordship the Nuncio,
to see if he tasted any of the forbidden things, but French cookery
is a fine cloak in these matters." Cooper was a bluff enough
Protestant of the humane Anglican persuasion who always stig-
matized New England's "Roundhead notions of religion," the
"rowdy religion—half cant, half blasphemy—that Cromwell and
his associates entailed on so many English men." But one would
hardly refer this animadversion on the Nuncio to anti-Catholic
bias. In a letter to his wife, about the Episcopalian Bishop Onder-
donk's propensity for fondling clergymen's wives, he shows the
same disinterested amusement. In fact, so far as Catholicism was
concerned, Cooper displayed something of the same sort of attrac-
tion-repulsion toward and away from it one may also note in
Walter Scott. In his last piece of published writing, he contrasts
unfavorably an American village's "half a dozen ill-shaped, and
yet pretending cupolas" with Catholic Europe's architectural distinction—"but this is one of the hundred instances in which the

thoughtful man finds reason to regret that the church, as it exists among us, is not really more Catholic."

Sometimes a man is best revealed through the wish-fulfillment *personae* he invents for himself in the shape of romantic heroes. Cooper's two most representative romantic heroes, *qua* romantic heroes, are the Red Rover, in the novel of that name, and the Skimmer of the Seas, corsair captain of the *Water-Witch,* who is described as smiling "with a look in which high daring and practiced self-command were blended with a constitutional *gaîté de coeur."* There, in revealing phrase, is the younger Cooper's dream-portrait of himself. What matter if, in practice, this *beau idéal* often degenerated into a middle-aged conservative's port-wine testiness? *N'importe.* Here is the gallant young seaman who once affected a queue, who courted the lovely Miss De Lancey so dashingly as a youth, who, in brisk maturity, as aide-de-camp to Governor Clinton, flaunted his sword, his cocked hat, his blue and buff uniform; and this same bright essence is preserved in the best of the romances.

Cooper's public life fulfilled the arduous criterion Jacques Rivière laid down, in his prophetic *Le Roman d'Aventure,* for the imaginative writer of the future: that he should adopt an active rather than a passive attitude toward life. Allowing for the differences in their respective eras, Cooper's life was as active as André Malraux's, and far more active than Ernest Hemingway's. He was naval officer, colonel in the militia, part owner of a whaler, traveler, United States consul for Lyons, and—not least of his many practical roles—vestryman of the Protestant Episcopal Church of America.

But it is the private Cooper—and, most especially, the domestic Cooper—who really engages our affections; and, unfortunately, this is the Cooper who does not appear in his books, except for occasional sunny flashes in *Satanstoe* and *Afloat and Ashore.* One finds this bonnier personality in the *Correspondence,* and in the memories of his friends and his children. This is the Cooper who talked with John Jay, whose coachman was the son of a Hessian soldier, whose betrothed was a great horsewoman—one thinks at once of Julia Mannering in *Guy Mannering,* and of Scott's spirited Charlotte Charpentier who was also a daughter of Huguenots. But Cooper was luckier than Scott in one important respect. His Greenmantle was something more than a romantic memory. He married his Greenmantle.

This is the Cooper who played chess with his wife on their wedding morning, and on many evenings thereafter. (One wonders if the Cooper chess set had elephant pieces like the chess pieces in *The Deerslayer*.) This is the Cooper whose wife, on his death morning, added the prayers in the marriage service to the morning prayers they always said together. This is the Cooper who was a great connoisseur of weather, who stopped a third of the way through volume two of *The Deerslayer* to note that "it is snowing famously at this instant," and whose last *Journal* entry read:

> Sunday. Numbers. Raining and cool. Most of us went to church, notwithstanding. About seventy persons attended. The Judge was there, having got home last evening. In the afternoon I read the service for my wife, who did not like to risk the weather. About five the wind went down, and it cleared. It seems as if all the clouds that passed in the last easterly storm, have been driven back by this from the west.[2]

There was one region of the stormy Cooper sky where the clouds never gathered: the clear west sector of his serene Anglican humanism, of his deeply reverential Episcopalianism which continued to deepen year by year throughout his life. In the orthodox sense of the word "religious," Cooper is the most religious of our major novelists. What other writer of his century made one of his romances a defence of Trinitarianism? Whenever he touches on the great Christian truths—and, more particularly, on the promise of the Resurrection—the cadences of his aureate diction rise to a noble solemnity. The crown of this Federalist Cincinnatus' political thought is simply and somewhat bleakly put in phraseology not unlike Belloc's harsh clarity. "If the laborer is indispensable to civilization, so is also the gentleman." But, in the higher realm of the spiritual, Cooper never makes the mistake of confusing the secular with the Christian ideal. Anticipating Newman, he distinguishes, in one of *The Chainbearer*'s asides, between the Christian and the gentleman:

> It is a great mistake to confound these two characters, one of which is a mere human embellishment of the ways of a wicked world, while the other draws near to the great end of human existence . . . the great substance of which, after all, the gentleman is but the shadow.[3]

It is no disservice to Fenimore Cooper's memory to say of him that, at bottom, he was first a Christian, and second a gentleman, and an American throughout.

Cooper's almost total obliteration from the contemporary literary consciousness is dramatized by his absence from that famous page, in *Green Hills of Africa,* wherein Hemingway utters his splendid heresy anent the origins of modern American literature:

> All modern American literature comes from one book by Mark Twain called *Huckleberry Finn.* . . . it's the best book we've had. All American writing comes from that. There was nothing before. There has been nothing as good since.[4]

Just before this point, Hemingway had explicitly rejected Poe, Melville, "Emerson, Hawthorne, Whittier, and Company"! He had exempted, along with Twain, Henry James and Stephen Crane. He makes no mention whatsoever of Cooper, unless one assumes that Cooper is included among the "others who wrote like exiled English colonials from an England of which they were never a part to a newer England that they were making."

Yet, in the strictest sense of the word, Cooper is a great American original. *The Pioneers,* for example, may not be a great book. It is certainly, for American letters, an extraordinarily seminal book. In the same sense in which all Russian literature drops out of the greasy creases of Gogol's *Overcoat,* so a good deal of later American literature—good, bad, and indifferent—is shaken out of the snow-flecked folds of the Federal cloak which Squire Cooper spreads so benignly before the pastoral fireplace of his *Pioneers.* Among other things: the dime novel; the western; Thoreau's hut on Walden Pond—Natty was before him on Lake Otsego; Huck's romanticist distrust of settlements; that Hemingway eidolon, the white hunter; even the basic elements of the detective story which Poe, afterwards, was formally to invent. And, by extension —portions of *The Prairie,* especially, are in question here—Faulkner's ravished Temple Drake and Caldwell's cannibalistic shoats.

One of Cooper's great Continental contemporaries and an English successor did not make the mistake of dismissing him so cavalierly. In Balzac's hands certain aspects of Natty Bumppo became transmogrified into the demonic criminal Vautrin, an identification which, incidentally, in no way invalidates Vautrin's connection with the historic *agent provocateur,* Vidocq. And through Vautrin into the faceless lineaments of the unnamed police spy in *Les Misérables;* and, by a second reflex, into still another proto-sleuth in Dickens' *Great Expectations.* Thackeray, who ranked Leather-Stocking with those "great prizemen of fiction," Uncle Toby and Falstaff, paid his creator the enormous compliment of adapting Natty's prairie death to the deathbed of his own Colonel Newcome. One can go even further. Cooper's redskins underwent the oddest sea change of all when they turned up, in the nursery imagination of James Barrie, as the Indian band of *Peter Pan*.

But we must probe somewhat deeper for the psychic provenance of the flight-and-pursuit framework of the adventure story which Cooper made his own, and which, for a time, helped relegate his stories to the mistaken category of the boy's book. Since Conrad endowed this particular pattern with a metaphysic, Kafka with a demonology, and Greene with a theology, it no longer requires defense as a significant esthetic device. Nevertheless, two specific points do call for affirmation here. First, the flight-and-pursuit situation is not only archetypal so far as the human personality is concerned; it was Cooper who, at the very beginning of American literature, inducted it into world letters. And most appropriately, too. For it has an especial connection with the American psyche. As Lawrence, writing on Cooper, percipiently remarks: "At the bottom of the American soul was always a dark suspense . . ."

Second, this pattern's indiscriminate association with Cooper has unfortunately caused his name to be too exclusively connected with certain other artists with whom, it is true, he does have definite affinities, but from whom his divergences are essentially far greater than any resemblances. Like Stevenson, for example, who, in *Kidnapped, David Balfour,* and *Treasure Island,* proved himself a master of pure adventure on a plane of sheer exquisiteness to which Cooper never attained.

Actually, Cooper has more in common with one of his much later admirers, Joseph Conrad. The early Conrad, especially, makes symphonic use of sea and sky and forest as Cooper did; and his most characteristic prose has the fine Latinate roll of Cooper at Cooper's infrequent best. Conrad's white men confront a Homeric age in Malaya, as Colonel Monro and Duncan Heyward had earlier confronted the heroic age on the bloody borderland between the white man and the red. Conrad's movement is psychologically operatic in the same way in which Cooper's is poetically operatic. The anthropological and social verisimilitude of Cooper's Indians was challenged at the very outset. Nevertheless, our great historian of the Indian, Francis Parkman, openly acknowledged his debt to Cooper, even as Hugh Clifford, historian of the Malays, did his debt to Conrad when he went to Malaya for the first time under the potent spell of *Almayer's Folly* and *An Outcast of the Islands,* even though his subsequent histories correct certain of Conrad's inaccuracies.

Conrad's fundamental admiration for Cooper is nicely put in his *Notes on Life and Letters*:

> For James Fenimore Cooper nature was not the framework, it was an essential part of existence. . . . that felicity and sureness of effect that belong to a poetical conception alone. . . . His descriptions have the magistral ampleness of a gesture indicating the sweep of a vast horizon. His method may be often faulty, but his art is genuine. . . . The road to legitimate realism is through poetical feeling, and he possesses that—only it is expressed in the leisurely manner of his time. He wrote before the great American language was born, and he wrote as well as any novelist of his time.[5]

This "magistral ampleness" allies Cooper with the panoplied rhetoric of Faulkner as well as, be it noted, with some of his clotted turgidities. Cooper's detractors have, however, preferred to concentrate on the technical awkwardnesses that disfigure him even more than they do Walter Scott. There is no need to enumerate these technical infelicities. Mark Twain pilloried them once and for all in a parody that is as savage as Thackeray's earlier parody had been affectionate. There is no particular point in attempting to defend them, either. They are indefensible.

Like the fabled girl with the curl, it may be said of Cooper that, when he is good he is very, very good, and when he is bad he is horrid—with a horridness that almost beggars description. His characteristic diction is an unfortunate, inflated late Johnsonese. He has borrowed from Smollett and Fielding—and from Scott, too—some of their more mechanical devices, more especially their comedy of humors which is tolerable in Smollett, better than tolerable in Smollett's successor, Marryat, and which, like Mr. Dick's kites, is destined to rise, in Smollett's spiritual godchild, Dickens, high into the empyrean of pure comedy, but which, in Cooper, attains only an unequaled ghastliness.

In the very nature of things, felicities and infelicities alike must always remain minor categories in the case of a writer like Cooper, whose greatness lies elsewhere than in personality, and who, moreover, seems singularly deficient in such usually essential qualities of a major novelist—especially one who is thought of as an historical novelist—as atmosphere, a sense of the past, local color, fictional density.

Not that Cooper, for all his spareness and almost total lack of personal charm, did not demonstrate certain marked felicities upon occasion. Sometimes his gilded, inkhorn stylistics rise, through rhetorical eloquence, into epithets of Corinthian regality —when, for example, in *The Red Rover,* he describes a northeast wind as "bringing with it the chilling asperity of the hospitable regions of the Canadas"; and again, in *The Pioneers,* where Canada is called "that polar region of royal sunshine." The prose of that chapter of *The Deerslayer* wherein Natty kills his first man and receives his first battle sobriquet is magnificently sustained— in point of fact, this chapter must be acknowledged one of the great set pieces of American fiction.

The worst of his novels is likely to be lit up, in the most unexpected places, by short passages of historical narrative that are in the grand tradition of Thucydides and Gibbon. Flags and ships, awaking Cooper's heraldic imagination, make him soar to lyric heights; and, when this Pegasean interlude occurs, it is always an organic thing, never an extraneous interpolation.

It must never be forgotten that there are certain special difficulties inherent in Cooper's artistic intention that did not beset the other novelists of his day, but which, now that the contemporary novel has moved so far away from its original narrative base in the direction of lyric and metaphysic, are readily apparent to us. In Cooper's time the novel, whether comic or tragic in idea, whether realistic or romantic in method, was necessarily more or less naturalistic in its overtones, a fact which ran counter to the old classic tradition of the West that always demanded what, for want of a better term, one may call "high style" for epic and tragedy, as Fielding's transitional volume, *Tom Jones,* bears uneasy witness. At his best, Cooper's basic purpose—though, very likely, he was not self-conscious enough, as an artist, to phrase this clearly to himself—was closer to the purpose of Vergilian epic and Euripidean tragedy than to the newer novel form which he had inherited from the eighteenth-century English writers; and he must pay a certain penalty for his pioneering here as elsewhere.

Now the foregoing paragraph is in no way designed to imply that Cooper was ever unconcerned with story. He was very much concerned with that eldest of the muses, the tenth and unnamed mother muse whose Arabian cognomen is Scheherezade. Cooper writes quintessential story. With him—but not with the novelists of the central tradition—story is in the center, and character is peripheral. Or, perhaps, it would be better to say that with Cooper action is character and character is action. When one is tempted glibly to brush off Cooper's preoccupation with "pure" story, one must realize how many things—and how subtle—are connoted by a comprehensive esthetic of "pure" story.

Ever since Lounsbury's day, even Cooper's comparative denigrators have been ready to admit the fertility of his inventive powers. They have been less willing to point out the richness and multiplicity of his themes. To isolate, at this juncture, but a few recurrent motifs, one may single out: a *nostalgie du temps perdu* —less frequent and less important, actually, than critics have assumed; the psychic-doubles who are surrogates for Everyman's divided soul; the majesty of death; the theological dogmas of Incarnation, Resurrection, Redemption, the Trinity, the survival of the individual personality; the ambivalences of divided loyalties on both the physical frontier and the moral frontiers of war and social and political change; the symbolic counter-claims of axe and rifle; the romance and the *mystique* of race and nationality; purification by the wilderness; the Ishmael figure; man's relationship with nature; the celibate hero; the aristocrat under democracy; the new American man.

Cooper's serious themes usually move, in stately tempo, within a frame of forest and sea, of high political idea, of the frontier as an idea simultaneously accepted and rejected and, in either contingency, invariably disliked. Some of his sea stories—*The Red Rover*, notably, and *The Water-Witch*—are set inside a frothy ambience of Shakespearean pastoral and near-Gilbertian musical comedy, with spruce midshipmen heroes and high-bred heroines in Arcadian masquerade. Cooper's geographical sense is as sharp as only a professional sailor's can be. Nevertheless, there are certain stories of his which seem to award Bohemia a seacoast, for the second time, and to locate Illyria on the moon.

In the words of *Guy Mannering*'s Dominie Sampson, Cooper's total published canon is pro-dee-gious. Within thirty years he produced more than fifty books of double-, if not triple-decker, dimensions; and this exclusive of numerous periodical articles, pamphlets, and reviews. Thirty-three of these—if one counts *Autobiography of a Pocket Handkerchief* (1843) as a novel, and it is surely as much or as little of a novel as *The Monikins*—are novels. The rest are divided into travel books, historical writing, and political tracts. His travel *Gleanings England* [1837], *France* [1837], and *Italy* [1838], particularly) are better than respectable specimens of their loose genre. His long *History of the Navy of the United States of America* (1839) is narrated with sobriety, even detachment, and with amazing objectivity, despite the bitter controversy which arose over his treatment of the Battle of Lake Erie.

In addition to D. H. Lawrence's too-simple classifications, "Fenimore Cooper's White Novels," and "Fenimore Cooper's Leather-Stocking Novels," there are several possible ways of breaking Cooper's novels down into categories. One might, for instance, divide them into Indian novels; novels of the sea; novels of the Revolution; novels political and sociological. Such a listing would be workable enough, but not exhaustive; and by no means mutually exclusive. Some categories would overlap—*The Pilot*, for example, is both a sea novel and a novel of the Revolution; *The Pathfinder* has to do with both wood and wave. Within these multiple categories, one can detect certain lines of development as well as a continuity of theme. The lover's quarrel with America, which begins with Cooper's second novel, *The Spy*, ends in downright Xantippean shrewishness by the time of *The Ways of the Hour*, his last piece of fiction.

The theological dimension deepens most impressively all the way through. Such themes as the ambivalence of his national-international alignment, as the cultural tension that racks all American writers from Irving to Hemingway, because they have two fatherlands—three, really, Europe, England, and America—as the Jamesian trauma of the emotional expatriate, though subsidiary matters for Cooper, are apparent from beginning to end. So is that other ambivalence, which reproduces the Europe-America clash *in petto*: the alternate attraction and repulsion of the frontier. Cooper was no passionate pilgrim, like Irving, James, and that Anglo-Indian outlander, Kipling. He was a spikily irascible, reluctant pilgrim, like our century's Sinclair Lewis. But he was a pilgrim none the less; and the equivocal lure of time long past, and of his seven years spent abroad, made American Cooper, to a certain extent, at least, what the artist must always be in part: a man without a country. Or better, perhaps: a man who must own to many countries.

These antipodes of the mind and heart are not American antipodes alone. They belong to the human personality at large; and to every literature. They are Barrie's Nursery posed against Never Never Land, Scott's Greenmantle set over against Julia Mannering.

But they are peculiarly sharp in American letters, as we may note them in the Twain antinomy of Huck and Tom. For Cooper they might be summed up as Natty Bumppo *versus* Judge Temple; as the Axe *versus* the Rifle; as the virgin forest of *The Deerslayer versus* the firelight on the paneled wall in *The Spy*, in *The Pilot*, in *Lionel Lincoln;* in several of the other novels as well.

Precaution (1820), Cooper's first novel, need detain no one very long. In title and tone almost a pure pastiche of Jane Austen, *Precaution* possesses the psychological atmosphere of *Emma*, the scene of *Pride and Prejudice*, the plot of *Persuasion*, but without the cool Austen intelligence. It maddens one with abstract Addisonianism and florid Johnsonese not even rendered tolerable by wit. In "the mild, the tender, the unassuming Clara," one encounters the kind of Cooper "female" who has made his name a byword for the insipid.

The Spy (1821) is another thing again. Not only is it the first of the really good Cooper novels, not only does it remain one of the best, but it is the first of his sheerly American books, striking a thrilling new chord: the romance of nationality. Just as Sydney Smith was asking his unfortunate question: "In the four corners of the globe, who reads an American book?," America as a subject for romance was being born. "The nation is passing from the gristle into the bone," wrote Cooper in a later preface to *The Spy*. Before that, writing *in propria persona* in the course of his romance, and noting "the richest lustre of an American autumn," he had commented that such "moments belong only to the climate of America"; and, as he wrote—and even today, as we read— emotion charges the very word, *America*.

Above all else, *The Spy* is archetypal Cooper, gathering into its misleadingly simple pages a rich congeries of typical Cooper motifs, each separate motif invested by the mythopoeia that marks Cooper's concept of his mysterious personages, Harvey Birch, the Spy, and Mr. Harper, who is General Washington incognito. In each other's company Harper and Birch appear like gods, like Jupiter and Mercury, moving again the august action of a war as fraught with destiny as Troy's high conflict. Even taken by himself, Harper is still a father god, associated with "the empire of reason"—Cooper's own epithet—and hence a symbol of the marmoreal stability for which Cooper, in his political nature, was so nostalgic. (Leather-Stocking, on the other hand, represents, among other things, a restless poetic response to the complexities of change.) Harvey Birch, Washington's spy of the neutral ground, is the first of Cooper's guardian presences, a mythopoeic emanation, almost, of the American landscape. He is also, like Leather-Stocking, a celibate hero, a tutelary wandering spirit, a protecting demigod, a redemptive figure. As he moves through mists and powder smoke, outlined on hilltops, misshapen "under the weight of his pack," as under the weight of the cross, Birch could be the Hanged Man of the Tarot cards. The cave where Birch hides Harper is still another archetypal symbol, one heavy with intimations of deity.

Unlike Leather-Stocking, however, Birch is an Ishmael figure, an outcast pariah against whom all raise their hands; and he is, besides, ambiguous, his identity unknown, his allegiance a matter of doubt. Westchester's neutral ground, between the contending British and American forces, is a half-world where many people "wore masks, which even to this day have not been thrown aside." Later on, Birch himself asks the kind of question that, with its suggestion of the ascertainment of spirits, is also curiously suggestive of the sinister ambivalence of Kafka's shadowland.

"Who do you call the enemy?" said the pedlar.

It is a question all too familiar now in our century of divided loyalties. Cooper is unconsciously preoccupied—the Byronic Pilot of the next book is another case in point—with men moving between two worlds as, in a certain sense, he always did himself, at least in the sense in which such later expatriates as James and Eliot were so to move—though with them the balance was to fall on the side of Europe, and with Cooper it fell on the side of America. There is even a real affinity between Cooper's anxious, moody, tortured patriots and Dostoevsky's revolutionists and *agents provocateurs* who are rarely revolutionists and *agents provocateurs* purely and simply, but often men of dual loyalties, uncertain of their own motivations.

A chronological estimate of Cooper's work would normally consider his third novel, *The Pioneers* (1823), here. But since *The Pioneers* belongs to the Leather-Stocking cycle—cycle is probably a better term than saga—consideration of it will be deferred until the time comes to look, *en bloc,* at this most towering achievement of Cooper's essentially mythic imagination. There are several additional reasons for thus stepping outside the chronological pattern of composition, and yet, when weighing the Leather-

Stocking stories individually, for reading them, not in the ideal order of Natty Bumppo's progress from heroic young manhood to apotheosis as elder prairie god, but in the staggered order in which Cooper wrote them, with the first composed coming third and the last written coming first in the corrected chronology.

For one thing, the order of composition is their true order in the important realms of both psychology and myth. It is proper that great mythic presences like *Le Gros Serpent* and *La Longue Carabine* should, by a radiant reversal, between *The Pioneers* and *The Prairie,* grow into youth and immortality, recapturing the Garden that was in the beginning—this is what Lawrence meant when he said, not altogether fairly, since each novel in the series has its own individual loveliness, that the Leather-Stocking books accomplish "a *decrescendo* of reality, and a *crescendo* of beauty." Again, Cooper's own concept of Leather-Stocking deepens as he deals with him from book to book.

As Jane Austen—or, at the very least, since the point is still a little in dispute, Jane Austen's school—was the occasion of Cooper's first novel, so his fourth book, *The Pilot* (1824), finds its *donnée* in Scott's *Pirate.* (Scott was to prove a constant creative irritant to Cooper ; and not always for the better. Scott's medieval novels, *Ivanhoe* and, more especially, *Quentin Durward,* would soon provoke Cooper's unsuccessful European trilogy.) At a dinner party in New York, where the seamanship of *The Pirate* was being praised, Cooper contemptuously dismissed it as the cunning *vraisemblance*—as if this were not a great deal!—of a landlubber ; and, by way of riposte, committed himself to write a more "authentic" tale of the sea. Thus, in a most un-Gilbertian manner, the American began his emulous apprenticeship to the greatest of all romancers, with one of the Scots master's lesser books, *The Pirate.* It is interesting to assess the two great rivals comparatively : gentlemen amateurs both and, in spite of this disabling fact, both writers of genius.

In his preface to *The Pirate,* Scott defends the liking for the supernatural, so inherent in his own romanticism, by pointing out that excessive rationalizing of the supernatural produces "a degree of improbability almost equal to an absolute goblin narrative." Cooper, whose mind is, perhaps, less haunted than that of any other great American writer, with the possible exception of Emerson, pooh-poohed the Scottish warlock's preoccupation with ghosts, witches, soothsayers, and black-letter magic. Although he, too, had his goblin pack of cards when he wanted to, Cooper always

scorned dealing them into "an absolute goblin narrative." Yet,
where Scott attained fairy tale and ballad—none better in the
whole scope of European letters—Cooper, quite unconsciously,
achieved real mythopoeia. Scott was homesick for the old dead
gods ; he played no part in calling new ones into life. On its highest
level, Cooper's drier, more sober genius is also more original than
Scott's, and, in the last analysis, far more classic. (At every juncture, one is faced with the constant paradox that Cooper's materials are romantic, but that his dry-point classicism of attitude is
not.)

If *The Pirate* is not a thoroughly good book, neither is *The Pilot,*
Cooper's first sea novel and his second novel of the American Revolution. That obsessive theme of his, the ambivalence of divided
loyalties, figures here again, this time within the mind of the Pilot,
who is the Scottish-born John Paul Jones. The Pilot himself, whose
face, on his first appearance, seemed "like the ocean at rest, contrasted with the waters around him," is another attempt in the
mythopoeic-patriotic vein. As Washington blended into the mountains in *The Spy,* as Leather-Stocking will later blend into the
woods, so is Jones intended to blend into the sea. But the trick
does not come off. The Pilot is as theatrically improbable as
Laura or Manfred. There are some good things. Above all, there
is a new thing under the sun, and a new sensibility at work. *The
Pilot* is the first real novel of the sea. Shepherd Hogg, in the *Noctes
Ambrosianae,* called Marryat "a Sea-Fielding." It is not nearly
so easy to categorize Cooper's sea books. He is neither a Sea-
Fielding nor a Sea-Smollett twice removed, nor a Sea-Scott, though
he does point forward to Melville and, after Melville, to Conrad.
What is indubitable is that he is the creator of the sea novel as a
special genre.

These are three of the traumata of experience which, when they
fuse with personal emotion and other themes from the deeper nooks
and crannies of his being, produce the genuine Cooper successes :
the Revolution as a political fact, the frontier as a social fact, and
Europe as an esthetic fact. Sometimes the hammer misses fire, and
the ball fails to reach its mark. This happens in *Lionel Lincoln*
(1825), the first and only member of an abortive group of historical novels to have been called *Legends of the Thirteen Re-
publics.* It is a rather interesting failure, with some capital military
set pieces in the battles of Lexington, Concord, and Bunker Hill.
Major Lincoln, Cooper's titular hero, is another of his divided
men. The Boston weather bites into one—" 'It's a stronger and a

bitter cold is ours, but it doesn't cut one like dull razors, like this
here of America.' " A parallel theme of wrong and retribution,
festering within an old Boston family, adumbrates Hawthorne.
Here is the kind of Puritan seed which will one day come to somber
flower in *The House of the Seven Gables, Jane Eyre, Bleak House,*
and *Little Dorrit*—in *Little Dorrit,* most of all, a book in theme
and atmosphere curiously cognate with *Lionel Lincoln.*

The Red Rover (1827), the second of Cooper's books to be
completed abroad—*The Prairie* had been finished in Paris previ-
ously—is also the first of what one might call his "pure" entertainments, using the term "entertainment" more in Stevenson's than
Graham Greene's sense. Except for an absurd conclusion, Cooper's
touch here, in this gay sea pastoral, is light and sure, and permits
one to match Cooper against literature's great romancers, several
of whom have long since surpassed him in the lists of pure romance.

The Wept of Wish-ton-Wish (1829), set against the somber
background of King Philip's War, is, however imperfect, Cooper's
Old Mortality, for he is fairer to the Puritan mind in this than
in any other of his books. Humane Episcopalian and traditionalist
that he is, his imagination can still kindle to Metacom's respect
for the old Puritan regicide in whose regard Conanchet exclaims:
" 'My pale father is a great warrior. . . . His hand took the scalp
of the Great Sagamore of his people!' " Nevertheless, Cooper never
manages to hit upon his objective correlatives quite so readily as
Scott, and *The Wept* remains a dreary waste of pages lit up now
and then by Miltonic imagery and by the grave oratorio poetry
that seems to wake in Cooper whenever Indians are in question.
Here and there sounds that other organ note of the immemorial
American forest. There is a powerful contest in religious dialectic,
with the balance held even, between Metacom and the Puritan,
Heathcote. A chord that, from this time on, will grow progressively
deeper in Cooper, is struck in this moving echo of the great promise
of the Resurrection. It is Conanchet speaking in his death elegy:

> Narramattah, thy people speak great traditions. They say that
> one just man died for all colors. I know not. Conanchet is a child
> among the cunning, and a man with the warriors. If this be true,
> he will look for his woman and boy in the happy hunting grounds,
> and they will come to him.[6]

The Water-Witch (1830) is an inferior *Red Rover,* full, like its
predecessor, of cavorting *à la* Douglas Fairbanks, rendered exciting—though, after *The Rover,* this particular excitement tends to

wear a little thin—by the usual pattern of pursuit and escape. A
corrupt exquisite is nicely handled; so is a Dutch merchant who
spouts a cozy kind of Knickerbocker poetry. The machinery of
the *Water-Witch* oracle is as tediously extravagant as anything in
Bulwer-Lytton. Still a third Shakespearean masquerade, added
to those in *The Pilot* and *The Red Rover,* it reminds us again, if
we need reminding, that one of Cooper's native lands is Illyria.
What is probably more to the point, in a balanced survey, is Ship
Master Trysail's question about an afterlife, put to Captain
Ludlow just before the French frigate is engaged. More and more
matters such as these become Cooper's noblest and most abiding
preoccupations.

The *Bravo* (1831), *The Heidenmauer* (1832), and *The Headsman* (1833) constitute Cooper's European trilogy. The theme,
linking the three books to one another, is neither incident nor
character, but idea—a preface to *The Bravo* suggests that this
idea is a "history of the progress of political liberty, written
purely in the interests of humanity." As novels, though *The Bravo*
is easily the best, they are all three of them extremely poor—
just how abysmally poor can be gauged by balancing *The Heidenmauer,* with its stiff German Reformation setting, against Scott's
better *Monastery* which deals with a slightly later period in
England; and yet *The Monastery* is but indifferent Scott at that.
An indubitably humane interest in theological controversy does
not save *The Heidenmauer;* nor does an equally humane interest
in social paradox relieve the deadly woodenness of *The Headsman.*

The *Monikins* (1835), an intolerably long fable of men as
monkeys, is Cooper's *Gulliver's Travels,* with the all-important
qualification that Cooper is no Swift. The animal parable, for
political purposes, is as old as Aesop and as new as Orwell. It
demands, for success, the unanalyzable gift of delight which the
good fairies, for their own good reasons, doubtless, seem to have
withheld from Cooper in his cradle.

Homeward Bound (1838) and its sequel, *Home as Found*
(1838), are the first of Cooper's novels of society as such—if, of
course, we choose to disregard that pastiche exercise, *Precaution.*
Their joint theme, the return of expatriate Americans in "a European mask," repatriating themselves; and their basic device—
which is that of "a set of characters, with different peculiarities,
who had freshly arrived from Europe, and to whom the distinctive
features of the country would be apt to present themselves with
greater force, than to those who had never lived beyond the in-

fluence of the things portrayed"—are sufficiently and prophetically Jamesian and, in addition, almost too excruciatingly biographical.

If one must establish a palm for the worst Cooper book of all, the heavy-paced Columbus novel, *Mercedes of Castile* (1840), appears as good a candidate as any for that invidious honor. The lovely Carib princess, Ozema—"It would not have been difficult to fancy Eve such a creature, when she first appeared to Adam, fresh from the hands of her divine Creator, modest, artless, timid, and perfect"—becomes a cliché of nineteenth- and twentieth-century romantic fiction. We meet her again as Fayaway in Melville's *Typee;* as a Tahitian enchantress in Nordhoff and Hall; as a Balinese in Michener.

The Two Admirals (1842)—English versus French ships in the Channel, loyal Admiral confronting Jacobite Admiral during the Forty-Five—brings Cooper, connoisseur of blue water, back to ships and the sea. Those favorite themes of his, divided loyalties and psychic doublets, turn up again. The death in Westminster Abbey of Sir Gervaise Oakes, the loyal Admiral, before the tomb of his old friend, Admiral Richard Bluewater who, in the end, had remained loyal to the Crown, is one of the greatest death scenes among the many memorable ones which Cooper wrote. What is more, the dialog in these particular pages is as admirably natural as anything in Thackeray. Nevertheless, on balance, *The Two Admirals* must be adjudged no better than an indifferent tale.

The story, considered sheerly as story, is better in *The Wing-and-Wing* (1842), a sea tale of a French privateer pursued by ships of Nelson's Mediterranean fleet in 1799. This is Hornblower territory and Hornblower's period. If one measures Cooper against Forester here, one finds that the English disciple of Marryat comes off the victor for the paradoxical reason that Cooper is basically too complex to show at his best with such *simpliste* themes. The star-colloquy between Raoul, free-thinking revolutionary, and Ghita, devout Catholic, reveals the inherent poetry that religion always brings out in Cooper. His intuitive sympathy with Catholicism, which now and then breaks through the palisades of his Protestant defences, is sweetly apparent here.

Wyandotté (1843) is, as an Indian novel, mercilessly realistic. Its central figure, Wyandotté—to grace the Tuscarora renegade with the warrior sobriquet that is Saucy Nick's "loftiest appellation"—is a sympathetically considered, more complex Magua, with Magua's grievance against both red and white. Wyandotté is an interesting composite of all the leading Cooper dichotomies and *personae* rolled into one: an outcast and hero, beset by clashing allegiances, with warring psychic doublets within his single personality. As a novel of the Revolution, *Wyandotté* gives this particular trauma of Cooper's a new and ambivalent turn. It grows clear, as he becomes older, that his jingoism is by no means a single seamless fabric. In *Wyandotté*, though he remains defiantly proud of America's separation from England, he simultaneously regrets the fact. The now familiar Cooper staple, a theological discussion before battle, puts in another appearance. These disparate elements do not save *Wyandotté* as a novel.

Afloat and Ashore (1844) and *Miles Wallingford* (1844) are the two halves of what was originally conceived of as a single novel. The first half, *Afloat and Ashore,* is, comparatively speaking, Cooper's *Copperfield* and *Pendennis*. These memories of youth have a mellow light over them that brings Cooper as close as he ever gets to that elusive quality, literary charm. Irascibility returns, however, in the second half, *Miles Wallingford,* wherein Cooper, reversing the point of view he maintained in *The Bravo* and the European travel books, declares for the desirability of the aristocratic principle.

It has become a cliché, in more recent Cooper criticism, to rank his *Littlepage Manuscripts* trilogy—*Satanstoe* (1845), *The Chainbearer* (1845), and *The Redskins* (1846)—next to the Leather-Stocking stories in importance; and to pit their contrasting subject matters, the one against the other, as specimens of Cooper, romancer and poet, balanced against Cooper, realist and sociologist. Actually, the Littlepage trilogy is neither so good as this contrast would imply, nor so divergent in attitude and material, either. The Leather-Stocking and Littlepage bodies of material are separated by different emphases; upon closer examination, their themes appear not at all unlike. For the Leather-Stocking tales are much more sociological than one supposes on a cursory glance; and there is a strong grain of poetry running through the Littlepage polemics, and through the details of the Anti-Rent war of the 1830's, against the great landed proprietors, which provided Cooper with his overt theme for these three novels. Almost every critic of the *Littlepage Manuscripts,* for example, has noted that three successive generations of Littlepage landlords serve as first-personal narrators for these three novels. What is equally significant but, apparently, not nearly so obvious is the parallel fact that a single Indian—known by the names of Trackless, Sureflint, Susquesus, and, finally, as the Upright Onondago—links the three

individual volumes of the series to an older and far more compelling tradition than the crackling parchments of Crown grants
and patroon leaseholds: the elegiac tradition of Tamenund and
the great Mohicans who are Cooper's unfailing symbols for a
red-skinned American Troad, fallen, yet heroic and immortal.

The first of the trilogy, *Satanstoe,* has been overpraised for its
re-creation of a pre-Revolutionary New York reconstructed partly
from the traditions of Cooper's own family, including the De
Lanceys, and partly from Mrs. Grant of Laggan's classic source
book, *Memoirs of an American Lady.* The pictures are, in the
pastoral way of a sampler sewn between embroidery hoops of pale
wood, pleasant enough. But *The Pioneers* had been truer pastoral.
Satanstoe is the "purple light" of springtide, a lilac-fragrant pastel
out of Fragonard; and we do not read Cooper, after all, for pressed
petals of memory, for lavender-sachet reminiscences.

The Chainbearer, the central novel, is also the central achievement of the trilogy. Even here, however, it may be said that the
best things in *The Chainbearer* are quite aside from Cooper's
overt intention, which is to establish a dialectic of property.

Cooper's *nostalgie du temps perdu,* for the heroic and pastoral
time, is always one of his most compulsive themes, and never
more so than when, as here once more, poignantly associated
with the passing of his defeated Trojan race, the Indian. The
Indian is Cooper's Aeolian harp, his book of Ossian, his Wordsworthian intimation of "old, unhappy, far-off things . . ."

> . . . and there was a moment when I fancied some Highland
> girl was singing near me one of the Celtic songs of the country of
> her childhood. But closer attention satisfied me that the words
> were really Indian; probably belonging to the Mohawk . . .[7]

The Chainbearer—who, as surveyor for the Littlepages, is evidently thought of by Cooper as a sort of culture hero—seems, in
his impact on the reader, almost another avatar of Natty Bumppo,
as, paradoxically enough, so does his mortal adversary, the brutal
squatter, Aaron Thousandacres whose "broad-shouldered, sinewy"
six-foot progeny was destined to become a stereotype in the
"Western" cinema from the day of William S. Hart right down
to yesterday's *Shane,* and undoubtedly beyond. Yet Aaron Thousandacres is simultaneously *The Prairie's* Ishmael Bush even as,
in that same book, Bush had been, in some ways, an aspect of Natty
Bumppo. Thousandacres kills the Chainbearer and, in an ensuing

gun-duel, is killed in his own turn. His dying dialog with the Chainbearer is a noble Christian document. It is also, on quite another plane—and surely this was once again unconscious on Cooper's part—a dialectical debate between the rebel and the conformist, between the hero and the Ishmael figure, in Cooper's own personality.

The Redskins, crude and unintegrated as it doubtless is in its propagandizing for Cooper's side of the property dispute, is, still and all, a vastly underrated book. Up to the time of this late volume, Cooper had seen in the Negro nothing of the tragic poetry he always saw in the Indian. For him the Negro had been, at worst, a vehicle for low comedy; at best, a picturesque property for the Pinkster, the old colonial Saturnalia of the New York blacks. Now, in *The Redskins,* a full century before Faulkner, though his Negro remains a lay figure considered as an individual character, he is willing to admit him, along with the Indian, among the guardian presences of the continent. The Indian, Susquesus, now the aged hero-saint, the Upright Onondago, is, as a living personality, much more successfully conceived. He is even allowed, in elegiac retrospect, to enter the company of the great Delawares.

It is easy to make sport of one aspect of Cooper's treatment of his Indians in this, the last but one of his Indian novels, when he sets up the pilgrim Indians for our admiration as opposed to the white-skinned Anti-Rent hooligans who masquerade as "redskins." It is nearly the end of Cooper's career before he lets his braves degenerate into protectors of the great landed proprietors. But, from a deeper point of view, there is something a little more here than merely the red man's taking up of the white man's burden. When the retinue of Chiefs on pilgrimage suddenly materializes before our eyes in an area that had not known the tread of the Indian for many a year, it is, for the author of Leather-Stocking, a twilight of the red gods he has loved. But it is not only degradation. In their stately processional the gods are still apparent.

Among the subsidiary themes, in *The Redskins,* are another attack on Puritanism and a moving invocation of Christ when the aged Susquesus notes: " 'There are red traditions and pale-face traditions. Both speak of the Great Spirit, but only one speaks of his Son!' "

By now the sands were running out for Cooper. Among the five novels he had yet to write in the remaining three years of his life, he would set down but one good book, *The Oak Openings. The Crater* (1848)—a year of fate in Europe—is, in intention, Cooper's

Typee and his *Mardi,* too, as well as his *Utopia* and his *1984;* and it is an intolerably bad book. *Jack Tier* (1848), a deliberate, harsh de-romanticizing of *The Red Rover* and *The Water-Witch,* is similarly unsuccessful from beginning to end. *The Oak Openings* (1848) turns out, however, to be another thing altogether.

Next to the five Leather-Stocking books, *The Oak Openings,* laid in Michigan during the War of 1812, is the very best of Cooper's Indian tales and deserves much more critical attention than it has hitherto received. The first part of the book reverts to pure narrative, for the first time in many years, and it is quite evident, in this late volume, that the hand of the essential narrator has lost little of its old cunning. The second part is given over to excitement of another kind, the theological excitement of religious idea on a plane of extraordinary exaltation. It is borne in on one with increasing force, as one reads the august colloquy on Christ between the Indians and the divine, Parson Amen, with its mighty echoes of the Passion and the Incarnation, that Cooper is the only major nineteenth-century creative writer—short of the great Russians—to work within a specifically religious dimension. Emily Dickinson hums ecstatically, like some metaphysical bee, from out her clear Puritan ambience. Melville is a Manichaean and Hawthorne a gently sceptical Euripidean. By contrast, Cooper is the most orthodox and traditional of Christians.

Beyond giving Stevenson the chart, the sea-chest, and the buried treasure of a much greater book, not much can be said for *The Sea Lions* (1849). It is a Trinitarian tract, with a wistful compulsion towards such Catholic doctrines as the doctrine of Purgatory, and a vast respect which, however, does not save it as a novel, for the "greatest of all our mysteries, the incarnation of the Son of God." Cooper's old double motif expresses itself, for the last time, in the two captains and the two ships of this Arctic tale of his. Of *The Ways of the Hour* (1850), a pioneer murder-mystery directed against the idea of trial by jury, it might be remarked that Cooper is no Wilkie Collins. The testy democrat-aristocrat takes a last prefatory fling at Jacksonian democracy and, in the act of so doing, voices this universal truth about the American ethos:

> When an American prates about aristocracy, it is pretty safe to set him down as knavish or ignorant. It is purely cant. . . . But the demagogue must have his war-cry as well as the Indian, and it is probable he will continue to whoop as long as the country contains minds weak enough to furnish him with dupes.[8]

The five Leather-Stocking novels are Cooper's crowning achievement, and one of the abiding glories of American letters. In the order of Natty Bumppo's time and generation as a man, they are: *The Deerslayer, The Last of the Mohicans, The Pathfinder, The Pioneers, The Prairie.* But Natty Bumppo is at once more and less than a man. Both from the standpoint of Cooper's evolution as a writer, and from the standpoint of the mythic curve described by Leather-Stocking's successive avatars in the books as they were written, it is better to look at the series in its order of composition: *The Pioneers* (1823), *The Last of the Mohicans* (1826), *The Prairie* (1827), *The Pathfinder* (1840), *The Deerslayer* (1841).

It should be evident by now that any mature approach to an assessment of Cooper's essential qualities must be, primarily, neither personal nor stylistic—though, in a very real sense, it is possible to speak of Cooper's art—nor sociological—though it is also clear that Cooper's insights into the mainsprings of society are, while limited in their scope, extraordinarily clear. No, Cooper's genius was mythopoeic rather than comic; poetic rather than naturalistic; closer, perhaps, to the conditions of music and painting than to the conditions of fiction; dealing, at its rare purest, in archetypes rather than types. Cooper, too, like Shelley, had his *"idola specus*—peculiar images which reside in the inner cave of thought." If he attained the archetypal only incidentally, or even accidentally, that, after all, is the best, perhaps the only way to achieve this hidden, healing spring of the human imagination—to stumble on it. It is the way in which primitives, who always live close to the archetypal, attain it. In this sense—in no other, really —Cooper is a primitive. He is never primitivist.

Story and song are the two most primitive ingredients of the literary experience. Cooper possesses both—for "song," in his case, read strong poetic organization. Song is the skald's, story the saga man's gift, more than they are the novelist's or the dramatist's. Cooper, then, is a primary writer in the most primary sense of the term. This is not necessarily to be construed as the highest praise, however. It is true that story is the primal, essential, and eternal literary element, and that all the greatest novelists and dramatists —Homer, Shakespeare, Dickens—are, Antaeus-like, strongest when close to Mother Story. Nevertheless, the purest story does not, of necessity, make the greatest book. The *Iliad,* mixed, is, quite possibly, greater than the *Odyssey,* pure. Cooper's own use of story is, as a matter of fact, much more Vergilian than Homeric; and it is not nearly so pure as many of his critics have assumed.

It contains, actually, in harmonious suspension, all the ethical, social, and political preoccupations of his critical side as well as the mythic intimations of his mythopoeia.

For all the wry classicism of Cooper's conscious self, the great five, among his romances, are a triumph of the romantic intuition, as, indeed, are most of the characteristically great American books, including even those of Emerson and Thoreau. Like most great books that express national ethos, these five breathe a spirit of place. They fulfill Frost's great injunction to the American artist: "Make of the stones of the place a pillow for your head if you hope to see angels ascending and descending." For Cooper, those stones are the pebbles of Ontario's shore, Otsego's Council Rock, the bluffs rising from the great plains that roll to the foothills of the Rockies. "Every continent," says D. H. Lawrence, "has its own great spirit of place." And the tutelary spirit who, gaunt in the sunset as he leans forever upon his long rifle, presides over our continent, is that figure of elegiac epic, Leather-Stocking.

Leather-Stocking's roots are many and complex. There can be small doubt that, in part, at least, he derives from Daniel Boone who is hailed, in one of Cooper's first-chapter footnotes to *The Prairie*, as "the patriarch of Kentucky," as a "venerable and hardy pioneer of civilization." The Boone figure had caught the imagination of the first quarter of the nineteenth century. This is the mythic view of the American as "new man" which rises to its apogee in the blare of Whitman and which, in an abashed kind of way, appears more mutedly in Henry James's Christopher Newman—the name itself, of course, is allegorical—of *The American*. Insofar as stereotypes have any validity, the soft-fleshed Babbitt stereotype is probably more valid now than this old vision of the sinewy hero, but the dream image still possesses immense authority, not least over the romantic soul of Babbitt himself.

It has been the fashion loosely to consider Natty Bumppo as a Rousseauistic reflex. Parrington, for example, thinks Cooper's hero is prompted by "the French school's" supplementing "the romance of his boyish recollections."[9] Then he goes on to say that Bumppo "is quite evidently man as he came from the hand of nature, uncorrupted by the vices of the settlements; indeed one might question whether the back-to-nature literature can show another figure so enduringly vital as the Leatherstocking." Insofar as Rousseau's noble savage is a philosophic archetype of man before the Fall of Man, he exhibits some kind of affinity with Leather-Stocking. Otherwise, aside from the fact that Leather-

Stocking always shows himself hostile to the infidelities of such *philosophes* as *The Prairie's* Obed Battius, surely this is far too simple an explanation.

Far from being Rousseauistic, Cooper's tutelary spirit of the American wilderness is actually closer to Eliot's numen in the drawing-room, Sir Henry Harcourt-Reilly, and, before him, to Oberon and Herakles. This is the quality Lawrence isolates when he calls Deerslayer "race-old," and remarks that he had no business marrying, for his "mission was elsewhere." It is true of Chingachgook and Uncas, too, those noble red presences who stand forever beside the tall white presence in his green hunting-shirt. Cooper is the definitive poet of Freneau's "painted chief and pointed spear"; but his chiefs are, in the last analysis, more gods than warriors. That is why Hawkeye's perception remains so virgin; why, in *The Deerslayer,* he refuses love but not—even though he is a forbearing god—death. That is why Chingachgook, at times, seems almost like Siva the Destroyer.

Hawkeye's mythic status—part man, part culture-hero, part god—helps explain the psychology of his emergence from his creator's subconscious. We see him first, in *The Pioneers,* a semi-comic figure, a broken old man in the stocks, a frontier Kent who has fallen on evil days. Then, suddenly, we realize, with Cooper, that this Kent is also a Lear; grandeur emerges even from the naturalistic-comic framework of *The Pioneers,* the least satisfactory of the five volumes of the Leather-Stocking cycle, but a book that, even so, is far more complex and more rewarding, too, than one might think on cursory inspection.

The Pioneers (time: *circa* 1793; place: Otsego, later Cooperstown), is, in its mixture of the ultra-realistic and the elegiac pastoral, a *Shepherd's Calendar* of the four seasons which strikes the proper eclogue note with an opening on Christmas Eve; with a winter contrast, as old as Horace, between the snow-capped mountain without and the roaring fire within. As indeliberate pastoral, *The Pioneers* must be accorded due indulgence in the usual pastoral conventions. But we do not progress very far before we realize that here is Vergil more than Hesiod or Herrick. A misty retrospect hangs, like a golden autumn haze, over his paragraphs. Cooper has never Scott's Homeric immediacy of execution, no matter how exciting the events he narrates. A stern Georgic chord is sounded, revealing the good side of Cooper's squirearchal conservatism—a passion for conservation—when Judge Temple rebukes the woodchopper for his wanton felling of the trees. One

of Cooper's most constant themes remains this very contrast between the new which he dislikes and the old which he admires, a
contrast which, in his own way, Scott also makes use of, though
Scott's treatment is actually more complex than Cooper's, since
he cannily accepts what he does not admire and romantically loves
what he rejects.

In his thematics Cooper tends to be a disconcerting mixture of
the eighteenth and—by anticipation—twentieth centuries. One
grows impatient with his over-use of the eighteenth-century stock
theme of the return of the disinherited, and this just as his European contemporaries, Balzac and Stendhal, are introducing the
new motif of the careerist provincial in the capital. A more prophetic intimation, in *The Pioneers,* is the beginning of the cult of
the gun—the *mystique de la carabine* which, in the American
mythos, has supplanted the older cult of the sword. Here is Natty
speaking in the one book that seems indifferent to his apotheosis—
Natty without Killdeer:

> There's a rifle, they say, out on the Cherry Valley, that will
> carry a hundred rods and kill. I've seen good guns in my day, but
> none quite equal to that. A hundred rods with any sartainty is
> great shooting! Well, well—I'm old, and the gun I have will
> answer my time.[10]

Though, in his great speech accepting arrest, Natty speaks pure
Vergilian, even as, in Scott, Helen MacGregor and Meg Merrilies
speak pure Homeric, the heroic dimension which will completely
invest the other four books is only implicit in *The Pioneers.* But
what will be, for Cooper, his characteristic mode of heroic communication—the aria-recitative—begins thus early; and sometimes the connective tissue of narrative rhetoric kindles, above
eloquence, into real literature. Chingachgook's hero-death, ringed
with fire like a Valkyrie, is the high point of the book. From this
time on we shall hear this Magic Fire Music sounding again and
again—in *The Last of the Mohicans,* in *The Prairie,* in *The Deerslayer.* Leather-Stocking's retreat to the wilderness is equally good
—the first of the several withdrawals of the god which will climax
the succeeding books:

> Elizabeth raised her face, and saw the old hunter standing, look-
> ing back for a moment, on the verge of the wood. As he caught
> their glances, he drew his hard hand hastily across his eyes again,
> waved it on high for an adieu, and uttering a forced cry to his dogs,
> who were crouching at his feet, he entered the forest.[11]

At the end of *The Pioneers*, Leather-Stocking was seventy-two or seventy-three. At the beginning of *The Last of the Mohicans* (time: *circa* 1757; place: Lake George, the forest, and Fort William Henry), he is a vigorous thirty-six or thirty-seven, and the metamorphosis into hero is already complete. By the time of *The Pathfinder* and *The Deerslayer*, Leather-Stocking has become god as well.

One suggestive indication that Leather-Stocking is, among so many other things, an intuition of numen lies in the fact that his name shifts, like a god's, from book to book, until, in *The Prairie*, like some father-god, he is never even called by his absurd given name of Bumppo. Cooper must, of course, have early chafed under the necessity of Bumppo's name. But, if there were any original fault in his thus christening his hero, it was a *felix culpa* certainly, since it may have helped drive him in the direction of this happy device of the hero-sobriquet, the god's changing appelation. Natty is always a minor god, be it noted, and, though he bears names of power, it might be said of this earth deity what Isaias said of a greater Name: *The Lord God shall call His servants by another Name, in which he that is blessed in the earth shall be blessed in God*. Natty admits to David Gamut his veneration of the name: " 'I'm an admirator of names, though the Christian fashions fall far below savage customs in this particular!' " The long colloquy between Deerslayer and Hetty, in *The Deerslayer*, is even more revelatory—for ourselves as well as for Leather-Stocking. For it is an integral part of the human condition that we are all Captain Nemos in search of our lost names. We bestride the earth, as Verne's hero did the *Nautilus*, in quest of otherness; of the abiding strangeness which is yet familiar, and which lies hidden in the heart of reality.

Considered sheerly as hero, though he partakes of the excesses of neither extreme, Hawkeye stands somewhere between the picaro of eighteenth-century narrative and the possessed, irrational hero of Gothic romance; and he looks forward to the omniscient *Diespater* of the detective story as well as to that sharp-eyed god's more raffish and fallible successors, our contemporary Byronic private eyes. On this particular level the hero—at this stage he is very close to the god, but yet not a god—must be alone, a lonely salamander, a celibate eft, a mateless phoenix; or, if like Philip Marlowe and Sam Spade, he happens to be promiscuous, he must be promiscuous with the casual, aloof brutality of a Jupiter.

But *The Last of the Mohicans* is not just Hawkeye's "accurate and fastidious eye." It is also the French and Indian War in vivid miniature. As common consent has fastened on *Pride and Prejudice* as the best of Jane Austen, so has common consent fixed on *The Last of the Mohicans* as the best of Cooper; and sometimes common consent is right, though recent criticism has come to prefer *The Deerslayer* and *The Prairie*. Certainly Cooper never displayed a surer sense of prose values which, never his strongest point, are here not only far better than usual but, absolutely speaking, uncommonly good. His descriptions are organically a part of his total thematics, not merely background. Like Conrad later, he gives us an abstract landscape in the dark varnished oils of his period, without any of the sensory sharpness of a Cather mesa or a Hemingway stream but with something, nonetheless, which those two more exquisite artists never attain. It is as if he evokes for us, in the solemn music of Wordsworthian recollection, the emotional inscape of the American forest wilderness.

The major motifs have high seriousness. If Cooper burks the theme of miscegenation in the case of Cora and Uncas, he succeeds in suggesting a deeper theme, the mystery of race. His Indians possess the truth of poetry. Everywhere, in these pages, one breathes a keen hero air. Uncas' appearance, before the conclave of Delawares, is the return-of-the-heir motif operating on an archetypal plane. Magua and Uncas hurl their *défis* at one another like Roland and Ganelon quarreling before Charlemagne. When Hawkeye throws Killdeer into the hollow of his arm, the gesture invokes Durendal and Hautclere. Hawkeye's utterances are filled with a grave music—a moral music as well as that which sounds to the ear—as are also Uncas' and Chingachgook's. The operatic-oratorio note, already evident in *The Pioneers*, swells mightily in the long debate between Uncas and Magua before Tamenund, Sachem of the Delawares, investing and determining the insistent note of Vergilian epic. By the final pages of the book, the relationship between Hawkeye and Chingachgook is no longer merely that of Indian warrior and white scout, of two strong men of divergent races and cultures united in a common bond of valor. They become, instead, twin numina, two great *genii loci*, two waiting presences, tutelary deities of the American continent, joining hands in amity over a coil of motives and cross-purposes. The Green Man and the Red Manitou.

The Prairie (time: *circa* 1804; place: the Kansas plains for which contend Sioux and Pawnee warring to the death), is

Cooper's own favorite among the Leather-Stocking tales, and, like many a later American classic, was completed in Paris. Old Leather-Stocking is in his eighties now—he says eighty-six at one point, but this does not quite fit the chronology of the books that are earlier in time. *The Prairie* has become, of late, the most highly praised of Cooper's novels, but for the socio-realistic dimension of the Bush family rather than for the poetic dimension of the death of the hero, and the accompanying mystic rapport, on the old trapper's part, with both the Western landscape that Cooper knew only from books, and with the animal creation for which the aged Leather-Stocking feels almost a shaman's empathy.

For those who wish to contrast them, both dimensions are summed up in two climactic and symbolic scenes: Ishmael Bush's hanging of Abiram White; and Leather-Stocking's peaceful death against the Western curtain of an American sunset where the "sheet of golden light" is like a trumpet blown for the passing of a frontier Trueheart, a prairie Valiant-for-Truth. For, in his death, the hero is a man again, not a god. There can be no doubt that the Bush dimension possesses extraordinary power—one need look no further for the ultimate esthetic matrix of Caldwell and Faulkner. Nevertheless the mythopoeic is once again superior and, in the death of the old hero, all of the underlying greater themes of the Tales—paternity, the mystery of race, the god in his aloneness, and the rest—are orchestrated in one mighty closing coda.

The operatic movement, the oratorio dialog, the stately tableaux painted after the fashion of George Catlin, are, if possible, even more strongly marked in *The Prairie* which, for this reason, offers the reader an admirable opportunity to notice the characteristic Cooper narrative method and even (if one is permitted the term) Cooper's monochromatic art. As always, however, the themes are more important than the thematics. It is evident that Cooper's sense of his mythopoeic function is, in *The Prairie*, for the first time a thoroughly conscious thing. Hawkeye, as *genius loci*, is very strongly and deliberately emphasized, from our first sight of him in heroic relief against a sunset down to his sunset death. The impression of Leather-Stocking as vegetation god, which will reach its apex in *The Pathfinder*, is strengthened by the Trapper's continual lament over the maimed trees.

Everywhere through the monologs and dialogs of Leather-Stocking keens the true Vergilian cadence—"much have I seen, and something have I suffered in journeying over it," he says of America, this Aeneas without Dido or Lavinia. The archetypal character of the preceding volumes is heightened as we behold the American Adam, who named the animals, now mourning for their degradation. The same archetypal quality extends also to the Euripidean recognition scene in which young Middleton, grandson of *The Mohicans'* Duncan Hayward, meets the old hero who had once succored his grandparents; as a pattern, it even embraces the Trapper's old dog, Hector, the hero hound who romps about with one of his own descendants in the person of Middleton's puppy. Hector is a dog of epic, in the line of Ulysses' great hound, Argos. Even more than this, he is a dog of faëry, like Irish Bran, like *Canis Major* which shines in the American heavens during the parching months. This recognition trick has a potent magic in it which never fails to thrill, whether it be in Dumas who employs it in *Le Vicomte de Bragelonne,* or in Thackeray who uses it in *The Virginians.* Other themes link up here, too: the continuity of tradition in human affairs; the mystery of heredity; "the old wars of the provinces."

Paradoxically enough, Leather-Stocking's humanity is simultaneously deepened. As Ulysses is a demigod, a wily warrior, and eventually a faithful husband, so is this old Trapper at once a demigod, a crafty fighter, and a most humane companion. In *The Last of the Mohicans* he struck down Heyward's horse so that it should not reveal the party's whereabouts to the pursuing Hurons. Here, in similar circumstances, he cannot bring himself to slay Obed's ass. The complexity of the Bush subtheme is highlighted by the fact that, in a sense, Ishmael Bush is a lawless Natty and Natty a law-abiding Bush. Natty has come some distance from his rejection of the law in *The Pioneers.* Now he is grudgingly reconciled to it. " 'The law!' " he tells Ellen Wade. " ' 'Tis bad to have it, but I sometimes think it is worse to be entirely without it.' "

Religious themes emerge importantly on several levels. Leather-Stocking, who in *The Pioneers* had cried a plague on church as well as state, here exposes the secret of the *philosophe's* cloven hoof and, in his colloquy with Obed Battius, refutes the Doctor's naïve Voltaireanism by speaking through the *persona* of the writer of the *Book of Job* in the melancholy cadences of *Ecclesiastes;* Middleton's marriage to Inez—even more, perhaps, the incident of Father Ignatius marrying the Protestant lovers—are reluctant but appropriate symbols of a union Cooper did not live to see in fact: a wedding of the old Catholic atmosphere with the newer Protestant tradition within the bosom of America. Though

the Pawnee, Hard-Heart, an Uncas *redivivus,* was modeled after
a living Indian, Petalasharoo, the familiar Indian patterns are
repeated. Mahtoree, for example, is a more elevated Magua;
Le Balafré a second Tamenund. The effects are none the less
superb. Cooper never surpasses the electric excitement of the
Indian *holmgang*—to use that irreplaceable old saga word for
single combat to the death—wherein Hard-Heart duels Mahtoree
to the death on the river island while the assembled Pawnees and
the Sioux look on.

In *The Pathfinder* (time: *circa* the spring of 1759; place: Fort
Oswego on Lake Ontario and the Niagara region), Cooper joins
together two of his narrative specialties, the wood and the waves—
as a connoisseur of fresh water, not salt this time, he catches
Ontario to the life—or, as he alliteratively puts it in the preface,
"seamen and savages." However little he knows of the "nice conduct of a clouded cane," Natty, now thirty-eight—one must always
be approximate on this nice point of Natty's chronology—still
realizes the beauty of a "clouded barrel," when the Iroquois are
afoot. The story as such is much too reminiscent of *The Last of
the Mohicans* wholly to captivate one's interest. Certain narrative
aspects do, however, merit attention. The quality of ultra-natural-
ism, the "smell of death"—this is the element which forced the
otherwise tough-minded Mrs. Trollope to solace herself with Scott
after a Cincinnati surfeit of Cooper's "raw-head and bloody-bones
adventures"—is seen at its Hemingwayesque most gruesome in the
scene in which the Iroquois arrange the dead Scottish soldiers in
the postures of living men. The siege of the blockhouse and the
island on which it stands will turn up again, in other latitudes,
in Stevenson's *Treasure Island,* after experiencing a sea change
under the marine magic of R.L.S.'s sheerer narrative spell. It
may even be that the suggestion for Jim Hawkins' apple barrel is
to be found here, too; and the island alternation of deathly silence
and stunning noise will later be a Stevensonian trademark. The
toy cutter, the white beach, and the green forest are still another
sharp-edged cutout snipped as with the quick Stevenson shears.
On another level, Cooper's three-page vignette of the French
Captain Sanglier, to which Balzac took such violent exception, is
an admirable portrait of a military type.

Pricked by these Stevensonian intimations, one feels that the
basic quarrel in Cooper is, perhaps, not so much between the realist
and the romancer as between the epic writer and the writer of

romance. There is in him, as a matter of fact, a tincture of both these strong latter Alcinoan dyes. As the epic proper looks forward to the saga, so the saga, in turn, looks forward to the novel. Romance, on the other hand, looks backward to the Arthurian cycle, and forward to those great narrators, beginning with Defoe and, one hopes, not ending with Clive Staples Lewis, for whom one can find no other term than novelist—yet they are at once something more and something less than novelists. Romance is the essence they distill, the ichor their pens flow, the brine their sea-bright faces are salt with. In these latter writers all four points of the epic-romance rhombus (epic, romance, saga, novel) stretch and elongate into the troubadour's pentagonal star. It is Cooper's greatest deficiency, as a romancer, that there is nothing of the troubadour about him. He lacks utterly what Malory called *glamourie*. But his improvisations are Arthurian; and, in two senses, he is a true saga man. His tales reproduce the exterior saga patterns of flight, pursuit, and the defence of the cave mouth; and the interior saga patterns of conflicting loyalties and duties.

Cooper wrestles, in *The Pathfinder*, quite powerfully with the humanity of Leather-Stocking. A long character evaluation at the end of Chapter 9 reveals that Cooper's intuitive perception of his own creation is somewhat at variance with the rationalization he here evolves to keep Pathfinder consistent throughout. All his determined efforts to assert and establish the fundamental humanity of his hero are undermined by unmistakable intuitions of numen which—in defiance of his conscious intention, as it were—persistently keep struggling through. In this long grapple between the realistic conception of Leather-Stocking and the mythopoeic concept of the semi-divine hero, it is the mythopoeic concept which finally emerges victorious, for, in the last chapter's dying fall, we are given the withdrawal of a god even more definitely than in the closes of the other books.

There is, however, one very interesting and, as it turns out, prophetically prescient manifestation of Pathfinder's human side as representative of American humanity. When Cap challenges the woodsman to declare the Christian denomination to which he adheres, he replies:

> Look about you, and judge for yourself. I'm in a church now; I eat in church, drink in church, sleep in church. The 'arth is the temple of the Lord, and I wait on Him hourly, daily, without ceasing, I humbly hope. No, no, I'll not deny my blood and colour; but am Christian born, and shall die in the same faith. The

Moravians tried me hard; and one of the King's chaplains has had his say, too, though that's a class no way strenuous on such matters; and a missionary sent from Rome, talked much with me, as I guided him through the forest, during the last peace; but I've had one answer for them all—I'm a Christian already, and want to be neither Moravian, nor Churchman, not Papist. No, no, I'll not deny my birth and blood.[12]

I'm a Christian already . . . That is superb symbolic sociology. Henry Seidel Canby has tried hard to prove[13] that Natty is a Quaker; and American Cooper, granted his desire, would undoubtedly have declared for "the King's chaplain" to whom he himself inclined to the point where, as an Episcopal romancer, he literally anticipates Charles Williams' themes of "coinherence" and "substituted love." But Cooper is a realist. Natty Bumppo is America; and, from Cooper's day to ours, Natty's way with religion has, by and large, been America's way.

It is almost certain that Cooper must have been psychologically unaware of the new mythopoeic twist he gives Pathfinder in this penultimate volume. Either way, it is immaterial; the fact fairly stares one in the face. Somewhere within the deepest recesses of his creative imagination stirred still another archetypal theme: the Euripidean theme of the protecting god, a theme that was already old when Baucis and Philemon gave the gods foaming milk to drink. In his avatar, as Pathfinder, as in his other avatars as Deerslayer, Hawkeye, the Trapper, but here more overtly than before or after, Leather-Stocking is a Herakles wrestling against death on behalf of a series of clean-cut young American Admetuses and their Alcestises. In *The Pathfinder* the lovers are Jasper Western and Mabel Dunham; and it only sharpens the crux of the matter that Pathfinder should want to, as he tells Mabel's father, " 'quit some of my wandering ways, and try to humanise my mind down to a wife and children.' " A demigod cannot "humanise," cannot abdicate. He must, instead, "divinise" his lonely, celibate spirit.

Here is precisely where such a good critic as Grossman goes wrong when he labels Leather-Stocking a great "negative" character; and where such a great critic as Balzac goes even further wrong when he describes Pathfinder as "a magnificent moral hermaphrodite." It is not so. Pathfinder is a wood god, and he must have nothing to do with marrying and giving in marriage—except, of course, for others. That is why, in *The Deerslayer,* he rejects and, in *The Pathfinder,* is rejected as a lover. That is why his travail of spirit, when Mabel Dunham first rejects his love, is so oddly and frighteningly mingled with grimaced mirth, as he laughs "amid his agony, in a way to terrify his companion by the unnatural mixture of anguish and light-heartedness." One of the hallmarks by which Herakles may be known is his thundering laughter, the laughter of the demigod. In the case of Leather-Stocking this Dionysian laughter is usually reduced in scale to no more than a ritual rictus, a kind of inner, Puritan, silent mirth. In *The Pathfinder,* during the love colloquies with Mabel Dunham, it swells into a virtual demoniac seizure, as if the god Pan had Pathfinder in his hairy clutches, and as if Pathfinder becomes a sylvan creature, laughing in the face of mortals. If he is hardly Donatello, Hawthorne's moral faun, he is, for the moment, not far removed from Mallarmé's amoral one.

The sense of numen is strengthened in the dissolving tableau of the finale. Winter is at hand. Pathfinder has brought birds ready cooked—"the friendly offerings of her protector"—to the grave of Arrowhead where Indian June still mourns her fallen husband. But it is time for the gods to go—red Chingachgook as well. They paddle, June between them, into the Ontario haze of Indian summer; and neither "Jasper nor his wife ever beheld the Pathfinder again," though once, grown old, the mother of sons, Mabel Dunham saw on the banks of the Mohawk "a man in a singular guise, watching her in the distance, with an intentness that induced her to inquire into his pursuits and character. She was told he was the most renowned hunter of that portion of the State —it was after the Revolution—a being of great purity of character, and of as marked peculiarities; and that he was known in that region of country by the name of the Leather-Stocking." *A being of great purity of character* . . . A woodland being, unaging, still protecting.

Mabel Dunham was Eve. Judith Hutter of *The Deerslayer* (time: *circa* 1740-1745: place: Lake Otsego), is the Lilith who, in the Apocrypha, comes before Eve. The mythic wheel has come full circle. Deerslayer is a youth now, serene, pure, valorous, untouched by experience, immortal both in a Keatsian sense and in the sense of numen. The sylvan vehicle of his apotheosis, *The Deerslayer,* is surely one of the three best of the Leather-Stocking stories, and, in more than one way, might even be considered the very best, though *The Prairie* is supreme in still another fashion, and *The Last of the Mohicans* has its own unique excellences.

There can, of course, be no question of applying to the Leather-Stocking series the close exegesis which the New Criticism has so profitably applied to such a later American masterpiece as, say, Eliot's *Four Quartets*. On close reading, nevertheless, the series is much more tightly and tautly knit than it seems to be. Themes cross, crisscross, weave and interweave. Each successive volume—whether regarded in order of composition or in ideal reading order, as Allan Nevins arranges the books in his continuous truncated edition, *The Leatherstocking Saga*—deepens previous themes and introduces new themes of its own.

The five stories can be arranged in a Spenglerian sequence of seasons, with *The Pioneers* as a Hesiodic overture announcing all four seasons, *The Deerslayer* embodying Spring, *The Pathfinder* Summer, *The Last of the Mohicans* Fall, and *The Prairie* Winter. In *The Deerslayer* the familiar preceding major themes are strengthened and continued. Profound new themes appear. An Antigone theme of divine decrees transcending man-made laws. A psychological intimation of original sin. A downright Dostoev-skyan dimension in the person of Hetty Hutter, a mental defective who is simultaneously an expiatory figure from a Limbo of the personality halfway between Dostoevsky's metaphysical half-world and the bleak lunar reaches of Greeneland. In spite of, through, and, perhaps, because of her mental infirmity, Hetty symbolizes and mediates a primal innocence which the other characters do not possess, except for Leather-Stocking, of course. There seems to be in Cooper's mind an eerie, undeveloped connection between Hetty's imbecility and the untutored naïvete of Deer-slayer—"it frequently appeared," notes Cooper, "to place him nearly on a level with the fatuity of poor Hetty." It is not the first time one has noticed that Leather-Stocking has something in common with Prince Myshkin. The long, almost uncanny conversation between Hetty and Deerslayer, on the subject of his various names—several are mentioned here for the first and only time, as if the youth were elementally old as well as eternally young—must be considered a pivotal passage for the entire series.

The brutal squatter, Tom Hutter, and the violent frontiersman, Harry March, are even more sinister, in their implications, than *The Prairie*'s Bush family which, after all, had been dowered with a harsh patriarchal grandeur. Again, as in *The Pathfinder,* Leather-Stocking's essential ambivalences continue to plague Cooper. For the twentieth time, it seems almost as if Cooper is consciously trying to rationalize the counter-promptings of his creative unconscious. In one way, the resultant near-equilibrium brings Leather-Stocking, as a youth, closer to average humanity than in the preceding books.

At the same time, intimations of the young god gleam through every bit as strongly as before. This time, however, Deerslayer wears his amaranthine woodland garland with a certain difference. This time his constant soliloquizing is more universal than personal—is, in fact, a general soliloquizing on the human condition that seems close to Robert Penn Warren's more sophisticated contemporary soliloquies on *la condition humaine* in his *Brother to Dragons*. At the same time, Deerslayer himself shifts from symbolic figure to allegorical personification. Where, in the previous volumes, he had been a symbolic consciousness of the American land, in this final volume he turns almost into an embodied conscience for America. " 'It is a hard thing to fear truth, Hetty,' " says Judith, " 'and yet do I more dread Deerslayer's truth, than any enemy! One cannot tamper with such truth—so much honesty —such obstinate uprightness!' " Moral and poetic dimensions coincide, in *The Deerslayer,* as they do in great music. Perhaps it is more than a pleasant accident that, on his deathbed, in one last letter to his friend Schober, Franz Schubert should have begged for more Cooper:

> In this distressing condition, be so kind as to help me to some reading. Of Cooper's I have read *The Last of the Mohicans* and *The Pioneers.* If you have anything else of his, I entreat you to leave it with Frau von Gogner at the coffeehouse . . .

In the closing chapter, while always remaining a protector, Deerslayer is also revealed as a contemplative priest sternly conscious of his individual need for celibacy; and as an inexorably judging angel. This latter quality is especially evident in the passage where Deerslayer rejects Judith's proffer of marriage and, in reply to her question asking whether he has been influenced by reports regarding her frailty, indicates that he has. Hippolytus was a prig; Deerslayer is an affronted god. For the last time, this particular ambivalence, between numen and human, displays itself. Cooper consciously rationalizes Deerslayer's refusal in human terms, and unconsciously—or, possibly, more consciously than we are willing to admit nowadays—also pays tribute to that high theme in *Comus* which Milton nobly denominates "the sunclad power of chastity." But he is also a compassionate god, as is revealed in the beautiful tensions of that very great scene, even among the great scenes of American fiction, wherein Deerslayer slays a man for the first time and receives the hero-name of Hawk-eye from the lips of his dying victim.

Cooper's golden Vergilian retrospect, his Wordsworthian and elegiac notes are at their strongest in *The Deerslayer*. So is the elevated religious tone which stamps Cooper as one of the most truly religious among the great American writers. One of the best moments in the book is Deerslayer's measured debate with Ching-achgook on the resurrection of the body. This religious plane in Leather-Stocking and in his creator, Cooper, is, atmospherically speaking, both Protestant Puritan—in spite of his aversion to Puritanism, Cooper is often possessed of a Covenanter's musical melancholy—and, strangely enough, the end product of something for which one can find no other adjective than Catholic. One ventures to suggest, on this same score, that an extra-literary reason for Cooper's enormous popularity a century and a quarter ago, and for his catastrophic drop in popular appeal, during this century, is precisely this religious dimension. To today's sophisticate his deeply pondered orthodoxy and his firm moralizing are alike obnoxious.

But already there are straws in the wind. Already we begin to appreciate once again the paradisal intimations in Chingachgook and Hist, that red Adam and his lovely Eve who, like all other daughters of Eve, came, at the last, to slumber "beneath the pines of the Delawares." Cooper is, for once, not afraid of passion. He seems released from clogging inhibitions in its representation when, as here, he can deal with archetypal man and woman in the Garden. And there are other archetypes at work here, too. One of the most powerful is the baptismal suggestion of the living waters of the Glimmerglass. Hetty's lake burial is sacramental. Everywhere, throughout these majestic books, one comes on intimations of grace.

The spare figure of Leather-Stocking, leaning on his long rifle, both hands clasping the barrel in immemorial epic pose, is burned deep in the American psyche. It is a good image for a nation with a mighty burden to bear, with a Roman destiny now thrust upon it. " 'No, no,' " says Pathfinder, " 'bloodshed and warfare are not my real gifts, but peace and mercy.' " And again: " 'No, no, Eau-douce, I do not seek blood without a cause; and my bullet is well leathered and carefully driven down, for the time of need. . . .

The deer never leaped that fell by my hand wantonly!'" The four notes E. M. Tillyard sets down for epic are: high seriousness; amplitude; deliberate organization; and the choice spirit which only comes out of the soul of a folk when the time and the place are ready—when a poet serves as mouthpiece for a large group of people, living in or near his own time. If we are permitted to elongate Dr. Tillyard's fourth criterion to cover people living some time after the poet's day, then, who else, for American letters, strikes these epic notes on quite the scale of American Cooper in his great Leather-Stocking stories which are at once something less and something more than novels?

ORESTES A. BROWNSON

1803-1876

The Critique of Transcendentalism

ALVAN S. RYAN

In a volume concerned with the evaluation of major American writers from a Christian perspective, perhaps the presence of an essay on Orestes Brownson requires some justification. He has, to be sure, been the subject of three biographies and of numerous critical studies in the past two decades. Professor Perry Miller gives him a prominent place in his anthology *The Transcendentalists,* and more recently the present writer has edited a volume of selections from his writings, the *Brownson Reader.* While this renewed interest in his work does not establish his stature as a major writer, it does indicate the end of the almost total neglect of his work. This neglect is most evident in the anthologies of American literature now being most widely used in American colleges and universities. Brownson is conspicuous by his absence. To my knowledge, only Frank Luther Mott and John T. Frederick, among literary anthologists, include a selection from his work, a passage from "The Laboring Classes."

From one point of view, the neglect of Brownson is both understandable and justifiable. He wrote no poetry, and his abortive attempts at fiction are scarcely worthy of attention. He was primarily a journalist and a general critic whose medium was the essay and review. As an essayist he might conceivably have maintained a place similar to that of Newman and Carlyle, or Mill and Huxley, among nineteenth-century prose writers, if his contemporary importance had been a pledge of his later reputation.

Why he has not done so can also be partly explained. Brownson

NOTE: This essay was completed before the publication of Mr. R. W. B. Lewis' illuminating study, *The American Adam* (University of Chicago Press, 1955). I call the reader's attention especially to his chapter entitled "The Real Presence: Parker and Brownson."

formulated his thought chiefly through long, discursive, and polemical reviews of other men's work; the form of the book under review too often determined the structure of his own essay, and he lacked either the capacity or the desire to give to most of his work the finish, the form and the stamp of personal utterance that make the works of far less penetrating thinkers live as literature. Yet Schlesinger says, and I think justly, that at its best Brownson's was "without question one of the best journalistic styles that America has known,"[1] while James Russell Lowell's reference to his "transparent and forcible prose" suggests the strength, although it suggests as well the defects of his style—a failure in subtlety and frequently a failure in attractiveness of rhythm or movement.

When all this has been said, it remains true that Brownson was not only a significant figure in his own time, but that a mid-century revaluation of his work may find in it much that the nineteenth-century *Zeitgeist* failed to recognize. His intellectual and spiritual odyssey remains a fascinating one. His early work, prior to his conversion to the Catholic Church in 1844, and his later writings as a Catholic, taken together, make a significant study in development. His importance for the student of American literature is in the fact that after some ten years as a leading figure among New England Protestant and Transcendentalist thinkers, as an eclectic in philosophy, and as an apostle of social and religious reform, he ultimately brought the Catholic tradition to bear upon the whole New England movement. With the exception of Isaac Hecker, who was not a leader of the movement, he is the only source of such criticism. He subjected Transcendentalism to a searching evaluation, and in describing it as a form of "learned gentilism" or Alexandrianism, endeavored to see it in the perspective of Western Christian thought. For the student of nineteenth-century thought who wishes to explore cultural filiations beyond national boundaries, Brownson is a valuable mediator between Europe and an America that was just arriving at its own social, political, and literary maturity. If he lacks the necessary qualifications to be numbered among the major writers, he is nonetheless worthy of more consideration than he has heretofore received.

It is my purpose to focus attention first on Brownson's role in his early years as a reformer and as a spokesman for Transcendentalism, and secondly on his criticism of Transcendentalism and of the works of such writers as Carlyle, Emerson, and Theodore Parker. If Perry Miller is right in affirming that Transcendentalism was fundamentally not a literary but a religious movement, then Brownson's ultimate evaluation of these writers as thinkers rather than as prose stylists has its relevance. Perhaps today, when we are less ready to accept Arnold's estimate of Emerson as "the friend and aider of those who would live in the spirit," Brownson's essays on Emerson can be read with fresh interest. It is my contention, at any rate, that in Transcendentalism Brownson saw raised the most fundamental religious and philosophical problems of his time, and that there can be no real understanding of his significance without a consideration both of his Transcendentalist phase and of the reasoning and the experience which led to his rejection of Transcendentalism in the years immediately prior to his conversion.

While it would be to no purpose to review here Brownson's early experience, it is important to recall that almost from the first he was a seeker who shared the evangelical fervor of the first decades of the nineteenth century. The paradox of his first religious affiliations is that he sought what he could believe in as the true church while at the same time he was committed by his Protestant heritage to the private interpretation of Scripture. He was successively a Presbyterian, a Universalist, and a Unitarian and even went on to project the Church of the Future before he finally came to rest in the Roman Catholic Church.

Brownson's quest for religious certainty has another dimension: his sensitivity to the question of social justice. He must be numbered among those who with almost prophetic awareness saw what would be the effect of the industrial revolution in America. In the first years of his ministry a somewhat vague religious impulse and a passion for reforming the world now conflicted and now were merged into a temporary harmony. As early as 1828 the utopian experiments and the writings of Robert Owen first attracted Brownson's attention, as he says in *The Convert*, "to the question of reorganizing society and creating a paradise on earth."[2]

After a brief period when Brownson was under the spell of Fanny Wright's eloquence, and was associated with the Workingmen's Party in New York, he left the Universalists in 1831 to become an independent minister. For two years he had been, as he says in *The Convert*, close to religious skepticism.[3]

Then, after hearing Channing's sermon on "Likeness to God" read to him by a friend, he was attracted to Unitarianism, and in 1832 he accepted a Unitarian pulpit in Walpole, New Hampshire. From here he frequently made the ninety-mile trip to Boston, and became acquainted with Channing, Ripley, and others of the Boston group. In 1834 he moved, at Ripley's suggestion, to Canton, Massachusetts, to become Unitarian minister there. At Canton his association with Transcendentalism may be said to begin.

Even though in 1834 the first meeting of the so-called Transcendentalist Club was still two years in the future, those who were to attend that first gathering were already developing their characteristic ideas in essays, sermons, and reviews. Both Ripley and Brownson enunciated in this year theological views which are to be heard frequently in the next decade—they are among the fundamental principles of the movement.

Ripley delivered the sermon upon Brownson's installation at Canton in May 1834.[4] Taking as his subject "Jesus Christ, the Same Yesterday, Today, and Forever," Ripley insists upon the distinction between what Theodore Parker was later to call "The Transient and the Permanent in Religion," and on which the Transcendentalists based their whole evaluation of historical Christianity. That which remains the same for religion is, says Ripley, the religious sentiment, although the forms of religion change. The "great spiritual principles" announced by Jesus Christ endure unchangeable, yesterday, today, and forever. "But," says Ripley,

> . . . let us not be misunderstood. . . . Religion is unchangeable in its essential elements, but not in its carnal forms. Everything connected with it is subject to change. Men's conceptions of its nature may undergo indefinite alterations. . . . The forms of religion may be varied. They have already changed many times; what shall prevent them from changing as often again? The religious sentiment seeks to express itself in forms, but it is confined to no fixed mode. . . . We assemble in our solemn temples, and worship in the fashion which our fathers have taught us; others may take our place who will deem our rites deficient or superfluous, and adopt more appropriate forms of their own; but what will be altered? Not the substance, but the shadow; not the reality, but the symbol.[5]

It is not too much to say that Brownson's study of Benjamin Constant during his two years in Walpole, New Hampshire, had inaugurated his Transcendentalist phase. When, a few months after his installation at Canton, he published his essay on Constant in the *Christian Examiner* (September 1834), he made it the occasion of sharp criticism of the institutionalism and the dry rationalism of his fellow Unitarians. The thesis of the review, which brings

Constant's thought to bear on the local debate, was the same
fundamental Transcendental thesis which Ripley developed at
Brownson's installation: namely, that the religious sentiment is
natural to man and that the intuitive experience of God is the
permanent element in religion. We must, he held, distinguish
between the religious sentiment and religious institutions. Institutions are not permanent, and even though the religious sentiment
seeks to externalize itself in a form, humanity in its progress
through the centuries outgrows each form and successively seeks
new forms in which to embody this religious sentiment. "The
sentiment now breaks away from that form, which, if one may
so speak, has become petrified . . ."[6] "We think," continues Brownson,

> the time has come for us to clothe the religious sentiment with
> a new form, and to fix upon some religious institution, which will
> at once supply our craving for something positive in religion, and
> not offend the spirituality which Christianity loves, and towards
> which the human race hastens with an increasing celerity. . . . The
> time has now come to rear the new temple. . . . We already see
> the germ of reorganization, the nucleus, round which already gravi-
> tate the atoms of a new moral and religious world.[7]

It is Brownson's further contention in his sympathetic review
of Constant that "religion and morality rest not on the understanding, not on logical deductions, but on an interior sentiment."
Understanding and affection, head and heart, are two distinct
orders of human faculties, and Brownson insists that the sentiments and affections are as worthy of trust as the understanding
or logical faculty. He goes further. "To us," he writes, "the sentiments seem to be peculiarly the human faculties. They give to man
his distinctive character."[8]

These views of Ripley and Brownson are typical of one important aspect of the Transcendentalist movement—its theological
emphasis. Brownson, not able to rest content with stating that the
time had come to clothe the religious sentiment with a new form,
soon began to outline his program for "The Church of the Future."
In July 1836 he established his Society for Christian Union and
Progress, and in November published the pamphlet "New Views
of Christianity, Society, and the Church."

"New Views" presumes to survey the entire history of Christendom in a few pages. The oversimplifications are gross, the terminology loose and approximate. By labeling the two forces which
alternately have gained the ascendancy in Western thought as

Spiritualism and Materialism, Brownson is able to make challenging but often mistaken generalizations. Catholicism, so he holds, for centuries emphasized Spirit at the expense of Matter; Protestantism represents the triumph of Matter over Spirit. Both traditions are, so Brownson believes, now dead, or mere "reminiscences." The one was an otherworldly religion that ignored man's condition in this world; the other substituted a striving for temporal goods. "We of the present century," he concludes, "must either dispense with all religious instructions, reproduce spiritualism or materialism, or we must build a new church . . ."[9]

Both Catholicism and Protestantism having failed to recognize the Atonement and the full significance of "the reconciliation of spirit and matter through Christ," it is now, says Brownson, the mission of all who believe in "Union and Progress" to bring about this reconciliation. In spite of his strictures against the earlier doctrines of the Unitarians as dry and cold, he looks to them to furnish the leaders of the new church.

It is clear that Brownson virtually equates Catholicism with Calvinism in his analysis. He declares, in fact, that aside from some few modifications produced by Protestant influence, Calvinism is only a continuation of Catholicism. Underlying the essay, then, is the familiar Transcendentalist position: namely, that from the warfare between Calvinist orthodoxy and rational Unitarianism must emerge a reconciliation of the two extremes, and that those Unitarians who reject the Lockean philosophy and the sensism and materialism of the eighteenth century are the only real party or church of the future.

Brownson's "New Views" bears a marked similarity to Ripley's article on Schleiermacher in the March 1836 *Christian Examiner*, which Miller calls a "transparent allegory" for New England. Schleiermacher found, according to Ripley's interpretation of his work, a synthesis between the new rationalism and "ancient Supernaturalism" by separating the central and absolute idea of Christianity from its temporary forms. Since Brownson acknowledged his debt to Schleiermacher in his Preface to "New Views," it is not surprising that Miller's comment on Ripley's article should be equally apposite to Brownson's thesis: "If instead of Supernaturalism one reads the Calvinists and instead of Rationalism the Unitarians, then the inference is obvious that the younger generation—repelled by Rationalism but incapable of fleeing back to Supernaturalism—have only the one choice of going forward, like Schleiermacher, toward the 'primitive consciousness.' "[10]

Brownson's "New Views" is but one example of his affiliation in 1836 with the new movement. On September 16, at Ripley's house, he had attended, with Emerson, Francis, Clarke, Alcott, and Ripley himself, the first meeting of the Transcendentalist Club. And in this same month, when Emerson's *Nature* was published, Brownson published in the *Christian Examiner* an article on Victor Cousin. The motifs of the essay, in Miller's words, "turn out to be so close to those of *Nature* that many pages of the latter . . . are wonderfully illuminated by comparison with this contemporaneous effort."[11] Certainly Brownson's later criticism of Transcendentalism is more readily seen as a criticism of his own views when such a passage as this from the Cousin essay is kept in mind: "The reason is God; it appears in us, therefore God appears in us. . . . The voice of the spontaneous reason is the voice of God; those who speak by its authority, speak by the authority of God, and what they utter is a real revelation."[12]

In 1838, Brownson founded his *Boston Quarterly Review*. C. L. F. Gohdes' chapter on the review in *Periodicals of American Transcendentalism* is a valuable treatment of the significance of its pages, most of them by Brownson himself, for students of Transcendentalism. The attention Brownson gave to Carlyle, to Cousin, to Alcott, and especially to Emerson, is indicative of his influence in spreading the doctrines of Transcendentalism during this period. One way to show the critical and independent quality of his defense of Transcendentalism up to 1840 is to contrast his treatment of Andrews Norton with his review of Emerson's "Divinity School Address."

Brownson reviews the "Divinity School Address" of July 1838 in the October issue of his *Quarterly*. Like nearly all of Brownson's criticisms of Emerson's work, it is warm in praise of his spirit and his intellectual and literary gifts even while it dissents from many of his conclusions. Brownson alludes at the outset to the excitement and severe censures the address has called forth, regretting "the abuse which has been heaped upon Mr. Emerson." "We like its life and freshness," he goes on to say, "its freedom and independence, its richness and beauty. But we cannot help regarding its tone as somewhat arrogant, its spirit as quite too censorious and desponding, its philosophy as indigested, and its reasoning as inconclusive."[13]

The moral doctrine of obeying the laws of the soul, expressed in Emerson's maxim, "Obey thyself," is to Brownson unsound. He affirms that morality rests on a sense of obligation to a law above the soul, imposed "by a supreme lawgiver."[14] He grants that to Emerson, "a pure-minded man," the laws of the soul are the higher instincts, but asks how in Emerson's own terms higher and lower are to be distinguished. We must look beyond the individual for a norm of conduct. A system of egotism, of "transcendental selfishness," seems to run through Emerson's writings. "We meet it everywhere in his masters, Carlyle and Goethe."[15] Moreover, the very term "instinct" implies passivity, whereas virtue is a personal activity, an activity of the will, "voluntary obedience to a moral law, felt to be obligatory."[16] To yield to instinct is to abdicate personality. Minimizing the powers of reflection and understanding, and failing to legitimate the instincts, Emerson "is merely reviving the old sentimental systems of morality."[17]

Turning to Emerson's theology, Brownson accuses him of confusing the religious and the moral sentiment, which are distinct. Even if they are identical, Brownson is not satisfied with Emerson's account. Emerson identifies the soul with God, "admits no God but the laws of the soul's perfection."[18] But God, Brownson insists, is independent; He is in us, but He is not us. Him we worship, and only Him. We dare not worship our own souls, yet this worship of the soul characterizes the transcendental egotism of Emerson's theology as well as his moral doctrines.

Brownson shares Emerson's fear that preaching "a historical Christianity" can too easily substitute the letter for the spirit, but here again he demurs. If Emerson means to "sever us from the past and to intimate that the Christianity of the past has ceased to have any interest for the present generation . . . we must own we cannot go with him. Christianity results from the development of the laws of the human soul, but from a supernatural, not a natural, development . . ."[19] Nor will Brownson allow that religion can, as Emerson suggests, dispense with either Christ or the Bible. "The church in general has erred by giving us only the historical Christ; but let us not now err, by preaching only a psychological Christ."[20]

Sharp as are Brownson's disagreements with Emerson, he ends by applauding Emerson for delivering the address, for attempting to encourage thought and to free men from routine and mere custom. Time will sift out Emerson's errors and his affectations, but "the influence of his free spirit, and free utterance, the literature of this country will long feel and hold in grateful remembrance."[21]

Andrews Norton published his chief work, *The Evidence of the Genuineness of the Four Gospels,* in 1838, and the next year his

attack on Transcendentalism as "The Latest Form of Infidelity"
appeared. Brownson commented on both at some length.

In his review of Norton's *Evidence* he rejects Norton's emphasis
on historical evidence and especially on the authenticity of the
miracles recorded in the Gospels. According to Norton's theory,
Christianity stands or falls on the basis of historical proof. This
Brownson will not allow. He says: "There are persons who believe
that the truths of Christianity bear on their face a certain stamp
of divinity, which the soul is capable of recognizing. . . . To these
persons the question of the genuineness of the Four Gospels is a
matter of comparative indifference."[22] Implying, without stating,
his agreement with these "persons," he outlines their belief: that
Christianity is a matter of experience, that religious truth springs
up spontaneously in the human mind; that there is divinity in man
to respond to the divinity that speaks from without. The emphasis
on miracles, with their appeal to the outward sense, is to Brownson
what one would expect from a disciple of Locke.

Brownson's strongest charge against Norton is that in denying
the authority of the inner light he shows himself the enemy of
democracy. Norton distrusts or patronizes the people. In religion
and politics he refers men to authorized teachers and leaders,
whereas the democrat believes "that Reason, the light which shines
out from God's throne, shines into the heart of every man. . . ."[23]
This linking of democracy with Christianity, as understood by the
Transcendentalist, adumbrates Brownson's thesis in "The Laboring Classes." It bears a close similarity, too, with the views Lammenais had promulgated a few years earlier in France. Brownson
had followed the French movement with interest and, as he wrote
after his conversion, the news of Lammenais' condemnation and
excommunication led him to conclude that "the old church was
dead, and her resuscitation no longer possible."[24] Brownson, in
short, insisted at this period in judging religious doctrine on its
availability to the people, and by such a test Norton's views were
hostile to both social and political equality.

Andrews Norton made no direct answer to Brownson's criticism.
But on July 19, 1839, he delivered, before the alumni of the
Harvard Divinity School, the "Discourse on the Latest Form of
Infidelity," by which he continues to be remembered. He charged
that the latest form of infidelity, Transcendentalism, in rejecting
historical evidences and historical Christianity to rely upon intuition, struck at the very root of Christian belief. "There can be no
intuition, no direct perception, of the truth of Christianity, no

metaphysical certainty." On the contrary, Norton affirmed, there is "no mode of establishing religious belief, but by the exercise of reason, by investigation, by forming a probable judgment upon facts."[25]

George Ripley replied to Norton in a series of three pamphlets. Theodore Parker, "who next only to Emerson—and in the world of action even above Emerson—was to give shape and meaning to the Transcendental movement in America,"[26] wrote his famous reply under the pen name "Levi Blodgett." Brownson's reply was delayed for a year until Norton, joining forces in desperation with the Calvinism against which Unitarianism was a protest, reprinted two articles which had first appeared in the January 1839 number of *The Princeton Review*. Brownson's essay, called by Miller "the best of the apologies for Transcendentalism that arose in answer to Norton's accusation of infidelity,"[27] appeared in his *Boston Quarterly Review* for July 1840. Brownson begins by applauding Norton for his courage in opposing publicly what he holds to be mischievous speculation, and for boldly bringing his charges into the open. Then Brownson denies that the term "Transcendentalists" accurately describes "the movement party." They agree chiefly in their opposition to Locke and "the old school." "Some of them embrace the Transcendental philosophy, some of them reject it, some of them *ignore* all philosophy, plant themselves on their instincts, and wait for the huge world to come round to them."[28] And though some read Cousin or Goethe or Carlyle, the movement is really of American origin. The Transcendentalists have been concerned primarily with legitimating their religious beliefs, and with establishing grounds for belief which are not— like Norton's evidences, probabilities and the testimony of history —confined to the learned few. These Transcendentalists would place the "unlettered ploughman" on a level with the "most erudite scholar" through affirming man's intuitive knowledge of the truths of Christianity.

Norton's view comes down, so Brownson charges, to believing that certain truths were revealed, or rather asserted, by the authority of God, and attested by miracles. Norton stresses the mere fact of their assertion, whereas Transcendentalists hold that once these truths are revealed, we can "know immediately, by intuition, by a mere looking upon them, that they are truths."[29] To Brownson there is a certainty in this intuition of truth, a certainty, moreover, that is open to every man, whereas Norton's historical evidences and proofs, by his own admission, amount only to a probability. And since the scholarship necessary to arrive even at such probability can be mastered only by very few, Norton virtually declares that the mass of mankind are absolutely disinherited by their Maker. Such is Brownson's charge, a charge which, in opposing intuition to the rational examination of evidence, leaves quite aside even the possibility of a Church with the authority to teach and to guard the integrity of Revealed Truth.

In his essay "The Laboring Classes," Brownson brought what he saw as the social and political implications of Transcendentalism to their logical terminus. A return to the "Christianity of Christ," so Brownson argued, would elevate the working classes to a position of economic and social equality. His sharp attack on the priesthood in this essay was in one sense a continuation of his defense of Transcendentalism against the Unitarian orthodoxy of Norton. To Brownson there was no basic distinction between the Catholic priest and the Protestant clergyman or between the Catholic and Protestant Church. He denied the necessity of the mediatorial function of priest, clergyman, or church, holding that there was only one mediator, Jesus Christ, who "preached no formal religion, enjoined no creed, set apart no day for religious worship."[30] In the conflict between prophet and priest in the Old Testament he found justification for his own mission, which he clearly assumes to be one of prophecy.

While Brownson later came to refer to "The Laboring Classes" as his "Horrible Doctrines," he insisted that he merely gave expression in the essay to thoughts which for years had pressed for utterance. The essay really restated his "New Views" in different terms; whereas the 1836 essay called the single organization of society the Church, the second called it the state. In both essays he turned Christianity into a social evangel, and in both he denied any distinction between the state as a temporal and the Church as a supernatural society.

Brownson's own interpretation of the effect of "The Laboring Classes" on his thinking, as he traces it in *The Convert,* is corroborated by a study of the essays he wrote in the next few years. He calls the essay the crisis in his mental disease, and says that the "universal scream of horror" with which it was received led him to re-examine his religious and political assumptions. Perhaps, as some scholars maintain, Brownson exaggerates the extent of his change, and is somewhat inaccurate about chronology, yet the essays from 1841 to 1843 present overwhelming testimony to the shift in his religious thought, especially with reference to Transcendentalism. This shift can be seen most clearly in the widely different evaluation he makes of two utterances of Theodore Parker's in 1841. I refer to Parker's sermon of May 17, 1841, "A Discourse of the Transient and Permanent in Christianity" and the lectures he gave in the autumn, which were later incorporated in *A Discourse of Matters Pertaining to Religion* and published in 1842.

In Parker's sermon, which led to his virtually being ostracized by most of his fellow Unitarians, he made the same distinction between the Christianity of Christ and institutional Christianity which Emerson, Ripley, Brownson, and others had been making for years. Theologies and doctrines constantly change or pass away, while the essentials of religion remain, and are perceived intuitively and as if by instinct. He declared that the authors of Scripture were inspired only as other men "equally pious and wise" are inspired, that since the fourth century the true Christian life has been out of the established church, that Jesus was a man as we are and a son of God, like ourselves. If, he argued, one takes a "heathen view" and makes Christ a God, the Son of God in a peculiar and exclusive sense, "much of the significance of his character is gone." However fully fellow Unitarians might agree with Parker's stress upon the humanity of Jesus, only a Transcendentalist could assent when he made the following assertion: "So if it could be proved . . . that Jesus of Nazareth had never lived, still Christianity would stand firm . . . . None of the doctrines of that religion would fall to the ground; for, if true, they stand by themselves."[31]

In his review article on the sermon,[32] a review somewhat longer than the sermon itself, Brownson discusses Parker's chief assertions in detail, and gives his support to nearly all of them. With Parker he holds that theology constantly changes; with Parker he would retain only the permanent in Christianity; with Parker he maintains that nobody really believes in the "plenary inspiration" of the Old and the New Testaments. There are occasional elaborations of Parker's thesis which take on significance in the light of Brownson's later conversion, as when he says: "The ingenious systems of Subtle Doctors, of Doctors Angelic, and Doctors Seraphic, have passed away . . ."[33] Most important, however, is the fact that Brownson argues ingeniously to show that Parker really believes in a supernatural revelation and that in his emphasis on the humanity of Christ he "is right as far as he goes." Much of what Parker says seems to trouble Brownson, but Parker's quarrel with those who would prematurely confine Unitarianism in the bonds of orthodoxy is also Brownson's quarrel, and he will not desert Parker in the crisis.

In the fall and winter of 1841-1842 Parker developed the central argument of his sermon in a series of five lectures. Brownson attended at least two, if not all, and in *The Convert* he describes their effect upon him, saying that they contained "nothing but a learned and eloquent statement of the doctrine which I had long defended, and which I have called the religion of humanity." "But," Brownson adds, "strange as it may seem, the moment I heard that doctrine from his lips, I felt an invincible repugnance to it, and saw, or thought I saw, at a glance, that it was unphilosophical and anti-religious."[34] The crucial difference was in the use he and Parker made of the religious sentiment as natural to man. Parker, so Brownson now saw, reduced religion to natural religion, to Carlyle's "natural supernaturalism," whereas Brownson made the religious sentiment the ground for showing that belief did not violate nature and reason, and thus removed his chief obstacle in the way of accepting supernatural revelation.

This account in *The Convert,* written thirteen years after Brownson's conversion, may be suspected by some to alter the facts unconsciously. One only needs to read the final number of the *Boston Quarterly Review,* however, to see that Brownson's account is accurate. The entire October 1842 issue (127 pages) is devoted to a review of the Parker *Discourse.* Comparing the review with the review of "The Transient and the Permanent" which Brownson published exactly a year earlier, one sees that the revolution in Brownson's religious thought has been almost total.

The central importance of Parker's book to Brownson's criticism of Transcendentalism is indicated by the fact that in 1845 and 1846, after his conversion, he devoted three articles to it in *Brownson's Quarterly Review* under the title "Transcendentalism." Because much of the argument of these essays repeats that of the 1842 review, while there are also important changes in interpretation, I shall compare them further on.

The change in Brownson's view of Parker's version of Transcendentalism did not, of course, come about through his study of Parker's writings. The two reviews merely indicate that a great change had taken place. It is in the essays which appeared in the intervening year that one can trace the movement of Brownson's thought from Transcendentalism to a repudiation of most of its characteristic doctrines.

In the January 1842 number of his *Review* there are essays that look both ways; a foolish consistency was never a hobgoblin to trouble Brownson. In this issue he reviews his own "New Views" of 1836 at some length, and reiterates most of its doctrines. After five years of "intense application" he has arrived at the same conclusions by a different process, "finds the book once again in his experience, and reaffirms it." He professes to believe in the Incarnation, but charges the church with having imperfectly apprehended the doctrine. The "ideal" is incarnated not alone in Jesus, but in every man; and the "Church of the Future" will be an organization "for the worship of God as revealed in all men."[35]

This is clearly the version of Transcendentalism Brownson held in 1836. But in the same issue of the *Review,* in the essay "Reform and Conservatism," he insists that while Transcendentalists are right in affirming man's power to perceive truths that transcend the senses, they are wrong in alleging that these truths exist in the soul. "They are objects of the soul's intelligence . . . exterior to it, and possessed by it only when it beholds them."[36] And in the same essay he says even more positively: "Alas! we have seen enough of mere individual reason. It is impotent when it has not, for its guide and support, the reason of God, speaking not only to the heart, but through revelation and the traditions of the race."[37]

These last quotations indicate the direction of Brownson's thought as expressed in his essays over the remainder of the year. In his April *Quarterly* he reviews his own *Charles Elwood,* and repudiates Constant's view of religion as "a sentiment of the heart, an indestructible law of man's nature,"[38] a view Brownson had held since 1834 and had shared with Ripley and Parker even in 1841 when he reviewed Parker's sermon. Likewise, he subjects the philosophy of Cousin, which he had followed for many years, to sharp criticism. He is clearly attempting to relate his philosophical and his theological studies, to arrive at a satisfactory answer to the problems of faith and reason which, as he makes clear in *The Convert,* have troubled him from his earliest years. His criticism of the subjectivism of Transcendentalism is part of his effort to open the way for the reception of the given and the objective not only on the level of reason but on the supernatural plane as well. He thinks he begins to grasp a true system of philosophy, yet he says near the end of his review of Elwood: "We pretend not, however, to have made any discovery that will supersede the necessity of divine revelation, or a childlike trust in the wisdom and goodness of Providence, whose ways are often dark and mysterious, and whose purposes are not seldom past finding out."[39]

In June 1842, Brownson published his pamphlet on "The Mediatorial Life of Jesus" as a "Letter to Rev. William Ellery Channing." Brownson addresses the elder Channing as "his spiritual father" and acknowledges the influence Channing's thought has had upon him since he first heard a friend read to him Channing's sermon on "Likeness to God." Then Brownson reviews his own beliefs as a Unitarian during the previous ten years. He has tried to find the grounds of religion in human nature, to resolve the providences of God into the ordinary operations of nature. With others of the movement party, he has tended "to sink God in nature." Many deny the doctrine of Providence and "in reading ancient history they seek to resolve all that is marvelous or prodigious into natural laws . . . . They see no longer the hand of God, but great Nature."[40] To hold this view, he now maintains, is virtually to deny God's existence by denying His freedom. God acts by the laws of His own being.

The remainder of Brownson's letter criticizes one by one the Transcendentalist attitudes on religion. Man is not naturally divine; what is divine is "superinduced upon his nature . . . by the grace of God. . . ."[41] Christianity assumes man's sinfulness, his alienation from God, not his divinity. Man cannot commune directly with God, but only through a mediator, who in the plain literal sense must be "very God of very God, and very man of very man."[42] Moreover, Brownson repudiates his view, stated in his criticism of Andrews Norton, that the historical fact of Christ's life was unimportant. "Christ, the literal person we call Christ, *is* Christianity. . . . To reject him historically is to reject Christianity."[43] This, he says, is the truth which they have had who have accused some of us of advocating "the latest form of infidelity."

Remembering Emerson's excoriation of historical Christianity as dwelling "with noxious exaggeration about the *person* of Jesus," one is not surprised to learn that Emerson found Brownson's letter "local and idolatrous."[44] It must have reminded him of Andrews Norton; it certainly indicated Brownson's repudiation of many of the doctrines of Transcendentalism he had espoused for years.

At this juncture in Brownson's thinking, his study of the work of Pierre Leroux was of central importance. He reviews Leroux's *De l'Humanité* (Paris, 1840) in the July 1842 issue of *The Boston Quarterly*, and later in *The Convert*, sums up the significance of

Leroux for his own conversion. Brownson's analysis is detailed, but it is only his comment on Leroux in relation to Transcendentalism that need concern us here.

Leroux's analysis of thought, his epistemology, especially his criticism of subjectivism, helped to crystallize Brownson's tentative judgment of the philosophical basis of Transcendentalism. "The object," in Brownson's reading of Leroux, "affirms itself in the fact of consciousness as object, as distinct from, and independent of, the subject. . . ."[45] Brownson opposes this view to that of the Transcendentalists, "that *man can be his own object, and that his life is all in himself, and therefore wholly subjective.*"[46]

Moreover, Leroux's concept of hierarchy and his doctrine of communion, according to which man lives only by communion with what is not himself, with nature, his fellow men and with God, ultimately led Brownson to examine the historical claims of the Catholic Church, although Leroux himself made communion with God a natural communion through humanity. Finally, Leroux's doctrine of individuals providentially elevated, his "Providential Men," opened for Brownson the possibility of supernatural communion he develops in his essays of 1843 and 1844. He held that through communion with those individuals who were providentially elevated by the Creator to "supernatural communion with himself," the human race itself might be elevated to a supernatural life. Thus, while Brownson still placed Jesus in the category of such providential men as Abraham, Moses, Socrates, and Plato, he now began to examine the claims of the historical Catholic Church. Without failing in his pledge to be faithful to his own rational nature, as he says in *The Convert,* he had glimpsed certain principles which "placed him on the route to the Catholic Church."[47]

Now that the course of Brownson's thinking during 1842 has been traced in some of its aspects, the disparity between his evaluation of Parker's sermon and Parker's published lectures should be more understandable. In opposition to Parker's identification of the law of God with the laws of human nature, Brownson had developed his conception of the Providential and his doctrine of communion. These became the basis of his argument in "The Philosophy of History," two essays which he contributed to the *Democratic Review* in May and June, 1843. Here he held that to confine God's intervention to the necessary and invariable laws of nature and of humanity is to imply Creation but to deny Providence, and that this view of Parker's and other Transcendentalists "will not suffice to explain and account for the facts of human

history."[48] Now Brownson read in the Old Testament and the
New the record of God's special intervention in human history.
He saw what was unique and historical as well as what was "universal" in religion. As he says in *The Convert*, he saw that "while
God binds nature, nature cannot bind Him," and he ends his
chapter "Providential Men" with the sentence: "I shall never
forget the ecstasy of that moment when I first realized to myself
that God is free."[49]

Since much of Brownson's re-examination of his own Transcendentalist assumptions during these months involved the problem
of knowledge, it is not surprising that he should in 1844 devote
three closely reasoned articles to Kant's *Critique of Pure Reason*
in his *Quarterly*, which he revived in January 1844 as *Brownson's
Quarterly Review*. Though space does not permit discussion of
these essays here, it is worth noting that in their repudiation of a
subjective theory of knowledge they complement his essays on
Parker, Leroux, and the "Philosophy of History."[50] Nor can the
other essays of 1844 be discussed. These are on such topics as "The
Church Question," "No Church, No Reform," and "Church Unity
and Social Amelioration." Some of them appeared after Brownson
had already begun to take instructions in the Catholic Faith in
May 1844. They show him searching no longer for the Church of
the Future, but for the authentic historical Church. In "The Church
Question," for example, he reviews the significance of the Trac-
tarian Movement; in April he concludes that the divine institution
already exists, "or there are no means of reform"; and in an essay
in July a new note is heard, when Brownson asks which church is
"the one true Catholic apostolic church."[51]

In his 1842 review of Parker's *Discourse* Brownson had commented in detail on the five books into which the volume was
divided: The Religious Sentiment, Inspiration, Christianity, The
Bible, and The Church. It was with Parker's thought alone that
he was concerned. But the three essays on Transcendentalism
which Brownson wrote after his conversion, while they once again
make Parker's book the point of departure, do not review the
book; instead, they sum up Brownson's judgment of the entire
movement. There are references not only to Parker, but several to
Emerson, some to Alcott, Carlyle, and Margaret Fuller, and to
Brownson's own earlier writings.

Having now traversed, in a quarter-century, a path from Pres-
byterianism through Universalism, Unitarianism, and Transcendentalism into the Catholic Church, he attempts to see Transcen-

dentalism in historical perspective. It was, so he now holds, a movement which looked upon the Protestantism of the early reformers as no longer tenable, as having yielded to the "blows of Bossuet, and other Catholic divines, in the seventeenth century."[52] What had survived of Protestantism survived largely as Deism or as infidelity, the complete denial of supernatural revelation. The reform party, unwilling to go back to Rome, to the older Protestantism, or to rationalism, must invent a new form, which was Transcendentalism. "It must neither assert nor deny revelation, and yet must do both in the same breath; it must be a believer to the believer, an unbeliever to the unbeliever; appear to the Christian to assert the supernatural order, to the infidel to admit only the natural order. . . . It boldly faced the difficulty . . . by asserting that the soul is furnished with a transcendental faculty or power which . . . places us in immediate relation with the world of spirit, as the senses do with the world of matter."[53] Distinguishing between institutional religion, as of human origin, and absolute religion, and denying any unique place to the Christian dispensation, Transcendentalists accepted the Bible along with the sacred books of all nations. All were valuable but imperfect attempts to symbolize permanent religious truths.

However different are their interpretations of intuition—and Brownson attempts to discriminate the various uses of the term— all Transcendentalists, according to Brownson, make man the measure of religious truth, and unrestricted private judgment the rule of faith. The God to whom Transcendentalists refer is either in the soul, and in the soul naturally, or, as with Emerson, there is no recognition of distinct substantive existences or distinct natures, but instead, one mighty Nature, the Over-Soul. Man and God thus stand in an immediate natural relation, for however frequently Transcendentalists employ the language of supernaturalism, the special spiritual sense, sentiment, or intuition they affirm is a natural power. But is man's natural relation the only relation he sustains to his Creator? "Do man's natural forces—that is, what he is and receives by virtue of his natural relation to God— suffice for the fulfillment of his destiny; or needs he the gracious, that is, supernatural, interposition and assistance of his Maker?"[54] These are now to Brownson the real questions, and his chief aim in the essays is to demonstrate that the Transcendentalists assert nature against grace, and exalt impulse and feeling above the very rational nature which is constitutive of human personality.

It should be emphasized that these essays, like many of Brownson's other essays immediately after his conversion, are over-vehement in their rejection of his earlier views. The tone is militant, unyielding, even at times almost mockingly contemptuous. Moreover, the attempt to employ a scholastic terminology which he had not made his own gives the essays a crabbed quality. One wonders why, if Transcendentalism is so obvious an error, and yields so easily to logical analysis, it could have held Brownson's allegiance for so long.

Ten years later, when he reviews Isaac Hecker's *Questions of the Soul* (1855), Brownson modifies his judgment of the movement. Hecker's sympathetic manner of addressing Protestants and Transcendentalists now seems to Brownson far superior to his own logical and polemical method, which tends to represent Catholicism in its negative character and to deny any truth in the Protestant position. Hecker recognizes that American Transcendentalists like Emerson and Parker were concerned with counteracting the Calvinistic view of human nature as radically corrupt. They could not countenance the annihilation of reason and nature in favor of grace. Their insistence on man's dignity was necessary and important. Addressing himself to Transcendentalists, Hecker finds, in Brownson's words, "something true and beautiful in many of those choice souls, who, however mistaken in their practical endeavors, sought earnestly for a time to live a higher life, and deserved something better than the sneers and scoffs they received from an unsympathizing world."[55] And Brownson stresses Hecker's assertion, in the face of Calvinism and Jansenism, that "man has a destiny, and to corrupt, to enfeeble, or to abandon those instincts, faculties, and activities which God has given him whereby to reach his destiny, this is the soul's suicide . . ."[56] Here, as Brownson now sees it, is the recognition of the truth in the Transcendentalist reliance on sentiment and instinct.

While Brownson is less favorable toward Hecker's next book, *Aspirations of Nature* (1857), his two reviews give evidence that he came to view more sympathetically the Transcendentalist endeavor to save nature and reason against Calvinism. Yet he insists that only in the Catholic doctrine of nature and grace are the polar exaggerations corrected. The reference to Calvinism and Jansenism in this context leads me to a suggestion which has occurred to me for the first time as I have reflected on the whole Transcendentalist debate, and have noticed how tenaciously the Transcendentalists held to their theory of the religious sentiment as natural to man.

Brownson himself had passed through a Calvinistic period at an early age, and it is not too much to say that in his recoil from Transcendentalism immediately after his conversion he at times comes close to Jansenism. What is more important is that this entire triangular debate among Calvinists, Unitarians, and Transcendentalists was carried on almost as if the classical conception of the natural moral law did not exist. When Parker, Ripley, Emerson, and the early Brownson affirm the divinity in man, and the natural religious sentiment, they are attempting in a confused way to assert the dignity of man as a rational creature against the extreme Calvinistic doctrine of total depraviy. To put it in another way, if Parker asserted the natural law as the participation of the Eternal Law instead of the Divine Law in man, he would be following the distinction of St. Thomas' *Treatise on Law*. The natural law "is nothing else than the rational creature's participation in the Eternal Law."[57] Why God should also reveal the Old and New Law to creatures who already participate in his Eternal Law is a question which St. Thomas discusses fully, but in all the writings that arose from the New England movement, there is, to my knowledge, only one reference to the problem. This occurs in Brownson's review of Hecker's *Aspirations of Nature* already referred to. Brownson distinguishes between what man can attain to naturally and what he actually does attain to, adding: "St. Thomas teaches us that revelation is necessary, practically necessary, to enable men to know even the natural law, especially in the case of the great mass of mankind."[58] This quotation suggests that if the Transcendentalists were right in asserting the natural law against Calvinism, their denial of the necessity of the Revealed Law largely stemmed from their acceptance of the Romantic doctrine of man's natural goodness.

Returning to the essays Brownson wrote immediately after his conversion, I think his recoil from Transcendentalism has a close connection with his essays on Newman. The severity with which Brownson attacked Newman's *Development of Christian Doctrine* in a series of essays beginning in the July 1846 number of his *Review* has often seemed puzzling to students of the two converts. Various motives have been suggested: Brownson's dislike of the Oxford converts and their intellectual subtlety, the encouragement given to Brownson by Bishop Purcell, and even a certain jealousy of Newman's eminence. No one, to my knowledge, has explored the possibility that Brownson's misreading of Newman—and Brownson admitted in 1864 that he had misinterpreted Newman—

can be accounted for with reference to the Transcendentalist doctrines which I have been discussing.

It should be noticed that Brownson seized upon certain expressions of Newman and largely confined his attack to these. What were they? That the mind of the Church worked out dogmatic truth "from implicit feelings," that certain of the Fathers had an "intense feeling" without "a digested idea of Purgatory, or Original Sin." "What in one age is feeling," says Brownson, "in a succeeding age becomes opinion, and an article of faith in a later age." Most important to Brownson was Newman's statement that Christianity "came into the world as an *idea* rather than an institution," from which Brownson concludes Newman's assumption to be that "Christianity can be abstracted from the church." Having quoted these passages, Brownson says: "We meet here an old, familiar acquaintance—a doctrine which we embraced for years before we became a Catholic, and which for years kept us out of the Catholic Church, as it now keeps out the greater part of our former friends and associates. Assuming that Christianity came into the world originally as an idea, and not as an institution . . . we held that, by seizing it anew, abstracting it from the institutions with which it has thus far clothed itself . . . we might organize through it a new institution, a new church . . ."[59]

Granted that Brownson is ignoring much else in Newman's theory, it is understandable that he should be startled by the surface similarity here between Newman's theory and his own earlier thought. For example, when Brownson wrote his favorable review of Parker's "Transient and Permanent in Christianity," he summed up Parker's theory thus: "We must distinguish between Christianity as it lies in the Divine Mind, and Christianity as it lies in our conceptions, in our doctrines, or systems of theology. The first only is *permanent,* the last is *transient.* . . . Hence, theology, like all human sciences, is subject to successive modifications, perpetual alterations. Christianity itself remains unchanged, but our scientific expositions of it change ever, and pass away."[60] Giving a disproportionate attention to whatever in Newman's book seemed similar to Parker's emphasis on the human element in religion, Brownson was led to the conclusion that Newman's theory was "essentially anticatholic and Protestant."[61]

Brownson's interpretation of Newman's theory actually anticipated in important respects that by which such Modernists as Loisy and Tyrrell attempted to enlist Newman in their defense.

Moreover, the Modernist heresy bears a striking similarity to the
view Brownson shared with Ripley and Parker in the 1830's and
against which he began to argue with such vehemence from 1842
on. Compare, for example, the following comment on Modernism
with some of the Transcendentalist formulations of the doctrine
of the religious sentiment: "The Modernists explained the fact
of religion by an immanent principle, a subconscious need which
the human being feels for the supernatural, and which gives rise
to what may be described as a religious sentiment. This sentiment
or 'religious sense' . . . is the seed from which all religion grows
and the essence of all that any religion has contained or will contain."[62] There is an equally close relation between the Transcendentalist and Modernist theories that dogma and doctrine are
subject to a real evolution, and when one recalls the Modernist
appeal to Newman on this score, Brownson's similar misreading
of Transcendentalist errors in Newman is made more understandable.

Among Brownson's later criticisms of Transcendentalism one
of the most penetrating is his characterization of it as a form of
"learned gentilism" or "gentile rationalism." He compares it with
the "old Alexandrian system, which sprang up in the third century
of our era, as the rival of the Christian Church. . . ."[63] This
Alexandrian syncretism attempted to mold the various forms of
gentilism into a doctrine that would rival Christianity, and even
borrowed the forms of its hierarchy and many of its dogmas. "It
called itself *Philosophy,* and its pretension was to raise philosophy
to the dignity of religion, and to do by it what Christianity professes to do by faith and an external and supernaturally accredited
revelation."[64] Brownson maintains that the nineteenth century is
distinguished by its return, with various modifications, to this
gentilism. He notes the gnostic element, for example, in Transcendentalism, the interest of Emerson in the Neo-Platonists, and notes
the similarity between "intuition," as understood by the Transcendentalists, and the ecstasy or trance of the Neo-Platonists.
Brownson's whole analogy between this third-century movement
and Transcendentalism illuminates much of the speculation and
activity of Emerson, Alcott, Parker, Brownson himself, and others.
For, as Brownson argues, the reform party, finding Protestantism
unsatisfactory and, like the Alexandrian Neo-Platonists, either
disdaining the Catholic Church or ignorant of its doctrines, attempted to form a new religion out of such materials as the old
supplied.

This analogy was no later invention of Brownson's. It was suggested in the essays attacking Transcendentalism which appeared in the *Princeton Review* in 1839. What is interesting is that Brownson had in 1840 accepted this characterization of Transcendentalism as sound. "We are now," he wrote, "in an epoch of history, analogous to that of the first three or four centuries of our era, and therefore our philosophy ought to be analogous to Gnosticism and to the Alexandrian Eclecticism."[65] Like the Alexandrians, French and German philosophers were seeking to reconcile reason and the Church, and Brownson argued that this reconciliation was precisely what was needed and precisely what Transcendentalism sought to achieve. To suggest why he should embrace this whole approach in 1840 and reject it as "gentile rationalism" in 1849 has been the purpose of this essay.

NATHANIEL HAWTHORNE
1804-1864

God and Man in New England

JOSEPH SCHWARTZ

ONE of America's most perceptive writers, Henry James, called Hawthorne "the most valuable example of the American genius." Although no one expects every critic to agree with James's estimate, no critic has placed Hawthorne below the first category in any critical ranking of American writers. The critics do differ, however, in their evaluation of the precise pattern of his ideas and his meaning.[1] And so the basic question must be answered again: what is the author saying?

Any study of literature concerns itself primarily with the author as artist; but a writer is not an artist alone. He cannot claim for his work the moral or intellectual immunity of the line or the plane or the color. He deals with words as symbols of ideas or emotions or attitudes. Indeed, he is forced to become a thinker of sorts, even a philosopher. Until we understand the attitude of Hawthorne toward many of the issues which gave meaning to the scope and direction of his art, confusion will make blunderers of us all. The works of Hawthorne, America's ablest romancer, are a rich source for any ideological investigation. The whole range of his fiction and nonfiction reveals a rare personality, a man of various interests and profound speculation. His chief interest was in the moral and religious character of man. Almost every short story or novel shows this searching concern.

There is justice and prudence in limiting our investigation to this point. Actually, the inquiry widens as we pursue our object. Consequently, we shall find ourselves dealing with such terms as free will, the natural desire for God, fatalism, and providence. In a restricted sense, one discovers that the history of philosophy has been an attempt to define these terms; just as the history of literature has been an attempt to put such abstractions into concrete statement for the benefit of mankind. This distinction between the duty of the philosopher and of the poet is at least the one made in the first important critical statement in the English language, that of Sir Philip Sidney, the contemporary of Hawthorne's beloved Edmund Spenser:

> Now doth the peerless poet perform both: for whatsoever the philosopher saith should be done, he givith a perfect picture of it in someone by whom he presupposeth it was done; so as he coupleth the general notion with the particular example. A perfect picture I say, for he yieldeth to the powers of the mind an image of that whereof the philosopher bestoweth but a wordish description: which doth neither strike, pierce, nor possess the sight of the soul so much as that other doth.

Because Hawthorne was still part of a tradition which did not fear the charge of didacticism, he rightly concerned himself with the intangibles, searching for the spiritual foundation of our temporal life, trying to understand the nature of good and evil, seeking to examine the sources and effects of sin. What complicates a study of this kind is the "artistic guise" which Hawthorne claimed for himself in the dedication of *The Twice-Told Tales*. But it is this same passage which gives us our guide for further investigation. In order to understand an author, he tells us, "You must . . . look through the whole range of his fictitious characters, good and evil, in order to detect any of his essential traits."

We cannot discover Hawthorne's ideas unless we search amid the tangled wonder of their artistic expression. His interest in philosophy as philosophy, though apparent, is not profound. His readings shows that he was aware of many of the current books dealing with philosophy. There are passages in the notebooks which mention philosophical terms exactly. But the "dismal and monotonous" desert of metaphysics (as he called it) was never thoroughly to his liking. He regularly read the "cloudy and dreary" metaphysical passages of the *Dial* when he wanted to induce sleep.[2] He disliked and neglected such subjects as a student.

His notebooks, however, are filled with abstractions, and here is the key to understanding his approach. Later, these abstractions were made concrete in the many short stories, sketches, and "moralities" which he wrote with such charm and felicity. He found discussions of metaphysics when not related to the human mind and heart in a concrete situation of life just as tedious as the conversations of the Transcendentalists. But when he could take a philosophical problem and apply it through his art to a lifelike situation, or when in real life he saw beliefs influence action, he became intensely interested. It was in this way, through observation and experience, that man's relation to God and man's relation to his own integrity or ethic became the essential problems of his artistic and intellectual life.

Born in 1804, Hawthorne grew up in a world confused by death and discovery. Intellectuals were watching with keen interest the dying gasps of Puritanical Calvinism, a theology so powerful that it had given form and order to the New England Mind. On the other hand, powerful new forces were investigating unexplored areas of theology and philosophy. What we might call the Christian Tradition in America was seriously weakened by this confusion. A brief record of the struggle will not be without point here; for Hawthorne was a thinking man, and there is reason for believing that he would know what was being discussed in his own day.

The essential theological controversy of the day centered largely around the free will of man. The Unitarians fought the old-line Calvinists on this age-old battleground. When, indeed, the Baptists gained strength, they were referred to with contempt as "free-willers" by the Calvinists. The struggle for supremacy confused many Christians; and the result was a weakening of faith for those who could accept neither the "Angry God" of Jonathan Edwards nor the sweet, benevolent Jesus of William Ellery Channing. The followers of both were vigorous in their polemic; but their vigor succeeded only in splitting what had been the single Christian idea in New England. Man's responsibility for his actions was vigorously debated, without fear of punishment, in public tribunals for the first time.

The Hawthorne family took sides early in the struggle. A study of his ancestors shows a progression from determined Calvinism to liberal Unitarianism, a pattern followed by many another New England family of the time. Only two American ancestors were militant Calvinists, Major William Hawthorne and his son, Colonel John—the witch-persecutor for whom Nathaniel apologized so profusely in more than one instance. By 1762 the sons of Joseph Hawthorne were leaving the orthodox church to marry girls of the Anglican communion. By the time of "bold" Captain Daniel and his son, Nathaniel's father, Calvinism had lost its hold on the Hawthorne family. Nanthaniel, Sr., was married in the orthodox church; but eventually his wife accepted the Unitarian religion, though never with the fervor of Sophia, Hawthorne's beloved wife. The famous Nathaniel was almost exclusively raised by his mother. There is no evidence to show that he was indoctrinated with the tenets of Calvinism, and little evidence to show that he was exposed to any deliberate religious proselytizing. It is remarkable that later in life he found God at all.

There are certain other factors which should be considered in the breakdown of a religion which so many critics have insisted Hawthorne fundamentally accepted.[3] The growth of the "new psychology" contributed to a new picture of man, a picture at variance with the black one painted by the Calvinistic theologians. The new psychologists around Hawthorne's time were beginning to investigate the nature of man in the light of his own capacities and talents. Thus, the will, as an effective power, received new recognition. Liberated from the shackles of an all-confining religious assumption of depravity, the psychologists were free to study the workings of the human mind, as it really worked.

This emphasis on moral philosophy, or practical ethics, as it was called, was coincident with the time of Hawthorne's college education. As a matter of fact, Hawthorne's philosophy professor was Thomas C. Upham, one of the most distinguished of the leaders in the Tri-Faculty psychology movement which did much to end the reign of Calvinism's hold on the mind. ("Tri-Faculty" is a term apparently borrowed from Herbert Schneider; he in turn had got it from the titles of books concerning the "new" psychology published in the first half of the nineteenth century. The powers of the soul were thought to be three: volition, imagination, and reason.) Upham's books stressed the free will of man, which would make for a completely different approach to an analysis of the relationship between God and man. Hawthorne's textbook was the work of Dugald Stewart, one of the Scotch philosophers. Here he learned as well about the concept of the free man. The picture of the nature of man to which Hawthorne was exposed proves to be diametrically opposed to the picture of man which the encrusted years of Calvinistic theology had drawn. These influences, it would seem, are more pertinent to Hawthorne's growth and development than the fast-dying influence of Calvinism. This is not even to mention the growing liberal movement in politics which many serious scholars feel was the final breakdown of the autocratic Puritan idea. Hawthorne himself was an ardent Jacksonian Democrat, actively enough engaged in politics to receive two choice political appointments. The philosophy of Jacksonian Democracy was utterly different from the narrow sense of election prescribed by Puritanical Calvinism.

The changes in theology, philosophy, and politics during Hawthorne's lifetime were both dramatic and far-reaching. That these changes were brought to his attention seems evident. We know that he described one of the chief philosophical innovations of his time as a mixture of "mist, moonshine, raw potatoes, and stardust." What is more important is that this sense of rapid change made it imperative for each man to be his own guide. At least the statement holds true for Hawthorne. He had to approach with new eyes and a new vision problems which Calvinism had settled to its own satisfaction. The result was that he reached new conclusions, more humane, if less dogmatic; more sincere, if less logical. Part of the beautiful, swift terror of his insight comes from the lonely path he thought he was forced to take in reaching conclusions concerning the verities of Heaven and earth.

In *The Education of Henry Adams,* Adams tells us of a boyhood faithful to all the exterior forms of religion. But he notes with sad anxiety that he and all his brothers and sisters threw off the mild discipline of Unitarianism as soon as they could. Like Adams, Hawthorne freed himself from any formal religion as soon as possible; but unlike Adams, he had no childhood memories to encourage and hasten the day of liberation. For all of the charges of Calvinism that have been raised against him, Hawthorne was reared in the most liberal religious tradition. He tells us in *Septimus Felton* that one's milieu has an effect on the "mind and moral nature." Following this lead, let us examine his environment in order to determine what religious attitudes might have been formed, destroyed, or ignored.

Hawthorne himself tells us that his youth was unfettered by any kind of dogmatism. His own opinion is re-enforced by the comment of his sister, Elizabeth, that as children they were under very little control. His sense of freedom and independence was developed at an early stage of his life. Elizabeth adds the significant comment that Hawthorne "developed himself." The free and romantic atmosphere of Raymond, Maine, where the Hawthorne family moved for economic reasons, helped to develop his sense of freedom. It was here, too, that Hawthorne acquired his love for nature and his habit of moralizing from the observation of nature. The consideration of nature as an emblem of God and eternity became a lifelong habit, especially noticeable in *The American Notebooks.* His early education did nothing to interfere with his natural spirit of independence. A crippled foot meant that his education had to be conducted at home. In an indirect way, this encouraged his sense of freedom of thought, since it prevented him from being subjected to the rigors of the contemporary school. Horace Mann tells us what kind of school it was, still under the control of Calvinism (schools were reluctant to change ideas, then as now), where the teachers expounded to the children "all the doctrines of total depravity, election, reprobation, and not only the eternity, but the extremity, of hell-torments."[4]

Spared this kind of earlier training, Hawthorne might have been subject to it at college, since Bowdoin was still under the influence of orthodoxy, or, to put it more exactly, since President Allen was vigorously orthodox. The faculty as well as the students constantly warred against him. It was here that Hawthorne met Longfellow (who was starting a Unitarian Society on the campus!) and was subjected to the influences of Upham and Stewart, both of whom taught the freedom of man. His reading shows that he became acquainted with the principles of Calvinism and with the principles of the many opponents of Calvinism. He was not fond of going to chapel; his interests were circumscribed by the nonphilosophical subjects. The life at Bowdoin was relatively unconfining; his spirit of independent thought was carefully preserved.

What can be surmised at this point is that neither Calvinism nor any of the newer religious dispositions claimed Hawthorne's allegiance. His closest friends in college and later were of the same noncommittal temperament. His native critical sense encouraged him to be suspicious of both the old and new. This native hue of resolution has confused many of his critics. They have called him gloomy, Puritanic, and despairing. This sense of fatality, which some see as a cloud hanging over his works, was the special target of attack by those who knew him best. Julian, Mrs. Hawthorne, James Field, and his best friend, Horatio Bridge, did much to dispel this cloud of gloom. His many other personal friends tried to make clear that he was independent and reserved by nature but not fatalistically inclined. The portrait of Hawthorne as a Calvinistic fatalist is an artistic one, but is less and less like Hawthorne the more we learn of him. In his graceful introduction to *Mosses from an Old Manse,* he wrote: "So far as I am a man of really individual attributes I veil my face." By his own injunction we are forced to turn to his own works, to probe where there is no veil, to discover the essence of his thought. The challenge of his art is even more stimulating than the challenge of his life.

More than any other writer of his time, Hawthorne was a God-concerned writer. He was innately religious, as his profound reverence for the mysteries of Christianity demonstrates. Many of his stories deal with religious subjects, with prayer, and with man's relation to God. His personal notebooks are filled with many habitual references to God. That he often wrote about religious subjects is not strange, for he felt that religion was not the property of the professional and exclusive religionists. His many caustic barbs were directed at the elements which surrounded a particular denomination; about the subject of religion in general he was deeply respectful. When he selected the one thing that he thought made his friend, Franklin Pierce, worthy to be President, it was that Pierce had learned the great lesson of life, "that religious faith is the most valuable and most sacred of human possessions." Why, then, did Hawthorne himself accept no formal religious faith? He could not accept the dogmas of the warring sects that contended for his approval. Given the milieu in which he grew up, it is easy to see why he insisted on individual belief, religion "as a matter between the Deity and man's soul." His natural antipathy for Calvinism made him suspicious of all formal religion. He deplored the fact that each sect should surround "its own righteousness with a hedge of thorns." His native sense of independence made him reject both the old and the new.

Julian tells us that, as far as he could remember, his father never attended church. Hawthorne was not silent on this issue, but curiously forward. While he was courting Sophia, she "commanded" him to go to church. His *No* was playfully, but firmly expressed. Though he loved the Sabbath, he had no set way of observing it. He speaks of his "inner man" going constantly to church, while many who went to church left their souls at home. Here is a case of a natural religious disposition unable to find any formal religious expression.

It would be well to cite here that famous passage from "The Old Manse" in which Hawthorne tells us of discovering his religious predecessor's library. It contained the works of theology, old and new. After leafing through them, he concludes that the lot of them are accumulations of "stupendous impertinence." The key to his idea of Christianity is voiced in a crucial passage: "So long as an unlettered soul can attain to saving grace," there is no need for the formalized religions with which he was acquainted. The "good orthodox" should be able to grasp the hand of the "good Unitarian," but since formalized religion made this impossible, he would have none of it.

The essential reason for which he rejected the old orthodoxy was because of its exclusiveness. In this one concept were all the weaknesses which he saw in Calvinism. He could not accept the idea of election. In the "Procession of Life," a blend of essay and narrative that Hawthorne wrote with such charm, he speaks out directly against the exclusive religionists. But it is in a little-known character study, "Man of Adamant," which, I think, ranks in power with "Ethan Brand," that he takes issue most effectively with the doctrine of intolerant election. Richard Digby, so sure of his own plan of salvation, retreats from the rest of the world after warning everyone that his is the only way to be saved. It was an abominable crime for men to trust to their own strength. It does little good that Digby hurls anathemas against the rest of mankind. His reward is a different kind of exclusiveness, for he turns into a man of stone, a symbol "repelling the whole race of mortals—not from heaven—but from the horrible loneliness of his dark, cold sepulchre." The false pride which comes from this view of exclusive election is always disastrous. Richard Digby's pride in his election to a religious truth turns him into a man of stone; Lady Eleanor's mantle, a symbol of her social pride because it made her different from everyone else, becomes the agent for her ravagement; and Ethan Brand's intellectual pride in the unforgivable sin destroys him.

This same intolerance, born of a sense of election, is described in "The Gentle Boy." Here Hawthorne is unsparing in his condemnation of Calvinism. And all of "Main Street" points graphically at the horrors of the Puritan way of life as it had been informed by the smug righteousness of the doctrine of election. The kind of God this represented was a horror to Hawthorne's sight. There is a striking incident in *The Scarlet Letter* that reveals just how much Hawthorne disliked the whole narrow theological system. He has Chillingworth, one of his darkest villains, use the theology of predestination or fatality as an excuse for the malice of his freely willed sins. The rigidity of orthodoxy was seen by Hawthorne especially in the exclusiveness of election—the high mystery of predestination. Hawthorne was repelled by this God of "dark necessity."

The alternative, as Hawthorne saw it, was an acceptance of the ephemeral mistiness of Unitarianism or the dreamy metaphysics of Transcendentalism. Both of these he rejected, because when he saw them he beheld "vapors piled upon vapors." His contemptuous dislike for Transcendentalism has been rehearsed by too many critics for me to echo it here. But what we sometimes forget is that he was equally disgusted with the "vaguely liberal clergyman of our own day." He referred to the volumes of the *Christian Examiner* and *Liberal Preacher*, modern sermons, and the controversial works of Unitarian ministers as "trash."

Hawthorne fictionalized his thought on this subject in his best satire, "The Celestial Railroad." In this biting fantasy he deals with the "cold, lifeless, vaguely liberal" Unitarian Mr. Smooth-it-away in no uncertain terms. The satire is penetrating and exact. Consult, for instance, the directory of ministers in Vanity City. "I need only mention the names of the Rev. Mr. Shallow-deep, the Rev. Mr. Stumble-at-truth, that fine old clerical character the Rev. Mr. This-today, who expects shortly to resign his pulpit to the Rev. Mr. That-to-morrow; together with the Rev. Mr. Bewilderment, the Rev. Mr. Clog-the-spirit, and, last and greatest, the Rev. Dr. Wind-of-Doctrine."[5] This brilliant satire reminds us that, when Hawthorne was requested to address the Unitarian Society in England, he refused. The names of the ministers clarify for us Hawthorne's objection to Unitarianism. If he thought this, it should not surprise us that he confessed that his faith in the office of clerical people decreased daily. Rejecting both the grimness of Calvinism and the mistiness of Unitarianism, Hawthorne, like an unfrocked clergyman whom he described, viewed "an impassible gulf between the man of yesterday and to-day." He paced to and fro on these borders trying to discover some measure of certitude for himself. His independent spirit sustained him. His discovery of God was a personal testimony of faith to the demands of his own nature. His natural desire for God was stronger than his powerful tendency to doubt.

Let us turn now to Hawthorne's positive concept of a beneficent Deity. His views will not have the religious neatness which a professional theologian might have given them; but they are strikingly articulate for a layman caught in the confusing currents of nineteenth-century speculative thought. The perceptive reader will notice that the total movement of Hawthorne's thought about God progresses from the lighthearted comments of youth to the more penetrating observations of maturity. Even in his old age, when he was ill and thought his power as a writer was leaving him, he was no less reverent toward the Christian mysteries than he had been in the prime of his speculative life and at the height of his creative powers. The awful mystery of God was most evident to Hawthorne in the world around him. He beheld a universe and observed the order and arrangement and beauty of it. He experienced vividly the value of its salutary effect. And like the first race of men, he looked for a cause. His reason and his heart could not be satisfied unless he accounted for both the order and the beauty. So he arrived at a knowledge of the nature of God from the manifestations of that nature in the perfections of the created universe. He is quick to warn us that the beauty and dignity of the natural world are not mere fancies of the poet's imagination; for the poet's ideal is "the truest truth." Those who would deny the poet's ideal "have been spawned forth by Nature with a contemptuous bitterness; she having plastered them up out of her refuse stuff, after all the swine were made."[6]

For Hawthorne, "beauty is never a delusion." Nothing is worthy of man's infinite capacity save the thought of Heaven. The whole earth is hallowed by the light of Heaven's sanctity. Hawthorne's personal faith in God is closely connected with his view of the universe as a pledge of paradise. Hawthorne is thrilled by "the golden pledge" of sunshine, "mere breath," a heavenly breeze, "tangled woods," common field—"promises of a blessed eternity": "O perfect day! O beautiful world! O beneficent God!" Never, he says, can my soul lose the instinct of its faith. The winningly virtuous Hilda *(The Marble Faun)* and the cameo-like Phoebe *(The House of the Seven Gables)* are the artistic products of a creator who believed this.

Hawthorne's innate religious sense led him by intuition more than anything else toward the idea of a beneficent Father. The human spirit has a natural desire for God, and the evidences of natural religion are strewn everywhere in our path. "The goodness of the Deity" can be pictured in a casual pool of water left by the tide in the sand. The mirror-image functions importantly in all of Hawthorne's works, as an artistic device and as a symbol, because the whole universe is in fact the mirror of God. This idea is expressed with keen exactness in "The New Adam and Eve." This graceful morality pictures the two innocents investigating the remains of civilization. They are perplexed and disturbed by what they find. Although terrified by the gallows, they are more confused by the artifacts which hide the glory of the created world. At last they discover a church and enter it. Though they have some idea of its use, they are amazed that mankind should have worshipped in such a confined area. "They go out of the church and kneeling at its threshold give way to the spirit's natural instinct of adoration towards a beneficent Father."[7]

In his positive view of the nature of God, Hawthorne stresses certain attributes which flow quite naturally from the idea of a beneficent Father. Contrary to the ordinary Calvinistic idea, Hawthorne's God is a God of love. This idea is so important that it demands our special attention. Roderick Elliston in "The Bosom Serpent" is so consumed by the jealous serpent of his own creation that he is blind to the most obvious fact of all, "the radiance of the Creator's face, expressing his love for all the creatures of his hand." Hawthorne's dislike for Milton's picture of God—a cold, intellectual Justice, with a delight in explaining things—is recorded. He felt that it was essential to Christianity that we should see our Judge as kinder to us than we deserve. That is why he disliked Michelangelo's "Last Judgment," since it pictured Jesus, the Saviour, as an "inexorable judge." The tone of the painting, the mood, was too severe. This was alien to his natural temperament and to his personal quest for sunshine. The lamp of man's faith, he said, was enkindled at a celestial fire. "It will surely lead us home to that heaven whence its radiance was borrowed."[8] The issue of this kind of faith is the crucial matrix of his two most fascinating romances: *The Scarlet Letter* and *The Marble Faun*.

The key to *The Scarlet Letter* is in the character of Arthur Dimmesdale, that "false and sin-stained creature of the dust." His perplexing nature provides the reader with some of the tale's most compassionate moments. His fundamental weakness is not his sin, nor even his hypocrisy, but his failure to recognize that God is a God of love. Hemmed in by the narrow theological system of his time, he cannot understand the nature of Him Whom he has offended. The central fact of his nature is indecision about the nature of God. This is precisely why he is the most miserable creature between Heaven and earth; and this is why Hawthorne withholds from him the natural sympathy which we would expect from so sensitive an author. His moral decline runs parallel with his confusion about God. At the very opening of the novel, Hawthorne is critical of Dimmesdale's religious sentiments. Ironically enough, as his hypocrisy corrodes his nature, his sermons become more powerful and persuasive. But his topic is always the horror of sin and the terror of hell. Hopelessness has made the topic of salvation impossible. Dimmesdale's confusion becomes indescribably tortuous.

It is down this painful road that Hawthorne takes the reader to the most compassionate scene in all of his fiction. It is the scene in the forest. Hester can no longer bear the thought of her lover's torment at the hands of Chillingworth, regularly called the "fiend." She is determined to save the minister. Although she tells him that he is dying of his own weakness, Dimmesdale can find no comfort. His anguished cry, "The judgment of God is on me," admits of no comfort. Since he does not know a God of love, he has only two alternatives. He can surrender to what he regards as a terrible sin (though it had "a consecration of its own") or he can make his sin known in order to experience the arid comfort which a meaningless public confession would give him. Hester tells him that "Heaven would show mercy." His concentration on the terrible God of Calvinism has left him "powerless even to repent." Dimmesdale's only reply is that he is "irrevocably doomed." Since he cannot recognize forgiving love as one of God's attributes, he chooses to run off with Hester. The error in this choice is indicated by Hawthorne in a chapter unequaled in world fiction before 1900—"The Minister in a Maze." Only in Dostoevsky do we find such keen psychological insight. Dimmesdale's free surrender to deliberate sin stupefied his potential blessed impulses. "The wretched minister" is tempted to do "some strange, wild, wicked thing." He would corrupt the faith of an aged deacon of the church, destroy the spiritual comfort of a pious old woman, teach the little children wicked words, and, most seriously, drop a germ of evil in the bosom of a young virgin.

His other alternative is the public confession. True to the Puritanic character, he chooses this. Once again we are back at the scaffold, Hawthorne's symbol of the religious and civil law of the Calvinists, "a system of fear and vengeance, never successful, yet followed to the last." This is the most terrifying, though triumphant, moment in the minister's life. The triumph is, however, only partial. At one moment he cries out that "God is merciful!" At the next moment, he doubts. His death scene is agonizing, because it is so incomplete. He still does not know. He is only sure that he must speak out his sin. But he does not know his destiny. The enmeshing entanglements of the human heart are revealed and laid bare; but the minister's maze still exists. The triumph of love does not belong to him. The minister, standing at the pinnacle of the religious and social order, was most confined by his narrow beliefs. Through his failure to attain to certitude, we see Hawthorne's dismay at the system he represented. But God who made us and loves us will not leave us "either to wander in infinite uncertainty, or perish by the way!"[9]

Hawthorne's artistic integrity was so great that he had to

present his ideas by indirection in *The Scarlet Letter*. In every instance the character was limited by his milieu. What we had to infer about the nature of God's love in that work is made explicit in *The Marble Faun*. The British title clearly indicates its central thesis—*The Transformation*. The transformation involved is that of Donatello, who grows from a thoughtless faun to the most spiritually developed person in the romance. In this superbly sketched tale of paradise lost and paradise regained, we reach the summation of Hawthorne's essential thought. His mind had never been so original, so inquisitive; his sensibility never so acute. His full powers, though not tightly organized, are here thought to bear on the central problem of the nature of God's love for man.

Donatello's problem is very much like that of Dimmesdale. Both men must face an enormous spiritual problem, caused by a terrible sin. But Donatello is a very different man. Virtue is much more a matter of private conscience for him. The formal constraint of Catholicism does not seem to weigh as heavily upon him as did the iron theology which dominated Dimmesdale's life. Donatello is not reluctant to accept his suffering, because of his perception of the nature of God. He must simply learn how to go about it. His fault is ignorance, not hypocrisy. Once he knows the way to the Lord, not even Miriam can stop him from taking it. The path of spiritual growth outlined by Hawthorne is so like the one sketched by St. Thomas Aquinas in "The Feast of S. Martin," that we are amazed at Hawthorne's knowledge of Catholicism as it affected a character drawn from that tradition.[10] Or perhaps the better suggestion is that Hawthorne came to the same conclusions by a different route. He deliberately created Donatello as a faunlike creature, almost independent of the normal influences which affect mankind. He stands apart. The process of humanizing him is, in fact, the process of spiritual growth. If anywhere, it is here that we would find Hawthorne's explicit conclusions. Donatello progresses from non-thinking naïveté through suffering to triumph. His story is easily documented.

When we first meet Donatello we are aware of Hawthorne's attempt to create a person wholly unconnected with the moral universe, a simple person of natural affections. He is partly lovable, completely beautiful, and totally amoral. Like the Faun he resembles, he "is endowed with no principle of virtue, and would be incapable of comprehending such." He has "deficiencies both of intellect and heart, and especially, as it seemed, in the development of the higher portions of man's nature." He is, as yet, "out-

side of rules." It is only when he kills on the instinct of simple
natural justice that he starts to become aware. Miriam offers him
her love as compensation for his action; but he refuses to accept
this consolation. Now the transformation begins. One of the first
things that he must learn is the relationship between divine and
human love. Saying, "Farewell, forever," he starts on a physical
journey very like the spiritual one which will save him. He returns
to Monte Beni to discover himself and to discover God. Hawthorne
arranges for Kenyon to be our commentator on Donatello's moral
growth. Kenyon represents, in his capacity as an observer, the
outward manifestations of Donatello's conscience. His function is
carefully symbolized by Hawthorne in the bust which he makes of
Donatello at this time, never complete, but showing a "growing
. . . sense" of the soul.

The tower at Monte Beni (in contrast to the scaffold) is the
chief symbol of the novel, a symbol of "the spiritual experience of
many a sinful soul, which, nevertheless, may struggle upward
into the pure air and light of Heaven at last." It is the artistic
parallel to the tower of purity, Hilda's home. Donatello's first experience is that of remorse for his sin, "a needful dark valley" to
pass through. Kenyon warns him not to stay there too long, or,
like Dimmesdale, he will never find the God of love. Donatello
surpasses Dimmesdale in this instance; he grows out of mere
remorse into a plan for positive action. "The Faun had found a
soul, and was struggling with it towards the light of heaven." The
spiritual regeneration is completed at Monte Beni. Donatello has
found the God of love which his spiritual confusion forced him to
seek.

> How it strengthens the poor human spirit in its reliance on His
> providence, to ascend but this little way above the common level,
> and so attain a somewhat wider glimpse of his dealings with man-
> kind! He doeth all things right! His will be done!

Now Donatello can accept Miriam once more, for he will not
use her love as a substitute for the love of God. His contrition has
led to his penance, and penance to salvation. Nothing is more
touching in the romance than Donatello's simple faith in visiting
the shrines on the road back to Rome. Donatello experiences one
more crisis. Miriam tries to dissuade him from accepting the
social punishment for his crime. She, once so much stronger and
more willful than he, must now learn from him. Miriam has not

made the same progress. She must suffer (as she recognizes) until, we hope, she merits the same peace of soul her lover has found. The Donatello of the end of the novel is almost unrecognizable. His calm authority, his spiritual peace, his dependence upon the love of God—all of these qualities inspire Kenyon's comment on the marvel of life: "We are all so changed!" Donatello's change is the direct result of his knowledge of the love of God. There are no loose ends to bother the reader. There is none of the vague emptiness of Dimmesdale's victory. We are satisfied in a genuinely tragic sense by a hero, who, because of his view of God, is a better man than he was when we first met him.

Hawthorne's faith in a beneficent Deity was strengthened by yet another attribute which was a part of his picture of God. His God was a God of hope. Without hope the soul would be corroded; men would forget their high destiny and fail to work for the achievement of their purposes. It follows from Hawthorne's insistence on a God of love that reason to hope would be given to man. Again we must turn to his comments on nature. The workings of the natural order were an emblem of the meaning of eternal hope. On a rainy day, a little speck of azure widens in the western heavens and we are told it is like "hallowed hopes, of the glory of another world," brightening forth like a rainbow. We create our own "moral rainbows" of hope from this view of nature. "The streak of sunshine journeying through the prisoner's cell" may be considered as "something sent from heaven to keep the soul alive." Let Hawthorne be explicit:

> God does not let us live anywhere or anyhow on earth without placing something of heaven close at hand, by rightly using and considering which, the earthly darkness and trouble will vanish, and all be heaven.[11]

In short, the basis for hope in God is the promise of eternity.

The pursuit of eternity (although the race is often a weary one) is a constant theme in all of his work, from the exuberant *American Notebooks* through the tired yearning of *Dr. Grimshawe's Secret*. The turmoil of the world will always die, "if we set our faces to climb heavenward." This is a significant idea in Hawthorne's work, especially because it was not an easy belief for him. He readily acquiesced to it, because it satisfied the fundamental needs of his nature as a person and as an artist; but the satiric side of his talent as well as his refusal to dogmatize might well have made

him a doubter. What seem to have impressed Hawthorne were
the possibilities of confusion in the actual world. His characters
are often confused by the twisted labyrinth of life, just as he
himself was in many instances. But a sun, shining above the
labyrinth, directs us aright. Has anyone counted his many references to sunlight, light, brightness, and illumination, especially
as these become emblems of hope? A lightning-storm at night
in the city is an apt comparison for him:

> Methinks the scene is an emblem of the deceptive glare which
> mortals throw around their footsteps in the mortal world, thus
> bedazzling themselves till they forget the impenetrable obscurity
> that hems them in, and then can be dispelled only by a radiance
> from above.[12]

Our hope in God is what promises a home in eternity. "The Lily's
Quest" is exact on this point. Lily and Adam find the answer to
the darkest riddle of humanity when they erect their temple of
happiness on a grave. "Now our happiness is for Eternity!" As
usual the ray of sunshine breaks through. The infinite longings of
Hawthorne's "inner heart" were for eternity, for that period of
the full flowering of the spiritual and undying principle in us. Thus
he connects the promise of eternity with his belief in the higher
destiny of man, born of the hope which a beneficent Father gives
to us. "We have strongly within us the sense of an undying principle, and we transfer that true sense to this life and to the
body, instead of interpreting it justly as the promise of spiritual
immortality."[13] Even in his darkest moments—out of the very
bitterness of death—he gathered the sweet assurance of a better
state of being. All earthly misery and, still more, all earthly
happiness could not be compensated for short of eternity; because
true happiness involves something more than earth can give to
us, something more than mere "mortal capacity" can enjoy.

While in Italy, Hawthorne viewed the many works of art which
the centuries of faith had created. In them he saw in many instances the solutions to his own problems. Most of all, he saw
the spiritual framework of the artistic order. His comments are
perceptive and revealing. They are an apt summary of his concept of the nature and idea of God. In the "Laocoön," for instance,
he saw the hand of God untangling the complications of life. The
piece was, he thought, the product of a most powerful mind, one
capable of reducing a complex idea to unity. One of his favorite

pictures was Guido's "Archangel," a copy of which he insisted Sophia paint for his study. He loved to study its representation of the immortal youth and loveliness of virtue, a human conception "deeply imbued with the celestial." Sodoma's "Scourging" reconciled for him the incongruity of divine omnipotence and outraged suffering humanity. It was when he viewed Raphael's "Transfiguration" that his thoughts on the relationship of God with men were most clearly defined.

> As regards the composition of the picture, I am not convinced of the propriety of its being in two so distinctly separate parts— the upper portion not thinking of the lower, and the lower portion not being aware of the higher. It symbolizes, however, the spiritual short-sightedness of mankind that, amid the trouble and grief of the lower picture, not a single individual, either of those who seek help or those who would willingly afford it, lifts his eyes to that region, one glimpse of which would set everything aright. One or two of the disciples point upward, but without really knowing what abundance of help is to be had there.[14]

This is Hawthorne's concept of God, as clearly as he could define it. That is why he called fatalism "a cold torture to the human soul." Hawthorne's natural desire for God led him to accept the concept of a beneficent Deity whose chief attributes were love and hope. A page from the secret history of "David Swan" fictionalizes this idea for us. His seriously considered personal theology, intuitively conceived, was fundamentally based upon his joyful acceptance of the idea of a kind Father. This was inevitably his source of calm strength (what Poe called "repose") when confronted by the disorganized habits of a confused age.

> Life is made up of marble and mud. And, without all the deeper trust in a comprehensive sympathy above us, we might hence be led to suspect the insult of a sneer, as well as an immitigable frown, on the iron countenance of fate. What is called poetic insight is the gift of discerning, in this sphere of strangely mingled elements, the beauty and majesty which are compelled to assume a garb so sordid.[15]

Hawthorne's natural theology had a powerful effect upon the artistic framework of his fiction. Like Henry James, he was convinced that character produces situation, that situation reveals character. In order to understand him at all, we must look through the whole range of his fiction. In doing this, we will discover that his concept of God strongly influenced his analysis of the nature of man. In pursuing this facet of my study I am well aware of the difficulty that Lowell's Hosea Biglow phrased so well:

> The moral questions ollus plain enough,
> It's jes' the human-natur' side that's tough.

What makes the succeeding analysis possible at all is Hawthorne's pronounced impulse to evaluate. All of his fiction is a clear demonstration of his desire to judge the difference between right and wrong in men's actions. Consequently, we may assume that there are some actions which man ought to perform, some which he ought not to perform, some which he may perform or omit as he pleases. This is such a deep-seated attribute of Hawthorne's nature that his tendency to grant or deny worth to certain actions becomes, for him, a *customary* judgment, influencing both his thought and his style. We cannot miss his moral earnestness, his propensity for moralizing. That is why Randall Stewart argues that his chief artistic occupation was the tracing of the psychological effects of sin on man's nature.[16] What makes this facet of my study so tantalizingly attractive is that Hawthorne adds to this impulse to judge a rich imagination, highly developed sensitivity, a transparent conscience, a keen sense of responsibility, Paul Pry's power of inquiry, and a marvelous flow of language that enhances when it equals his powerful and fecund thought.

Hawthorne's personal view of God helped him to accept the traditional idea of Christian dualism in his analysis of the nature of man. Heaven is our home, but we win it by our life on earth. In one of those aphoristic remarks which fill *The American Notebooks,* he capsulated man into a working definition which applies here: "Mankind are earthen jugs with spirits in them." This is a representative statement and a consistent one. It expresses a fundamental dualism which runs throughout Hawthorne's work. Depending upon the tone of the story or essay, he emphasized alternately the "earthen jug" aspect of man or the spirit in him. But the essential fact about man, that he was a union of body and soul, is the stable factor in Hawthorne's analysis of the human character. His consciousness of the beauty of the body and the wonder of the natural world made him deny the Transcendental idea of unity.

However, his belief in a God of love who prepared a home in eternity made him regularly emphasize the spiritual in man. For instance, any sort of bodily torment was a reminder to Hawthorne of the soul that is within us, not within the jurisdiction of the shadowy demons of pain. We need only refer to his portrait of Donatello, who becomes a real man only when the soul within him develops. It was because of his emphasis on the soul in man that he rejected the doctrine of evolution. "Evolution is not true, for we have a soul, and are very distinct from animals. The soul possesses an accumulation of wisdom, and an eternity to grow more in wisdom."[17] The cumulative evidence for this point of view would flow far beyond the limits of this short essay; the central problems of his artistic endeavors were always spiritual ones.

In trying to formulate his view of man, essential for drawing character, Hawthorne was perplexed by the same ideas which confused him in his search for God. He was forced to accept or reject the Calvinistic view of universal depravity or the Unitarian concept of human perfectibility. There were those, of course, who were searching for a *via media;* but they could not lead the way. All that Hawthorne could do was join in the search. From this intense personal effort of discovery came a strikingly clear view of man, even if the roughhewn edges were not always smoothed.

From the earliest record of Hawthorne's written work we see his constant objection to the idea of universal depravity. As a theory for judging human nature it was completely alien to his natural temperament. "Drowne's Wooden Image" is only one of many sketches in which Hawthorne makes quite the opposite point. "Yet who can doubt that the very highest state to which a human spirit can attain, in its loftiest aspirations, is its truest and most natural state . . . ?" The pronounced spiritual principle in man made necessary evil an impossible explanation. He warns us in many instances that we should not deny the spiritual life in any man. Just as the river reflects the sky in its bosom, so each human breast reflects an infinite heaven in its depths. There is no settled resolve toward good or evil, he tells us in "Fancy's Show Box," until the moment of execution. This alone would deny the natural depravity of man. Again and again "the infinite spiritual capacity" of man is pointed out. The doctrine of universal depravity says that evil is the nature of mankind; man cannot elevate himself; he is saved only by predestined election. By his insistence on the spiritual aspirations of man, by his symbolic reading of nature, we can see that Hawthorne rejected the idea that man's fallen nature is inherently evil.

That Hawthorne knew this doctrine well, we can see in "Young Goodman Brown." He has the Devil state it exactly for us: "Evil is the nature of mankind." Chillingworth's darker moments are much like this. Because Goodman Brown believed this on account of his strange experience in the forest, he became a desperate and distrustful man. "They carved no hopeful verse upon his tombstone, for his dying hour was gloom." The outcome of the story warns us of the dire consequences of believing such a doctrine. "The Birthmark" also warns us of the invariable triumph of the gross fatality of earth, if we do not reach "a profounder wisdom" that tells us that our mortal life has some of the texture of the celestial. The Venus de' Medici inspires him to think of "the high destinies of the human race," just as, many years before, a beautiful lily growing out of a dank pond symbolized for him man's choice of assimilating good influences as well as evil ones. It is man's nature to choose; we are not determined to evil.

The heart, he felt, was the essential informing factor of the total human personality, "the great conservative." It is like a cavern, he allegorized, made up of many passages. There are sunshine and flowers at the entrance, deeper a terrible gloom with monsters of diverse kinds; but deeper still are found the flowers and sunshine of the entrance, here made perfect. "These are the depths of the heart, or of human nature, bright and peaceful; the gloom and terror may lie deep; but deeper still is the eternal beauty."[18] This passage helps us to understand the real meaning of "Earth's Holocaust," a morality so diversely interpreted. We can burn up all the worn-out trumpery of the world; but this will be of little avail until man purifies his own heart.

If Hawthorne had accepted the idea of universal depravity, or a necessitarianism of any kind, in his analysis of man, he would have been unable to write either "The Great Stone Face" or The House of the Seven Gables. The short story is an eloquent sermon (if too structured to be superb artistically) which opposes the idea of depravity. The power and triumph of Ernest was that he shaped his own life, by modeling it on an ideal to be pure and great. No original necessity, to use Chillingworth's idea, made him unable to form his own life. We live by our own choice "among poor and mean realities" or "a life of good deeds and holy love." This same idea is expressed in The House of the Seven Gables, the book which Hawthorne thought it was most natural for him to write. The exquisite artistry of its lighter touches and graceful posturing make its message even more compelling.

Hawthorne is not directly concerned here with universal depravity, although he succeeds in voicing his usual attack on Puritanism.

He is concerned with a related topic: does necessity of any kind, heredity or environment, determine our actions? Are we motivated to do evil by some necessity against our will? From the weakest, Hepzibah, to the strongest, Phoebe, the answer is *No*. Although Hepzibah has almost lost her power to act because of inactivity, she moves like a tigress in defense of her beloved Clifford. Even Clifford throws off the shackles of the past and experiences an hysterical kind of freedom in that remarkable train ride. Holgrave tells Phoebe that a dark necessity—the family feud—hangs over them. She rejects the whole moral of his story, as he himself does later. The powerful force of inherited evil is firmly conquered by the union of the families and the promise of happiness which the author so carefully phrases at the end of the romance. It would seem that in matters of conduct man is free to exercise the loftier elements of his nature.

The American Notebooks provide us with two passages which should be cited in this connection. In the first instance Hawthorne is sketching a possible morality:

> A series of strange, mysterious, dreadful events to occur, wholly destructive of a person's happiness. He to impute them to various persons and causes, but ultimately finds that he is himself the sole agent. Moral, that our welfare depends upon ourselves.[19]

It is difficult to see how a believer in universal depravity could have written this analysis of conduct. It seems to negate the necessary evil of man's nature. Again:

> A person to look back on a long life, ill-spent, and then to picture forth a beautiful life which he would live, if he could be permitted to begin his life over again. Finally to discover that he had only been dreaming of old age—that he was really young, and could live such a life as he had pictured.[20]

The passage speaks for itself. Man's ability to choose the morally good would be the exact opposite of the idea of universal depravity. That man is necessarily evil is contradicted by the whole procession of his characters: Hilda, Phoebe, Hester Prynne, Kenyon, Donatello, and the numerous shadowy personages that move with such quiet grace through his many moralities.

If Hawthorne was terrified by the Calvinistic idea of universal depravity, he was disgusted with the Unitarian idea of human perfectibility. He was more often an optimist than a pessimist; but his optimism was always solidly based upon the mature analysis of man. More than most writers of his time, Hawthorne had a clear concept of the nature of sin. What he called a "moral war-fare" was constantly going on in man's soul. His "lament for life's wasted sunshine" was serious and infectious. One of the reasons that he sought with such might for the succor of a kind God was his view of the evil in man. This potentially destructive power amazed him. The perfectibility of man's nature was something reserved for eternity. What we might call a consciousness of original sin was strong in him. "What is there so ponderous in evil?" he asked in *The House of the Seven Gables*.

Though the design of God was always clear to him, man's parti-cipation in this pattern was highly irregular. Hawthorne saw vividly into all of the dark corners of life. He looked down quite as much as he looked up. Though his heart told him that looking up was the sole reality, he was not entirely satisfied. He had to know from whence sin came. He had to study its effect upon man, a study not since equaled in American Literature. But it is a study that can be fully understood only when we recognize that it was framed by his recognition of virtue. The free performance of evil certainly ruled out Calvinistic necessity on any score; but it did more than that, it made him look at man as he really is—a curious amalgam of good and evil. The power of his perception of evil depends upon his own sure knowledge of the good. His exploration of the depths of human nature went far beyond the boundaries established by Unitarian orthodoxy.

"Sin, alas! is careful of her bond-slaves," he wrote. This might serve as the epitaph of his analysis of the nature of evil. His chief interest was in exposing the nature of evil, rather than in dissecting the unhappiness which it caused. We need read only "The Haunted Mind" to see how powerful evil can be. His keen interest in the secret sin of men in high places and in men of spotless reputation shows an implied criticism of the so-called "guiltless" type. On more than one occasion, he warned the reader not to dissociate himself from men of any kind—good or evil—for we are all brothers through our common guilt. The real validity of such a character as Chillingworth depends upon his cogent analysis of evil as a part of man's trial. Even the incredible Westervelt gains purpose and stature because of Hawthorne's healthy respect for sin. The mysterious, dark stranger of Miriam's past reminds us also that he doubted the perfectibility of human nature. No one can forget the bigoted, wicked, and bloodthirsty Puritanic types in *The House of the Seven Gables*.

The perceptiveness that Hawthorne displayed in "Ethan Brand" has caused many critics to insist that producing this kind of sketch was his proper métier. Here the vast power of evil is given the immense scope of a human soul. Brand would find the unpardonable sin! The pursuit of evil raises him to a kind of worldly eminence. But he is rotten inside, corrupted in every particular. His face is frightening; his laugh that of a fiend. Suicide is his only recourse. The unpardonable sin was his cultivation of the intellect to the point of eliminating the universal and humane impulses of the heart, the source of man's virtue. His sin drove him apart from his brother-man and, like the Man of Adamant, he lost the key of holy sympathy to our common nature. Nowhere else has Hawthorne presented the face of evil with such a terrible aspect. I suppose that is why "Ethan Brand" has been used to demonstrate Hawthorne's belief in universal depravity. We sometimes forget what Brand says: "Freely, were it to do again, would I incur the guilt. Unshrinkingly I accept the retribution!"

On a social level, Hawthorne also rejected the doctrine of man's perfectibility short of eternity. This is the central problem of Hawthorne's only realistic romance, *The Blithedale Romance*. Hawthorne's nonfictional comments on reformers and reform movements were always caustic. This is not to say that he was not interested in reform. His objection was to the formalized treatment given man by the reformer. In two ways such movements offended his analysis of the nature of man. First, they minimized man's freedom of choice, and, second, they neglected to account for the existence of evil in this world. Coverdale, our spokesman in the novel, is immensely attracted to Hollingsworth, one of Hawthorne's most complex characters. But Hollingsworth would turn the experimental community into a philanthropic venture for the rehabilitation of criminals. Coverdale's natural critical sense rebels against this superficial analysis of the nature of man's sinfulness. Eventually, Hollingsworth drives everyone from him but the only person who can sustain him, Priscilla. He would drive men like oxen, Coverdale comments, into the performance of virtue. Life was just not that simple. In any event, the plan was too dangerous, for it obsessed the reformer until he denied man's freedom. "The spirit of benevolence" which motivates such a reformer is unrealistic in its dependence upon man's ultimate earthly perfectibility. Later, this same spirit transforms itself into a dangerous disregard for man's inherent right to reform himself. Hawthorne was contemptuous of all the reform movements of

his time because of his own wary respect for the power of evil.
His insistence on the cause and cure of sin in the individual heart
would seem to be the reason.

I am sure that Hawthorne's view of the nature of man was the
wisest analysis in fiction form in America in the nineteenth
century. Man's spiritual aspirations, which ultimately culminate
in eternity, are the most important results of his nature and the
truest record of his character. Rejecting both universal depravity
and human perfectibility, Hawthorne found his own *via media* in
his excellent balance of mind and heart. The various aspects of our
nature can be exercised for good when we have the right view of
our destiny or for evil if we seek it as our end. An author's estimate
of the nature of man must, in a large measure, depend upon his
estimate of God. Hawthorne's emphasis on eternity as the final
home of man, as the completion of the perfect round, tells us something of his conclusions about man. It seems to say that the quest
which begins in the human mind and heart with the dawn of
understanding and feeling is a pilgrimage that can end only in
eternity. The thirst for happiness which grows out of the properties of the soul can never be slaked by anything short of a goodness that is infinite. Human nature, as Hawthorne has described
it, enables man to accept or reject the accomplishment of infinite
achievement; but, he adds, to accept the infinite argues "a profounder wisdom" than to be limited by "the gross fatality of
earthly life."

Hawthorne's view of God and man is, of course, severely limited
by the personal origin of his concepts. At times in his analysis of
God he falls into the same kind of vague liberalism which he so
often deplored. His basic certitude was often disturbed by superficial events. Too often, he resolved his problems by dismissing
them. Thus, his faith lacked definition when he most needed it.
Temporal reasons circumscribed his capacity for hope. His beautiful power of love was too often tested by earthly circumstances.
Thus, his natural tendency to doubt became an agonizing torture
to his soul. That all of these things are true we know from the
many complex problems which bloom from his fertile imaginings.
These things do not surprise us. Our pleasurable amazement
comes from those conclusions he did reach. So often the parentless
child of his century went wandering over meaningless deserts. Or
else the orphan would retreat into an inadequately prefabricated
refuge. Hawthorne, too, had his deserts. It is to his credit that
he never accepted the mirage as the real thing. And if his wander-

ings were circular, they were at least guided by the stars. All that he had was the mirror of the universe; that he saw so much should embarrass those who have so much more. His secure place as one of the greatest writers in the nineteenth century rests as much upon the discoveries of his mind (this is rare!) as it does upon the manners of his artistry.

In one of his short stories, Hawthorne defines a bold and daring esthetic—the realization of artistic perfection. This is surely a parallel to his own analysis of man's relation to God. This is not the facile and easy idealism that would have broken under the strain of his tremendous artistic impulse. This is genuine idealism born from his belief in a right order of things. The essential truth about his nature, both as man and artist, is revealed in this illuminating letter to his wife: "I first look at matters in their darkest aspect, and having satisfied myself with that, I begin gradually to be consoled, to take into account the advantages of the case, and thus trudge on, with the light brightening around me."[21] This light was permanent and consistent, though shadows often obscured it. We need not apologize for his sadness, a sadness born of doubt. This was the world as he saw it, a strange mixture of good and evil. His honesty and his integrity demanded that he record it all in a matchless style that is more often poetry than prose.

To pay sufficient tribute to his honesty, we should, I suggest, remember the intense manner of his search for the true and the beautiful. "When the artist rose high enough to achieve the beautiful, the symbol by which he made it perceptible to mortal senses became of little value in his eyes while his spirit possessed itself in the enjoyment of the reality."[22] Precisely because of this, the symbol, the artistry, the tone, became more beautiful than any stylistic calculation could have made it. Part of the radiance of his view of God and man rubbed off on his work. It is only a matter of justice that we give him the title he carved for himself, truly "The Artist of the Beautiful."

HENRY WADSWORTH LONGFELLOW

1807-1882

Poet of the Feeling Heart

JOSEPH E. O'NEILL, S.J.

ONE spring morning over a century and a quarter ago, the packet ship *Cadmus* made its way out of New York harbor bound for France. Among the passengers was the recently appointed Professor of Modern Languages at Bowdoin College, Henry Wadsworth Longfellow. The professorship, however, was newly created, the college was small and unknown, and the nineteen-year-old professor was still callow and unlearned, although he did have some right to the title of poet. During his senior year at Bowdoin, nineteen poems had appeared in the *United States Literary Gazette* alone. Ten others had slipped easily into the pages of *The Portland Advertiser* and *The American Monthly Magazine*. One poem, a tribute to Shakespeare, while failing to win the contest in which it had been entered, had nevertheless been printed in a book, and in addition "a few poetical articles of a suitable character," requested by Carey and Lea for their gift-book annual, *The Atlantic Souvenir,* had been written and delivered, and would appear in the issue for 1827.[1] In spite of paternal and editorial warnings against too hasty publication, it must have seemed to the youthful poet that he could with some justification congratulate himself upon a modest but genuine *annus mirabilis*.

More properly, it had been an *annus juvenilis,* for the verse was entirely imitative, literary, and unreal, despite the pronouncement of William Cullen Bryant that "really beautiful poetry" was being written for the columns of the *United States Gazette* "by H. W. L., we know not who he is. . . ."[2] To Bryant and the public, and perhaps to the young poet himself, it may have seemed that a new poetic star had arisen in the not-too-brightly lighted American firmament. However, the radiance was to dim considerably, even in the poet's own estimation, for of all these boyhood poems Longfellow was to include only seven in his first published book of verse and, forty years later, even these seven were to be denied a place among the final *Voices of the Night.*

Of course, Longfellow's mature estimate is the correct one, as even a cursory glance at these smooth but empty lines will reveal. From the very patriotic but plagiaristic "The Battle of Lovell's Pond," to the soft and sentimental "Song of the Birds," the melancholy tones of the Graveyard School are clearly heard in the sighing and moaning of the winds. When it is not the winds, similar sound effects are produced by beauty, the spirit, evening, winter, and life. The eye is appealed to for the evocation of the mortuary mood, and well-worn stage properties like mouldering urns, broken lutes, and unstrung lyres are scattered about in convenient proximity to graves and sepulchres. We can admire the biblical terseness of these lines from "Youthful Years":

> Sorrow is for the sons of men
> And weeping for earth's daughters,[3]

but they are the only good thing in an otherwise feeble piece. The glow of admiration quickly fades before the plethora of grief with which these poems are afflicted. Of course the sorrow is only a literary one, for Longfellow was not unhappy at the time. Nor was he ill, as the nature of much of the imagery might lead one to suppose. For instance, the tubercular hero of "The Poor Student" lives in an unhealthy and depressing atmosphere of "decaying" hope, "faded" loves, and cares that have "blasted" and "wither'd" the zeal and beauty of his youth. Clearly, the spirit of "Thanatopsis" broods darkly over all. Little wonder, then, to find "nature soon decay" and to learn that his "worn and wasted spirit" has sought its "last cold couch" and "a dreamless sleep, that knows no waking."[4]

It is impossible to grieve over the fate of so literary and anemic a hero or to believe that his creator had uttered so much as a single genuine sigh over his untimely end. Without doubt, the young poet pacing the deck of the Europe-bound *Cadmus* had written too much, too quickly. A fatal facility and a too-easy acceptance by literary editors had resulted in juvenilia that would one day return to haunt him most embarrassingly.[5]

As if aware that her presence at this time were really harmful to the creation of genuine poetry, the Muse suddenly abandoned

Longfellow for a dozen years. With inspiration gone, facility vanished also and three years in Europe did nothing to recapture either gift. Apparently the poetic fires had been permanently extinguished. Longfellow, at least, thought so, for we find him writing to his sister from Göttingen in March of 1829: "My poetic career is finished—Since I left America, I have hardly put two lines together."[6] What happened, it would seem, was a kind of pilgrim's progress in reverse. The youthful descendant of Pilgrims had become a Pilgrim himself, looking reverently to the Old World as "a kind of Holy Land, lying afar off beyond the blue horizon of the ocean."[7] The lands of crusader, saint, and king had early cast a potent spell over this romantic young republican but, as ever, the reality was not all that he had dreamed it would be. Still, it was the real thing, and literature and life, with all their pleasant and unpleasant aspects, had driven all thought of poetry from his mind. Although, like the student in *The Tales of a Wayside Inn*

> He loved the twilight that surrounds
> The border-land of old romance,[8]

this was no dreamy innocent abroad, no naïve visionary, but a young man with a purpose. That purpose was to become famous in the literary world. "The fact is," he had written to his father while still at Bowdoin, "I most eagerly aspire after eminence in literature; my whole soul burns most ardently for it, and every earthly thought centers in it."[9]

This is the language of youthful enthusiasm but it was meant sincerely and deeply and, be it remarked, Longfellow accomplished what he set out to do in spite of savage criticism, illness, sorrow, and the busy life of a teacher. The record speaks for itself—professor, scholar, translator, prose writer, and, above all, world-famous poet at whose shrine an adoring public in America, England, Europe, and even the Orient, paid sincere and continuous homage for nearly a hundred years. No other American man of letters was so well known, none so widely read, and none so deeply loved, almost to the point of dulia, by the thousands of "the mighty average of humanity."[10] In a word, Longfellow's is one of the greatest American "success" stories ever written.

At the moment, however, it was not poetry that concerned him but the people and languages of France, Spain, and Italy. Despite a certain amount of provincial prejudice, Europe took him a fairly easy captive and he fell a willing victim to the charm of the French countryside and the wit of its people. Italy alternately fascinated and repelled him, as it did almost every American. But it was to Spain above all that his young heart went out; the memory of it stayed with him all his life. There were to be three more visits to Europe, but Longfellow never went back to Spain, preferring to leave unbroken the spell it had cast upon him. Years later he was to recall the memory of that youthful delight in the nostalgic lines of "Castles in Spain":

> White hamlets hidden in the fields of wheat,
> White cities slumbering by the sea,
> White sunshine flooding square and street,
> Dark mountain ranges, at whose feet,
> The river beds are dry with heat—
> All was a dream to me.

Nevertheless, the young man had not dreamed away his time. During his eight months in France and eight more in Spain, he proved himself no mere romantic tourist but a serious student, at least to the extent that he kept a diary in French and Spanish for nearly two weeks. Moreover, he was able to write his father: "With the French and Spanish languages, I am familiarly conversant, so as to speak them correctly, and write them with as much ease and fluency as I do the English."[11] A year in Italy added to his store of foreign languages and, it would seem, something of life as well, for he experienced physical illness and the pangs of love—but survived both.

Longfellow then went on to Vienna, Prague, and finally to Germany in the middle of January 1829. After a gay month of social activity in Dresden, partly owing to having brought with him letters of introduction from Washington Irving, whom he had met in Madrid, Longfellow joined his friend Edward Preble at Göttingen. Settling down at the university he studied diligently, mostly, it seems, in French, Spanish, and Italian literature. He came to know the professors and fell in love with the idea of a German university, which he hoped could be put into effect in Portland, his native town. The months passed pleasantly enough between study and a trip to London. Finally he left Göttingen in June, went on to Paris, and in July sailed from Liverpool for home with the satisfactory consciousness that he had a good knowledge of French, Spanish, and Italian and had made at least a beginning toward a mastery of German. His real love for that language and literature was to come later.

At Bowdoin he began his duties with enthusiasm, even though

he found he was to be librarian as well as Professor of Modern Languages. This was a field almost completely virgin in America and Longfellow soon discovered that it was necessary to edit much-needed textbooks in English, Spanish, and French. While teaching French, Spanish, Italian, and, in 1831, German also, he was busily translating the *Coplas* of Don Jorge Manrique, and contributing articles to the *North American Review* and the *New England Magazine*. The latter he revised and published in book form under the title of *Outre-Mer: A Pilgrimage Beyond the Sea* (1833-1834). Part autobiography, part fiction, the book is a series of Irvingesque sketches of the lands and people of his youthful travels, a slight but, on the whole, attractive and, at times, even charming hodgepodge. The first fruits of his European travels, they reveal an observant eye, a Protestant mind, and a smooth and graceful style.

With the publication of *Outre-Mer,* Longfellow evidently fancied himself destined to success in the field of prose. He had done little poetic work during the years at Bowdoin and had, in fact, become something of a scholar. He had become a husband, too, having married Mary Storer Potter of Portland in 1831. Meanwhile, he had begun looking around for another and better teaching job, contemplating the Round Hill School in Massachusetts, New York University, and even the distant University of Virginia. But a call came from close at hand. Charles Ticknor, the incumbent of the Smith Professorship of Modern Languages at Harvard College, was about to resign, and as he had recommended Longfellow as "an accomplished scholar particularly in modern literature,"[12] the authorities offered and the young professor quickly accepted the new and delightful post. There was even an understanding that he might go to Germany to perfect his knowledge of the language, which he was only too happy to do, despite the uneasiness and reluctance of his wife. April of 1835 found him once again sailing out of New York harbor, in the company of Mrs. Longfellow and two young ladies from Boston, Miss Goddard and Miss Crowninshield. He was still a young man but this time he was a better professor than poet, his new college was more famous than Bowdoin, and he himself was a scholar and author with something of a reputation abroad.

His aim now was a mastery of the Northern languages—Danish, Icelandic, Swedish, Finnish, and Dutch. Once again he accomplished what he set out to do, succeeding in acquiring a reading ability in these and in Portuguese and Provençal as well. In

Scandinavia he worked hard under difficulties, bought books with
enthusiasm for Harvard College library, and worried over his
wife's health. Meanwhile, the poetic fires began to glow again and
the feeling that he might yet write something lasting and memorable in the poetic way seems to have returned, for some months
later in Rotterdam he notes in his journal:

> Sat up late at night writing poetry—the first I have written
> for many a long, long day. Pleasant feelings of the olden time came
> over me; of those years when as yet a boy, I gave so many hours
> to rhymery! I wonder whether I am destined to write anything in
> verse, that will live?[13]

Actually, it was not "many a long, long day," since he had
written poetry only a few months earlier. Longfellow had apparently forgotten that while he was in Stockholm in June he had
transcribed in this same journal the following lines:

> Toll! toll! toll!
> One more immortal soul
>   Hath taken flight to-day
>   From its tenement of clay,
> And cometh not back again.
> When the blast of Autumn calleth
>   The leaf falleth,
>   The flower dyeth,
>   The bird flyeth,
> And this is like unto man's death.
> But in Spring, the gentle rain
>   Falleth not in vain,
> Nor the sunshine from the sky.
> For they give breath
>   To the flower that in Autumn dyeth;
>   And the bird that in Autumn flyeth
> In Spring cometh back again.
> Not so the immortal soul!
>   The pilgrim of Eternity,
>   He taketh his scallop-shell,
>   He taketh his sandal shoon,
>   And he goeth forth eftsoon,
>   And biddeth his friends farewell,
> And ever and anon the solemn bell
>   Tolleth his funeral knell;
> For he cometh not back again.
>
>   The body to the tomb,
>   The spirit to its doom!

> We spread the sable pall
> Sorrowing most of all,
> That we shall see his face no more.
> In Spring the gentle rain
> Falleth in vain
> And the sunshine from the sky.
> For they cannot restore
> The mortal forms that die.
> The pilgrim of Eternity
> Goeth forth—and cometh not back again,
> For evermore!

Andrew Hilen, to whom we are indebted for its publication, calls this a "morbid" and a "melancholy poem."[14] Though certainly melancholic, it is not unwholesome but normal and universal. The lightly musical rhythm and the familiar but perfectly appropriate diction and imagery make it a strangely effective little dirge for mortality. It is curious that Longfellow never bothered with it again. Simple, sincere, and without sentimentality, it is better than anything he had yet written and much that he would yet write.

In a sense, the lines were unhappily prophetic, for Longfellow, while in Rotterdam, had now to suffer his first great sorrow, the death of his young wife soon after childbirth, on November 29, 1835. The blow was a severe one and it took all his courage to meet it. Two months later he confesses to his father that "the sense of my bereavement is deep and unutterable."[15] Sorrow quickly followed sorrow, and at Heidelberg where he had gone to continue his study of German he learned of the death of his brother-in-law and friend, George Pierce. It was a winter of heartache and hard work; manfully he stuck to his task of mastering German and read hard and long—over sixty authors including Heine, Novalis, Hoffmann, Uhland, and especially Goethe and Jean Paul Richter.[16] Wearily he turned to travel in the spring and summer. At Thun in Switzerland he became acquainted with Nathan Appleton, a wealthy merchant of Boston, who was traveling with his young and beautiful daughters Mary and Frances Appleton. Their companionship, especially that of the seventeen-year-old, dark-eyed Frances, helped to lighten his burden, and when he left them to return to America there was a new brightness in his heart. Longfellow had fallen deeply and lastingly in love.

For the next six years the young professor boarded in lovely old

Craigie House—a place where Washington had not only slept but had had his headquarters—teaching modern languages and lecturing at Harvard, writing poetry and prose, persistently wooing the beautiful, intelligent but icy-hearted Frances Appleton. The struggle was long and hard, and Longfellow poured it all out in prose and poetry. The story of his German wanderings and readings, his unrequited love and consequent soul-sufferings burst upon Beacon Hill and a small section of the world in only the thinnest of disguises. "Mary Ashburton" and "Paul Flemming" were recognized only too well, and the romantic pages of *Hyperion* (1839), though they may have been, as Hatfield avows, "the most important single document having to do with his transmission of German culture to the English-speaking public,"[17] failed utterly to transmit his passion to her heart.

The story was hinted at also in verse, and his courageous efforts to overcome the inertia of a state of dreamy but emotionally real preoccupation with the dead in the manner of Novalis and Matthisson are recorded in those "psalms" of life and death[18] that were to attain such remarkable and lasting popularity. "A Psalm of Life" is the most famous of all, his most ringing call to action, a versified blending of the doctrine of action he had learned from Goethe and the spirit of an inscription which "Paul Flemming" had read upon the wall of a chapel in Germany and taken deeply to heart: "Look not mournfully into the Past. It comes not back again. Wisely improve the Present. It is thine. Go forth to meet the shadowy Future, without fear, and with a manly heart."[19] It is not a good poem but it is one of the sincerest poems ever written. Along with that other psalm, "Hymn to the Night," and its equally famous though somewhat less convincing cry for peace, the success of *Voices of the Night* (1839) was assured, and the nine hundred copies of the first edition were sold within a month. Definitely, a new poet had arisen.

Wisely Longfellow attempted to tap further the golden vein of popularity by turning away from the soulful sighings of German Romanticism and trying his hand at a more muscular type of verse, namely, ballads. Having successfully thrown off sadness and the dreamy voices of the night, he now achieved the spirited and vigorous lines of "The Wreck of the Hesperus" and "The Skeleton in Armor," the latter especially being a compact ballad of swift action, simple but effective characterization, and appropriate though literary imagery. One cannot say as much for the other pieces in *Ballads and Other Poems* (1841). "God's-Acre" has the strength of a homely image:

With thy rude ploughshare, Death, turn up the sod,
And spread the furrow for the seed we sow,

but the rest of the poem is mediocre. "Excelsior" is surely not
"silly symbolism"[20] but neither is it (as one Spanish critic called
it) "the *Sursum Corda* of the American muse,"[21] and although
"Maidenhood" just manages to restrain itself from spilling over
into cloying sentimentality, it is certain that "The Village Blacksmith" is a prime example of Longfellow's unhappy tendency to
offer emotional moralizing in the name of poetry and religion.

Meanwhile, Longfellow was working on a play, "The Spanish
Student," for which he held high hopes, literary and financial.
The original enthusiasm petered out, however, and it failed also
to kindle that of his friends Sumner, Ticknor, and Felton. Moreover, difficulties in finding a publisher arose, and the whole thing
becoming a wearisome burden, he left the manuscript with his
lawyers and sailed for Europe in the spring of 1842. The irritation
of irksome duties in Cambridge and the pangs of unrequited love
in Boston had forced the poet to request a six months' leave of
absence.

Once in Europe, Longfellow began to recover his health and
good spirits. For his lovesickness, however, there was only one
complete cure, and this was to be found in Boston, not at the
baths of Marienberg, near Boppard on the Rhine. At the moment,
he was beginning to come alive again. He made the acquaintance
of the poet Freiligrath, who became his friend and translator,
and under the spell of fabled Europe turned automatically to the
writing of poetry. "The Belfry of Bruges" is the poetic reward
for having climbed the famous tower just as dawn was breaking, in order to drink in the sights and sounds of the romantic
old city. Laudable as a tourist's capsule guide to the past, it is
not very praiseworthy as a poem. A few months later on the
Rhine he did much better with "Mezzo Cammin," a genuinely
poetic lament over the unfulfilled aspiration of his youth done
unconsciously in terms of the sights and sounds he had seen and
heard and the vision he had dreamed in the belfry of Bruges. It
is, moreover, a felicitous presage of the success he was to attain
in that difficult but artistically perfect form, the sonnet.

The sorrow and the care did not kill, however, and Longfellow
was soon able to convince himself of the need for an extension
of his leave of absence. President Quincy of Harvard was somewhat more resistant and, the extension being denied, Longfellow

went across to London, where he became the guest of Dickens. In October, he set sail for home and as he lay rocking in his berth, probably still somewhat under the emotional influence of Dickens' *American Notes,* he composed the disappointingly feeble pieces which found publication in December under the title *Poems on Slavery* (1842). It was early to take a stand on the question and Longfellow's friends were pleased and even astonished. Sentimental in tone, rhetorical in style, and melodramatic in content, they are little more than tracts in verse. Typical of the seven poems is "The Good Part," a distressing example of a poet imitating himself as he presents us with a female counterpart to the virtuous village blacksmith, a parallel extending even to the phrasing and the imagery. Easily the best is the short and eloquent poem "The Warning"—eighteen lines of verse written ten years before as part of a much larger work, the unpublished Phi Beta Kappa poem.

If the *Poems on Slavery* are too frail to bear the weight of some future "tower of song with lofty parapet," so, too, is the more ambitious effort, "The Spanish Student," which finally achieved publication in June of 1843. It is not a complete failure —it has Shakespearean overtones, it has humor, it has some eloquent lines, and it has the simple and beautiful lyric, "Serenade." The careful use of imagery drawn from religion accentuates the virtue of the heroine and is artistically correct, but that is all. The poet has tried too hard. The result is an artificial construct drawn up according to established specifications but it is not really alive.

Upon his return from Europe in December of 1842, Longfellow, rested and refreshed, took up his scholastic duties once again. He had not been completely cured but the moment was not far off and a new chapter in his life was ready to be written. His seven years of persistent courtship were about to come to a truly happy ending. The ice about the heart of the beautiful Frances Appleton melted and dissolved in a gush of tender sentiment, and "Mary Ashburton" and "Paul Flemming" were united in matrimony on July 13, 1843. It was a union that was to bring deep happiness to both until, eighteen years later, almost to the day, Mrs. Longfellow was to burn to death in an accident in their home, Craigie House. But the tragedy of that "martyrdom of fire"[22] was still mercifully hidden in the darkness of the future.

The years between were to be busy, peaceful, and eminently productive. In point of fact, they constitute Longfellow's highest point of literary achievement. His youth was over, he was married, he was a professor, a scholar, a translator, and a poet. On the morning of his fortieth birthday he wrote the sonorous ending to the first and greatest of his long poems of this distinctly American period. *Evangeline: A Tale of Acadie* (1847) was the result of two years of devoted labor on a subject that was perfectly fitted to his nature and his talents. It was moving, it was part fact and part fiction, it dealt with a beautiful and virtuous woman, and it had the pathos of a steadfast but unfulfilled love that roamed from region to region over this broad continent of ours. Although he did not visit any place connected with his story of the displaced Acadians, he did a good bit of research and seems to have drawn upon recollections of his European travels to depict the country of Acadia and the deeply fervent faith of its Catholic people.

It was not an easy thing to do, in spite of his affinity for the subject, for the heroine is a model of virtue, it is a tale that calls for a sympathetic insight into Catholicism, and the meter is the most difficult of all to handle in the English language. That the poem is a unique success cannot be denied. It has its moments of sentimentality and although it never descends to the "fatuous facility" for which Harriet Monroe condemned it,[23] neither does it quite rise to the eminence of Hawthorne's praise—that it has "the simplicity of high and exquisite art."[24] The truth seems to be that it is a remarkably sustained effort, a minor masterpiece of poetic art. There have been "over two hundred and seventy editions, one hundred and thirty translations," and "more than two hundred and fifty books and articles have appeared dealing with the subject."[25] This is not absolute proof of poetic excellence but it should render somewhat foolish all airy and cavalier treatment of this serene and beautiful poem.

Longfellow now turned to prose and began at once upon a novel. It was to be American in scene and character and over the next two years he worked at it slowly but lovingly, "con amore," as he said.[26] But love was not enough and *Kavanagh* (1849) is weak and ineffectual, very much in the manner of the dreamy and poetic Mr. Churchill whose literary ambitions never came to fulfillment. The plot is slender, the characterization conventional, and although there is occasional humor, the book is interesting only for its remarks upon the value of universality over nationality in American literature. Emerson wrote that it was "the best sketch we have seen in the direction of the American Novel"[27] and

Hawthorne called it "a true work of genius if ever there were one."[28] But these are clearly the voices of friendship. Longfellow's undoubted narrative ability lay in poetry, not in prose.

Longfellow's next effort was in verse but in a medium that was never to be entirely natural to him, the dramatic. *The Golden Legend* (1851) is his greatest effort at capturing the medieval past. Based upon Hartmann von der Aue's *Der Arme Heinrich* and strongly influenced by Goethe's *Faust*, it is a tale of life and death clothed in the imagery of light and darkness. The heroine is another Evangeline, beautiful, devout, faithful to God and to her Prince. Her willingness to go down into the darkness of death in place of her fearful lord is an act of supreme virtue which brings light to her selfish and deceived Prince, and the play ends in the triumph of innocent love over the triple darkness of sin, the devil, and death. To Longfellow it was a happy blending of the Romantic and the Christian and was therefore truly "golden."

This was not the opinion of the anonymous reviewer in *Blackwood's Edinburgh Magazine,* who found it "an ill-constructed drama, almost aimless in purpose, and without even an intelligible moral," although "there is nearly as much fine poetry in Mr. Longfellow's *Golden Legend* as in the celebrated drama of Goethe."[29] Other critics have spoken well of it, Ruskin and Saintsbury for instance, but their praise is for his concept of the medieval spirit.[30] Actually, Longfellow caught only the superficial aspects of medieval Catholicism—there is a sense of faith but no real awareness of the vital role of the Church in the lives of monks and lords and ladies. It is Catholic to a degree, it shows insight, piety, and some learning, it has some fine lines and an excellent imitation of a miracle play, but the evidence is inescapable that Longfellow's flair was not for the dramatic but for color, atmosphere, and story.

On April 20, 1854, Longfellow gave his last lecture at Harvard. For years he had coveted freedom from the academic routine. Now it was his and he began almost at once to win further fame as a poet. With daring, imagination, and an astonishing facility, Longfellow soon wove one of his happiest poems out of the rich fabric of Indian myth and legend. *The Song of Hiawatha* (1855) was never intended to be a sociological or naturalistic treatment of the American Indian, nor is there any good reason why it should have been. It is what it was meant to be—a charming tale of fantasy and remote historical fact. Hiawatha is unlike any Indian that ever lived because he is a demigod, a culture hero, and

Longfellow has surrounded him with a simplicity and a childlike quality of playful humor that has often been imitated and parodied but has never been equaled or surpassed. Bliss Carman said of the poem "it has an air of pristine innocence"[31] which indeed it has, but it is the innocence that comes not only from a healthy mind and heart but also from a sense of craftsmanship and the delicate, sure touch of the artist.

Very much the same traits are seen in the third of Longfellow's major productions that deal with an American theme, *The Courtship of Miles Standish* (1858). This finest of Puritan pastorals is done in somewhat plain and rugged hexameters, doubtless to suggest the simple and homely nature of his people and their lives. The whole thing is artfully conceived; for instance, the clever use of imagery drawn from the business of war amusingly underlines the characterization of the brave but somewhat pompous little hero of Plymouth Colony. It is impossible to deny that with the stories of Miles Standish, Hiawatha, and Evangeline, along with the eloquent and patriotic paean, "The Building of the Ship," Longfellow has made a lasting and valuable contribution to the treasury of American myth and legend. This did not go unnoticed by his contemporaries; it was Whitman who wrote: "I should have to think long if I were ask'd to name the man who has done more, and in more valuable directions, for America."[32]

There was always the double strain in Longfellow, interest in both native and foreign materials. After the tragic death of his wife in 1861, the poet turned, not to Germany and its mystic voices of the night as he had done a quarter of a century before, but to Italy and the great literary love of his life, "Christian Dante."[33] With the aid and advice of his friends he finished his translation of the *Divina Commedia,* and when it was published in 1865-1867 it had prefixed to it six of the finest sonnets he ever wrote. The flow of poetry, once begun, did not stop. Over the years he published *Tales of a Wayside Inn* (1863, 1872, 1873), an excellent collection of stories in his most accomplished manner. In theme and subject they represent his plunder of the literary world. The countries of Europe that he knew and loved, even the East as well, were called on to furnish his chosen guests in Sudbury Inn with their fascinating variety of stories. Longfellow is not Chaucer, but these tales in verse have some small measure of Chaucer's simplicity, wit, and fundamental soundness of heart and mind.

There was a final trip to Europe in 1868, almost a triumphal tour of England, France, and Italy, with honorary degrees from

Cambridge and Oxford, and a cordial and private reception by Queen Victoria. This did not mean an end to activity, however, for on his return the poet published what he fondly hoped would be the monumental and major work of his life: *Christus: A Mystery* (1872). It is a trilogy of plays in verse: *The Divine Tragedy, The Golden Legend,* and *The New England Tragedies.* Regretfully, one must use the word "failure." It is not only the fact that no one can improve on the New Testament—*The Divine Tragedy* is hardly more than a colorless paraphrase—nor that his generally sound artistic sense failed him in allowing him to follow a descending scale that starts with divine love, continues with human love, and ends in a bathos of hate and religious persecution. The fundamental reason for the failure is the fact that Christ is not the center of the trilogy. *Christus* was intended to depict the triumph of universal love, but the God who died for love of man is only a pale figure in *The Divine Tragedy,* is present only by implication in *The Golden Legend,* and is not even symbolically a part of *The New England Tragedies.* Yet this is not to say that these last twenty years of Longfellow's life are a period of failing powers. Some of his finest work in the short forms of poetry was still to be done. It was not yet night nor had he yet reached *Ultima Thule.*

Longfellow died on March 24, 1882, but that was not really the end of the story. He lives on in his work, a form of immortality that has not always been discussed with impartiality and common sense. One of the reasons for the confusion as to the nature of the real values of his poetry is that in Longfellow the man and the artist are one. His lines have always flowed so easily and naturally from his character and his life that friends and enemies alike were apt to be deceived into judging the value of the poetry by the worth of the man and mistaking personal virtue for impersonal art. There is many a gap between inspiration and achievement, and in Longfellow the fertile seed of moral idealism did not always blossom into the fine flower of poetic success. It frequently failed to do so because of the nature of his own character and psychological makeup.

No great poet has ever refused to listen to the voice of reality and to look it in the face for as long and as steadily as possible. But Longfellow's vision was by nature blurred, he neither would nor could look at reality except through a luminous, golden mist of emotion. Not only did emotion affect the cast of his mind, but it was, in a way, the very source and origin of his ideas on philosophy, art, love, and religion. With him it was a case of the deep well of feeling from whose depths ideas floated up into consciousness. It is significant that the feelings, the emotions, the passions,—all the movements of the heart and of the soul—are continually visualized in his poetry as water, flowing or still. The presence of the same image also reveals the intimate association in Long-fellow's mind between thought, feeling, and poetry, a doctrine clearly expressed in poems like "Seaweed," "The Tides," "The Poet and His Songs."

In the great battle between the head and the heart, Longfellow was clearly on the side of the heart. That this was to lead to a fatal weakening of poetry was not, of course, apparent to Long-fellow himself, and as a matter of fact he felt at times that he was writing about thoughts rather than about emotions. At least once he states that "poetry is the flower and perfume of thought."[34] Yet his undeviating position was always to the effect that thought should not impinge upon the affections nor interfere with them in any way, either in life or in literature. In his journal for June 17, 1848, he wrote: "A hot day, and a hair-splitting sermon from Dr. W. He ought to have lived in the days of Thomas Aquinas. To me, a sermon is no sermon in which I cannot hear the heart beat."[35] Longfellow did not stop to reflect that Thomas Aquinas was not writing sermons but philosophy. Evidently Dr. W. improved, for later in the same month Longfellow notes: "Dr. Walker preached a good sermon, in which he said it was useless to apply the reasoning faculties to things beyond their jurisdiction and in the realm of the affections. Bravo, for a philosopher!"[36]

This is the great Romantic doctrine of the importance of the heart in the life of man. That it was dear to Longfellow is confirmed by his use of the symbol of the heart which, for him, even more than the soul and the intellect, is the image of man in epitome, at his best and at his worst. In Longfellow's poetry the heart stands for each of man's faculties as well as for his body and his soul; in a word, the heart is the symbol of the whole man.

A most important corollary of the doctrine of the primacy of the heart is the theory of the value of the heart as a guide to truth and as a standard of moral measurement. This, of course, is a reaction against the Calvinistic view of the heart as totally corrupt. Father Isaac Hecker put this as clearly as possible in an article written in 1887:

> Against Calvinism we had a particular grudge. Among the truths I had gained in company with Brownson was that the affections of the heart are guides to truth as certain as the logic of the understanding—that is, when the heart is pure. But ac-

cording to Calvinism the human heart is never pure, and, with all its affections, is totally depraved.[37]

With Father Hecker Longfellow would surely have agreed— witness his insistence upon the holiness of the affections, by which he meant love in all its natural forms, domestic, social, universal, love of man and love of God. This doctrine of the heart as virtue is the core of Longfellow's religion and the source of the strength and weakness alike of his life and poetry. The difficulty is that he failed to make a clear distinction, and sometimes made none at all, between the devout affections as emotion and the devout affections as acts of the will. Whether he realized it or not, in thus putting the stress upon love as emotion rather than upon love as will, virtue was elbowed out of its proper province, a move disastrous both to religion and to poetry.

For when this is done, the poet becomes a creature of feeling, passionately beating his wings in a spiritual vacuum or simply grinding out pietistic preachings in verse. Having rejected completely his forefathers' diet of strong Calvinistic meat and drink, Longfellow is sometimes to be found dining on little pink cakes and the very weakest of tea. The sentimental puerilities of the following lines from "Prelude," with their picture-postcard clouds and angels, reduce theology to the level of shoddy, commercial "art."

> The Land of Song within thee lies,
>   Watered by living springs;
> The lids of Fancy's sleepless eyes
> Are gates unto that Paradise;
> Holy thoughts like stars, arise;
>   Its clouds are angels' wings.

This unfortunate juggling of the emotions so that they come to be equated with the will began early in Longfellow's life. In a letter to George W. Wells of December 18, 1824, he had written: "I conceive that if religion is ever to benefit us, it must be incorporated with our feelings, and become in every degree identified with our happiness."[38] But this is surely to reduce religion to the plane of physical therapy in which its function becomes nothing more than an anodyne. Longfellow, however, did not always make this confusion. He is particularly clear and distinct in "The Pilgrim's Breviary" from *Outre-Mer* when speaking of the Spanish Catholic "peculiarly beautiful and impressive" practice of the Ave Maria at twilight:

There is something beautiful in thus measuring the march of

time. The hour, too, naturally brings the heart into unison with the feelings and sentiments of devotion. The close of the day, the shadows of evening, the calm of twilight, inspire a feeling of tranquility; and though I may differ from the Catholic in regard to the object of his supplication, yet it seems to me a beautiful and appropriate solemnity, that, at the close of each daily epoch of life—which, if it have not been fruitful in incidents to ourselves, has, nevertheless, been so to many of the great human family—the voice of a whole people, and of the whole world, should go up to heaven in praise, and supplication, and thankfulness.[39]

One notes the distinction between the heart and the feelings, the implication of the heart as will, the nature of religion as an act of praise, supplication, and gratitude to God—in a word, the worship of God. This is, of course, the Catholic viewpoint which Longfellow has caught here, but it cannot be said that he is always so perceptive in his comments upon Catholicism.

One might with justice describe Longfellow's attitude towards the Catholic Church as precisely the same as Hawthorne's toward England, "Our Old Home," with exactly the same psychological reaction, the disturbing one of being simultaneously attracted and repelled. The result is that at times we can expect generous tributes and at times unkind and prejudiced remarks. Along with the sympathetic portrait of monasticism in "The Legend Beautiful," there is the fabliau-type tale in "The Monk of Casal-Maggiore." The poet of *Evangeline* and "The Saga of King Olaf" is also the author of "Torquemada," "The Cobbler of Hagenau," and "The Bells of San Blas." If to Longfellow Catholicism was not quite the Scarlet Woman who so troubled his Puritan forbears, neither was she the proper spouse for a Protestant and a Republican. One of the few ungracious acts of his life was to refuse a medal offered him by the King of Italy on the ground that the King was a Catholic potentate. Nevertheless, Longfellow was genuinely attracted by all that was beautiful and good in the vast storehouse of Catholic culture and creed, and many of his poems are enriched by his borrowings. But he was not drawn to the truth of Catholicism. This was owing to his Unitarian indifference to dogma and to the character of his intellectual and emotional capacities. I do not mean to imply that he was without intellectual conviction and deliberate assent of the will in the matter of belief. That there is a God, that He is our heavenly Father, that there is a divine providence, that there is a personal immortality, are doctrines clearly revealed in his poetry and as strongly held in his life. There is occasional reference to the Holy Ghost, but it does not seem probable that he believed in the divinity of Christ. His fondest hope was for a universal church where all men would unite in love and worship, and this is the doctrine that he preaches in *Hyperion,* in *Kavanagh,* and through the mouth of the Theologian in *The Tales of a Wayside Inn.*

On the negative side it seems certain that he had no real sense of sin. He was not, of course, completely blind to the existence of moral evil in the world and his vision of life was strong enough for him to see that "beneath the sparkling surface there is ever a muddy undertow, which works up from the bottom and seams the purer waters with its darker hue."[40] This was a reflection induced by the sight of the crowds thronging the boulevards of Paris, and noted in his journal for September 11, 1836. But the very next entry, six days later, has this revealing observation apropos an acquaintance who called soon after breakfast: "We walked together on the Boulevards this morning; but I am sure he saw nothing, for he was deep in an argument on predestination and the depravity of human nature—points of doctrine to which he clings with great pertinacity. 'Death and the judgment to come' make this Felix to tremble. I told him that in general I was pretty quiet and calm in regard to these matters, and troubled only when at times a horrible doubt cut into the cool, still surface of my soul, as the heel of a skate cuts into smooth ice."[41] In spite of such occasional doubts, Longfellow completely rejected the Calvinistic doctrine of original sin as an outmoded aberration of the human mind. "Drove to town to a christening," he wrote in his journal for November 13, 1852. "The little baby, the clergyman informed us, had been 'conceived in sin,' and he proceeded to cast out of him the 'old Adam.' How strange all this sounded!— in Boston, in the middle of the nineteenth century!"[42] And again on July 23, 1848, he had observed: "Went to church. The services began with the chanting of the Beatitudes, which was touching. The sermon was by a young man going to China as a missionary, who evidently thinks Calvin superior to Confucius."[43]

But Longfellow evidently did not think Calvin superior to Confucius and that is why it is difficult to accept as a real awareness of the nature of moral evil his many references to sin as well as all those poems in which sin plays a major role. "The Sifting of Peter," for instance, is a poem which seems most clear and unequivocal in the matter of sin, the danger of temptation, and the need for penance. The last two stanzas are as follows:

Wounds of the soul, though healed, will ache;
The reddening scars remain, and make
    Confession;
Lost innocence returns no more;
We are not what we were before
    Transgression.

But noble souls, through dust and heat,
Rise from disaster and defeat
    The stronger;
And conscious still of the divine
Within them, lie supine
    No longer.

There is no doubt that Longfellow was deeply sincere in writing such lines, but does he realize what he is saying? Is it not, after all, a rather literary "Confession" and an equally literary "Transgression"? It is hard to believe that Longfellow was intensely aware of the corruption of sin and the deadly effect upon the individual, as, for instance, Hawthorne and Melville were aware.

One should not, of course, expect the impossible, and Longfellow, by nature and temperament, was incapable of theological or philosophical speculation. Quite frankly he noted his bewilderment in the matter, on July 9, 1848: "In the evening, went to hear Dr. Bushnell, of Hartford, preach before the graduating Theological class. A long discourse on Atonement. Before five minutes, I was quite bewildered. Two hours it lasted, and we came out in a drenching rain."[44] That there was a simple lack of intellectual vitality in Longfellow is inescapable. Unlike Melville, he was not by nature "a pondering man"[45] and the complexities and profundities of the great religious and philosophical questions that tease the mind for solution were outside the range of his interests and capacities.

Instead, he had the kind of mind that preferred to ignore the existence of "the old, dull pain" that so troubled him in Hawthorne's writings.[46] As a result, he was only too glad to reject the dogma of fallen man and original sin. His inclination was always to believe in the purity of the heart and the ultimate triumph of good. Insisting upon the holiness of the affections, he never seemed to realize the danger of self-deception and error. Of course the affections are "holy" if the heart is "pure." The difficulty is in practice—when is the heart pure and how can one be certain? These have always been questions entailing much self-scrutiny, fasting, and prayer, a fact well attested to by his

Puritan ancestors who strove mightily to arrive at a reasonable
and reassuring degree of moral certainty in the matter.

But all this does not seem to have agitated Longfellow. His
letters and his journals give no indication of any serious or pro-
longed examination of the state of his own soul. Here are his
reflections on the last day of the year 1845: "So closes the year
1845. Peace to his ashes! Peace to the embers of burnt-out
things; fears, anxieties, doubts, all gone! I see them now as a
thin blue smoke, hanging in the bright heaven of the past year,
vanishing away into utter nothingness. Not many hopes deceived,
not many illusions scattered, not many anticipations disappointed;
but love fulfilled, the heart comforted, the soul enriched with
affection!"[47] These are the words of a man who is content and
at peace. They are not the words of a man intensely concerned
about his own spiritual life. There is only an occasional reference
to conscience—four of them, to be exact. Once he observes that
his unanswered letters hang upon him "like an evil conscience,"[48]
twice he notes with dismay his own idleness in the matter of
artistic creation,[49] and he has one flat statement to the effect that
in the matter of conscience "there is no middle course."[50]

Hardly more convincing are the only two poems that refer to
personal guilt of any kind. In "Weariness" he contrasts the "pure
and white" souls of his little children with his own "lurid" past:

> How red my setting sun appears,
> How lurid looks this soul of mine!

This is the only serious charge he ever directed against himself
with the exception of that of idleness in the matter of poetic
creation, as in the other poem of direct accusation, "Loss and
Gain":

> I am aware
> How many days have been idly spent;
> How like an arrow the good intent
> Has fallen short or been turned aside.

There are, of course, numerous references to sin, wrong, passion,
lust, greed, and, above all, hate. For hate was the one great sin to
Longfellow as love was the one great virtue, and in this he was
undoubtedly correct. But that he ever had a deep realization of
the evil effects of sin upon the individual and upon society is
difficult to believe since it has not flowered forth in any moving
poetry. His hatred of hate is evident but it is somewhat weakly

expressed in those poems that condemn the particular forms of hatred that disturbed him—slavery, war, and the persecuting spirit. Thus, *Poems on Slavery* are poetically feeble, the anti-war poems such as "The Occultation of Orion," "Christmas Bells," "The Arsenal at Springfield," are more eloquent than poetical, and the persecuting spirit of Puritan prejudice which he attempted to capture in *The New England Tragedies* never becomes a vivid reality in a dramatic way. Although he could see the fundamental truth behind the symbol of Medusa—"What a fable lies hid in that classic tale. Beauty, sin, despair!"[51]—he was never able to present it with a truly imaginative re-creation of the power and effects of moral evil. There are poems which attempt it, but they are not successful. "The Masque of Pandora" is really a poetic fable of the story of original sin, but although Longfellow has caught the idea that punishment and suffering are needed for pardon, it is clear that the evils let loose upon the world by the curious and foolish Pandora are more physical than moral in their effects:

> Fever of the heart and brain,
> Sorrow, pestilence, and pain,
> Moans of anguish, maniac laughter,
> All the evils that hereafter
> Shall afflict and vex mankind.

All this is true of the earlier poems as well. In "The Goblet of Life," "The Bridge," "Hymn for My Brother's Ordination," "Sandalphon," and others there is much more awareness of pain, care, and sorrow than there is of sin and guilt. Longfellow's severest critics here have been the Calvinistic ones. The Rev. Augustus Hopkins Strong stated the case exactly when he wrote of Longfellow: "Sin to him is a misfortune and a disease, but never guilt and ruin."[52] And again, in the same excellent essay: "Longfellow was by nature and by education a Pelagian. The problem of moral evil never seriously vexed him. Born and nurtured amid peaceful and moral surroundings, with a quiet and studious disposition, gentle and social in his ways, he never knew any deep conviction of sin, never felt the need of an atoning Saviour, never shrank from the holiness of God."[53]

In thus abandoning his Puritan heritage and closing his eyes resolutely to the presence of moral evil in the world, or at least to the explanation of it in Calvinistic theology, it would seem that Longfellow allowed himself to slip past the point of no return, the moral point of intellectual conviction that separates a real awareness of sin from a merely emotional acknowledgment of it. No great poet has ever done this—neither the author of Job, nor Aeschylus, nor Dante, nor Milton, nor Shakespeare. In Longfellow's case the effect was to render a large portion of his poetry distressingly pale and anemic. What he needed was a coagulating substance, a heavy dose of the kind of intellectual fibrinogen that ran in the bloodstream of his Puritan ancestors. This is why the great work of his life, the one poetic effort which, had it been successful, would have established him forever as a religious poet, is so signal a failure. In spite of thought, devotion, and perseverance, *Christus* is a weak and disappointing trilogy. The figure of Christ is reverently handled but the terrible force of His great enemy is never made real and vivid. It is pain that is stressed, rather than the fearful cause of the pain—the sins of mankind:

> Golgotha! Golgotha! Oh the pain and darkness!
> Oh the uplifted cross, that shall forever
> Shine through the darkness, and shall conquer pain
> By the triumphant memory of this hour![54]

But Christ, the Redeemer, came to triumph over sin and to open the gates of heaven to fallen man. And as the figure of Christ is palely done, so too is that of Lucifer, His great enemy. He is the one character in *The Golden Legend* that could have put bone and muscle into the somewhat unbelievable story. Instead he is represented, not as the epitome of evil, but as a mild, clever, almost sentimental and sympathetic figure, as when, for instance, he soliloquizes on the confessional:

> Here sits the priest; and faint and low
> Like the sighing of an evening breeze,
> Comes through these painted lattices
> The ceaseless sound of human woe.

Remarkably tame lines, surely, for the Prince of Darkness and the enemy of Christ and mankind! There are other scenes in which Lucifer plays a mischievous and even wicked part but none in which a significant awareness of evil is really manifest. His ultimate defeat is certain, abrupt—and Romantic. Only once, and that in the Epilogue, does he really suggest the darkness of evil:

> Lo! over the mountain steeps
> A dark, gigantic shadow sweeps

> Beneath my feet;
> A blackness inwardly brightening
> With sullen heat,
> As a storm-cloud lurid with lightning.

But the final effective impression is weakened by the author's comment on Lucifer:

> He, too, is God's minister,
> And labors for some good
> By us not understood!

So Longfellow lost his chance to create something permanently effective through the handling of a religious theme. Instead of the play of light and dark as an imaginative symbol of physical life and death, he could have made a more significant use of this particular form of imagery by having it stand for grace and sin, the life and death of the soul. But he failed to see the richness inherent in his own imagery and his vision never went much beyond the externals of his story. Thus he noted in his journal for November 3, 1851: "I have added a new scene to The Golden Legend—the Prince and Elsie at the Castle. Not long; just a little point of light after so much gloom and shadow of death."[55] There is no question but that Longfellow had the symbolic imagination to a certain degree. He was always able to see the spiritual reality behind the physical fact, and this appears again and again in his poetry, as for instance, in these lines from "Haunted Houses":

> The spirit-world around this world of sense
>   Floats like an atmosphere, and everywhere
> Wafts through these earthly mists and vapors dense
>   A vital breath of more ethereal air.

But the symbolic imagination failed him in the long run because he could not fuse the spiritual fact and the physical object in a permanently vivid and intense moment of artistic creation. It failed him, also, because it did not have enough vitality upon which it could draw—for instance, an awareness of the supernatural, of grace, and of the love of God.

But it failed him most of all because he possessed only a superficial sense of the Christian past and because his religious center was moral rather than doctrinal. At times, it is true, he alighted upon the center of religious fact as when he spoke well of immortality, of submission to the Will of God, of Trust in Providence, of universal love, but all too frequently he merely hovered about the outskirts of the great truths of religion, dissipating his poetic strength in moralistic injunctions of a platitudinous nature. But morality has never lent itself to the richness of symbolic and imaginative thought, its tendency being always towards a legal clarity and precision. This is why his use of religion does not square with his undoubtedly real poetic talent. When he does use religion well it is generally for background, to underline a character, or to suggest a fitting atmosphere, as in *Evangeline, The Courtship of Miles Standish*, "The Saga of King Olaf." But these are artistic purposes and these poems are successful, therefore, for other than religious reasons. In a few poems he has even succeeded in the matter of didacticism joining hands with religion. "The Legend Beautiful" has absorbed the didactic element in the story itself because the story is the lesson and because it springs squarely out of the great truth that love of man is love of God. "King Robert of Sicily" is another instance in which the moral is not tacked on at the end but grows out of a great religious truth: *Deposuit potentes de sede, et exaltavit humiles.* And the charming tale of Christ and the Sultan's daughter, which Elsie narrates to the Prince in *The Golden Legend*, is not merely a pretty little legend but a poetic phrasing of the great dogma that Christ died for man out of the depths of His love.

But these are exceptions and they succeed also for the technical reason that Longfellow managed to overcome the didacticism through the strength of his undoubted narrative ability. Unfortunately, his reputation as a religious poet has been based upon his sermons in verse, his sincere but obviously didactic lyrics, and although they are the source of his immense popularity in the nineteenth century they are also the nadir of his poetic weakness. Howells was wrong, then, in saying that "his art was essentially a religious art, as religious as Dante's, as Milton's, as Wordsworth's."[56] His art was essentially moral and ethical, and, in fact, it was precisely because of this that the poet who comforted and strengthened so many thousands for so many years and who so truly practiced what he preached that the sweet breath of his life reaches us strong and fair today cannot be called a religious poet at all. The truth is that his finest poems are not his most Christian ones; they neither teach nor preach but evoke a mood, create an atmosphere, tell a story. "My Lost Youth," "A Dutch Picture," "The Tide Rises, the Tide Falls," are immeasurably superior to all those sermons in verse which, at their worst, earned him the dubious distinction of being called "a sort of male Mrs. Hemans"[57] and, at their best, chose to honor God through the poetically feeble way of didacticism.

It is difficult to read poems like "The Broken Oar," "Snow-Flakes," "Nature," "The Sound of the Sea," "The Jewish Cemetery at Newport," without being aware of the presence of conscious artistry. Even those that seem at first sight to be completely literary in origin, poems like "Chaucer," "Milton," and "Shake-speare," on further study reveal themselves to be blessed with the solid artistic virtue of a happy correspondence between the word and the thought, the image and the meaning. The early morning freshness of Chaucer, the surge and sweep of the Miltonic line, and the roar of daily life in Shakespeare are all suggested with a deceptive simplicity and ease. What Longfellow is doing, of course, is making vivid use of the sensuous in poetry, an accomplishment for which he is generally not given credit.

Longfellow's visual perception was not notable for its sharpness and precision. The nature of his camera eye was for the panoramic effect, the broad sweep of space and sky, and he was especially happy when his vantage point was some high place from which he could look down, whether it was the great tower of Bruges or simply the lofty turrets of the moral imagination

> . . . where the eye
> Sees the world as one vast plain,
> And one boundless reach of sky.[58]

Despite an undoubted fondness for the blurred and the indistinct, the luminous haze in which so much of his poetry seems to be written, there is in Longfellow a genuine love of vivid color and bright light.

In his early poetry there was a tendency to overload his palette and to spread his pigments with too lavish a hand, as in the excessively rich and lush lines of "Autumn" and "The Spirit of Poetry." Although he learned to be more sparing with his brush as time went on, he never lost his Romantic fondness for warm red, bright gold, and the striking contrasts of black and white. It is the painter's eye responding to the glow of fruit and flower that notes the "fiery blossoms of the peach,"[59] the apples that "burned among the withering leaves,"[60] and the "fields with poppies all on fire."[61] He watches the "hot and burning stars"[62] blazing in beauty or in malignancy but most of all he loves the sight of

> . . . autumnal foliage and the glow
> Of sunsets burning low.[63]

Over and over the setting sun paints "the dusky windows red,"[64] flamboyantly incarnadines the "oriel of the West,"[65] makes the world stand out in sharp and clear-cut splendor:

> Leafless are the trees; their purple branches
> Spread themselves abroad like reefs of coral,
>   Rising silent
> In the Red Sea of the winter sunset.[66]

To Longfellow there was a potent association between the golden hours of poetic activity and the golden season of the year. October was his favorite month and autumn the season he always welcomed with eager hopes of creative fulfillment. It is not surprising to find many an effort to catch the "mellow richness"[67] of this "imperial Charlemagne"[68] of seasons and

> The wonder of the falling tongues of flame,
> The illumined pages of his Doom's-Day book.[69]

This is true of the long poems as well. *Evangeline* is flooded with brilliant light and color in lines like:

> Bright with the sheen of the dew, each glittering tree of the
>   forest
> Flashed like the plane-tree the Persian adorned with mantles
>   and jewels.

Although color is deliberately subdued in *The Courtship of Miles Standish,* there is a flash of brightness illuminating the bridal procession:

> Down through the golden leaves the sun was pouring his
>   splendors,
> Gleaming on purple grapes, that from branches above them
>   suspended,
> Mingled their odorous breath with the balm of the pine
>   and the fir-tree,
> Wild and sweet as the clusters that grow in the valley of
>   Eschol.

The restrained sensuousness of the image, with its delicate blend of the Bacchic and the Scriptural, perfectly suggests the modest joy of this sober though gracious "Puritan pastoral."[70] But it is *The Song of Hiawatha* which is the poem of color, par excellence. There is shining and gleaming everywhere and the whole is brilliant with color, gaily and lavishly applied. Animistic nature is seen with a child's exuberant delight in the primary hues,

warm reds and yellows, bright blues and greens. There is hardly
a page without its liberal splashing of color which, like the poem
itself, is innocent of subtlety and depth but is truly fresh, shining,
and happy. Moreover, it is a poem of sound effects as well, filled
with the interesting noises of the forest and of human life. There
is screaming, coughing, hissing, panting, humming, chirping,
flapping, and rattling. Above all, there is singing, of pine trees, of
birds and bees and mosquitoes, and of arrows flying through the
air. Because it is a poem of the long ago and the far away it is
full of "far-off murmurs, dreamy whispers," the plashing of
"dreamy waters," the buzzing of insects in "the drowsy air," and
all the sounds of sleep

> As of waves upon a seashore,
> As of far-off tumbling waters,
> As of winds among the pine-trees.

The note of distant, sleepy sound is the harmonious and functional
complement of the shadowy and dreamy visions with which the
poem abounds.

Whoever is willing to look for it will always find progress and
development in Longfellow. For instance, there is a continuous
sound of music in his lines from the early devotional type of
poem like "Thanksgiving," in which the strains are too familiar and
literary to be heard at all, through the studied sound effects of
"Midnight Mass for the Dying Year" and the somewhat mechanical use of onomatopoeia in "The Arsenal at Springfield." In the
last-named poem, although the image of an organ is carried out
for twelve stanzas, the sounds are never integrated; they are
merely *there*. A decade later in "My Lost Youth," Longfellow
wrote one of his finest poems, a skillful weaving together of sight
and sound. The thundering of "the sea-fight far away" makes an
effective and unobtrusive contrast with "the friendships old and
the early loves" that

> Come back with a Sabbath sound, as of doves
> In quiet neighborhoods.

The passage from sight to sound through the entire poem is so
smooth and easy that the whole is a little masterpiece of the
remembrance of things past. Part of the charm is undoubtedly
owing to the delicate rhythm and to the poetic suggestiveness of
the refrain:

> A boy's will is the wind's will,
> And the thoughts of youth are long, long thoughts.

This is a long way and a far cry, indeed, from the tinkling and obvious rhythms of his more famous didactic pieces. Moreover, it marks the progress from the artificial and affected to the organic and the functional, since what counts ultimately for poetic success is not so much the presence of the sensuous as the way in which it has been wedded to the emotion and the idea. With Longfellow this harmonious unity was achieved whenever he touched upon certain favorite themes, moods, and emotions—patriotism, the sea, artistic inspiration, above all, the thought of the past with its remembrance of lost youth, vanished days, and departed friends.

For there is a note of sadness running through his poetry that is more than German *Weltschmerz,* more than Romantic melancholy. It was part of Longfellow's nature to think of the past with nostalgia for the joy he had known and it was his good fortune to capture easily, movingly, with a silvery grace of utterance, the mood of regret for days that are no more. From 1840 to 1880, almost the whole of the poet's creative life, one hears repeated the same low chords, an echo, doubtless, of other poets sighing in the same way, yet sincere, universal, the authentic tone of humanity. There are many examples. In "The Fire of Drift-Wood" the pain of the remembrance of other days is heard in a sound familiar to all who have left youth and friends behind:

> The leaves of memory seemed to make
> A mournful rustling in the dark.

The silence and sterility of old age is pathetically present in "Autumn Within":

> There is silence: the dead leaves
> Fall and rustle and are still;
> Beats no flail upon the sheaves,
> Comes no tumult from the mill.

"Curfew" is a tone-picture of simple but haunting symbolism in which the light and sound of life fade silently into night:

> Darker and darker
> The black shadows fall;
> Sleep and oblivion
> Reign over all.

These are more than the lament of an individual, these are the plaints of mortality perfectly caught. Nowhere are they heard more truly than in the memorable lines of "The Tide Rises, the Tide Falls." The poem is a little parable of life, a short history of man and his works in the face of implacable nature—the lonely traveler in the deepening twilight is the "pilgrim of Eternity" on the shores of time. All through the night the sea has done its obliterating work and in the morning the traces of man are gone. Gone, too, is the traveler, nevermore to return—

> And the tide rises, the tide falls.

We are the traveler but the magic is Longfellow's, and the sound of the chord he has touched is deep, universal, and true.

The charges against Longfellow have long been known: he was academic, he was didactic, he was superficial, he was sentimental. They are all true, but only to a degree and they are not true all the time. When they are present it will generally be found that they are present together, for they are all related, one with the other and, like his poetic virtues, they are the inevitable result of his own nature as a man and his own principles as an artist. Ultimately, no man's wisdom is all his own and all men are academic who depend on what has been written before them.

In Longfellow's case literature was of supreme importance because it was a precious record of the noblest ideas and ideals of the noblest men and women. As such it could be interpreted, transmuted, and handed on to the thousands of people who would benefit by its moving vision of the good and the beautiful. This was the only reality, or at least the main reality, that interested Longfellow, and it is only to this extent that he yielded to the Romantic idea of literature as an escape from the shocks and buffetings of life, a secure and delightful nook for delicate feelings too easily bruised by the rough impact of the world and for ears too easily jarred by the tumult of the times. For a while it seemed as if he would succumb completely to the lure of such a dream world but we know that he resisted courageously and successfully.

On the evidence of his life and work Longfellow was a man of action in the true sense of moral and creative activity. Although there was always with him an intense yearning for rest, there was always, even to his old age, the ambitious desire to be active, to be alive, and to create. That it is never too late is the spirit and moral of "Morituri Salutamus":

> For age is opportunity no less
> Than youth itself, though in another dress,

And as the evening twilight fades away
The sky is filled with stars, invisible by day.

Since literature was an expression of the ideal and so an invaluable aid in teaching us how to live, the function of the poet inevitably became a moralistic and didactic one, as he put it plainly enough in "The Singers." But the good teacher does his best to be simple and clear, and of course these are the qualities above all others that Longfellow aimed at in his poetry. There is no doubt that he attained them. At times, unfortunately, his simplicity thinned out into banality and his clarity became a synonym for the merely obvious. This was a logical outcome of his distressing tendency to confuse thought with emotion and his inability and unwillingness to gaze very long at the primary facts of existence.[71] Although he was bound, therefore, to be superficial and sentimental, he had nevertheless the compensating virtues of sincerity and serenity, and these in turn were partly the result of his own nature and partly the fine flowering of his strong religious spirit which supported him well in the major crises of his life and never deserted him in the many minor irritations which continually provoke the successful man of letters.

All in all, Longfellow's poetic successes outweigh his failures. He was a man of his era and he was the right man for his time in America. Doubtless it would be satisfying to discover that his work contains anticipations of tension, ambiguity, and complexity but, as a matter of fact, these are the precise qualities he strove mightily to avoid. Serenity, clarity, simplicity were his aim in literature as in life, and they are the polar opposites to the qualities sought for in present-day poetry.

At his best he had the Classic virtues of moderation and restraint and the Romantic virtue of aspiration for the ideal in whatever times and places it may seem to have been found. He progressed steadily from the artificial and the illustrative to the real and the symbolic. He wrote well and lastingly in the narrative and in the lyric, with special success in the sonnet. He knew the sound of the sea and the sound of mortality and he caught both in some few poems of simple and unforgettable beauty. He gave us foreign culture and made us proudly aware of American myth.

That he was a poet of minor rank is incontrovertible. It seems equally certain that he is one of the best of minor poets. He was not a genius but a highly talented, finished artist, and he was a Christian gentleman of whom any nation might be proud.

EDGAR ALLAN POE

1809-1849

The Incorporate Silence and the Heart Divine

JEREMIAH K. DURICK

It is still very difficult to pronounce a final critical verdict on the work of Edgar Allan Poe. Unlike most of the other American writers of the nineteenth century, he is commonly regarded as a "mystery" quite as unfathomable as he was when, as the Angel Israfel, he troubled the dark waters of his own day. In spite of the continuous industry of scholars and critics, solutions of the Poe mystery give answers as dusty and as paradoxical as any proposed by that hardy race of critics, the "Ishmaelites," about *Moby-Dick* and Herman Melville. It is also still possible to arouse over Poe controversy as acrimonious as any that has raged over the lively body of *Leaves of Grass*, because he was a master of mystification and self-deification long before pilgrims worshipped at the Whitman shrine in Camden. And Thoreau, courting solitude at Walden, was perhaps less wedded to isolation than Poe at Richmond or Philadelphia or Fordham.

On first looking into Poe's works, the proverbial schoolboy is likely to become an avid fan of this master of the "weird" or an equally ardent scorner of his jingled dreams of fair women. Few young people read much of Poe before their initial enthusiasm or revulsion is intensified by one or more legends from the Great Poe Myth. Merely a sniff of the mystery makes partisans of us all, and the descent into this maelstrom is easy! The critic, come-of-age, whose own early impressions of "supernal" beauty or of Poe-esque horror cannot be totally obliterated, finds himself facing a situation with few parallels in world literature. He finds that whereas most great writers "grow" on us, Poe tends to diminish in stature as we grow older. As we try to digest the "genius" of Lowell's *Fable*, we must also swallow the "fudge." I make this observation, not unmindful of the tendency of certain contemporary critics to see Poe's craftsmanship as a forerunner of Flaubert, James (who disliked Poe), and Proust.[1]

It is somewhat less difficult to "place" Poe in American literary history because his enemies by the very violence of their opposition often proclaim his historical importance, while lamenting or belittling or denying his influence. What would American literature be without Edgar Allan Poe? The answer to this question may be found in part in the most impressive bibliography of critical and scholarly study thus far accorded to any American writer. Even the Melville revival has failed to attract more competent or zealous scholars: Harrison[2] and Woodberry[3] of an earlier day, Killis Campbell[4] and Arthur Hobson Quinn[5] of our own, to name only the more illustrious. Scholar-critics like W. C. Brownell[6] and Norman Foerster,[7] with little fundamental sympathy for Poe's outlook on life or for his esthetic ideals, have treated him with as much respect as they have shown to any of the great New England writers. Eminent contemporary critics, including T. S. Eliot[8] and Edmund Wilson,[9] have evaluated Poe's place in modern literature without the faintest trace of condescension. Allen Tate's "Forlorn Demon" of the "Angelic Imagination" becomes "Our Cousin, Mr. Poe" in the very next chapter.[10] After delivering himself of such pathetically "just" verdicts as: "The readers of Poe are usually of high-school age or mentality. The imitations of Poe are in the pulp-paper magazines. . . . The rhapsodies on Poe are mostly by third-rate critics,"[11] Malcolm Cowley goes on to discuss Poe's flair for invention, his showmanship, and his well-known influence, by way of Baudelaire, on modern European literature. Yvor Winters is perhaps alone among recent scholars and critics to deny Poe's historical significance, but even he grudgingly admits "that the course of romantic literature would have been different (perhaps) in America, had Poe never been born."[12]

While the battle still rages between "factual" biographers and romantic rhapsodists, while the critical pot still boils over in little magazines and in the groves of Academe, the common reader (of "high-school mentality"?) continues to read and reread with unabated enjoyment a handful or two of Poe's poems and tales and to accept his "greatness" as the uncrowned laureate of the "middlebrow." This acceptance is made doubly respectable by schoolteachers and handbook-makers, who "place" Poe among the "classics" of our literature as calmly as they acknowledge the historical eminence of Irving and Cooper and much more easily than they accept Melville. "Leave Poe's paradoxes to the partisans and to the New Critics," they seem to say, utterly oblivious of the fact that their own "critical" estimates are based on controversial platitudes and premises that have become a part of America's literary folklore.

II

Let us begin with a favorite platitude: Poe never wrote a story more grotesque than his life, nor dreamed a dream more incredible than the nightmare of his own mortal years.

It is possible to summarize the "facts" of Poe's life simply and concisely. Professor N. Bryllion Fagin has given us such a summary in less than four pages in his excellent study *The Histrionic Mr. Poe*.[13] As Mr. Fagin admits, his account tells us nothing of Poe's "experiences in love." Nor does he do more than allude to his subject's "excessive conviviality." He fails altogether to mention the alleged drug-addiction. Naturally Mr. Fagin makes no attempt to regard the dream-poems and the tales of terror as revelations of the inner life of a strange psychopathic personality. In short, this most admirable "factual" summary omits all the stuff of Poe's life which has give rise to the fundamental platitudes of the Poe controversy, not to mention the chief items in the character indictment of the Rev. Rufus Wilmot Griswold, Poe's literary executor—and dark angel.

To conclude from this that it is not the "facts" behind the platitudes that bedevil the critics of Poe would be to dismiss as worthless the monumental labors of Professor Quinn and Hervey Allen,[14] and the painstaking scholarship of scores of other investigators. Quinn's capacity for infinite detail is matched by Allen's talent for exploiting to the fullest the romantic possibilities of secondary source material. Killis Campbell in *The Mind of Poe*[15] had already done an admirable job in laying the ghosts of the Griswold legends, but Quinn's point-by-point refutation of Griswold's charges and insinuations ought to be the last word on the work of this pious master of detraction. Oddly enough, the romantic defenders of Poe's name need to take good strong doses of Quinn's facts, because their own defense has given, unwittingly, comfort to Poe's enemies. They have also helped to distort the viewpoint of the common reader by suggesting that Poe's abiding appeal is partly at least a *succès de scandale*.

It would be foolish for the most ardent partisan to deny Poe's shortcomings: his unstable temperament, his ambiguous relationships with women, his fits of depression, his inability to hold his liquor, his histrionic talents for throwing a veil of mystery about himself. Not for nothing was he the child of actors; not for nothing did he attempt to wipe out the "stigma" of his lowly birth at Boston on January 19, 1809, by adopting the ideology and the manners of a Virginia gentleman. The counsel for the defense must admit that Poe was more or less responsible for creating the myths for Griswold to twist beyond recognition or for modern psychoanalytical critics like Mr. Krutch[16] to explore to their subconscious depths. It is imperative for any student of Poe's life to know that there is an impressive body of evidence in Quinn's biography and elsewhere to refute or to mitigate the charges expressed or implied in our list of shortcomings. This evidence is drawn from the testimony of casual acquaintances as well as from friends and partisans. One closes the books of Poe's most objective biographies readily subscribing to the old French dictum: To know all is to forgive all.[17] Perhaps the best refutation of the still widely held belief that Poe lived his writing-years in a constant state of inebriation is the solid five-foot shelf of work he left behind him, writing as various in kind as any that has ever appeared in America from the pen of a single author. In less than forty feverish years Poe managed to produce not only the miscellaneous grist of the journalist's mill but also a select and constantly revised body of imaginative work such as usually characterizes only the completely dedicated artist.

Perhaps the only safe conclusion we can draw about the allegedly romantic episodes in Poe's life story is that no honest biographer dares to equate either dream or nightmare with reality. The critic, none the less, cannot dissociate his life from his work, for like Byron's and Shelley's, Poe's best and happiest moments (and his most foolish) must always be looked at through the colored glasses—dark or yellow or rose—for which he made the frames—and, sometimes, the pigment, when the Byronic mood seized him.

Like Pope and some of Poe's fellow Romantics, he himself helped to create the widely accepted legend of his precociousness. Were we to accept Poe's word for it, he was lisping in numbers lyrics like "To Helen" when he was fourteen years old. Of his early bent toward poetry there can be no doubt. When in 1827 he published privately in Boston his first volume of verse, *Tamerlane and Other Poems,* he wrote a preface in which he attributes

the "greater part" of the poems to the year 1821-1822, and adds:
". . . they were written by one too young to have any knowledge of
the world but from his own breast."[18] This seems like romantic
hyperbole, but we do have the testimony of his Richmond schoolmaster, Joseph H. Clarke, erstwhile of Trinity College, Dublin,
that he had seen a "lost" manuscript-volume belonging to these
early years. There is also the persistent legend that the Allans—
even the generally unsympathetic John Allan—had encouraged
young Poe to compose sentimental effusions marked more by
adolescent moon-calf than by hints of unripened genius.

Even were all the poems in *Tamerlane* written nearer to their
date of publication, it is only fair to Poe to note, as Quinn points
out, that Bryant was the only American poet of major rank to
have issued a volume by 1827, although Whittier and Longfellow
were two years older than Poe, Emerson six years his senior, and
Holmes was born in the same year.[19] Poe's undeniably precocious
dedication to poetry and his characteristic style of composition
are apparent in this fledgling work—now one of the rarest and
richest prizes for the bibiophile.

It was during these apprentice years that young Poe met Mrs.
Jane Stith Stannard, the mother of his schoolboy friend. She became at once the object of his passionate veneration and the
ultimate inspiration for "To Helen." His claim that this poem was
also written in his fourteenth year seems very dubious in the
light of the criticism of Professor Campbell, who calls attention to
its "maturity" of phrase, and argues that Poe would have been
unlikely to defer its publication to the 1831 volume, had it been
composed before 1827.[20] The version we usually read did not
appear in print until 1845. Incidentally, "To Helen," with its
memorable, haunting lines:

> To the glory that was Greece
> And the grandeur that was Rome,

even more than "The Raven," reflects the "magic" of Poe's ways
with words, but, on close reading and analysis, betrays an immaturity in handling imagery as reprehensible to modern critics
as his "jingling" was to Emerson.[21]

The 1827 *Tamerlane,* published by Calvin F. Thomas in Boston,
went as unrecognized as its penniless author or its ambitious young
printer. Already in the black books of John Allan, because of the
gambling episode at the University of Virginia, Poe in desperation enlisted in the United States Army under the name of

Edgar A. Perry. It is unnecessary here to enter into the controversies over Sergeant Poe's successful soldiering or to give an account of his eight months at West Point. A great deal of nonsense has been bandied about in regard to Cadet Poe. The itch to write—and to write poetry—persisted throughout his military career. He published *Al Aaraaf, Tamerlane and Minor Poems* in Baltimore in 1829 while waiting for his appointment to the Military Academy, and *Poems,* second edition, in New York shortly after his dismissal from the Point, thanks largely to the subscriptions of his fellow cadets, probably under an amusingly erroneous impression about the book, which they thought was a collection of comical and satirical verses!

By 1832, more desperate than ever for money but still determined to make his living by his pen, Poe turned to the prose tale. From Baltimore, where he was already probably living with his aunt, Mrs. Maria Poe Clemm, he sent five short stories to the *Philadelphia Saturday Courier.* None of these is now ranked among Poe's masterpieces, although the best of the five, "Metzengerstein," begins with this characteristic sentence: "Horror and fatality have been stalking abroad in all ages,"[22] and all of them contain similar intimations of the kind of immortality awaiting their author at maturity. Any disappointment Poe may have experienced at failing to win a prize from the *Courier* was compensated for by the award he received on October 12, 1833, of $100 from the *Baltimore Saturday Visitor* for "MS. Found in a Bottle." The following January the tale called originally "The Visionary" appeared in *Godey's Lady's Book.* The tale in its revised form bears the title "The Assignation" and is generally now regarded as one of Poe's most powerful and readable stories. It is one of a half-dozen stories that seemed to this writer to wear well after several rereadings.

The days of apprenticeship were now at an end. The 1831 volume of poems included "Israfel," "To Helen," "Irene," and "The City in the Sea." The prize short story had brought Poe to the attention of John Pendleton Kennedy, through whose influence he began his editorial connection with the *Southern Literary Messenger.* The preface to *Poems* (1831), commonly known as the "Letter to B——" (Elam Bliss, Poe's publisher?), which appeared in July 1836 in slightly revised form in the *Messenger,* also indicated that a new and significant critical voice had been raised in America. We can say, then, that by 1834 Poe had definitely arrived in the world of letters. Henceforth his threefold genius—

as poet, as storyteller, and as critic—would be able to find the outlets of the "accepted" professional writer and editor. Poe had arrived on his own power—and mostly alone. From this day forward he was a man with a pen for hire, who, amid poverty and personal struggles, must continue his solitary way up the hill of Parnassus.

Poe's growth as an artist is chiefly manifest in his continued revision of the poems and stories that seemed most perfectly to fulfill his earliest esthetic ideals. The remarkable thing about his spirit of dedication is his unremitting perseverance against all the contingencies of circumstance to give his readers what they wanted or expected from him, in a style often worthy of a better cause. As we reread today stories like "William Wilson" or "The Cask of Amontillado," the memory of our own adolescent delight in the macabre vanishes as we recognize that here, to borrow Poe's own words about Hawthorne's *Twice-Told Tales*:

> A skilful literary artist has constructed a tale. If wise, he has not fashioned his thoughts to accommodate his incidents; but having conceived, with deliberate care, a certain unique or single effect to be wrought out, he then invents such incidents—he then combines such events as may best aid him in establishing this preconceived effect.[23]

This single effect is invariably an improvement, sometimes a triumph, over the raw material from which the story was fashioned. One need not apologize for the teller of Poe's best tales any more than he need defend the poet who made a deeply-felt frustration the theme of "The Haunted Palace" and a series of more or less real bereavements the subject of "Annabel Lee."

Poe must have learned quickly to distinguish between the demand of deadlines and the imperatives of his own dedication to his art. Let his audience cry for the Gothicism of Germany: he will give them the terror of his own mortal soul and make them think that is what they wanted. His ability to establish rapport with his readers and at the same time to offend most of the literary bigwigs of his day is part of the Poe paradox. It may explain also why he founded no "school" but discovered a popular genre—the detective story, and why his "spiritual" progeny consists of schoolboys—and French Symbolists! And yet perhaps the best refutation of the allegation that Poe has no imitators comes from T. S. Eliot's simple confession: ". . . one cannot be sure that one's own writing has not been influenced by Poe"![24]

To tell the full story of Poe's literary development is no more the aim of this paper than it is to unravel the twisted skein of his life. For the next fifteen years (1834-1849) Poe was to display such talents as an editor and such versatility as a writer that it now seems strange that the legends of his moody temperament should outshine his capacity for hard work and that his penchant for dissipation should overshadow his maturing genius. Poe had already learned—perhaps as early as his boyhood schooldays in England—to live in two worlds: the world of dreams now given a name, if not a local habitation, on the printed page—and the workaday world in which he lived in terrible isolation, unbroken even by his pitiable union with Virginia Clemm.

III

Although Poe never could come to businesslike terms with a world he never made, it does not follow that he was not deeply interested in certain aspects of it. The legend of Poe's living only in a world of fantasy and drugged senses is another vulgar error. He may have dared to dream dreams "no mortal ever dared to dream before," but neither poppy nor alcohol ever blunted his naturally keen powers of observation. His knowledge of the natural world, achieved through observation and through books, was not extensive, and yet it was sufficient for his purposes as a writer. This is especially discernible in his marvelous sense of place in a tale of ratiocination like "The Gold Bug" and also in tales of death such as "The Fall of the House of Usher," in which the terror is made credible by Poe's mastery of topographical detail. Although he had little or no regard for the "realistic" story as such, his longest piece of fiction, "The Narrative of Arthur Gordon Pym," is a masterpiece of verisimilitude which invariably invites comparison with Defoe and Swift. "The Gold Bug" takes us back to his days in the Army when he was stationed at Fort Moultrie, and "Gordon Pym," grounded on written "sources," assumes reality because Poe's powers of observation can guide, if not govern, his imagination. His love of invention, which, as Mr. Cowley points out, he shared with hundreds of his fellow Americans, made him the progenitor of science fiction. But who would now dare say that the worlds of Tom Swift or of Tom Corbett, Space-Cadet, can be created by a man devoid of mechanical sense and powers of observation?

Let us pass over lightly the question of the influence on Poe of classical and academic learning. Poe was a very competent student of the ancient languages at the University of Virginia, according to Miss Margaret Alterton.[25] Like his powers of observation, his erudition has been often underrated—but never by himself. He was given to pretending to learning he did not possess, and yet he was sometimes guilty of howlers inexcusable in a critic merciless in his own attacks on the errors of other writers. His learning was necessarily perhaps merely sufficient for the day, but, as the careful researches of Campbell and Margaret Alterton show, Poe knew almost as much as the needs of his art required and a great deal more than the average journalist of his day. One is often amazed, for example, at the breadth and solidity of his knowledge of science and should be impressed by Poe's obvious respect for learning wherever and whenever he found it.

The charge that Poe was little concerned about the problems of his day is regrettably well founded. His contempt for the social reformers of New England (he called the Transcendentalists "the Crazyites") is well known. His attitude toward politics was aristocratic, as became a Virginia gentleman. Politically he had no ambitions and about the devious ways of the politician, few illusions. When he did choose to utter pronouncements on society and the art of governing, he sounds far less like a friend and disciple of Attorney-General William Wirt than like a forerunner of H. L. Mencken. Poe's disdain for the legislator and his contempt for the "people" can be illustrated by the following selection from his *Marginalia* (brief "marginal" items from his editorial pen) which appeared in the *Southern Literary Messenger* in June 1849:

> In drawing a line of distinction between a people and a mob, we shall find that a people aroused to action are a mob; and that a mob, trying to think, subside into a people. . . .

> Samuel Butler of Hudibrastic memory must have had a prophetic eye to the American Congress when he defined a rabble as —"A congregation or assembly of the States-General—every one being of several judgment concerning whatever business be under consideration." . . . "They meet only to quarrel," he adds, "And then return home full of satisfaction and narrative."

> We, of the nineteenth century, need some worker of miracles for our regeneration; but so degraded have we become that the only prophet, or preacher, who could render us much service, would be the St. Francis who converted the beasts.[26]

The sardonic tone of Poe's political epigrams can be matched by some of his comments on the books and authors unlucky enough to come under his critical lash. To the admirer of Poe's poems and better-known stories his mastery of satire and invective comes as something of a shock. It is erroneous, nevertheless, to think of Poe as "un-American." Like other good—and even great—Americans, he was exercising his democratic right to castigate perverted manifestations of popular sovereignty. As we shall see, Poe's unconcern for social problems even more than his contempt for the people is symptomatic of a malaise deeper than aristocratic affectation and more disturbing than an alleged deficiency in understanding of American "traditions."

The undemocratic *obiter dicta* quoted above could explain why Vernon L. Parrington and his disciples summarily dismissed Poe from the *Main Currents in American Thought,* contending that he was alienated from "the more generous southern ideals." Parrington himself, nevertheless, does sympathize with Poe and, in sentences quite uncharacteristic of his treatment of belletrists, writes: "[Poe] suffered much from aloofness, but he gained much also. In the midst of gross and tawdry romanticisms he refused to be swallowed up, but went his own way, a rebel in the cause of beauty, discovering in consequence a finer romanticism than was before known in America."[27]

Whatever one may think of Poe's allegedly un-American political views, he was, allowing for his moment and milieu, a phenomenon in our literary history as native as Davy Crockett. Such is the opinion of a critic as shrewd as William Carlos Williams. In his chapter on Poe in *In the American Grain,* Dr. Williams calls our attention to the distinctively American quality of Poe's idiom.[28] True enough, this idiom is often disguised by foreign allusions and phrases, but let us not forget that Whitman, far less versed in foreign tongues than Poe, attempted to conceal his own cultural limitations by inventing foreign-sounding, grand-opera words and phrases. As Dr. Williams so well says: "He was the first to realize that the hard, sardonic, truculent mass of the New World, hot, angry . . . was, in fact, not a thing to paint out, to smear, to destroy—for it *would* not be destroyed, it was too powerful—it smiled!"[29] And, more pointedly, Dr. Williams maintains: "Poe gave the sense for the first time in America, that literature is *serious,* not a matter of courtesy but of truth."[30]

Immediately relevant to the discussion of Poe's intellectual equipment and its serious application to literature is the fact that he was gifted with an unusually lucid mind, while his imagi-

nation was nurtured on an agony as Romantic as any dreamed
of in the philosophy of his British and European contemporaries.
Perhaps this is the very essence of the Poe-paradox.

There is no need to point out the limitations of Poe's esthetic
theories or to see in "The Philosophy of Composition" and his
other theoretical pieces mere rationalizations of his own practices
as a writer. Some critics have argued that the theorist ruined the
poet. What a pity that a mind as clear and as perspicacious as his
should leave its most characteristic marks on the solution of cryp-
tograms in plot-ridden stories and on the invention of the detective
tale! The latter is, of course, no mean feat in itself, as the recent
history of this popular genre amply testifies. What really strikes
the close student of Poe is the almost complete lack of ethical
content or concern in his thinking. This is the real root of that
deeper malaise already alluded to in previous comments on Poe's
social and political cynicism. His ethical unconcern touches directly or indirectly everything he wrote, from his "entertainments"
to his lyrical verse, and includes his one attempt, "Eureka," to
write a "philosophical prose-poem." It goes much deeper than his
attack on the "heresy of the didactic" in the poetry of his contemporaries. It is the true basis for the claim of Poe's enemies
that he is the spiritual father of "art for art's sake" and the
godfather of Bohemia Literaria. To the modern sociological critic
he is anathema not only because he has no concern for man's
fate but also because everything human seems foreign to his
proud isolated ego.

IV

Poe's contempt for the didactic tradition was, nevertheless,
good medicine for the American poets and poetasters of his time.
They had inherited the didactic convention of English neoclassical
verse and the ethical involvements of evangelical Protestantism.
At a time when the dogmatic truths of religion had suffered serious
body-blows from the Enlightenment and later from the Unitarian
and Transcendentalist theologians, Christian moral teaching
tended more and more to replace dogma in "secular" literature as
well as in the Protestant pulpit. This was the age when literature
became scripture as Scripture (alas!) was already rapidly coming
to be regarded as mere literature. Those of us who remember our
early schooldays made our first acquaintance with poets from
teachers bent on having us learn "lessons" from poetry. Bryant,

Longfellow, and Lowell were good preachers, while Poe was reserved for "declamation" contests. (If we couldn't learn lessons from E. A. Poe, he could at least serve as a horrible example of the evils of drunkenness and perhaps of other nameless iniquities.)

Poe's medicine was bitter and sometimes even emetic, as in his vicious attacks on Longfellow. His own critical practice should have been tonic to a "business" already fast succumbing to the logroller (Poe rolled a few logs himself!), and his sharp reviews of the work of his contemporaries, a cleansing caustic. He could be harshly severe with established reputations, and his treatment of nonentities was savage. For example, in reviewing *The Sacred Mountains*, by the Rev. Joel T. Headley, Poe could be completely devastating:

> "Quack" is a word that sounds well only in the mouth of a duck; and upon our honor we feel a scruple in using it:—nevertheless the truth should be told; and the simple fact is, that the author of *The Sacred Mountains* is the Autocrat of all Quacks. In saying this, we beg not to be misunderstood. We mean no disparagement to Mr. Headley. We admire that gentleman as much as any individual ever did except that gentleman himself![31]

Unfortunately the critical times were out of joint for Dr. Poe, and his patients began to look for evidence in their physician of madness and the devil's hoof. Small wonder Poe founded no "school" —not even a school of literary surgery.

Now our Puritan ancestors in America were not without interest in literary theory, but up until Poe's time and including his most notable contemporaries, no American (the academic-minded Lowell excepted) had taken the critic's task very seriously. As a matter of fact, no American critic of the nineteenth century shows Poe's capacity for sustained and organized thinking about literary theory. One may argue that Poe was virtually illiterate in the critical classics of the Western world and even question how much Poe was able to get out of reading his kindred spirit, Coleridge. Miss Alterton thinks that Poe owed much to the *Biographia Literaria*. The fact remains that Poe was an American pioneer in recognizing the significance to himself and to others of a rationale of poetry and the short story. His theorizing on the latter was, to be sure, largely incidental, but Poe, the artist, was first of all a poet who embedded poems in his most carefully wrought tales and thought of his ideal storyteller as a spoiled poet.

The tenets of Poe's critical creed are so well known that it is not necessary to repeat them in detail. Poe himself was deliberately repetitive, making pretty much the same points in "The Poetic Principle," "The Philosophy of Composition," and in various observations and asides in his critical reviews.[32] The key points may be reduced to Unity, Beauty, and Brevity—with Death and the Woman as the chief sources of inspiration. Even a complete synthesis of all Poe's poetics will not give us a very comprehensive philosophy of poetry. Let us not, however, underestimate the significance of an esthetic creed which emphasizes quality and intensity as well as unity. This emphasis makes for a conception of artistic integrity unique not only for Poe's America but also for a Romantic age in which diffuseness was often confused with imagination and quality regarded as expendable. But this conception of the poet's art, implicit in his thinking as early at least as 1831, fell on barren ground and had to wait for the French poets, with their passion for theory, to put it to work. In America, Poe's poetics has not been without influence, but that influence has been largely confined to schoolbooks and manuals on how to be a writer.

V

Poe's single lengthy excursion into philosophic realms was still more unhappy in its results. He had little or no talent for metaphysical speculation, but he did have, like many other writers of his day, a deep curiosity about science and pseudo-science. When he turned in his philosophical prose poem, "Eureka," to "first causes," he was still haunted by his passion to discover the Oneness of things—a passion which he shared with Coleridge—and those he considered his own mortal enemies, the New England Transcendentalists. Unfortunately, Poe tended to identify simplicity with unity. To him, as Alterton and Craig point out in their most careful analysis of "Eureka," "multiplicity in search of unity is identified with mortality in search of immortality."[33] Even when we allow for the liberty granted the poet, the curiously compounded terminology of this prose poem makes for maddeningly difficult reading. The lucidity of Poe's prose is lost in a potpourri of terms from physical science and the jargon of philosophical idealism. Strangely enough, certain modern scientists to whom Professor Quinn submitted his analysis of "Eureka"[34] vouch for the accuracy of Poe's astronomical knowledge, and one philosopher cited by Quinn points out the startling resemblance between Poe's theory and Einstein's! It seems incredible to us that "Eureka" was first presented as a popular lecture, but still more so that it was well received.

The problem of the One and the Many with which Poe wrestled in this prose poem had been especially disturbing to his contemporaries both in Old England and New. The previous epoch had been generally satisfied with materialistic answers to the central problems of psychology and cosmology, but the Romantics were nothing if not "transcendental," and men of letters as well as philosophers, speculating on the nature of man and of the universe, had turned to an idealism in which, to use Emerson's famous phrase, the self is "part or particle of God." Poe, whose contempt for the New England Transcendentalists we have already mentioned, was, for all his preoccupation with physical science, a good disciple of Coleridge—perhaps also of Plato. At times Poe does use what seems to be the unmistakable language of the materialist, talking of the "Cloud-Land of Metaphysics,"[35] regarding terms like "God" and "spirit" as incomprehensible.[36] He argues that there is no immateriality because whatever is not matter simply does not exist. And yet he can also talk of God's "purpose" in creation, of the "Divine Volition," and of matter as a means, not an end.[37] This confusion of terms makes "Eureka" itself a "Cloud-Land" and Poe's philosophy of nature as pantheistic as Emerson's. He finally works up to the contemplation of: "A novel Universe swelling into existence, and then subsiding into nothingness, at every throb of the Heart Divine? And now—this Heart Divine— what is it, *It is our own.*"[38] (The italics are Poe's.) Professor Braddy suggests the possible connection between Poe's nihilistic philosophy and the "Nevermore" of "The Raven"![39]

Poe professed to believe in immortality just as he professed to believe in God, but by the time he reached maturity there is little evidence to show the theological or moral influence of the Episcopal Church in which he was reared. As a matter of fact, the religious influences of Poe's youth as a Virginia gentleman were strongly colored by a fashionable deism which, as "Eureka" shows, he never completely shook off. His "Heart Divine" was Emerson's Over-Soul, but, unlike the Sage of Concord, Poe had little or no concern for the ghosts of morality which continued far into the nineteenth century to haunt the New England mind. The ethical void, already noted in Poe's outlook on society, quite plainly had its roots in the determinism implicit in his cosmology. "Eureka" is Poe's "Song of Myself!" He is Whitman's Everyman—and every atom of him "as good belongs" to the "Divine Volition."

Now "Eureka" was written and published one year before Poe's death. It represents what some critics have looked upon as the final step in his mental development. It is perhaps unfair to judge a professedly prose poem by philosophical or theological standards; nevertheless, for all its assimilation of nineteenth-century science, "Eureka" is an immature work. Baudelaire, it is worth remarking, virtually ignores these attempts of Poe at theological speculation. Early in life Poe apparently lost whatever he may have held of orthodox Christian belief and never recovered it. His greatest French disciple did make a partial recovery by a life of suffering, although it is revealed to us through the idiom of romantic blasphemy. At least, as T. S. Eliot points out in his penetrating review of Christopher Isherwood's translation of the *Journaux Intimes*: "Baudelaire perceived that what really matters is Sin and Redemption."[40] Without ever alluding to Poe, Mr. Eliot recognizes in Baudelaire's "theological innocence" a kinship between these two tortured souls that is relevant to our analysis of Poe's agonizing attempts to work out a philosophy of life in "Eureka":

> Baudelaire's notion of beatitude certainly tended to the wishy-washy; and even in one of the most beautiful of his poems, *L'Invitation au voyage,* he hardly exceeds the *poésie des départs.* And because his vision is here so restricted, there is for him a gap between human love and divine love. His human love is definite and positive, his divine love vague and uncertain.[41]

VI

Because he regarded each individual as almost one with the "Heart Divine," Poe thought he had solved such "riddles of Divine Injustice" as the existence of evil. The riddle of death continued just the same to preoccupy his creative imagination in his poems and stories. The place death held as one of the two supreme and proper subjects of poetry may be discounted somewhat for his fiction, because death was part of the stock-in-trade of specialists in Gothic terror. But Poe's use of the death-motif is something more than Romantic convention, Gothic or graveyard—something more significant that riddle-solving or breaking cryptographic codes, or using the repetend. This motif was deeply personal, having haunted him from the day of Mrs. Stannard's death to the last mortal moments of Virginia Clemm. Death—and the Woman! D. H. Lawrence speaks of Poe as fascinated with the idea of his own self-destruction because: "Doomed he was. He died wanting more love, and love killed him."[42] Lawrence here expresses his own favorite theme, but even the common reader, innocent of Lawrence's anti-eroticism, recognizes in Ligeia and Ulalume and Madeline Usher a morbid love of easeful death as real as Keats's temptations to suicide. It is possible to be carried far afield by these intimations of morbidity in Poe's work. It is likewise possible to see in the characters of his tales as well as in his poems self-revelation for which there is little substantial evidence. Factual-minded scholars and defenders of Poe have, however, gone to the opposite extreme in denying the validity of autobiographical elements in any of his work except in the poems addressed to women. Are we to dismiss as irrelevant to our understanding of Poe the theme of death? Are we to deny the obvious "high seriousness" of "Eureka" and the shorter "philosophical" pieces? How can we disregard the Romantic frame of reference against which Poe as artist worked? These questions are not rhetorical, and their answers attest the critic's right to regard Poe's morbidity as something more personal than mere pose.

However distasteful it may be to his admirers, Poe did look upon the Universe as a "plot of God"[43] and life itself as a tragedy —a human tragedy in which "The Conqueror Worm" is the hero. And yet in the "Sonnet-Silence" physical death becomes "the corporate silence." Man need not dread this "silence"; rather, let him commend himself to God! This may be prayerful boasting of the kind he dared not utter "in the ghoul-haunted woodland of Weir" or in the outer-space philosophizing of "Eureka," but Poe's "view of Death" contained no element of Bryant's Stoicism. Not even the philosophy of the "Heart Divine" could minister consolations to his lonely, restless heart.

Lawrence was right: Poe needed love—not merely the physical love of which he was allegedly incapable, but the Love Divine which reconciles the oneness of beauty and death. There is something so awfully pathetic about Poe's personal tragedy that invites the critic to homily, even though he rejects the moralizing platitudes of schoolmarms and pious clergymen.[44] One cannot fail to see in Poe's agony over the "Incorporate Silence" his need of the "Heart Divine" and in his quest for unity, a passionate pilgrimage during which he attempted to synthesize all things, human and divine. His tragedy was essentially one of isolation in time and in place. His life was, to tear Lawrence's words out of their context, regrettably "lurid and melodramatic." There was nothing either of the "lurid" or of the "melodramatic" about Poe, however, which could not have been saved by love, an earthly love which could have helped "humanize" his poems and stories, a Love Divine that would have taught him to look through and beyond the "Incorporate Silence." Poe was from childhood a lonely soul, ambitious to make a name and a place for himself as a person and as an artist. At every turn his ambition seemed frustrated or misdirected—and his sense of isolation, intensified by the vicious circle of his tragedy, made the "Incorporate Silence" of Nirvana seem like the only ultimate worth idealizing. Fittingly enough, his best work and the best passages in all his work remain a loveless, exotic monument to a lonely man. Little wonder, then, that Poe's most sympathetic critics, if not his most avid fans, can be found today among the dwellers in "Axel's Castle"—disciples of Baudelaire, Valéry, Yeats, and the rest. Perhaps there is no final solution to the mystery that was and still is Edgar Allan Poe, until we are able to reconcile his double destiny as literary idol of the schoolboy and grandfather of modern symbolism.

HENRY DAVID THOREAU
1817-1862

Christian Malgré Lui

MICHAEL F. MOLONEY

WHEN Henry David Thoreau went out to Walden Pond on a
March day in 1845 to consolidate a conviction that had been
growing for some years, he posed a problem to which subsequent
students of his life have given conflicting answers. It was inevitable
that in the twenties and thirties of this present century the hegira
should have been interpreted in terms of social and economic protest.[1] It was equally inevitable that the impingement of Thoreau's
pantheism upon his inherited Puritanism and his acquired but
perhaps somewhat superficial orientalism should have led to the
evaluation of the Walden episode as a search for spiritual certainty.[2] Both of these explications strike me as possessing essential
truth but as fixing a wrong emphasis. With all of the centrifugal
pressures to which it was subjected, Thoreau's life was dedicated,
as few American lives have been, to literary purpose. Primarily,
he was a man of letters. Quite literally, I think, he went out to
Walden Pond to write a book.[3] To be sure, a part of *Walden* was
already in existence before its author took up his squatter's residence on his friend Emerson's acres and much of it was to be
written long after he had left his idyllic bachelor's hall. Still, the
Walden years were conclusive in Thoreau's creative life and
their end product was one of the supremely great books yet written
in America.

Literature, to be sure, is not created *ex nihilo*. It is the result of
the meeting and fusion of thought and art. Thoreau's passion for
nature, his reaction against the growing materialism of his day, his
deep-seated ethical, and less deep-seated but no less genuine, religious concerns—these are the materials upon whose intractability
his creative imagination and his magnificent gift for phrase sought

to impose a final form. There have been better-trained observers of nature, better-balanced social philosophers, more revealing students of the inner life. But a great writer, fortunately, need not be an equally great thinker. If, as H. J. C. Grierson suggested in a famous essay[4] written thirty years ago, only Dante, Lucretius, and Goethe are metaphysical poets in any philosophically exact use of that term, there is still welcome in the muses' mansion for the many metaphysical poets whose verses reveal a tumult of ideas, tortured, it may be, confused, occasionally triumphant, but always personal, and whose art molds itself around the angular contours of those ideas and illumines them with its characteristic grace.

Like the minor metaphysicals of the seventeenth century, Thoreau was an acute if limited thinker. He was intense rather than profound. But he had a passionate sincerity which kept him from the facile pontificating into which Emerson too easily fell. Moreover, the ascetic discipline of his external life preserved his mental processes from slackness. Even when the great bulk of the posthumously published journals is included, it can honestly be said of Thoreau that he treated his reader with respect, in Coventry Patmore's meaning of that phrase. He is never carried away by the sound of his own voice. When such athleticism of the mind, exercised on the central problems of man's existence, is joined with an innate and assiduously cultivated gift of expression, literary greatness is inevitable.

It was Emerson's *Nature,* called by Henry Seidel Canby "that most seminal of all American books,"[5] which gave Thoreau the external warrant for his internal conviction of the importance of the cosmos in man's existence. It is unthinkable, however, that Emerson's essay "turned" Thoreau to nature. A man, at least when he is so strong, so "prickly" a character as Thoreau, is not likely to be directed by another into ways of thinking and acting which will dominate the rest of his life. What Emerson's *Nature* did give Thoreau was a confirmation of his own intuitions. To the country boy who knew the Concord countryside "like a fox or a bird," the meeting with Emerson's ideas just as his Harvard years were drawing to a close must have come as a revelation. Here in the words of a famous townsman a half-generation his elder was the gospel for which he hungered. Emerson's now familiar phrases then were fresh and unshopworn:

To go into solitude, a man needs to retire as much from his chamber as from society. . . . There is a property in the horizon which no man has but he whose eye can integrate all the parts, that is, the poet. . . . In the woods, we return to reason and faith. . . . The tradesman, the attorney comes out of the din and craft of the street and sees the sky and the woods and is a man again. . . . Every rational creature has all nature for his dowry and estate. . . . Nature stretches out her arms to embrace man, only let his thoughts be of equal greatness. . . . Every natural fact is a symbol of some spiritual fact. . . . Parts of speech are metaphors, because the whole of nature is a metaphor of the human mind. . . .

Whether or not the *Bhagavad-Gita* was a parallel influence with Emerson's *Nature* (as Canby holds)[6] is open to some doubt. There is no question, of course, of Thoreau's interest in oriental philosophy to which the first reference in the *Journal* appears under the date of August 22, 1838. It is generally agreed that Emerson introduced him to the Chinese and Hindu thinkers and it was during his residence at Emerson's home in 1841 that the *Journal* entries become extravagant in their praise of the Eastern books. This enthusiasm is persistent and long maintained. Almost ten years later, he writes: "What extracts from the Vedas I have read fall on me like the light of a higher and purer luminary, which describes a loftier course through a purer stratum—free from particulars, simple, universal."

At this time he contrasts the religion and philosophy of the Hebrews with that of the Hindus to the disadvantage of the former. The Hebrews, he asserts, represented a "wilder and ruder tribe, wanting the civility and intellectual refinements and subtlety of the Hindus." In a letter to Harrison Blake dated November 20, 1849, he quotes: "The Yogi, absorbed in contemplation, contributes in his degree to creation: he breathes a divine perfume, he hears wonderful things. Divine forms traverse him without tearing him, and, united to the nature which is proper to him, he goes, he acts as animating original matter." Upon this he comments: "To some extent, and at rare intervals, even I am a Yogi."[7] *Walden* itself has overtones from his Hindu readings, notably the parable of the Kouroo artist.

But while the literary influence of the Hindu scriptures is undeniable, whether they contributed significantly to his characteristic attitude toward nature is debatable. The source of Thoreau's enthusiasm would seem to be more simply explained. He was a thoughtful and solitary boy reared in rural Concord, with whose inmost thoughts and experiences the fields and streams, the swamps and woodlands of his native countryside were early identified. This process was certain to be stimulated by the predominance of Wordsworthian romanticism in the reading to which a bookish youth in that epoch would have surely turned. That an intimate and personal love of the good earth has existed side by side in America with callous indifference to natural beauty and its immense affirmative potential in human life is a fact abundantly testified to in Thoreau's century by authors as divergent as Cooper and Twain, as Irving and Lanier. That this love still persists can today be witnessed to by the millions of Americans brought up on farms or in small towns, almost any one of whom is certain to have numbered a Thoreau *manqué* among his boyhood acquaintances.

This insistence upon the essentially native character of Thoreau's approach to nature is confirmed, I believe, by an attentive reading of his works. Those competent in such matters inform us that the *Bhagavad-Gita* is the meeting place of the Sankhya and Yoga philosophies—that is, of the rationalization of the active and contemplative lives. Provision in the *Gita* for life in the world as well as life withdrawn from it is incontestable, but the stubborn fact remains that the emphasis in Hindu philosophy is on withdrawal—that way lies perfection. Moreover, the end of the Hindu pursuit of perfection, the objective of the withdrawal, is complete depersonalization, the absorption of the individual in the All.

Now Thoreau is one of the most individualistic of literary personalities and there is no evidence that his quasi-rejection of human fellowship and his absorption in nature had any other purpose than the sharper definition of his personality. His quarrel with society was exactly on this point. The mills of society produced only one order of grist and it was to escape that impersonal fate that Thoreau took the action he did. Consequently, it is scarcely fanciful to insist that Thoreau has far more in common with the desert saints of the early Church or with the hermits of the Middle Ages than with the Hindu sages. Like them, Thoreau went out from society to save his soul; the baring of that sensitive, gentle, acidulous, poetic soul to the wonder that is nature was for him an act of dedication and worship. His writing is the record of his soul's progress.

Thoreau's first book, *A Week on the Concord and Merrimack Rivers,* is disappointing as a revelation of his nature doctrine. In many ways it is a beautiful achievement, but there is a certain self-consciousness about it which sheathes in a formal rhetoric sometimes hopelessly ill-fitting the keen, hard observations and commentaries of the early portions of the as-yet-unpublished *Journal*. It was in the *Journal,* where he had not to concern himself with gauging the public taste in rhetoric, that Thoreau's particular attitude toward nature first found characteristic expression. Thus the entry for March 27, 1841: "I must not lose any of my freedom by being a farmer and landholder. . . . The farmer's muscles are rigid. He can do one thing long, not many well. His pace seems determined henceforth; he never quickens it. . . . When the right wind blows or a star calls, I can leave this arable and grass ground, without making a will or settling my estate." And for December 29 of the same year: "These motions everywhere in nature must surely be the circulations of God. The flowing sail, the running streams, the waving tree, the roving wind— whence else their infinite breath and freedom? I can see nothing so proper and holy as unrelaxed play and frolic in this bower God has built for us."

This sense of awe before nature, this capacity for absorption in her mystery, which is the true note of Thoreau, is not something to be associated only with his youth. In his mid-thirties he can write: "I suspect that the child plucks its first flower with an insight into its beauty and significance which the subsequent botanist never retains." The same year the hay in the barn on Baker Farm turns him back upon himself: ". . . such stacks of quiet and undisturbed thought, when there is not even a cricket to stir in the hay, but all without is wet and tumultuous, and all within is dry and quiet. Oh, what reams of thought one might have here!" A few weeks later: "Nature must be viewed humanly to be viewed at all: that is, her scenes must be associated with humane affections, such as are associated with one's native place, for instance. . . . A lover of Nature is preeminently a lover of man." Finally, in March 1853: "Man cannot afford to be a naturalist, to look at Nature directly, but only with the side of his eye. He must look through and beyond her. To look at her is fatal as to look at the head of Medusa. It turns the man of science to stone."

But all of these passages, fine as they are, are only the prelude to the synthesis which is ultimately achieved in *Walden*. We know that Thoreau drew on the journal both before and after the Walden residence for the materials that went into the book immortalizing his adventure, but it is beyond doubt that the two years of retirement at the Pond were climactic years. At this time he acquired final confidence in himself. It is easy to scoff

at Thoreau's Walden residence as a very tame business, indeed—
this withdrawal of a mere two miles from Concord to a cabin
from which he could and frequently did repair to his neighbors
or friends when the need or the inclination for human companionship struck him. Certainly, by pioneering standards the Walden
episode was neither heroic nor spectacular. It was not a feat of
physical courage or endurance.

In the realm of the spirit, however, its heroism has not, perhaps,
been sufficiently appreciated. Brook Farm was a group protest
against the materialism of the age; it was also the expression of
a confident minority voice of the age. Thoreau's protest was more
individualistic. He was, at the beginning of the Walden residence,
almost twenty-eight years old. He was a graduate of Harvard
college, where he had had an undistinguished career. Although
possessed of mechanical talent which had contributed appreciably
to the family graphite business, he had refused to submit himself
to the processes of trade and was already acquiring the reputation,
among the solid citizenry of Concord, of a ne'er-do-well. There
is abundant evidence in *Walden* and elsewhere of his sensitivity
of this score. The acerbic quality of many of his censures of the
social and economic ideas against which he was protesting can
hardly be explained in any other way.

When Thoreau went out to Walden, he went, I think, to strike
a blow in defense of the poet's right to existence and in main-
tenance of the dignity of the poetic profession. There is no doubt
that he thought of himself as a poet. In the *Journal* for April 11,
1852, there is the statement: "Every man will be a poet if he
can; otherwise a philosopher or man of science. This proves the
superiority of the poet." There are many other passages in the
Journal emphasizing the worth of poetry and the place which
this awareness held in Thoreau's thought. Moreover, the conception of the poet as priest and interpreter of nature and by that
fact lawgiver to mankind which runs with variations through the
Romantic era, finding its boldest expression in men so different
as Wordsworth and Shelley, was the staple of Thoreau's thoughts.
He went out to Walden Pond because with the immense ferment
in his mind he could not do otherwise. "The mass of men," he was
to say, in one of his most brilliant apothegms, "lead lives of quiet
desperation."[8]

But so did Thoreau, in a quiet different sense. His whole
life, however idle it may have appeared to the more superficially
prudent of his fellow citizens, was a struggle to get done the job

he had to do. "I have thought that Walden Pond would be a good place for business,"[9] he writes in a long mockingly ironic passage, and the "business" he there transacted was the poet's desperate business of getting to know his own thoughts. From this point of view, a passage occurring early in the chapter on "Sounds" is highly revealing:

> There were times when I could not afford to sacrifice the bloom of the present moment to any work, whether of the head or hands. I love a broad margin to my life. Sometimes, in a summer morning, having taken my accustomed bath, I sat in my sunny doorway from sunrise till noon, rapt in a revery, amidst the pines and hickories and sumachs, in undisturbed solitude and stillness, while the birds sang around or flitted noiseless through the house, until by the sun falling in at my west window, or the noise of some traveller's wagon on the distant highway, I was reminded of the lapse of time. I grew in those seasons like corn in the night, and they were far better than any work of the hands would have been.[10]

Nature, then, was for Thoreau the means whereby he might discover what manner of man he was. But it was also the key to the true reality outside himself. "I perceive that we inhabitants of New England live this mean life that we do because our vision does not penetrate the surface of things. We think that *is* which *appears* to be." He adjures his fellows to

> ... settle [themselves] and work and wedge [their] feet downward through the mud and slush of opinion, and prejudice, and tradition, and delusion, and appearance, that alluvion which covers the globe, through Paris and London, through New York and Boston and Concord, through Church and State, through poetry and philosophy and religion, till [they] come to a hard bottom and rocks in place, which we can call *reality*. ...[11]

The search for literary origins usually leads into dangerous terrain and in the case of Thoreau, after the general impact of Emerson, and Coleridge and German idealism and the Vedas, and of course Plato and Homer is acknowledged, one comes back to the conviction that here is no man of parts, now echoing this idea, now that, but, on the contrary, a confident and poised individual who has dominated his borrowings and subdued them to himself.

Whatever he sees in nature is assayed by the same test. Therien, the woodchopper with his unspoiled joy in existence, the night-hawk circling in the sunny afternoon, the sedge bending under the weight of the reed-birds, the shifting coloration of the ice of the pond—these he sees, not with the eye of the anthropologist or the biologist or the physicist, but with the eye of the poetic imagination. With all the closeness of his objective examination, the reality which he seeks is the reality which the poets call beauty. In the opening of the chapter, "Where I Lived, and What I Lived For," he plays with the idea of property ownership: "I have . . . surveyed the country on every side within a dozen miles of where I live. In imagination I have bought all the farms in succession, for all were to be bought, and I knew their price."[12] But the satisfaction which he seeks is not assured by title deed duly registered with the proper local authority. The deed to such satisfaction must be registered in a far higher court:

> I have frequently seen a poet withdraw, having enjoyed the most valuable part of a farm, while the crusty farmer supposed that he got a few wild apples only. Why, the owner does not know it for many years when a poet has put his farm in rhyme, the most admirable kind of invisible fence, has fairly impounded it, milked it, skimmed it, and got all the cream, and left the farmer only the skimmed milk.[13]

Initial difficulties, more imaginary than real, beset the acceptation of Thoreau as a social thinker. Many of his countrymen will certainly feel there is something quixotic about a man who will go to jail rather than pay a poll tax but who will accept his freedom when the tax is paid for him. This seems uncomfortably close to betrayal of principle. Many, too, will almost certainly feel that the Walden retirement as an economic gesture has its comic aspects. The individualist who would declare himself free from industrial enslavement builds his freehold with a borrowed axe. Yet it must not be forgotten that another unworldly man, the great Mahatma Gandhi, who, despite his supposed impracticality, exercised a profound influence on the destinies of four hundred million human beings, found inspiration in Thoreau for his most effective political and economic ideas.

It would be difficult, of course, to defend the consistency of Thoreau's social protests in the minutest details but in their essentials they leave little to be desired. He was certainly not without profound social consciousness. He refused to pay a poll tax because he thought the commonwealth of Massachusetts was at best inconsistent, if not hypocritical, in its attitude toward slavery. He took part in the activities of the underground railway. He defended John Brown before the halo of martyrdom had been fixed upon him. He warmed Johnny Riordan with his practical charity. But, generally, he was suspicious of the efficacy of the state in its official capacity or of organized groups within the state to alleviate the lot of the individual. "I came into this world, not chiefly to make this a good place to live in, but to live in it, be it good or bad."[14] Taken in isolation, this sentence has a cold and contemptuous ring, but tempered by the profound pathos of his observations on Johnny Riordan and his earnest compassion for John Field and his underprivileged brood, it deserves another reading. As he himself says, "a man has not everything to do," and such being the case a man must do what seems most immediate to him. The most immediate task for Thoreau was the ascertainment of self. "I went to the woods because I wished to live deliberately, to front only the essential facts of life, and see if I could not learn what it had to teach, and not, when I come to die, discover that I had not lived."[15]

It is of the utmost importance to remember that Thoreau did not advocate that everyone follow his example. Every man must confront his own particular Walden Pond, must accept its challenge or suffer the consequences of his refusal. If Thoreau thought his Walden was worth writing a book about, this was true primarily because he was born with that book in his vitals and the prevenient pangs of parturition made themselves felt very early in his life. In this case, as is true of many great books, the book which demanded writing had a prophetic message.

To us, born into the immense complexity of the twentieth century, the life of Concord a hundred years ago must seem bucolic by comparison. It is the prerogative of genius to sense beneath the incipiencies of civilization the implications of their fruition. It is the glory of Thoreau that in his "Civil Disobedience," in *Walden,* and in "Life Without Principle" he had a burning awareness of the potential threat to the human person which lay hidden in certain political and economic developments of his day. Perhaps the most eloquent statement of his economic protest occurs in the opening pages of the first chapter of *Walden*:

> I see young men, my townsmen, whose misfortune it is to have inherited farms, houses, barns, cattle, and farming tools; for these are more easily acquired than got rid of. Better if they had been born in the open pasture and suckled by a wolf, that they might have seen with clearer eyes what field they were called to labor in. Who made them serfs of the soil? Why should they eat their sixty acres, when man is condemned to eat only his peck of dirt?

Why should they begin digging their graves as soon as they are born? They have got to live a man's life, pushing all these things before them, and get on as well as they can. How many a poor immortal soul have I met well-nigh crushed and smothered under its load, creeping down the road of life, pushing before it a barn seventy-five feet by forty, its Augean stables never cleansed, and one hundred acres of land, tillage, mowing, pasture, and wood-lot. The portionless, who struggle with no such unnecessary inherited encumbrances, find it labor enough to subdue and cultivate a few cubic feet of flesh.[16]

Alongside this should be set two passages from "Life Without Principle":

If I should sell both my forenoons and afternoons to society, as most appear to do, I am sure that for me there would be nothing left worth living for. I trust that I shall never thus sell my birthright for a mess of pottage. I wish to suggest that a man may be very industrious, and yet not spend his time well. There is no more fatal blunderer than he who consumes the greater part of his life getting his living. The poet, for instance, must sustain his body by his poetry, as a steam planing-mill feeds its boilers with the shavings it makes. You must get your living by loving.[17]

It is remarkable that there are few men so well employed, so much to their minds, but that a little money or fame would commonly buy them off from their present pursuit. I see advertisements for *active* young men, as if activity were the whole of a young man's capital. Yet I have been surprised when one has with confidence proposed to me, a grown man, to embark in some enterprise of his, as if I had absolutely nothing to do, my life having been a complete failure hitherto. What a doubtful compliment this to pay me! As if he had met me half-way across the ocean beating up against the wind, but bound nowhere, and proposed to me to go along with him! If I did, what do you think the underwriters would say? No, no! I am not without employment at this stage of the voyage. To tell the truth, I saw an advertisement for able-bodied seamen, when I was a boy, sauntering in my native port, and as soon as I came of age I embarked.[18]

These passages are sufficient to confirm the significance of the social and economic gospel Thoreau was so eminently fitted to announce. He was by nature an ascetic. He had, as few men have ever had, the Franciscan awareness of the joys of material poverty and of their relation to the riches of the spirit. The purity of his doctrine of detachment came easily to him because he was by instinct solitary. His authenticated attraction for two women

establishes his physical normality, but it is difficult to imagine
Thoreau as husband and father under any circumstances. Consequently, as a secular Assisian he spoke to a disbelieving age of
the vanity of its pursuits.

The greatness of American civilization was manifesting itself
freely in Thoreau's generation. The immense energy which was
to subdue a continent and exploit its resources with fearful un-
wisdom was approaching full tide. The accelerated accumulation
of gross wealth and crass political power was evident on all sides.
At such a moment, the finer spirits would necessarily be tempted to
retreat and the Transcendental movement, in its main lines, is
perhaps best interpreted as a retreat from the hectic, brawling
contemporary scene by minds unable to cope with its rude vigor.

It was not in Thoreau's nature to give ground other than temporarily, to recruit his powers. The soundness of his position lay
in his insistence that man can remain in the world without sub-
mitting to it. Before the bright young men in the advertising
agencies had assumed the direction of our national energies and
the supervision of our culture, he knew that careful evaluation of
needs, not the endless multiplication of desires, is the only avenue
to sanity of mind and health of body. The Sunday supplements
now point with alarm to the feverish pursuit of dollars which
ends in coronary thrombosis at forty. By these warnings Thoreau
would not have been impressed. To live safely that a heart muscle
might be induced to function for eighty rather than forty years
would have seemed futile to him. To live wisely, that is, to be the
master, not the servant, of possessions, was his objective. Likewise,
in the mid-twentieth century Thoreau would be as little attracted
by the statist, of whatever persuasion, as by the rugged individualist. It would be dangerous to attempt to determine what his
attitude toward any particular piece of contemporary economic or
social legislation would be, for he was an intelligent man whose
preconvictions would not have been inflexibly maintained in the
face of changed conditions. But he was suspicious of reformers
because he believed reform was something that had to be worked
out by the individual from within rather than by his neighbors
from without. He might have brought himself to see the necessity
of the projection of government into the lives of men in the
modern manner, but he would have wholeheartedly deplored the
conditions which necessitated that projection.

The problem of Thoreau's religion does not admit of easy solution. He early "signed off" from the Christianity of his youth. He

did not go to church. At times he writes with what seems calculated irreverence: "There is no science in men's religion; it does
not teach me so much as the report of the committee on swine."
More frequently, he declares himself free from identification with
any sect or even religion, as, for example, in the undated *Journal*
entry for 1850:

> I do not prefer one religion or philosophy to another. I have no
> sympathy with the bigotry and ignorance which make transient
> and partial and puerile distinctions between one man's faith or
> form of faith and another's—as Christian and heathen. I pray to
> be delivered from narrowness, partiality, exaggeration, bigotry.
> To the philosopher all sects, all nations, are alike. I like Brahma,
> Hari, Buddha, the Great Spirit, as well as God.

Yet what even so honest a man as Thoreau writes about his
religious convictions can be meaningful only when considered
against the background of his times. Doctrinal Protestantism
under the impact of the Enlightenment was disintegrating in
Thoreau's youth. Recollection of the rigid controls of the New
England Puritan theocracy tended to exaggerated reaction, particularly among intellectuals. The example of Emerson, who too
had "signed off" from formal affiliation was doubtless a significant
personal factor. But more important was the general intellectual
climate of New England, heavily charged in the early nineteenth
century with Hegelianism. The inevitable result of the impact of
German idealistic philosophy was to further dilute the already
far-from-concentrated content of the current theology.

Against such a background, Thoreau's negations, far from
revealing an unsympathetic attitude, are better considered as a
clearing of ground for his statement of affirmatives. No careful
reader will doubt that he was a reverent man. More often than
not, his reverence will be associated with nature as when he writes
in the *Journal* for 1851: "My profession is to be always on the
alert to find God in nature, to know his lurking-places. . . ." This
reverence is more than pantheism. Pantheism could not, although
Plato might, inspire him to write: "Our whole life is startlingly
moral. There is never an instant's truce between virtue and vice."[19]
Moreover, in the magnificent passages on chastity in the same
chapter on "Higher Laws" in *Walden* there is a wisdom higher
than Greek. "The generative energy, which, when we are loose,
dissipates and makes us unclean, when we are continent invigo-
rates and inspires us. Chastity is the flowering of man; and what

are called Genius, Heroism, Holiness, and the like, are but various fruits which succeed it. Man flows at once to God when the channel of purity is open."[20] It would be reckless to claim these lines as specifically Christian, especially since in the context Thoreau seems to suggest Vedantic sources. Still a man's heritage is unescapable and the texture of Christianity was woven closely into Thoreau's conception of life. Mystic he was not in any exact sense, although he has been loosely called such—certainly not according to Maritain's definition of mysticism as the "experiential knowledge of divine things obtained by the gift of Wisdom." No more was he a mystic in the Hindu acceptation. To say this is not to be deprecatory. Of the multitudes who have served God and man with saintly zeal, comparatively few have belonged to the mystic brotherhood.

Thoreau's vocation was of a different order. At a time when Yankee ingenuity was subduing the earth, and the gospel of success was proclaimed from every street corner and town hall, he came to preach an older and more abstemious doctrine. Intuitively, he seems to have experienced the conviction that behind the Puritan virtues of thrift and industry and provident concern with material things lay the rather more than half-neglected truths which gave these things meaning—truths which Puritanism itself, in its best moments, remembered. In an age which was rapidly reducing all values to one value and all standards to one standard, and these not of the highest, he set himself in the name of humanity against the tide. *Walden,* which describes his relationship with his epoch is, ultimately, a humanist manifesto, the most pregnant that American humanism has produced. Man is Thoreau's primary concern, not God. However, he was still near enough to the Christianity which he outwardly rejected to be quite certain that man without the Spirit is not man. He would have man cease from the unrelenting pursuit of possessions to consider his true self, confident that though the thin current of Time, the river in which he goes afishing, slides away, it will have mirrored the God who "will never be more divine in the lapse of all the ages."

As a protest against the crassness of the *Zeitgeist,* then, *Walden* deserves its remembrance. But it has earned remembrance of a more positive sort. To do small tasks greatly is a high calling. Of this truth Thoreau, in his own way, was quite as convinced as was St. Thérèse of Lisieux; his testimony to the significance of the "little way" is not unworthy of a place beside hers. *Walden* bears unswerving witness to the dignity of human life, which can never

be essentially trivial since it is near neighbor to the infinite. In
his reverence for simple things Thoreau's sanity touches the hem
of sanctity.

Thoreau, the thinker, it should be evident, is not to be dismissed lightly. To the most pertinent facets of human existence
he had committed long hours of lonely meditation. Because his
mind was acute and perceptive, the fruit of those meditations still
retains its pungent flavor. His view of human destiny was not,
however, all-embracing. He was not a system maker. His intuitions
were often very sharp and very sure but his illuminations were
intermittent rather than steadily maintained. For that reason it
seemed reasonable to insist at the beginning of this essay that
unless violence were to be done him he must be evaluated primarily as a creative artist, rather than as a thinker. The difference
is one of emphasis. In philosophy, economics, history, we are
concerned with the ideas expressed as such. The medium of
expression is of secondary importance. Where the thinker is also
a great master of expression, a Plato or an Augustine, we are
confronted with a more complex problem of evaluation. But with
the artist it is always the impress of the personality that is primary. Obviously, that stamp cannot be fixed in nothingness nor
can it be permanently fixed in wax. The quality of the artist's
thought must be of such consistency as to take firmly and finally
the seal of his art. From this point of view, no reasonable critic
can complain of the texture of Thoreau's thought.

The art of Thoreau must stand or fall on the merits of *Walden*.
A Week on the Concord and Merrimack Rivers is too huddled;
in Canby's words it ". . . became perilously like a library of the
shorter works of Henry Thoreau."[21] It is on occasion overwritten.
It is, to a degree, immature. *The Maine Woods* and *A Yankee in
Canada* are travel books, hurried and sometimes imperceptive.
"Civil Disobedience," "Life Without Principle," and "Cape Cod"
are essays in which there is much brilliance of execution, but the
best things in them were done better in *Walden*. The organic character of the organization of *Walden* has been argued by F. O.
Matthiessen.[22] With that demonstration of unity, achieved in
part through the presentation of the personal history of the writer
and in part by the chronology of the seasons, it would be difficult
to quarrel. But after admitting that here is the mold which
Thoreau deliberately imposed on his material, one may still ask
whether or not the inchoate materials set to the mold. And even if
the answer is a negation does this argue Thoreau's failure? I should
say not. For to demand of *Walden* the type of unity which is

required of a five-act play, or even of a three-volume novel, is
to ask of it something which it does not pretend to give.

Walden belongs with a literary genre which was naturalized
in England in the seventeenth century. It descends ultimately
from Seneca, its first eminent English practitioner was Francis
Bacon. But its masters were Sir Thomas Browne and Robert
Burton and, to a lesser extent, Thomas Fuller and Izaak Walton
and Abraham Cowley. Historians have called the seventeenth
century the century of "baroque" culture. Since Wölfflin gave it
currency as a term of art criticism, the word "baroque" has acquired meanings so multitudinous that, like the terms "romantic"
and "classic," it has become almost meaningless.[23] One interpretation, however, of baroque culture seems to remain constant. It is
a product of an age in which the accustomed verities have been
shaken, in which men dissatisfied with or unsure of immediate
tradition feel themselves compelled to an aggressive confrontation
of life. A baroque age may be a period of intense internal exploitation.

The seventeenth century was such an age. Its central intellectual
feature was the conflict of the ancient otherworldliness of the
Christian past with the secular this-worldliness of the new learning. This did not involve a conflict of science and faith in the
vulgar nineteenth-century sense. But it did pose for thinking
minds the problem of first allegiances. This brought a turning in
of men upon themselves, a vivid and frequently agonizing self-
examination whose history is written in Bacon's essays, in the
Religio Medici, and in the *Anatomy of Melancholy*. The voice of
that new self-consciousness was the voice of Senecan prose with
its off-beat rhythms, its concentrated brilliance, its unitary self-
sufficiency.

It was to the seventeenth century that Thoreau turned for a
literary master. The accents deeply imitative of Browne are evident in this early passage from the *Journal*:

> I am freer than any planet; no complaint reaches round the world.
> I can move away from public opinion, from government, from
> religion, from education, from society. Shall I be reckoned a
> ratable poll in the county of Middlesex, or be rated at one spear
> under the palm trees of Guinea? Shall I raise corn and potatoes
> in Massachusetts or figs and olives in Asia Minor? sit out the day
> in my office in State Street, or ride it out on the steppes of Tartary?
> For my Brobdingnag I may sail to Patagonia: for my Lilliput to
> Lapland.

This is apprentice work, gifted apprentice work, to be sure, but as yet without the personal impress. It took years before the imitation of Browne could be translated into a personal style in which the highly stressed but eccentric rhythms fit themselves with perfect coincidence to the twists and turns of the thought. The following later passage from the *Journal*, which could be duplicated indefinitely, indicates the final mastery of the Browne manner:

> As the wood of an old Cremona, its very fibre, perchance, harmoniously transposed and educated to resound melody, has brought a great price, so methinks these telegraph-posts should bear a great price with musical instrument makers. It is prepared to be the material of harps for ages to come, as it were put asoak in and seasoning in music.

The bizarre metaphor with its metaphysical yoking of disparates, the punning intimacy of language, illustrated by the radical meaning assigned to "resound," the half-poetic, half-commonplace effect of "put asoak in," the tantalizing misdirection of rhythmic expectation, beautifully handled in the first sentence of the passage, where two anapests and an amphimacer of the opening phrase seem to be building into a formal oratorical period, but which, by an abrupt reversal, lead instead into deliberately prosaic accents designed to suggest the mind thinking aloud—these are the typical notes of the "Attic" or Senecan prose as Browne handled it. Thoreau's mastery of it is unmistakable.

The intricacies of a great prose manner mastered, one thing alone was necessary to transmute the manner into a style. That was the self-assurance derived from a significant subject. I have insisted that Thoreau went out to Walden Pond to write a book, a book in which his whole life culminated. I am not moved by those who lament the unwritten books never quarried out of the voluminous *Journals*. I doubt that Keats, given another twenty-five years, could have written another "Ode to a Nightingale." Certainly I see nothing in the *Journals* that promises another *Walden*. But one was quite enough. Although a much lesser book, it is quite as expressive of the genius of its author as are the *Divina Commedia* and *Paradise Lost*. Actually, was not Thoreau's theme their theme? Was he not asking the same questions—What is life's meaning? How is salvation possible? How can Paradise be regained? These are the queries that perennially disturb man's smugness, and no book which answers them, as *Walden* does, honestly and eloquently, can lack conviction.

In the manner of the great baroque masters, *Walden* is, despite Matthiessen, rambling and discursive. Like the *Religio Medici* and the *Anatomy*, it is an essay, or better, a volume of essays, and its essential unity comes from the mind of the author. That mind is sometimes curt, impatient, contemptuous, but never cynical. It is more often than not generous and compassionate. Always it is alert, receptive, witty, thoughtfully intense. These are the qualities which, when joined with an adequate style, mark the great essayist. It is unfair to Thoreau to quote from *Walden*, though few books are more quotable: "I have travelled a good deal in Concord . . . ; the cost of a thing is the amount of what I will call life which is required to be exchanged for it . . . ; I have never yet met a man who was quite awake. How could I have looked him in the face? . . . It is not worth the while to go round the world to count the cats in Zanzibar." It is unfair because, with any essayist, the test is not the bravura passage but the steady revelation of the man in an art which rises and falls with his spiritual pulse-beat. By such a test Thoreau belongs with the immortals.

HERMAN MELVILLE
1819-1891

Loyalty to the Heart

GEOFFREY STONE

IN THE summer of 1850, when he had begun work on *Moby-Dick*
(though presumably in a first version) and was approaching the
height of his creative powers, Herman Melville wrote an essay in
appreciation of Nathaniel Hawthorne. Hawthorne had just published one of the best of American novels, *The Scarlet Letter,* but
Melville's discursive encomium had the *Mosses from an Old Manse*
of 1846 for its occasion—perhaps for no better reason than that
an aunt then staying with her nephew and his new family in Pitts-
field had given Herman a copy of the earlier book. Nathaniel was
much pleased with "Hawthorne and His Mosses," though he was in
fact less the subject of the essay than he himself or anyone else
could have understood at the time. Knowing what its author's
next book was to be, we can see that the piece celebrates a literary
type better represented by Melville than by Hawthorne—whom
Melville some twenty-five years later would more accurately
describe as "one at home in death."

What so fixed and fascinated him in Hawthorne, said Melville,
was the dark side of the New Englander's soul, "shrouded in a
blackness ten times black." And "this great power of blackness
in him," Melville explained, "derives its force from its appeal
to that Calvinistic sense of Innate Depravity and Original Sin,
from whose visitations, in some shape or other, no deeply thinking
mind is always and wholly free." Again, when Melville goes on to
speak of Shakespeare, in whose company he places Hawthorne,
we are better equipped than the reader of 1850 to understand that
he may be thinking of himself as also in that company:

> Through the mouths of the dark characters of Hamlet, Timon,
> Lear, and Iago, he craftily says, or sometimes insinuates the things

which we feel to be so terrifically true, that it were all but madness
for any good man, in his own proper character, to utter, or even
hint of them. Tormented into desperation, Lear, the frantic king,
tears off the mask, and speaks the same madness of vital truth.
. . . In Shakespeare's tomb lies infinitely more than Shakespeare
ever wrote.[1]

Here Melville, the critic of Shakespeare, makes the same assumption that later critics of Melville have made. Since the appearance of Raymond Weaver's biography in the early twenties,[2]
Melville has time and again been exhumed, almost always with the
excuse that only by knowing what the man hid can we learn what
the books reveal. That, of course, is a tacit admission of the books'
failure. A story or a poem ought to render up its own meaning.
While a creative work is always derived from the author's personality, since his subject matter is limited to what takes place in
that personality as a result of the world's impingement on it, if
we must revert to the personality to find what is actually in the
work, there is a manifest failure of "creation": our object of attention becomes the man rather than the book, though the book
has made the first claim on our attention.

But to seek the completely self-subsistent book is to follow a
counsel of perfection. When we have such works, or the appearance
of them, generally we know nothing of the author, as with Homer,
or very little of him, as with Shakespeare. We can, nevertheless,
avoid turning with undisciplined curiosity from the work to the
man. Without falling into the error from which the New Criticism
sometimes suffers—which is to write as though there were only
poems, never poets—we can still keep our eyes on the text with a
fair steadiness and not assume there must always be a difference
between its apparent and evident intent, given only to the scholarly reader of laundry lists or the psychoanalytic expert in dirty
linen. Modesty before our betters' efforts to speak their minds en-
joins us to call in adventitious aids to interpretation only when
there is a plain enough failure in communication.

There are some failures of communication in Melville, but they
are fewer than would appear from the writings of his more recon-
dite commentators. Certain things in him will seem deeply obscure
unless we understand the ambience of ideas in which his mind
worked, but this obscurity is rather the shortcoming of our ignorance than any failure of Melville's. Certain things, too, we can
see more clearly articulated in his works than he himself can have
seen them because we stand at a remove, in time and involvement,

that gives us without much effort of our own the disinterested eye
for seeing how these things hang together. As Hawthorne, according to what Melville told Sophia Hawthorne, saw allegorical
significances in *Moby-Dick* that had at first escaped its author,
so can we discover extensions of the book's meaning. Most books
that endure do so by a process of growth; new areas of experience
accrete to them with each generation of readers. A good book is
not a transcript of reality but reality made more easily available
to us through the author's God-given imagination, and in time
the book comes to us with the added wealth of reality it has uncovered for its other readers through the years.

The sources of the ideal figure that Melville saw particularized
in Shakespeare and Hawthorne readily suggest themselves. We
know them with greater certainty because of the efforts of a recent
generation of Ph.D.'s, who have painstakingly uncovered most of
what Melville may have read or even heard, but a little knowledge
of the age and some literary intuition will also indicate these
sources. The figure of Melville's essay is interchangeable with the
figure he was shortly to create, Ahab, and derives from Calvinism,
from Elizabethan and seventeenth-century literature and the Platonic notions that were common in it, and from the idea of the
hero as he was conceived in the Romantic revolt. None of these
sources was peculiarly American, but the especial combination of
them that Melville drew on was something characteristic of the
first half of the American nineteenth century, so that Melville is
very much an American and a product of the Protestant mentality
that has done so much to form the American character.

The Calvinism of the earlier Melvilles in America had in Herman's father thinned out into Unitarianism, but the general disposition of mind that attaches to a creed will often outlive that
creed's particular dogmas. Though Alan Melville postulated a
one-personed God, we may suppose that in his unformulated beliefs, in his unreflecting day-to-day responses, there was a touch
of the exaggerated dualism so frequent in the thought of those
who have been touched by Calvinism. This almost Manichaean
picture of the nature of the world has an extraordinary vitality,
as we can see by its persistence in minds as different as those of
John Quincy Adams, Mark Twain, and John Jay Chapman—the
one despairing of salvation, the other contriving a myth he did
not dare to publish in which the world was shown to be pure evil
because it was pure nothing, and the last thrusting into a fire the
hand that had offended him. Melville's father died when the boy

was twelve, and shortly thereafter his mother joined a Dutch Reformed church of the most orthodox confession, so that such of Herman's adolescence as was passed at home must have put him under the influence of a strict Calvinism.

The signs are that Melville early gave up profession to any formal religion, for his first two books, to the small extent that they touched on the matter, suggested adherence to a sort of natural religion in which the Golden Rule could take care of all human problems. Indeed, *Typee* and *Omoo* were attacked by missionary societies as the works of a pagan, and that in a sense they may have been: of the youthful pagan for whom there are not yet any big questions since his animal faith assures him life is worth living. Yet orthodoxy, as something he did not quite subscribe to, always had for him a Calvinist complexion. In *White-Jacket,* his fifth book and the one preceding *Moby-Dick,* he made explicit a fairly conventional religious position—in an effort, it may have been, to win himself back from the despairing estimate of the human condition he had already shown in *Mardi.* Toward the end of the book he announced that "our final haven was predestinated ere we slipped from the stocks at Creation," as though he sought what cold comfort—the thought that what must be, must be—the doctrine of predestination held. (He did, being the man he was, make this very abdication of the will into an example of the Romantic exaltation of it, saying in the cadences of Sir Thomas Browne: "Each mortal casts his vote for whom he will to rule the world; I have a voice that helps to shape eternity; and my volitions stir the orbits of the furthest suns. . . . Ourselves are Fate.") In *Billy Budd,* written in the last year of his life, he called the idea of man's natural goodness "a heretic thought," and original sin, as we have seen, he associated with innate (or total) depravity.

The polar notions of natural goodness and total depravity recur frequently in Melville's writing, embodied in characters who are either wholly uncorrupted or wholly corrupted. In *Typee* he included some reflections on the noble savage, whom he had found, with a slight taint of cannibalism, in Polynesia, and on the soiling influences of civilization, but the full eighteenth-century doctrine of the natural goodness of man, with all its corollary notions about society, education, and religion, he never entertained. Those of his characters who are naturally good rather appear as "sports"; they are rare human specimens and in point of numbers they are probably inferior to the totally depraved in his work.

This proportion agrees with the usual Calvinist estimate of the numbers of the elect and the damned, and it seems not altogether farfetched to suggest that the Calvinist sorting of the sheep from the goats in the real world lay behind Melville's similar attempt in fiction. But he makes no easy moral judgment on his evil characters—Jackson in *Redburn,* Bland in *White-Jacket,* Babo in "Benito Cereno," Claggart in *Billy Budd.* They do wicked deeds because wicked deeds seem "the legitimate operation of [their] whole infernal organization." No more does he reward his good characters with worldly prosperity. From Yillah, the dream girl of *Mardi,* to Billy, they all come to temporal disaster. If one thinks of evil as a positive force—which it must be when there are persons who produce it by the inevitable operation of their natures—then it stands a fair chance of triumph in a world of which it is a constituent part.

The opposition of light and darkness in Melville's work is not so stark and simple as this might seem to indicate. However crude a dichotomy his metaphysical assumptions might tend toward, at his best he was too sensitive a writer to deny in experience what did not accord with them. The chief character he created, Captain Ahab, though his name is that of the apostate king of Israel who worshipped Baal, is no monolithic personification of the evil of overweening pride. "Ahab has his humanities," lacking which his pursuit of the white whale would be less humanly significant and, in fact, would be merely "the hideous and inhuman allegory" Melville once denied it was. Coleridge somewhere calls allegory the translation of abstract notions into picture language, and *Moby-Dick,* whose allegorical quality Melville on another occasion admitted, reveals one of its aspects when looked at under this definition. Ahab himself gives us a very clear statement of what has been translated into what when he says:

All visible objects, man, are but as pasteboard masks. But in each event—in the living act, the undoubted deed—there, some unknown but still reasoning thing puts forth the moulding of its features from behind the unreasoning mask. If man will strike, strike though the mask! How can the prisoner reach outside except by thrusting through the wall? To me, the white whale is that wall, shoved near to me. Sometimes I think there's naught beyond. But 'tis enough. He tasks me; he heaps me; I see in him outrageous strength, with an inscrutable malice sinewing it. That inscrutable thing is chiefly what I hate; and be the white whale agent, or be the white whale principal, I will wreak that hate upon him.[3]

Any of their creators who had had the talent might have put this speech into the mouths of the heaven-defying Renaissance and Romantic heroes, and the view of things it propounds—the notion that nature imperfectly bodies forth superior realities—is a species of untranquil Platonism. To mention Platonism is not to imply that a systematic philosophy can be found in *Moby-Dick*; it is rather to say that the Platonic atmosphere is one congenial to the symbol-making and myth-creating task Melville undertakes in the book. The Platonic turn of mind finds in each material fact the portent of some spiritual reality. Plato notoriously condemned poets because they do not deal in facts, but poets know that their fictions will be accepted so long as they seem statements of fact symbolizing some wider truth. In a sense, all makers of fiction, poetic or prose, are Platonists.

While a symbol in its simplest meaning is something that stands for or represents something else and, like allegory, is a picture of something abstract, the contemplation of the symbol, as formulators of religious disciplines have long known, can reveal much actually dwelling only in the thing symbolized. Melville's success in the handling of symbols derives from the tangibility and substance he gives them. Because they are present to our sense and observation, though vicariously, of course, they give us the opportunity fully to explore their implications. This "realism" is also necessary to the general disposition of mind Melville is attempting to convey. His is an apprehension of "the instinct of the knowledge of the demonism in the world." Ontologically this instinct may be false, but it is certainly a fact of experience for those who set matter and spirit in fundamental opposition. Curiously enough, the believer in such an opposition is obsessed with a feeling of the ponderousness of *things*: the very solidity of creation oppresses him because he believes it is by an evil accident that he has been immured in the all-too-substantial flesh.

Here also, it seems to me, is the reason why everything in *Moby-Dick* is on a scale rather larger than life. The huge in art is recurrent, and it can be argued that it is an attempted compensation for man's physical puniness in contrast with much of nature; but Melville's evocation of the huge was not alone an assertion of the creative powers of the creature. While there is a quality of defiance in the gigantism of *Moby-Dick*, that gigantism is further there to represent the ambiguity Melville is concerned to depict. On one side stands the "queenly personality" asserted by Romanticism, man, as he put it in a letter to Hawthorne, declaring "himself a sovereign nature (in himself) amid the powers of heaven, hell, and earth," and on the other side stands the simple immensity of the material world that, as though with a malign intelligence of its own, at every turn thwarts the sovereign personality.

It was a vision encouraged by nineteenth-century science's extension of the frontiers of the physical world. Though through science the century progressively dominated nature, men of the time were in turn dominated by nature's very quantity and, as to their knowledge nature's extent increased, they grew more and more to feel that its intention could not be benevolent. Nature's impersonality, its sheer bulk having removed it from any consideration in human terms, made them lose faith in their own personal uniqueness, and with this went their religious faith. Faith partly went through loss of belief in the literal truth of Genesis; but an eighteenth-century heritage of Deist optimism was also destroyed, and nature, seen as indifferently following its own laws, could no longer be made to accord with an idea of inevitable progress that made man the heir of all the ages.

Melville would eventually, in *Clarel,* write a long poem about men who had lost their faith. How close he himself came to the classic type of nineteenth-century atheism (it still endures, of course) is hard to say. My own guess is that for a long time his thinking oddly gave credence to a God in whom he could place no trust—"oddly" not because such thinking is rare but because, as Melville saw, it implies that "man's insanity is heaven's sense." His preoccupation with this ambiguity had once, before he came to the writing of *Moby-Dick,* seriously hampered his creative powers (in *Mardi*) and it would in time very nearly extinguish them (in *The Confidence-Man*), but in the two examples cited he seems to have been involved in a personal way that his command of symbol allowed him to escape in his one great book.

In the five books written before *Moby-Dick,* Melville's use of symbol is not constant, and if we allow that he had been brought up in an atmosphere of Protestant thinking that the material world existed only to reveal the immaterial eternal verities, we may also allow that his use of symbol was not always conscious. Symbolic significances can be seen, gifted as we all are now with a Freudian hindsight, in the captivity in the valley and the injured leg of *Typee,* but to Melville's overt intention they can have been no more than devices for his story—or perhaps he did have a bad leg. *Omoo* is a fairly literal account of his adventures in

Tahiti and devoid of symbolism. *Mardi* starts out to be a novel of adventure in the contemporary realistic convention but soon falls away into weak and confused allegory, in the end drawing the admission from its author, "I've chartless voyaged." There are incidences of symbolism in both *Redburn* and *White-Jacket* —Redburn's long hunting coat and the canvas reefer of the narrator of *White-Jacket* are identical devices—but both books offer themselves as straightforward pieces of autobiography, though the latter book is subtitled *The World in a Man-of-War,* thus implying a symbolic parallel.

That sort of parallel, however, is more strenuously and obviously pursued in *Mardi.* Like *Moby-Dick,* the book is an attempt to represent the human condition in the terms of a sea voyage. If it fails where *Moby-Dick* succeeds, it is not so much because of the confusion of thought it displays (its discrete parts make consistent enough arguments) as because of the baldness of its allegory and the lack of detachment mentioned before. To take the second fault first: Ishmael, the narrator of the better book, tells us little if any more if we identify him with Melville, while Taji, the narrator of *Mardi,* leaves his own motives so obscure that we must search for them in Melville's. A partial explanation for this can be found in the fact that Taji is both narrator and protagonist of *Mardi,* so is in no position to comment on his own motives, while Ahab is the protagonist of *Moby-Dick,* leaving Ishmael free to explain him; but the very choice of either means of telling the story appears to indicate the degree of personal involvement in the respective instances.[4]

The sensuous thinness of *Mardi* makes it, as a novel, unconvincing. There seems nothing inevitable about the symbols and figures of allegory used, so that one has the impression that Melville came to certain general conclusions, then looked around for figures of a picture-language in which they might be represented. True enough, from *Gulliver's Travels* to *Animal Farm* there have been successful stories of entirely didactic intent, in which the lesson to be taught has plainly been arrived at before the fiction that embodies it, but the fiction itself always carries conviction and its people (even when they are speaking horses or pigs) seem to indicate the lesson as much as the lesson indicates them. The story can even be so much a *Ding an sich* that the superficial reader can quite ignore the lesson. Swift has found his way into the nursery and Orwell into the films, where they chill no spines, and Melville, who thought that *Typee* might be given to babies with "their gingerbread," has had *Moby-Dick* presented as an adventure story for boys.

Mardi is Melville's first book of avowed fiction and the first to show any large literary ambitions. The two books following, like the two preceding, are drawn from personal experience (though we can now document autobiographical inaccuracies which the contemporary reader only suspected) and are modest in the achievement they aim at. Melville, it might be said, did not begin writing in a "literary" way. His first two publications as a writer of travel stories brought him the friendship of Evert Duyckinck, a New York editor of considerable culture, and access to Duyckinck's library, in which he began to make up for what reading he had missed in his brief formal education and his years at sea. The result upon him of that reading was *Mardi,* where he essayed, without yet having the abilities, the sagelike role we have seen announced in the essay on Hawthorne. The requisite abilities were to be developed, though not fully achieved, in *Redburn* and *White-Jacket.* The subject matter of these books—which to Melville may well have seemed closer to his own experience than scholars now deem it—did not allow the too-easy fancy of *Mardi* and in making the demand on him that he be credible taught him the art of bringing out the "certain significance [that] lurks in all things." It is not a question of Melville's having deepened in wisdom when he came to write *Moby-Dick;* perhaps he had then no better grasp of the copybook maxims than he had when he wrote *Mardi;* but he had arrived at the harmony of his faculties in which he could write a book that stood entirely on its own merits.

He would not subsequently write any long work that could be said to stand thus, though four books would be in their ways equally ambitious. (A book, he soon remarked, can drink a man's blood.) Setting the books that seek to show "God's foot upon the treadle of the loom" against those that are primarily concerned with adventure (in which can be listed *Israel Potter,* though it is a work in which he drew entirely on other than his own experiences), we can see that he was never much a novelist of the typical nineteenth- or twentieth-century sort. Only one of the longer imaginative works, *Pierre; or, The Ambiguities,* has the aspect of a regular novel, with the necessary paraphernalia of background, characters, and plot, but even here Melville's interest is always more in the existential ambiguities that give the book its subtitle than in personal idiosyncrasies and particular milieus. In *The Confidence-Man,* the one work of Melville's that can be called just plain dull, we have a parable showing the failure of human charity, a foregone conclusion once we allow what Melville hints at in the final pages—that there is no transcendent Love for men to draw on. The long narrative poem published in 1876 examines a great nineteenth-century question, the conflicting claims of science and religion. Melville's sympathies are obviously with religion and, I should say, with Roman Catholicism at that, though the arguments given for traditional religion are "practical" ones. But men of course do very little that is truly worth while from practical motives, and when Melville in the poem wishes to make a final affirmation, it is of the heart's supremacy—the organ to which he had proclaimed his primary allegiance years earlier. The short novel done in the last year of his life was written to justify the ways of God to man. And in its way it justifies Melville's enduring championship of the heart, for in it the heart has at last changed.

"The reason the mass of men fear God, and *at bottom dislike* Him, is because they rather distrust His heart, and fancy Him all brain like a watch," Melville said in his correspondence with Hawthorne. In the same letter he declared: "I stand for the heart. To the dogs with the head!" Yet the conflict of head and heart in his works is not easy to analyze, because, as he himself was aware, it is rarely easy to say where one begins and the other ends. Head and heart are perhaps least difficult to distinguish between in *Mardi*. All the exuberances, the digressions, the exalted cribbings from Browne, Rabelais, and Carlyle are actually the products of the head, however much it was something still youthful in Melville's heart that allowed him to set his head to these tasks. These are contrived out of the nimbleness of his superior wit. The nimbleness is not quite adequate when Melville essays fantasy, for he is only *too* fanciful, and his South Seas background dissolves; but in satire, which is doubtless a more "rational" activity than fantasy, his success is considerable and his treatment of topical subjects often shows a prophetic rightness.

It is in the book's sad little allegory that Melville speaks for the heart, and apparently the heart's anguish was too intense to be clearly expressed. The allegory occupies only a few pages of the book, though it is supposed to be its continued theme. The narrator rescues a beautiful blonde maiden who is being borne off by South Seas islanders as a human sacrifice. For a brief period he is her lover; she disappears; and he sets off in search of her, all the while pursued, in fashion that is menacing only in its dreamlikeness, by the sons of the man he killed in rescuing the blonde Yillah. When he rejects the advances of a dark temptress, he learns that she has done away with Yillah, and he turns his canoe toward the open sea, announcing: "Now, I am my own soul's emperor; and my first act is abdication!"

Perhaps some specific hurt to Melville's heart prompted this fiction. Just what it was we cannot say; but neither can we be much clearer about what he is saying more generally in the heart's case. Before Taji has faced to the boundless sea, his companions have set off for Serenia, a sort of natural paradise of natural religion of a diluted Christian variety that, so far as can be determined, he has rejected for reasons of the heart rather than of the head. With Yillah gone, there is nothing to which he can reconcile himself. And what are the apparent implications of this? If Taji is the heart's champion and his final act is suicide, what is implied is the heart's rejection of creation, for the suicide is less intent upon destroying the experiencing subject than upon eradicating the world he finds insufferable. Such an act, for the advocate of the heart, is quite contradictory, since the heart only knows itself through the world's impact on it. Nevertheless, not the portrayers, but the philosophers, of human actions are the ones who must avoid the contradictory.

Moby-Dick concludes with a scene in some ways similar. Its narrator, the sole survivor of the whale-wrecked whaling ship, floats in a coffin, "and the great shroud of the sea [rolls] on as it rolled five thousand years ago." Ishmael has said earlier in the book that "Ahab's quenchless feud seemed mine," but Ahab, not Ishmael, dies in pursuing the feud. Ishmael's survival is the indication of *Moby-Dick's* moral superiority over *Mardi* and over the next two more ambitious works, *Pierre* and *The Confidence-Man*. All four books end in disaster. This is no doubt in part owing to Melville's models—the bloody Tudor-Stuart dramas and the Gothic romance—but the disasters do have a character of inner necessity, even when circumstances and motives are as obscure as they are in *Mardi*. But in three of the books the author seems to demand our assent to the conclusion that disaster is universally inevitable: the human creature is of his nature forced to make a demand on the world that the world will defeat.

In explaining Ahab's pursuit of the white whale, Ishmael says of him: "He piled upon the whale's white hump the sum of all the general rage and hate felt by his whole race from Adam down; and then, as if his chest had been a mortar, he burst his hot heart's shell upon it." This direct assault upon "all the subtle demonism of life and thought" finds the heart and head working together much of the time more adroitly than in the earlier book. The chap-

ters of cetological information that come between the chapters
of action, the involved quincuncial speculations with their often
magnificent rhetoric, the metaphors that throw an analogical
ladder from the world of the senses to the metaphysical world—
they are all achievements of the intellect in creating the book's
atmosphere of myth, and the myth is one of the proud heart. In
that sense there is no conflict between the head and the heart,
for here the head is at the service of the heart.

Yet, in a strange way, the head is serving the heart to its own
destruction. Nineteenth-century science provided a great deal of
what might be called the physical substance of *Moby-Dick* and,
as has been said before, the portentous hugeness of all that surrounds the voyage of the *Pequod* reflects the scientific vision of
the time, but the attitude ultimately is not one of scientific
mechanism. There is an inquiry after the "unknown but still
reasoning thing . . . behind the reasoning mask" that recalls
seventeenth-century efforts, with their proneness to the magical,
after a unity of thought that would explain the microcosm and
the macrocosm with a single set of rules. Because Ahab's vision
is touched with Manichaeanism, the still reasoning thing proves
to be hostile, and the inquiring mind discovers another in opposition to it. The queenly personality, to realize its claims, must out-
wit this other mind or placate it, and either attempt is magic. So
rationality abdicates that the heart may proclaim its defiance
and dominion, and the heart, we are told, bursts.

In *Moby-Dick* we are permitted to stand at a proper distance
from this dilemma. Since Ishmael (who, with obvious significance,
is rescued from his coffin by the ship *Rachel*) escapes destruction,
the dilemma can be neither universal nor inevitable, no matter how
recurrent and widespread it is in the human condition. The mythical quality of the story also allows us to stand our distance, offering
the charity even characters in fiction can demand of us but under
no compulsion to admit that, despite any of God's grace, there go
we. It is true that the mythical story seeks to account for something wider than itself, and so has something like a universal
extension, but that extension is to be used imaginatively by the
listener, on whom always devolves the task of interpretation. In
the conventional novel genre of *Pierre*, the book that followed
about a year after *Moby-Dick*, this freedom is lacking because we
must be convinced of the essential rightness of the "deductions"
the author makes from the actions he depicts. As a plain matter
of fact, we often enjoy novels the philosophy of which is unac-

ceptable to us, but that is obviously owing to our conviction that the author's ability to observe and portray the concrete in human affairs is better than his ability to discover their larger portent.

Just as record, there is a good deal of psychological verity in *Pierre*, which is the story of an absurdly lofty young man who gets involved in an amorous relationship—one that costs him his fortune, his health, and eventually his life—with a girl whom he assumes to be his dead father's bastard. This verity, however, seems generally to be out of line with what Melville is proposing as the profounder truths about his hero. What appears for the critical reader is a portrait of a neurotic who, finding the world will not meet the demands of his exorbitant self-love, formulates a philosophy of nihilism to justify his disappointment. But what Melville asks us to conclude is that the pursuit of the highest virtue will always end in what Pierre calls the "monstrousest vice"—to which the answer is, even though there may be a smack of Pharasaism about it, that if Pierre had only used a bit of common sense, he would never have come to such a pass. Melville no doubt saw this as well as we can, and he tried to contrive his story in such a fashion that common sense should seem inoperable in Pierre's case. Again, the contrivance, like the insistance that at the heart of everything lies an ambiguity, lacks a convincing inevitability, and we are aware of a failure in accomplishment that leaves us with a rather uncomfortable sense of superiority to the author.

Pierre's difficulty with the head and the heart is that in their interaction they lead one another astray. The mind asks for certitude, only to learn, by dwelling on the heart, that "appallingly vacant as vast is the soul of man," while the heart, insisting that "that which shall not be still *ought* to be," learns there is no "philosophy that a mortal man can possibly evoke, which will stand the final test of a real impassioned onset of life and Passion. . . . Events are brass." Events are indeed brass, which is just what Pierre would not have them be. So he, like Taji, must conclude that the realm in which events take place is a maleficent creation and agree, with his half-sister, that there can "be no perfect peace in individualness." To have been born is the great evil because the rest of creation is somehow not worthy of the human creature.

By the time of *The Confidence-Man*, the last prose fiction Melville published, the human creature was no longer proudly defying his ordained fate. In *Pierre* he has been "the fool of Truth, the fool of Virtue, the fool of Fate," but in *The Confidence-Man* he is, when not a scoundrel, just a plain fool. I have said that this book,

like the others, ends in disaster. The disaster, however, is not
expressed in physical violence. The book is pretty well devoid of
physical action. It tells the story of a Mississippi River steam-
boat's voyage in which a succession of passengers are gulled, often
as much for the pleasure of it as for the money, by a mysterious
confidence man who appears in a number of disguises, engaging
his victims in long discourses that make up the bulk of the book's
text. The discourses, and the cheating to which they are incidental,
are to argue, and to demonstrate, that charity does not exist, and
on the final page, with the extinguishing of a lamp in a cabin,
we are told by implication that the light has also gone out of the
world: all mankind is involved in the disaster of the loss of God or,
more exactly, a loving God. Without a God of love, Melville was
quite aware, there could be no charity among men.

The story itself lacks charity; there is a constant note of
misanthropy that does not appear in the other works. "Whatever
befall us," Melville had said in an earlier book, "let us not train
our murderous guns inboard; let us not mutiny with bloody pikes
in our hands." This is just the moral abomination that *The Confidence-Man* commits; the author is using his pike on his fellows.
The rage in the other books has a quality of bafflement about it;
it is the absurdity of Titanism that makes it tragic, and we can
sympathize with the person "tormented into desperation" till he
thinks his madness "vital truth" without our ceasing to estimate it
madness. But now the heart has grown rancorous and the rage is
turned against men. In the narrow lucidity of hate the head serves
the heart well, skillfully, though in the event quite drearily, providing the extended ironical exercise the book is in showing that
charity simply will not work and even those who hypocritically
preach it for their own purposes cannot count on it. There is a
bitterness here quite literally beyond words, for Melville would
not write anything again for a long time to come.

Recording in his journal a conversation had with Melville when
the younger man visited him in Liverpool shortly after finishing
The Confidence-Man, Hawthorne wrote that Melville had said
that he had "pretty much made up his mind to be annihilated."
By this Melville meant that he had given up hopes of immortality
(as a person, not as a writer), but atheism is a doubtful corollary.
The Confidence-Man seems more infused with rage against God
than denial of Him, and Melville was clearly one of those persons
whose religious difficulties are less concerned with the question
of God's existence than with what one's personal relationship
with Him is to be. If God were to be taken out of the dictionaries,

he would be found in the streets, Melville had earlier written to
Hawthorne and, on the trip to the Near East, in the initial stages
of which he had visited Hawthorne, Melville noted another place
where God was to be found. "It was in these pyramids that was
conceived the idea of Jehovah," he wrote after seeing the pyramids
near Cairo.[5] And a few days later he observed:

> They must needs have been terrible inventors those Egyptian
> wise men. And one seems to see that as out of the crude forms of
> the natural earth they could evoke by art the transcendent mass
> & symmetry . . . of the pyramid so out of the rude elements of the
> insignificant thoughts that are in all men, they could rear the tran-
> scendent conception of a God. But for no holy purpose was the
> pyramid founded. Casts no shadow great part of the day.[6]

Twenty years later the shadow of God was upon the narrative
poem Melville made from his visit to Palestine (and, as with most
of his books, from printed sources as well). *Clarel: A Poem and a
Pilgrimage in the Holy Land* describes the journey of a group of
troubled persons from Jerusalem to the Dead Sea and back again.
These pilgrims pass over the stony ground of the Holy Land to
verify in their own experiences the geography of Scripture, seeking, it might seem, for some material sign to stay the faith materialism has sapped. The poem gives more attention to character
than is usual in Melville's writing; there is a real attempt to bring
out personal idiosyncrasies and to give the illusion of living and
observed individuals. Two, at any rate, are plainly drawn from
life: Melville himself, who

> . . . supplemented Plato's theme
> With daedal life in boats and tents . . .
> Too frank, too unreserved, may be
> And indiscreet in honesty[7]

and Hawthorne, whose

> . . . virgin soul communed with men
> But thro' the wicket.[8]

But the two chief characters are undoubtedly constructions of
Melville's imagination. One is Ungar, a former Confederate soldier
of Maryland Catholic and Indian ancestry, a voluntary exile
from America now in the military service of the Turkish Sultan,
who in the long arguing that goes on in the course of the journey
upholds the traditional point of view regarding religion and society. The other is Derwent, an Anglican clergyman, a Christian
of the most latitudinarian kind, for whom is

> The object clear: belief revised,
> Men liberated—equalized
> In happiness. No mystery,
> Just none at all; plain sailing.[9]

Though we are given to understand that most of the pilgrims have lost their faith because of the corroding effects of science on religious belief, the opposing claims of science and religion as they appeared to men in the second half of the nineteenth century are not gone into in great detail in the dialogs that swell the poem to two volumes. Melville must have been as little impressed as he was sympathetic with the scientific argument for the non-existence of God or, what amounts to the same thing, the existence of an impersonal God. The most eloquent of the speakers is Ungar, who pleads for Catholicism, though he himself seems not to practice it. Clarel, a former divinity student who has lost his religious belief, is far more concerned with the difficulties of giving the total assent of the will demanded by faith than he is with the rational arguments for and against belief. The sort of belief offered by Derwent engages no one in the poem; it is "an over-easy glove," a blindly determined optimism not to be assumed by those who cannot deny "doubt bleeds, nor Faith is free from pain."

The long conflict of head and heart in Melville's works at last in *Clarel* reveals itself clearly for what it is: St. Augustine's conflict of the two wills, the turmoil and unease in the person when, as St. Paul observed, he does not what he will but does what he will not. It is true that Melville does not state the case thus. When, early in the poem, one of his characters, standing before the arch from which Pilate is said to have shown Christ to the mob, upbraids the Son of God for the offer of salvation, it is because this offer has ended the time when

> The natural law let men prevail;*
> Then reason disallowed the state
> Of instinct's variance with fate.[10]

Here, it might be said, the argument is that if the heart had not been led to entertain hopes contrary to reason, men might still be living in a state of meaner but attainable happiness. And such, of course, the argument on its surface is. Yet "the dream that drags out its repulse" simply is not satisfactorily explained in this

---

* Melville had a fondness for poetic inversion not always demanded by meter. The meaning of the first line is doubtless the one made plain by its natural order: "Men let the natural law prevail."

way. It cannot have been even to Melville, for, when at the end of
the poem he returns Clarel to Jerusalem, with no more certainties
than he had before the "weary length of arguing" began and with
his sorrows much increased by the sudden death of his fiancée,
the author can only tell the young man: "Clarel, thy heart, the
issues there but mind." One runs the risk of presumption in saying that a man of Melville's intelligence and insight (and there
are analytic passages of great brilliance in *Clarel*) had missed the
point; but it is obviously not the best counsel to tell a man to
follow the dream that will thwart itself. If, however, we think of
the matter in the terms of the two wills, the injunction makes
more sense. We need not equate one will with the head, the other
with the heart. Just as the two wills are not really separate en-
tities but a manner of speaking, so is the conflict of head and
heart a way of describing the soul's disquiet when, led astray by
pride in one of pride's infinite disguises, it has lost the path that
leads to the knowledge of God. That knowledge is not the mere
result of ratiocination; it is the active experience of intelligence
that comes with love. Melville, we can deduct, sensed this. As
Clarel at the poem's end turns from the Via Crucis and "vanishes
in the obscurer town," surely the love taken from him by Ruth's
death also symbolizes God's love, whether Melville consciously
intended this or not. Perhaps he could not make this his conscious
intention because God for him was still the figure he had glimpsed
in the pyramids.

In the fifteen years that remained to him after the publication
of *Clarel,* Melville issued two more volumes of verse—little, privately printed collections—but in the last year of his life he set
his hand again to prose, in which he had presumably made no
sustained imaginative effort for thirty-five years. He turned once
more to the sea and produced a short novel of fablelike quality.
Though his prose had some awkward moments, it could still evoke
that air of wonder and feeling of the concrete that had been present
in *Moby-Dick* and certain of the short stories. If his next-to-last
prose fiction has a quality of thinness, this very last one has the
grit and grain of an encounter with reality.

There is a legend of Melville's "long seclusion," by which is
meant the years from 1856, when *The Confidence-Man* appeared,
to 1891, when he died, and, being a legend, it ignores the fact
that during this period he published four books of verse (counting
the two volumes of *Clarel* as a single book). But there is a good
deal of retirement implied in the fact that Melville chose a medium

so uncongenial to his best talents as verse and, measuring the verse against what he could at times do in prose, we can say that this seems the work of a man who has deliberately sought limits to his self-expression. *Billy Budd,* which was not published until long after his death, renounces that retirement; the prose vehicle is a means of public statement, for even in the nineteenth century verse was becoming a kind of private utterance. *Billy Budd* is not more "personal" than any of the poetry; it is not at all autobiographical or self-declamatory; but it is written about Melville's central concern: how can we justify the ways of God to man?

Though Melville was a man much given to pondering philosophical problems, ready, as Hawthorne remarked, to talk "about time and eternity, things of this world and the next . . . and all possible and impossible matters . . . deep into the night," he was, in terms of accomplishment, not a philosopher but a creative writer, a poet in the inclusive sense, a maker and a depicter of human actions. *Billy Budd* is not a syllogistic demonstration that the full operation of God's providence is necessarily beyond man's knowledge, nor by turning to it can we discover the process of reasoning—if there ever was any such process—by which Melville arrived at "acceptance." "Drowning men do drown!" Melville had once protested, and they still drown in his last work: the innocent sailor is hanged for an apparent crime because the ways of this world demand it. The tale itself is Melville's solution, and the ingredients in it are not so very different from his other tales.

The basic conflict and ambiguity are still there. Ahab felt his topmost greatness lay in his topmost grief, by which he meant the rage that was doomed to failure. Pierre discovered two sorts of time in the world, chronometrical and orological, one to be observed for survival and the other for virtue. Captain Vere, who condemns Billy, sees the existence of two orders of justice, earthly and heavenly, one in its execution apparently violating the other. Evil is still a positive force in the world, but the entire disposition of things is no longer malevolent toward man, though this is because the feelings of the experiencing agent have changed rather than the external circumstance. A victory over pride has been achieved: man no longer seeks to tear aside the pasteboard mask and fall headlong into vacancy; he can accept the brazen fact, for, though it must always surpass his particular understanding, it is part of an order that in the end works to his benefit. Heart and head may conflict, but the single will overcomes their divergence and directs them to a common goal.

Parallels have been seen in *Billy Budd* to both the Crucifixion and the Fall, and no doubt anyone seeking to write a parable of the human condition would somehow have to reckon with the two events by which it has been chiefly determined. We should, however, be false to the whole quality of Melville's thought in saying that this story in his Christian testament. Billy's death is in no way redemptive in the Christian sense—his acceptance of it and his forgiveness of those responsible are examples of the peace available to the hero, the man whose virtues are his own—and Captain Vere is not a figure of omniscience but someone who has arrived at the sad wisdom that what is must be. The symbolic import of Billy's death is that the best among men must always suffer for the evils the rest of us do.

What might Melville have become in a different ambience of religious thought, one that had made the full Christian tradition more readily available to him? It is, of course, a question quite impossible to answer finally, for works of literature, as I said at the beginning, are the results of a particular personality's encounter with specific circumstances and problems, and Melville was a man who above all felt compelled to be himself. Had Melville known another God than the one he found in the pyramids, his loyalty to the heart surely would not have had so much rage and defiance in it, and his final renunciation of rage might well have shown more joy, but if we may call ourselves wiser than he in seeing the faults of this loyalty, that wisdom is his gift to us.

WALT WHITMAN
1819-1892

Ego in New Eden

ERNEST SANDEEN

ALL of the romantic poets exhibited an intense consciousness of
self that shone through a wide range of moods, from the exultant,
defiant, or ecstatic to the tortured or melancholy. This persistent
self-awareness Walt Whitman brought to a logical finality; with
him the subjective context of romantic poetry became the subject
matter. In the typical romantic poem the ego of the poet is deeply
implicated, but Whitman made the ego itself the chief object of
contemplation. In *A Backward Glance O'er Travel'd Roads* (1880)
Whitman explained that when he had asked himself at the start
of his poetic project how he could best express his "own distinctive
era and surroundings," he saw "that the trunk and centre whence
the answer was to radiate . . . must be an identical body and soul,
a personality—which personality, after many considerations and
ponderings, I deliberately settled should be myself—indeed could
not be any other."

The reader of *Leaves of Grass* may suspect that here Whitman
in his old age was rationalizing the impulses that had launched
him upon his poet's career but he will not question the statement
as an accurate description of the point of view in the poetry. In the
first edition of *Leaves* in 1855, the introductory poem which was
finally, in 1881, aptly entitled "Song of Myself," occupied over
half of the pages, excluding the prose preface. Even in the last
edition that Whitman supervised, after he had added hundreds
of poems to his lifework, this poem with its significant title remained central and germinal. In fact, all of the poems in *Leaves*
are essentially "songs of myself."

There is little in Whitman's poetry except the ego, but most of
his poems are more complex than mere monologs. It is more ac-

curate to describe them as interior dialogs in which one of the speakers is invariably the poet himself. In some of the poems the poet and the reader are the *dramatis personae,* as, for example, in "Song of Myself" or in "Starting from Paumanok," where both poet and reader are continually being broken down into the innumerable persons listed in the catalogs and then made whole again to confront each other, as it were, face to face. In "Crossing Brooklyn Ferry" the reader is any one of the multitudes who in the future will enjoy the experience of the ferryboat which the poet is now enjoying.

Other poems, and certain passages in the poems already cited, show the poet conversing with nature. Here it is usually the poet, not nature, who plays the passive role of listener, the poet understanding and translating the esoteric language of "the large few stars," "the sagging moon," the trembling throat of the thrush, or the sea with its husky-haughty lips. In still other passages the poet engages in dialogs with God, but these are more difficult to localize because in Whitman's poems the poet, the reader, nature, or all three together, have a disconcerting way of suddenly becoming themselves transfigured into divinity.

The basic dialog, however, the one that does the most to produce the impression of dialog in the poems, takes place between the poet and himself. "I cannot understand the mystery," Whitman wrote in an early notebook (1847-1848), "but I am always conscious of myself as two—as my soul and I."[1] The interior colloquy suggested here can be heard throughout the *Leaves,* now as barbaric yawps ringing from housetop to housetop in the morning, and again as whispered intimacies under the stars. What is more, the careful listener may conclude that Whitman and his soul are, at last, the only characters in the Whitman drama. Varied and numerous as they are, all of the other characters may be but the masked images either of the poet or of his alter ego.

It was the long conversation which Whitman had with his countrymen from 1855 to his death in 1891, in his poetry and in his prose writings, that gave a distinctive coloration to the reputation he achieved. Both at home and abroad he has been and is still regarded as an American nationalist poet, perhaps the only one we have had. In our own time of ideological warfare, his explicit prose statements as to the nature of his democratic faith have inevitably been emphasized. Contemporary readers with widely divergent partisan loyalties have all found much to praise and much to deplore in Whitman's political-social philosophy. In the neutral perspective of history, however, Whitman may come to be regarded as a writer who maintained the democratic dogma in its wholeness. For he respected both of the twin principles handed down from the founding fathers, that of individual freedom and that of equality, and he asserted the dynamic dependence of each upon the other.

In *Democratic Vistas* (1871), "out of a brief, general, sentimental consideration of political democracy" Whitman found "the origin-idea of the singleness of man, individualism, asserting itself. . . . But the mass, or lump character," he added, ". . . is to be ever carefully weigh'd, borne in mind, and provided for. Only from it, and from its proper regulation and potency, comes the other, comes the chance of individualism. The two are contradictory, but our task is to reconcile them."

For Whitman, then, the essence of democracy lies in the dialectical tension between the individualistic ideal and the communal ideal. The poem which has stood first in *Leaves* from the fourth edition (1871-1872) on, begins with a summarizing aphorism:

> One's-self I sing, a simple separate person,
> Yet utter the word Democratic, the word En-Masse.

But generalizations like this which appear in some of his verses as well as in his prose were merely skimmed off the top of his poetic vision. Essentially his perception of the democratic reality was an intuition, an experience, not a theory. The individual involved in the democratic contradiction was not a political or social abstraction but a concrete person; he was "one's-self" or more specifically "myself." The other half opposing the self in the dialectic of demos was not a conceptualized multitude; it was the myriad "you" or "they," the series of partial portraits which crowded the catalogs but could never be exhausted.

Most important of all, the relation between the self, the simple separate person, and the collective mass was not conceived in a scientific, or philosophical way; it was personal and intimate. Whitman's whole purpose in his poems would seem to be to dramatize a state of rapport between himself and his fellow human beings, especially his fellow Americans, which was more than intellectual, which was, rather, elemental and primitive.

The bond that Whitman felt between himself and America was so close that each could be identified, at least in part, with the other. There was the movement out from the poetic ego to the multitudinous reader and there was the reciprocal movement from the multiple ego back to the poet. The subject became the object, and the object became the subject. Whitman's poetic vision is both lyrical and dramatic; there is the subjective lyricism of the private ego, but there is also the dramatic ebb and flow of the ego as it confronts, merges with, and then re-emerges from the reality outside itself.

"Song of Myself" began with an invitation to the reader to identify himself with the poet.

> I celebrate myself, and sing myself,
> And what I assume you shall assume
> For every atom belonging to me as good belongs to you.

Through the rest of the long poem, however, the situation was reversed, for the most part, and the poet identified himself with his readers, that is, with his fellows. A good example is Section 15 of the poem, which consists largely of a long list of persons, ranging from the President with his cabinet to the opium-eater and lunatic, from the "pure contralto" singing in the organ loft to the quadroon girl and the prostitute, and including duck-shooter, deacon, farmer, printer, machinist, policeman, marksman at a Western turkey-shooting, ballroom dancer, trapper, squaw, peddler, Yankee girl, canal boy, flatboatmen, and many others. The section ends with these lines:

> And these tend inward to me, and I tend outward to them,
> And such as it is to be of these more or less I am,
> And of these one and all I weave the song of myself.

It was at this deep level of mutual identification and fusion between the single self and the multiple selves that Whitman sought to solve, or dissolve, the democratic paradox of the one and the many.[2]

Because Whitman's perception of the self was poetic and dramatic, not philosophical, the self for him was necessarily existential and particular. At the same time the fact that the self could identify itself with other selves, equally particular, argued a quality of universality. In other words, Whitman's own inner experience corroborated the transcendental doctrine of Emerson that if a man penetrated his own ego deeply enough he would realize more than himself, he would realize universal selfhood. In Whitman's poems, the celebration of the self becomes the celebration of the "divine average."

The most characteristic of Whitman's devices, the catalog, has been the most often and the most severely criticized. Even sympathetic readers have conceded that this device is a weakness. Emerson's observation has become classic: "I expect him [Whitman] to make the Songs of the Nation but he seems contented to make the inventories."[3] Yet the catalog was the means by which Whitman tried to accommodate the Emersonian paradox, the universality of the concrete, individual self. The catalog adds up to a whole which is more than the sum of the parts; it is a still higher level of universality, or more accurately, of concrete universality. It comes to a portrait of America in the middle of the nineteenth century. Whitman's catalog is a poetic equivalent to the philosopher's generalization or the scientist's hypothesis. Philosopher and scientist present an abstract formula which implies the data on which it is based. Whitman presents the data which suggests, not an abstract generalization, but a generic image.

However, it is the self of the poet in its double movement of filling these images of American personality with itself and being in turn filled by them that finally unifies these images in a single portrait. The self-consciousness of the poet acts as a lens which brings the various lines, shapes, and colors into focus, and "composes" them to form the picture of American character.

The figure of the American which emerges from *Leaves* is, with certain exceptions, what we would expect, given Whitman's time and place in history. He is a man of the outdoors, first of all. It is true that Whitman was the first, perhaps the only, romantic poet to sing the praises of the city. For this reason he has often been taken as symptomatic of the change taking place in nineteenth-century America from an agrarian to an urban way of life. But if so, he also illustrates how the imagination lagged behind the reality, for he is emphatically the poet of the open air. Even in the city what he loves is the surge of the outdoor crowds, in the street, on the ferryboat or on the omnibus. The city man he most admires is the fireman, the ferryboat deck hand, the horse-car driver, and the teamster.

Whitman's collective portrait of the American is extensive enough to include lawyer, physician, priest, and banker, but their inclusion is perfunctory and mechanical. Whitman's American is the common man, self-reliant, practical, non-intellectual, and non-professional. He is the hunter, the western trapper married to a red girl; he is the butcher-boy, the hairy-chested blacksmith; he is that picturesque giant, the Negro teamster. When Whitman stops to listen to America singing, what he hears are the varied carols of the mechanic, the carpenter, the mason, the boatman, the deck hand, the shoemaker, the hatter, the woodcutter, the ploughboy, the mothers and young wives at their work of sewing or washing.

The twentieth-century reader needs to be reminded that Whitman's generic American is not proletarian. The distinctive quality of the collective, egalitarian mass is that it is interpenetrated with the proud, self-reliant ego which the poet represents. Perhaps Whitman himself best summarized his characterization of the American when he wrote an anonymous review of his first edition of *Leaves*.

> An American bard at last! One of the roughs, large, proud, affectionate, eating, drinking, and breeding, his costume manly and free, his fact sunburnt and bearded, his postures strong and erect, his voice bringing hope and prophecy to the generous races of young and old.[4]

This description of Whitman's American suggests a parallel, perhaps unconscious, with a generic type already well developed in the American imagination, namely, the Westerner, the backwoodsman. Constance Rourke in her classic work, *American Humor: A Study of the National Character,* shows how this "Gamecock of the Wilderness" arose on the national scene soon after the battle of New Orleans, the event which symbolized the growing self-awareness of the West. He soon made his way into the theater, first in the West, then in the East and finally in London. His "tall" exploits appeared in newspapers throughout the country and were especially copious in that lively "Chronicle of the Turf, Agriculture, Field Sports, Literature, and the Stage," William Trotter Porter's *The Spirit of the Times*.

Absorbing what was legendary and representative in such historical characters as Daniel Boone and Davy Crockett, or perhaps, more accurately, providing the model by which they grew into legendary figures, he tended to merge, partially at least, with other American mythic heroes such as the Yankee, and Mike Fink, the Mississippi flatboatman. The backwoodsman, Miss Rourke says, "was appropriated; his eccentricities were considered not only western but American, and he was warmly applauded therefor."[5] Like the Yankee Jonathan who preceded him and the lumberjack Paul Bunyan who followed him, this western figure was a comic hero in a comic mythology. Because the frontier, though primitive enough, was never completely cut off from the highly developed civilization which surrounded it,

American mythology differed from other mythologies in that it originated in a self-conscious state of mind. The American demigod with his typically epic exaggeration could only be accepted under the guise of humor.

There is nothing comic about Whitman's American hero, but he nevertheless shows his blood relationship to the Gamecock of the Wilderness. He may not be the humorous figure that the backwoodsman is—at least he is clearly not intended to be—but he has the same self-consciousness in appearance and manner. There is a trace of affectation in his very "nonchalance" and apparent indolence of dress and behavior; there is the hint of a defensive attitude in his "postures strong and erect." He has other qualities, too, which resemble those Miss Rourke attributes to the backwoods hero: the obsession with strength and size; the tendency to boast, to swagger, to indulge in rhapsodic monologs about himself; the addiction to "sudden silences"; the love of masquerade and costume; the relish for high-flown oratory and bombast; his moments of " 'sudden glory' that [have] a touch of the supernatural."[6]

In other less direct ways Whitman portrays the frontier America of his time. Whitman's American, at least as represented in the ego of the poet, is typically on the move. He saunters, without destination, along the open road; in the regional catalogs of "Song of Myself" and other poems, he moves over the continent in seven-league boots; he sometimes extends his itinerary and as freely roams over the whole earth, as in "Salut au Monde." In "Crossing Brooklyn Ferry," he not only crosses the East River; he crosses the barriers of the ages and joins hands with the generations of Americans to come. In "Passage to India," retracing with breath-taking rapidity the course of empire and civilization as it has taken its westward way back to the Mother East, he is swept up into the super-historical, cosmic journey of the soul.

The free verse itself, the use of slang and colloquial expressions are deliberate adaptations to fit the informal, unconventional American character which the poems incarnate. Naive as these recourses may seem to the literate reader, it is impossible to say they are wholly unsuccessful. Even the ambiguity of tone which resulted from them, that of a curiously self-conscious primitivism, may be described as typically American.

As we have seen, Whitman is both an individualist and an egalitarian. In his later prose writings, where he often adopts a kind of prudent platform decorum, he emphasizes the virtues of conventional nineteenth-century individualism and sounds the conventional note of alarm at the possibilities of unreason in the masses. But in the candid depths of his poetry he is revealed as an ardent egalitarian. He loves the people for what they are, not like Emerson or the more zealous but less enlightened reformers, for what they might be if they realized their theoretic potentialities. His dialog with his countrymen through which he creates his image of America is, as he himself insisted, a dialog of lovers.

The crucial problem in interpreting Whitman's poetic vision is the nature of his love. What strikes the reader of *Leaves* at once, especially in the early editions, is that his love of people is intimately physical. His lines abound in sensual and sexual images. As he admitted in his own anonymous review of the 1855 edition, "If health were not his distinguishing attribute, this poet would be the very harlot of persons. Right and left he flings his arms, drawing men and women with undeniable love to his close embrace, loving the clasp of their hands, the touch of their necks and breasts, and the sound of their voices."[7] Actually this first edition of *Leaves* creates a more vivid impression of the "harlot of persons" than of "health."

The reader need not play the role of amateur psychoanalyst, but only draw upon the psychological data which has become common knowledge to conclude that Whitman displays the emotional attitudes of retarded sexuality. Within the first twelve lines of his 1855 edition, the poet has told us that he is in love with the atmosphere—

> I will go to the bank by the wood and become undisguised
>   and naked,
> I am mad for it to be in contact with me.

A few lines later he tells us that, while others discuss, "I am silent, and go bathe and admire myself." He can even transform his self-love into a religious doctrine:

> Divine am I inside and out, and I make holy whatever I
>   touch or am touched from;
> The scent of these arm-pits is aroma finer than prayer,
> This head is more than churches or bibles or creeds.
> If I worship any particular thing it shall be some of the
>   spread of my body.

There follows a detailed "anatomy" of his own body, concluding with these lines:

> I dote on myself . . . there is that lot of me, and all so luscious,
> Each moment and whatever happens thrills me with joy.[8]

Closely related to this autoerotism and another indication of his sexual immaturity is Whitman's homosexuality which was brought into full view with the publication of the "Calamus" poems in the third edition of *Leaves* (1860). Here he celebrates that love which he calls "adhesiveness," a term he borrowed from phrenology and converted to his own use to mean "the manly love of comrades." These poems are manifestly homosexual in motivation and the writer is keenly, painfully aware of the fact, despite the denial he made in his late years of any such awareness. Even the poet's ruses of mystification seem calculated to highlight and dramatize rather than conceal "the secret of [his] nights and days." However, the point of greatest interest for the student of Whitman's poetry is the importance which Whitman attaches to this group in his total poetic program. For example, there is this three-line poem (in its later, revised form) :

> Here the frailest leaves of me and yet my strongest lasting,
> Here I shade and hide my thoughts, I myself do not expose them,
> And yet they expose me more than all my other poems.

In another poem of this group he cries out, "O adhesiveness! O pulse of my life!"

Another notorious group of poems was included in the 1860 edition, immediately preceding the "Calamus" collection. Entitled "Enfans [*sic*] d'Adam," later changed, fortunately, to "Children of Adam," it contained poems "celebrating" the love between men and women, a love which Whitman designated by another term taken from phrenology, "amativeness." Although the passion which Whitman sings of in these poems is frankly anatomical and is asserted with sufficient violence, it seems unreal at last; the rhetoric is formal, the love-relation basically programmatic.

It is tempting to speculate that Whitman might have written the "Children of Adam" poems as a kind of social obligation to acknowledge the world's way of love in return for the right to assert his own. But even in the relation of "manly attachment" a feminine-masculine duality existed. This it is which probably explains the insistence upon the equality of the female with the male which runs like a refrain throughout Whitman's poems.

For Whitman in the "Calamus" relationship plays the feminine role. Full of yearning as he may be, he is not the stormy lover,

seeking to possess; he is the shy beloved who longs to be possessed.
It is the poet who is wooed and caressed. His lover holds the poet's
hand. Sleeping beside him "under the same cover in the cool night,"
his lover lets his arm lie lightly around the poet's breast and "ever
at parting kisses [him] lightly on the lips with robust love." Even
the reader of *Leaves* is invited to play the male lover's part: "Here
to put your lips upon mine I permit you." Whitman also slips into
the receptive role in the "Children of Adam" poems. For example,
in the poem, "From Pent-up Aching Rivers" where the poet is
supposedly making love to a woman, it is not long before the parts
are reversed and he is speaking of "the soft sliding of hands over
me and thrusting of fingers through my hair and beard."

The revelation afforded by the "Calamus" poems helps to illu-
minate several passages in the poems that appeared before and
after the 1860 edition of *Leaves*. It gives heightened significance
to those passages especially which interrupt the flow of Whitman's
stormier rhetoric and introduce an altogether different movement
—lyrical, quiet but deep in feeling, wistful. An example is the
passage in "Song of Myself" beginning "Twenty-eight young
men bathe by the shore." It is a little drama in which a maiden
lady surreptitiously and with intense longing watches the naked
young bathers from behind the blinds of her window. Her situation
is summed up in the line, "Twenty-eight years of womanly life,
and all so lonesome." In one of the "Calamus" poems, "These I,
Singing in Spring," Whitman tells of a walk he takes through
the countryside, alone,

> . . . yet soon a troop gathers around me,
> Some walk by my side and some behind, and some embrace
>   my arms or neck,
> They the spirits of dear friends dead or alive, thicker they
>   come, a great crowd, and I in the middle.

"And I in the middle"! The phrase occurs elsewhere in Whitman's
Leaves, once in "Song of Myself": "My right and left arms round
the sides of two friends, and I in the middle." The pathos of the
phrase comes from the reflection that probably it describes an
ardent wish rather than a reality.

The appearance of *Leaves of Grass* remains as spectacular to
the student in 1958 as it was to Whitman's contemporaries a
century ago. Despite all the biographical data and early writings
of Whitman which have been dug up in the interval, there is little

or nothing in his early life or early verse and prose to predict the author of *Leaves*. During the years 1847 to 1855, some great change took place in Whitman which was no less than a change in personality. Some critics like Dr. Maurice Bucke and F. O. Matthiessen believe the change was due to a sudden vision or illumination; others like Henry Seidel Canby believe it came about in the way of a natural, gradual development. But all agree on the fact of the startling transformation. The one outstanding characteristic of his early writing is anonymity, the anonymity of the conventional. But *Leaves* is unique in perception and style. As Randall Jarrell has pointed out, even its obvious faults are inimitable.[9] With the literary metamorphosis came a corresponding one in Whitman's dress, manners, and personal habits. The fastidious dandy became one of the "roughs."

As we have seen, Whitman's love, "the secret of my nights and days," was a love to hide yet a love which it were death to hide. Certainly this predicament of self-consciousness which he suffered played a decisive role in bringing about the great change in him just described. Without presuming to "explain" the mystery of his poetic originality, the student may reasonably suppose that this change involved a momentous inner decision, arrived at suddenly or gradually—the decision to accept himself and to accept himself in his totality, sexual anomaly and all, body and soul, what might be evil in him as well as what might be good. He had solved the dilemma which was himself by ceasing to struggle with it, by simply accepting it and affirming it. He was rewarded by being restored to wholeness and by an ecstatic sense of freedom. The first (unnamed) "Song of Myself" was the chant of his liberation.

> Sure as the most certain sure . . . . plumb in the uprights,
>   well entretied, braced in the beams,
> Stout as a horse, affectionate, haughty, electrical
> I and this mystery here we stand.
>
> Clear and sweet is my soul . . . . and clear and sweet is all
>   that is not my soul.
> . . . .
> Welcome is every organ and attribute of me, and of any
>   man hearty and clean,
> Not an inch nor a particle of an inch is vile, and none shall
>   be less familiar than the rest.

And a few pages further on:

> Whimpering and truckling fold with powders for invalids
> . . . . conformity goes to the fourth-removed,
> I cock my hat as I please indoors or out.
>
> . . . .
> I chant a new chant of dilation or pride,
> We have had ducking and deprecating about enough.[10]

It has already been suggested that Whitman did not fully reveal
the nature of the ego which he asserted with such vigor in the
Leaves of 1855 and 1856 until he published the third edition of
1860. The first two editions seem to express primarily the immediate exuberant emotions of liberation which were generated
from his new orientation. It might be argued that the expression of
these emotions committed him to a course which led to an ever
more intimate, and ever more clearly defined, revelation of himself.
At any rate, the decision to accept himself in all his erotic pecu-
liarity is publicly confessed in the third edition. Both the fact of
his revolutionary decision to accept himself and the nature of the
self which he has accepted are fully revealed in the first poem of
the "Calamus" group:

> In paths untrodden,
> In the growth by the margin of pond-waters,
> Escaped from the life that exhibits itself,
> From all the standards hitherto publish'd, from the pleasures,
>   profits, conformities,
> Which too long I was offering to feed my soul,
> Clear to me now standards not yet publish'd, clear to me
>   that my soul,
> That the soul of the man I speak for rejoices in comrades,
> Here by myself away from the clank of the world,
> Tallying and talk'd to here by tongues aromatic,
> No longer abash'd (for in this secluded spot I can respond
>   as I would not dare elsewhere,)
> Strong upon me the life that does not exhibit itself, yet
>   contains all the rest,
> Resolv'd to sing no songs to-day but those of manly attach-
>   ment,
>
> . . . .
> I proceed for all who are or have been young men,
> To tell the secret of my nights and days,
> To celebrate the need of comrades.

Certain attitudes in *Leaves* can be understood in a new way if
it is supposed that they grew out of a strenuous struggle for self-
justification. For example, the self-deification in certain passages

need not be taken literally as the blasphemy which it appears to be. It is more probably overcompensation for the sense of inferiority from which the poet believes he has freed himself and it is reinforced by the exhilaration of his release.

His extreme but convincing egalitarian sympathies are also clarified in the light of an urgent need for self-approval. Whitman's hero, the ego who plays the title role in "Song of Myself," is as proud, as willful, and as lawless in his behavior as any aristocrat, but he is no Nietzschean superman scornful of the weak and contemptuous of the multitude.

> To a drudge of the cottonfields or emptier of privies
> I lean . . . on his right cheek I put the family kiss,
> And in my soul I swear I never will deny him.

If Whitman's hero-ego is understood as an image by which he seeks his own salvation, the reason for his democratic inclusiveness becomes plain. He must accept even the social and moral outcast because he is himself an outcast asserting his claim to be accepted. The banquet he sets is "for the wicked just the same as the righteous"; he "will not have a single person slighted or left away"; he invites the "keptwoman and sponger and thief. . . . the heavy-lipped slave . . . the vererealee." Whitman not only receives the outcasts; he becomes their champion. In a poem entitled "Native Moments," which appeared in the 1860 edition, the motive for Whitman's sympathy with the pariah is suggested. This poem, placed in the "Enfans d'Adam" group, is really a "Calamus" poem. It shows the poet, in imagination, giving himself up to "the drench of [his] passions," sharing "the midnight orgies of young men":

> . . . I pick out some low person for my dearest friend,
> He shall be lawless, rude, illiterate, he shall be one condemn'd
>   by others for deeds done,
> I will play a part no longer, why should I exile myself from
>   my companions?
> O you shunned persons, I at least do not shun you,
> I come forthwith in your midst, I will be your poet,
> I will be more to you than to any of the rest.

It is already apparent that if Whitman were chiefly concerned with creating a self-image which would allow him to accept himself as he was, he must reject the conventional distinctions between good and evil. This rejection, in fact, seems to have been part and

parcel of the original inspiration which led him to his loud affirmation of the ego. In the earliest notebook of his which has survived,
dating back to 1847 or 1848, he says: "The first inspiration of real
wisdom in our souls lets us know that the self-will and wickedness
and malignity we thought so unsightly in our race are by no means
what we were told, but something far different, and not amiss
except to spirits of the feeble and the shorn."[11] In his first experiments with the verse form of *Leaves*, contained in the same
notebook, he writes:

> I am the poet of sin,
> For I do not believe in sin.[12]

The first poem of the 1855 edition of *Leaves* announces that the
poet is "not the poet of goodness only. . . . I do not decline to be the
poet of wickedness also."

> What blurt is it about virtue and about vice?
> Evil propels me, and reform of evil propels me . . . . I stand
>   indifferent,
> My gait is no faultfinder's or rejecter's gait,
> I moisten the roots of all that is grown.[13]

Following his declaration, in the 1860 "Proto-Leaf,"[14] that he will
write "the evangel-poem of comrades and love," Whitman says:

> I make the poem of evil also, I commemorate that part also,
> I am myself just as much evil as good, and my nation is—
>   and I say there is in fact no evil,
> (Or if there is I say it is just as important to you, to the
>   land or to me, as any thing else.)

Implicit in Whitman's repudiation of orthodox morality is the
romantic distinction between "nature" and "society," or "nature"
and "civilization." Under the code of civilized society he had
stood condemned, self-condemned; he had suffered an "unnatural"
suppression of an essential part of himself, he had suffered self-
division and humiliation. In order to accept himself as he was in
his wholeness, he must reject the artificial, trivial standards of
society and adopt the larger, more genuine and more "healthy"
standards provided by nature. In his decision to assert his ego in
its universal significance, "nature" was the authority which he
invoked. The meat and drink he provides are for "natural hunger."
His "intricate purpose" is like that of the April rain or that of
the mica on the side of a rock.

Even if the validity of Whitman's naturalistic morality were granted, it is difficult to see how he could harmonize his own homosexual impulses with this standard of primitive innocence. Yet he apparently believed that the "manly love of comrades" was natural and universal. He proceeds "to celebrate the need of comrades" for the benefit of "all who are or have been young men." This kind of love is a matter of national importance:

> I believe the main purport of these States is to found a
>   superb friendship, exalté, previously unknown,
> Because I perceive it waits, and has been always waiting,
>   latent in all men.
>   *("To The East and to The West.")*

But "the need of comrades" is not confined to America. In a moment when he is "yearning and thoughtful," Whitman imagines that he sees "other men in other lands yearning and thoughtful," men in Germany, Italy, France, Spain, China, Russia, or Japan,

> And it seems to me if I could know those men I should
>   become attached to them as I do to men in my own lands,
> O I know we should be brethren and lovers,
> I know I should be happy with them.
>   *("This Moment Yearning and Thoughtful.")*

Nor is the principle of "manly attachment" restricted in time; it permeates history. Whitman sees it "as base and finale . . . for all metaphysics" (in a poem added to "Calamus" in 1871, "The Base of All Metaphysics"). He has studied "the Greek and Germanic systems," he has studied Kant, Fichte, Schelling, Hegel, Socrates, Plato, and "Christ divine," yet underneath them all he clearly sees "the dear love of man for his comrade, the attraction of friend to friend" as well as the attraction of husband and wife, "of children and parent,/Of city for city and land for land."

This belief in the universality of his own immature erotic emotions was not a temporary phase in Whitman's development. In a long footnote in *Democratic Vistas* (1870), he vigorously reiterated his faith in "the adhesive love, at least rivaling the amative love . . . if not going beyond it. . . . I say democracy infers such loving comradeship," he concludes, "as its most inevitable twin or counterpart, without which it will be incomplete, in vain, and incapable of perpetuating itself."

His attempt to read into all men his own private eros was Whitman's pathetic fallacy—"pathetic" in more than one sense.— If Whitman were naïve, it was not because he failed to recognize

his sexual inversion but because he was able to convince himself
that it was normal among all healthy males. When he tried to elevate "adhesiveness" to a principle of national unity or of world
brotherhood, his error was not only naïve; it was grotesque. Yet
his mistake, astounding as it seems, is of value to the student, for
it marks the most sensitive spot in Whitman's self-image. It was
his anomalous sexual yearnings which had, in the first place, imprisoned him within the walls of his own disapproval; if this
part of himself could not be absorbed into the ego-image which was
now to release him, all was lost. Whitman's attempt to universalize
his inverted sexual desires was an error to which he was driven
by the logic of his own self-redemption.

Taking *A Backward Glance O'er Travel'd Roads* in 1880, Whitman declared that his " 'Leaves' could not possibly have emerged
or been fashion'd or completed, from any other era than the
latter half of the Nineteenth Century, nor any other land than
democratic America." The statement sounds like the formal acknowledgement which any author might make of the debt he owed
to the environment in which he worked. But for the student of
Whitman this statement has special significance. It is more than
a formality; it is a confession.

There is no doubt that the America of his day provided the
faith which empowered Whitman to redeem himself, and to
escape from the dungeon of self-condemnation in which he had
languished. This America presented to him a generic image out
of which he could construct not only an acceptable but a heroic
image of himself. His vision of America, like his self-image, was
half real, half idealized; it was created partly out of the present
but mostly out of the future; it emerged from his actual experiences and also from his reading of such American prophets as
Ralph Waldo Emerson.

Leaves of Grass can be described as the meeting place of a
highly self-conscious poet and a highly self-conscious nation, for
Whitman in the 1840's and 1850's found America to be in a predicament much like his own. As a new, undeveloped country,
America, like Whitman, experienced a conflict between feelings of
inferiority and impulses of exaggerated self-assertion. Every
American could sense the disparity between the crude reality of
his homeland and the superior culture of the European fatherland,
even when he did not acknowledge it. By the time Whitman began
writing *Leaves*, however, the aggressive spirit of national self-

confidence, though clouded with threats of sectional conflict, had gained ascendancy. Whitman in the midst of his own emotional and social difficulties felt himself buoyed up by the expansive, optimistic spirit of his environment. He could identify what he had felt as his own moral deficiency with the cultural deficiencies which all Americans felt. But he could also rationalize his psychological inadequacies, as his fellow Americans had rationalized their cultural inadequacies, into positive virtues. There is a subtle connection between the sexual immaturity of Whitman and the cultural immaturity of Whitman's America.

American pride, which was partly defiant, partly unconscious and naïve, was precisely what Whitman needed to aid him in solving his own problem of self-censure and self-isolation. However, proud and independent as they were, his fellow-Americans showed the pride of equals, not of superior and exclusive aristocrats. They were not a nation set apart; they were mankind. "Here at last," Whitman wrote in 1855, "is something in the doings of man that corresponds with the broadcast doings of the day and night. Here is not merely a nation but a teeming nation of nations."[15] Sharing in the national pride, then, Whitman could feel that he belonged to the whole human community and was supported by it.

Because it was a nation which, in its ideals at least, represented humanity, America excluded no one. It was as notable for its broad tolerance and sympathy as for its pride. One of the first entries in the earliest Whitman notebook extant (1847-1848) sums up this paradox of a national pride which is non-exclusive: "True noble expanded American Character is raised on a far more lasting and universal basis than of any of the characters of the 'gentlemen' of aristocratic life. . . . It is to be illimitably proud, independent, self-possessed, generous and gentle. It is to accept nothing except what is equally free and eligible to any body else."[16] In the Preface to his 1855 *Leaves* he lauds the "common people," who best express "the genius of the United States," for both "their self-esteem and wonderful sympathy" (p. iii). In these and other similar statements Whitman is not mouthing patriotic platitudes. He is making an act of faith and hope in his countrymen which is of serious personal concern to him. We have already seen Whitman's hunger for sympathy in the loneliness and yearning of his secret predicament, and we have seen the anguished offers of sympathy to all kinds of "shunned persons" which he was ready to make in return.

We have also noted that in order to redeem the morally ambiguous passions which were an essential part of him, Whitman had rejected orthodox moral standards and had adopted a posture of primitive innocence. Here again, America, or—more accurately —one of the myths inspired by America, was of use to him. America had become an apt illustration for the theories of European romanticism, an untouched wilderness which invited escape from the complexities and vices of civilization and offered a return to nature and primeval virtue. America loomed up as a new Eden where the human race could slough off its old failures and make a second new start.

It was not entirely a fiction. Thousands of immigrants rejecting the chafing social, economic, and political restrictions of the Old World had actually found an entirely new world of opportunity and freedom in America. The lawlessness of the frontier settlements in the West indicated that many Americans had also thrown off the moral restrictions of the Old World. The very title "Children of Adam," which Whitman gave to his group of poems celebrating the human body and sex, suggests how literally he adopted the myth of a new Eden. The group begins with one "Adamic" poem and ends with another.

The composite image of Whitman's ideal American—a common man, untutored, earthy, bearded, tanned, endowed with full-bodied passions which he expresses freely in his Adamic innocence, proud, unconcerned, yet full of tenderness for the weak and unfortunate—this image is a projection of the poet's intimate personal needs. The fact that Whitman preferred the "powerful uneducated person" for his friend in real life suggests that when he portrays this rugged outdoor hero in his own poetic person, as in "Song of Myself," he portrays not himself but his imaginary lover. Whitman created his generic American out of certain types he found in the America of his time, and he created him in the image of the rough athletic lover his heart desired.

Whitman was an ardent prophet of American democracy because he had so much at stake in the venture. His inspiration was no command from the mountaintop; it was rather the cry of his deepest, inmost wants. If he made a religion out of America, or promulgated the religion of America created by his predecessors, he did so because he himself most needed the salvation it offered.

For reasons not altogether clear, Whitman appears to have passed through a period of self-doubt in the years 1859-1860. However that may be, in 1860 he stood on the verge of what was to be a tremendous experience both for himself and for America, an experience which would restore him to a lifetime of unbroken faith in his poetic venture. "It is certain," he declared in 1880 (*A Backward Glance*), "that, although I had made a start before, only from the occurrence of the Secession War, and what it show'd me as by flashes of lightning, with the emotional depths it sounded and arous'd . . . that only from the strong flare and provocation of that war's sights and scenes the final reasons-for-being of an autochthonic and passionate song definitely came forth." As if to make his point more emphatic he adds, "Without those three or four years [of his Civil War work] and the experiences they gave, 'Leaves of Grass' would not now be existing."

The conduct of the common soldier in the Civil War convinced him, once and for all, of the heroic character of the American people. One night, early in 1864, when on a visit to Culpeper, Virginia, Whitman watched a Union infantry contingent march past through the deep mud; they were "full of gayety, endurance, and many fine little outshows, the signs of the most excellent good manliness of the world." As he watched, it occurred to him that he had "never before so realized the majesty and reality of the American people *en masse*. It fell upon me like a great awe" ("Down at the Front," in *Specimen Days*). When he wrote *Democratic Vistas* in 1870, he itemized and castigated the vices of the dark period of Reconstruction, but he was still convinced that the moral health of America, beneath all the appearances, was fundamentally sound.

At this point the importance of the Civil War for Whitman begins to appear. In 1855 the robust American whom he had created in the image of his love lived, for the most part, in the realm of the ideal. In the Civil War years Whitman saw him in the flesh, or thought he did. But he not only saw his common-man hero at his most heroic, he became associated with him in what must have been for Whitman a most satisfying relation. As a nurse or, more accurately, a visitor in the war hospitals in Washington, D. C., Whitman, for the first time in his life, could openly take his feminine role in society. What is more, he found his feminine feelings responded to. The soldier-patients, ill or wounded, were lonely, depressed, and were yearning for home and kindred, especially for their women folk. They probably were not indifferent to the maternal kindness and tenderness of a man like Whitman.

In a letter which appeared in the New York *Times*, December 11, 1864, Whitman relates how he read to one seriously wounded

young man from the New Testament at the young man's request.
"I felt that he was even then the same as dying. He behaved very
manly and affectionate. The kiss I gave him as I was about leaving,
he returned fourfold."[17] Whitman wrote to his mother on September 15, 1863: "Mother, can you wonder at my getting so attached
to such men, with such love, especially when they show it to me—
some of them on their dying beds, and in the very hour of death,
or just the same when they recover, or partially recover? I never
knew what American young men were till I have been in the
hospitals."[18]

It is hardly surprising that Whitman was confirmed in his
belief that the sentiments of manly love were universal. To his
intimate friend, Mrs. Abby Price, he wrote a frank account of his
relation to his patients:

> In the hospitals, among these American young men, I could not
> describe to you what mutual attachments, and how passing deep
> and tender these boys. Some have died, but the love for them
> lives as long as I draw breath. These soldiers know how to love
> too, when once they have the right person and the right love
> offered them. It is wonderful. You see I am running off into the
> clouds, but this is my element.[19]

But Whitman was not merely exploiting an unusual situation
for the satisfaction of his own unusual and ardent desires. The
real significance of his work in the war hospitals lies in the deeper
satisfaction he took in having become a useful citizen, not despite
his feminine qualities but because of them. Here at last he could
merge himself, just as he really was, in a great common cause with
his fellow Americans. The letters he wrote during this time reveal
his almost pathetic eagerness to prove the good he was doing. He
distributed small gifts among the soldiers, he read to them and
wrote letters for them, but he early concluded that he performed
his greatest service by his healthy presence and by the invisible
dynamic of his love.

It was as if he were acting out, in real life, the role he had
written for himself in his earlier verses.

> The friendly and flowing savage . . . . Who is he?
> . . . .
> Wherever he goes men and women accept and desire him,
> They desire he should like them and touch them and speak to
>   them and stay with them.
> . . . .

Behold I do not give lectures or a little charity,
What I give I give out of myself.
. . . .
To any one dying . . . . thither I speed and twist the knob
    of the door,
. . . .
I seize the descending man . . . . I raise him with resistless
    will.

O despairer, here is my neck,

By God! you shall not go down! Hang your whole weight
    upon me.
. . . .
I am he bringing help for the sick as they pant on their backs,
. . . .
You will hardly know who I am or what I mean,
But I shall be good health to you nevertheless,
And filter and fibre your blood.[20]

The early declaration of faith and love had been vindicated in
the actualities of the war hospitals. Whitman would never doubt
again, though he would encounter long years of ill health, of
neglect and loneliness. No wonder that ever after, he asserted
emphatically the decisive effect of the Civil War on his *Leaves*.

Whitman's philosophy begins, and perhaps ends, in psychology,
that is, in an intuition of the self. As we have seen, his experience
of his own ego revealed a duality, "my soul and I," but a duality
which was also, paradoxically, a single personality. His discovery
of the psyche and the implications of that discovery Whitman
narrated in a parable contained in "Song of Myself." The experience he represents here may have prompted him to adopt the new,
affirmative attitude of self-acceptance which made him the poet
of *Leaves of Grass*.

Backward I see in my own days where I sweated through
    fog with linguists and contenders,
I have no mockings or arguments . . . . I witness and wait.

I believe in you my soul . . . . the other I am must not abase
    itself to you,
And you must not be abased to the other.

Loafe with me on the grass . . . . loose the stop from your
    throat,
Not words, not music or rhyme I want . . . . not custom or
    lecture, not even the best,
Only the lull I like, the hum of your valved voice.

I mind how we lay in June, such a transparent summer
    morning;
You settled your head athwart my hips and gently turned
    over upon me,
And parted the shirt from my bosom-bone, and plunged
    your tongue to my barestript heart,
And reached till you felt my beard, and reached till you held
    my feet.

Swiftly arose and spread around me the peace and joy and
    knowledge that pass all the art and argument of the
    earth;
And I know that the hand of God is the elderhand of my own,
And I know that the spirit of God is the eldest brother of
    my own,
And that all the men ever born are also my brothers . . . .
    and the women my sisters and lovers,
And that a kelson of the creation is love;
And limitless are leaves stiff or drooping in the fields,
And brown ants in the little wells beneath them,
And mossy scabs of the wormfence, and heaped stones, and
    elder and mullen and pokeweed.[21]

It is obvious that the self-discovery told of in the parable is an
erotic one; it is a narcissistic experience. But the ancient myth
has been changed in important respects. The first Narcissus was
condemned to stare at his reflected image until he pined wistfully
away, but this new Narcissus consummates his self-love in a
mysterious self-marriage. He plunges into the pool of self and yet,
miraculously, he does not drown. He re-emerges and finds, around
the edge of the pool, a brave new world peopled with innumerable,
beautiful "selves." These selves, joined together by the same love
which binds the poet to his soul, form a wide community: God
and all the men and women ever born. Perhaps even the leaves,
the brown ants, the scabs, the weeds, and the stones are meant to
be included.*

The remarkable result of this inner marriage is probably due
to the equality which is maintained between the partners, despite

---

* The Freudian would probably interpret the parable as a description of the
libido (the force generated by the sexual instincts) flooding the ego (representing
the self-preservative instincts) and overflowing so as to be invested in objects
outside the self. It is the Freudian hypothesis that narcissism is the primal stage
of sexuality and that outside objects come to be invested with libido at all only
because the accumulation of narcissistic libido in the ego becomes intolerable past
a certain point. In short, for the Freudian, Whitman's parable tells the story of
growing up sexually.

the intimacy of their union. Neither the soul nor "the other I am" is "abased" to the other. If the "I" had been completely surrendered up to the soul, for instance, there would not have been the movement out from the self to embrace the universe in its love. The movement would have been reversed and would have ended in total self-inclosure, a psychic death.[22]

Whitman may have been well aware of the danger. At least he always associates the soul with death in his writings, just as he associates the body with life. In some notes he made in 1861 for a preface which was never published, he said his *Leaves* was "made first, to be the Chant, the Book of Universal Life, and of the Body,—and then, and just as much, to be the Chant of Universal Death, and of the Soul."[23] From first to last Whitman shows in his work that he feels the strong attraction of death. In "Cradle" and "Lilacs" he indulges in his "death wish" with erotic voluptuousness. The sea which lisps the "delicious word death" leaves him softly all over; the dead are lost in a "loving floating ocean," they are "laved in a flood of bliss," "the body gratefully nestling close" to death.

Yet Whitman's poetic imagination never completely surrenders the poet to this dark, seductive power. Denis de Rougemont describes the erotic mysticism of the Western romantic tradition as a union with the Divine in which the distinctive self of the mystic is obliterated. This form of mysticism is *"infinite transcendence,* man's rise into his god. And this rise is *without return."*[24] However, there is a return, according to Rougemont, from the Christian mystic's transcendent experience, a return to the here and now. The Christian mystic will live his life in a new perspective, but he will live in the temporal world. Whitman's is an erotic mysticism; certainly it is not Christian. Yet it follows the rhythm of Christian mysticism as described by Rougemont.

In the concluding stanzas of "Cradle" and "Lilacs," the poet returns to life from his immersion in death. He deliberately, firmly, puts behind him the images and symbols of his preternatural experience, and comes back to the everyday world refreshed and reassured. Perhaps this ebb and flow of self-immolation and self-retrievement, "the merge and the outlet again," accounts for the fact that Whitman's poems on death, unlike most romantic poems on that subject, are not melancholy. In *Democratic Vistas* Whitman predicted "some great coming literatus, especially poet, who . . . will compose the great poem of death. Then man will . . . take his right place, *prepared for life,* master of fortune and misfortune" [italics added]. Throughout his work there is a constant, even tiresome insistence upon the equality of the body and the soul. The reason would seem to be his awareness of the danger which sounded for him in the siren song of death.

Another observation to be made of the self-marriage enacted in Whitman's parable is that the poet, the "I," the body, is the receptive female partner while the "soul" is the aggressive male partner. In his poems celebrating "adhesiveness," we have seen that the *persona* of the poet takes the feminine role and is extremely conscious of his sensuous, physical being. Some of the love-poems make it clear that he also associates his lover with the soul.

> Fast-anchor'd eternal O love! O woman I love!
> O bride! O wife! more resistless than I can tell, the thought
>   of you!
> Then separate, as disembodied or another born,
> Ethereal, the last athletic reality, my consolation,
> I ascend, I float in the regions of your love O man,
> O sharer of my roving life.

We have observed that Whitman's yearnings for manly love led him to a contemplation of death, that is, of what transcends the physical and the mortal.

Whitman extended his experience of the erotic union of body and soul to nature and to the cosmos. For instance, among some of his early notes for a proposed series of lectures on religion is found this interesting analogy:

> There are in things two elements fused though antagonistic. One is the bodily element, which has in itself the quality of corruption and decease; the other is the element, the Soul, which goes on, I think, in unknown ways, enduring forever and ever.

> The analogy holds in this way—that the Soul of the Universe is the Male and genital master and the impregnating and animating spirit—Physical matter is Female and Mother and waits barren and bloomless, the jets of life from the masculine vigor, the undermost first cause of all that is not what Death is.[25]

It is apparent that "body and soul," "woman and man," "matter and spirit" are for Whitman equivalent terms to designate the same duality. And this was the duality he had discovered erotically in his own ego.

Out of this union of the male soul and female matter is born the world of phenomena, the world of differentiation or of what Whitman calls "identity"—

> World of the real—world of the twain in one,
> World of the soul, born by the world of the real alone, led to
>   identity, body, by it alone . . .
> *("Thou Mother With thy Equal Brood")*

"Identity" is a favorite word with Whitman and he gives it a special emphasis if not a special meaning. It represents for him the mystery of uniqueness in a person or a thing—a mystery because the uniqueness springs from the fusion of two universals, matter and spirit. Although the distinction is never very clearly stated, Whitman seems to attribute the unity of the universe to the soul, and to attribute to matter the differentiation of "identities." In any "identified" person or thing, however, the unity of the spiritual and the material is absolute.

> Strange and hard that paradox true I give,
> Objects gross and the unseen soul are one.
> *("A Song for Occupations")*

The cosmic process by which the world of the soul is led to identity by the world of the real is evolutionary. We saw that Whitman, in his poetic ego, fused the unique person, Walt Whitman, with the generic American. In a similar way he is both the individual who has "receiv'd identity by his body" and the universal soul ranging freely through space and time, backward as well as forward.

All of these ideas, as ideas, were common enough, even conventional, in Whitman's day. In fact, he could have derived all of them from Emerson, whose essays he read in a profoundly susceptible mood. But Whitman used these ideas as instruments to express his own erotic self-awareness. For example, the basic transcendental concept of the union of matter and spirit Whitman transformed from an abstraction of thought into a concrete, sensuous reality.

> Urge and urge and urge,
> Always the procreant urge of the world.

> Out of the dimness opposite equals advance, always sub-
>   stance and increase, always sex,
> Always a knit of identity, always distinction, always a breed
>   of life.
> *("Song of Myself")*

All of the Transcendentalists professed to be looking for the roots of natural life, but compared to the shaggy, primitive Whitman, Emerson and even Thoreau look like pale-faced scholars. The philosophical naturalism which was romantic in origin begins, with Whitman, to change into realism. He makes it easier to see a relation between Emerson and Dreiser.

Whitman did not pretend to be a philosopher, but he did profess to be a religious prophet. His own vision of selfhood, of America, and of the universe he regarded as religious rather than literary in inspiration. Further, he regarded all genuine poetry as scripture and the genuine poet as "the true son of God." In brief, he followed the trend of nineteenth-century romanticism in confusing literature and religion.

The main tenets of Whitman's religious belief are clear: he believes in the unique worth of the individual; he believes in immortality; he believes in God. His faith was sincere and grew deeper and firmer the longer he lived. His articles of faith, however, did not to the same degree become more clearly defined or more consistent.

Whitman placed a high, even a sacred value upon the individual human being. But this emphasis hardly seems justified if it is the fate of the "identified" individual upon death to be swallowed up in the undifferentiated world-soul which was also an essential part of Whitman's credo. One possible way out of the transcendental inconsistency was to adopt the Oriental belief in the transmigration of souls, and it is significant that Whitman, like Emerson, felt the attraction of this doctrine. He believes, he writes in "Song of Myself," that he will "come again upon the earth after five thousand years." Later in the same poem he says:

> And as to you life, I reckon you are the leavings of many
>   deaths,
> No doubt I have died myself ten thousand times before.

But it cannot be said that Whitman was consistently committed to this notion of immortality. At other times, in defiance of his pantheism, he affirmed a belief in personal immortality. In 1888 he confided to a group of his friends: "I believe in immortality, and by that I mean *identity*. I know I have arrived at this result more by what may be called feeling than formal reason—but I believe it: yes, I know it."[26]

There are similar, and related, uncertainties and inconsistencies in Whitman's ideas about God. If the soul of the individual is but the soul of the cosmos incarnate, then it follows that the individual is himself divine. This position was implied in the transcendental pantheism which Whitman adopted and it was especially attractive to him because of his need to create a heroic self-image.

> What do you suppose I would intimate to you in a hundred
> ways, but that man or woman is as good as God?
> And that there is no God any more divine than Yourself?
> *("Laws for Creations")*

Given Whitman's essential pantheism, this deification of man, found frequently in his work, is not as blasphemous as it sounds to the orthodox Christian. In other passages his belief is nothing more definite than a personal sense of assurance.

> Something there is more immortal even than the stars,
> (Many the burials, many the days and nights, passing
> away,)
> Something that shall endure longer even than lustrous
> Jupiter,
> Longer than sun or any revolving satellite,
> Or the radiant sisters the Pleiades.
> *("On the Beach at Night")*

Even when he marches with the soul through the evolving aeons, however, Whitman sometimes places the Deity outside the framework of change as the fixed objective toward which the cosmos is moving. "Our rendezvous is fitly appointed . . . . God will be there and wait till we come."[27] There are other passages in Whitman which, like this one, indicate a belief in a personal God, but it may well be that Whitman was speaking figuratively.

Whitman's religious world was that of "natural supernaturalism," already strange to us in the middle of the twentieth century but familiar enough to the nineteenth. It was a paradoxical world where there could be no miracles because everything was miraculous, where no God-become-man could be recognized because all men had become gods, and where there was no room for the truly supernatural because all things had been deified. It was a world created by the romantic revolution in which the rationalism of the Enlightenment was repudiated because it was thought to have destroyed the spirit of religion as well as the organized forms of religion. The romantics wished to recover the religious spirit but, strangely enough, they agreed with the prophets of the Enlightenment that the religious forms were dead and would soon disappear. They were chiefly interested in the religious emotions, especially those induced by the sense of mystery. Having repudiated Scripture together with religious institutions, they took "Nature" for their revelation and authority much as their predecessors had done. But whereas Nature had revealed clearly defined "laws" to the rationalist, to the romantic mind Nature revealed the hazy mysteries of soul. Thus nature, including human nature, became supernaturalized.

This was the religion which Whitman preached to his fellow Americans, following Emerson as the forerunner who had been crying in the wilderness of the New World. Whitman believed that the faith he sought to inspire combined the best elements of all previous religions without being subject to the limitations of any single one.

Whitman himself provides the best summary of his New World religion:

> I will see, (said I to myself,) whether there is not, for my purposes as poet, a religion, and a sound religious germenancy in the average human race, at least in their modern development in the United States, and in the hardy common fibre and native yearnings and elements, deeper and larger, and affording more profitable returns, than all mere sects or churches—as boundless, joyous, and vital as Nature itself—a germenancy that has too long been unencouraged, unsung, almost unknown. With science the old theology of the East, long in its dotage, begins evidently to die and disappear. But (to my mind) science . . . as evidently prepares the way for One indescribably grander—Time's young but perfect offspring—the new theology—heir of the West—lusty and loving, and wondrous beautiful. (*Preface,* 1872)

Initially Whitman had been deeply concerned with the religion of American democracy because he desperately needed the faith it provided in order to save his own ego. But after he had perfected his personal faith during the years of the Civil War, he began to take more seriously than before his responsibilities as a national prophet—the role to which his own inner needs had originally committed him. One manifestation of his changed attitude was that he now became a writer of frequent occasional poems as well as of prose pieces which were really long editorials on national life and letters. Another sign was his disposition toward greater moderation, as shown in his extensive revisions in which many of the more reckless phrases and images were toned down or deleted. The "Calamus" poems were allowed to stand but he rejected some of the most personally revealing ones, especially those expressing despondency and near-despair. Further, in his prose writings (usually in footnotes) he rationalized the "Calamus" sentiment into a political-social doctrine.

Whitman's post-War prefaces, in contrast to the defiant manifesto which the 1855 preface was, betray a prudential anxiety about his lifework. In 1876 he confesses that he has "felt temporary depression more than once, for fear that in 'Leaves of Grass' the *moral* parts were not sufficiently pronounc'd." In more serene moments, however, he has been consoled by the thought that his poems prepare the way for and necessitate morals, "just the same as Nature does," and that therefore "they are what, consistently with my plan, they must and probably should be" (*Preface*, 1876, footnote). Whitman is at great pains in these later prose writings to rationalize his initial intentions as a poet. The purely personal motives are ignored and instead there emerges the figure of a man who has decided to be a poet, a national poet, and who carefully and deliberately plans the best means by which to realize his ambition. Whitman's account of how he began to write *Leaves* is even harder to believe than Poe's explanation of how he wrote "The Raven."

Whitman also became less defiantly nationalistic in his later years. In his essay "Poetry and the Future" (1881), he was even willing to admit the value of foreign literature and literature of the past for would-be American writers. As for the poems which Whitman wrote after the War, they show a corresponding change of emphasis. Aside from the many verses in which he was merely repeating himself at a very low level of inspiration, his best poems of this period are oriented toward the "soul" rather than the "body," to return to Whitman's basic dualism. Mr. Gay Wilson Allen has pointed out that with the supplement which Whitman published in 1872 he had begun what he intended to be a new volume of poems which would be complementary to *Leaves of Grass*, a volume he now regarded as finished. In his preface to *Two Rivulets*, published in 1876, he explained what his plan had been: "It was originally my intention, after chanting in 'Leaves of Grass' the songs of the body and existence, to then compose a further, equally needed volume, based on those con-

victions of perpetuity and conversation which . . . make the
unseen soul govern absolutely at last." However, in February
1873 he had suffered a severe stroke which left him partially
paralyzed for several years and from which he never fully
recovered. In May of the same year he suffered another hard blow
in the death of his mother. Therefore in 1876 he had to admit
that "the full construction of such a work [his contemplated
second volume] is beyond my powers, and must remain for
some bard in the future."

"Passage to India," the title poem of the 1872 supplement and
the nucleus of the proposed second volume, is the only longer
poem of the post-War period which, in sustained poetic quality,
will bear comparison with such poems of the earlier period as
"Song of Myself" and "Cradle." "Passage to India" is not only
one of the best but also one of the most representative poems of
Whitman's later period. It is an occasional poem, at least at the
beginning; it is an international, "one-world" poem; and it is a
poem in which "the unseen soul" is made to "govern absolutely
at last."

At the same time, "Passage" shows that the change in Whitman
is one of emphasis only, that there is no break in the continuity
of his work. For example, the journey motif, the most characteristic of Whitman's structural devices from first to last, is here
elaborated as never before. There are at least three different
"journeys" envisioned, on three different ascending levels. The
first journey which is contemplated is a physical one which spans
the globe. It has been made possible by "the great achievements
of the present . . . the strong light works of engineers," the Suez
canal, the Transcontinental railroad, and the Atlantic cable. The
recent completion of these three projects was the immediate
occasion for the poem.

There is a second voyage, however, which the poet imagines,
a voyage through time as well as space and toward a unity which
is more than physical. This is the movement toward the spiritual
and cultural community of mankind, contained prophetically in
"myths and fables of eld," in "the far-darting beams of the
spirit," in "the deep diving bibles and legends," and in "the daring
plots of the poets." Between the ancient dreams and the modern
facts there arise before the poet the figures of the early explorers
of the New World. To these the poet also pays tribute, especially
to that supreme hero of Whitman's later years, Christopher Columbus. Just as the poems and legends of the past underlie the

physical oneness of the world achieved by modern engineering, so too poetry is needed to complete the process.

> After the noble inventors, after the scientists . . .
> Finally shall come the poet worthy that name,
> The true son of God shall come singing his songs.

This poet-prophet will not only celebrate the modern wonders; he will reveal to the feverish children of men the significance of the restlessness and dissatisfaction which have driven them westward across the earth.

> Nature and Man shall be disjoin'd and diffused no more,
> The true son of God shall absolutely fuse them.

Their journey around the world completed, mankind find themselves back at the point where they started. Whitman interprets this circular movement symbolically, as a spiritual return to primitive innocence. "Passage indeed O soul to primal thought . . ." He instructs his soul ("I with thee and thou with me") to begin its circumnavigation of the globe, following the course

> Of man, the voyage of his mind's return,
> To reason's early paradise,
> Back, back to wisdom's birth, to innocent intuitions,
> Again with fair creation.

There is nothing new for Whitman in this nostalgia for Eden, but it is significant that here he does not associate his Adamic myth with America. This Eden belongs to the geography of mind and time but if in addition there is any reference to earthly geography, it is to the oldest, not to the newest of civilized lands.

With the next stanza, however, comes the realization that this return of the mind to man's beginning in paradise is but prolog and symbol. In fact it is soon apparent that all that has gone before is but prolog and symbol for the third "journey" which now begins.

> O we can wait no longer,
> We too take ship O soul,
> Joyous we too launch out on trackless seas,
> Fearless for unknown shores on waves of ecstasy to sail,
> Amid the wafting winds, (thou pressing me to thee, I thee
>   to me, O soul,)
> Caroling free, singing our song of God,
> Chanting our chant of pleasant exploration.

The poet's contemplation of the human race moving around
the finite earth through the centuries has been only a preparation
for the bolder vision which now seizes him, a vision of his own
unearthly voyage with his soul through the seas of infinity.

Here we have come back to that familiar pair of lovers, "my
soul and I," who play such a large part, if not all the parts, in
Whitman's drama. In "Song of Myself" we saw these lovers
in their youth. On that June morning as they lay together on the
grass their love was consummated and they were pledged to
travel together on their way through the world. In "Passage,"
we see them in middle or old age as they face together another
journey, the journey beyond their earthly life. They are still
as much in love as they were in youth. They still accept each
other without reservation, without reproach or blame, and they
set out on their celestial voyage with undiminished faith and hope.

> Sail forth—steer for the deep waters only,
> Reckless O soul, exploring, I with thee, and thou with me,
> For we are bound where mariner has not yet dared to go,
> And we will risk the ship, ourselves and all.

In trying to place his poetic vision in such a perspective that
it can be evaluated, it is instructive to compare Whitman with a
contemporary of his, the Danish writer, Sören Kierkegaard.
Neither of the two men knew that the other existed but both
of them experienced the same modern crisis of self-consciousness.
Kierkegaard, however, approached the crisis from a more purely
intellectual background; he was trying to rescue the idea of
human freedom from the web of historical determinism which
he saw as a threat in the philosophy of Hegel.

Yet Kierkegaard, like Whitman, found a basis for freedom in
psychology rather than philosophy. His focal point was what he
called his "category of the individual," more specifically the individual's inner life. Kierkegaard believed that a man was to
be liberated, not by thought but by the will, by inner action.
Descartes had begun with doubt; Kierkegaard began with despair,
for "despair is a far deeper and more complete expression, its
movement much more comprehensive than that of doubt. Despair
is precisely an expression for the whole personality, doubt only
an expression for thought."[28]

The reason Kierkegaard urges despair as the first step toward
liberation is that it is a free choice which forces the individual
to face himself and accept himself as he really is. "So then choose

despair, for even despair is a choice; for one can doubt without choosing to, but one cannot despair without choosing. And when a man despairs, he chooses . . . himself, not in his immediacy, not as this fortuitous individual, but he chooses himself in his eternal validity."[29] Here again Kierkegaard insists upon an inner act of the will instead of an abstract action of the mind. The liberated individual, says Kierkegaard, "knows himself, but this knowledge is not a mere contemplation . . . it is a reflection upon himself which itself is an action, and therefore I have deliberately preferred to use the expression 'choose oneself' instead of 'know oneself.' "[30]

Kierkegaard goes on to illustrate this act of self-possession with an analogy which immediately recalls Whitman's parable of self-marriage in "Song of Myself." "If I desired to be clever," Kierkegaard writes, "I might say at this point that the individual knew himself in such a way as Adam 'knew' Eve in the Old Testament sense of the word. By the individual's intercourse with himself he impregnates himself and brings himself to birth."[31]

Kierkegaard also resembles Whitman in the image of human society which unfolds from his self-union, for this society is one and yet it is made up of unique individuals. "It is the secret which the individual life shares with itself," Kierkegaard explains, "that it is at once an individual life and at the same time the universal."[32] "Every man is the universal-human and at the same time an exception."[33] Kierkegaard puts the democratic paradox in an extreme form: "The truly extraordinary man is the truly ordinary man. The more of the universal-human an individual is able to realize in his life, the more extraordinary he is."

Yet the similarities between Whitman and Kierkegaard in their experience of selfhood are similarities of form only; in the content of their experiences the two differ radically. For Kierkegaard the real inner self is the ethical self, the conscience; for Whitman it is the pre-ethical self, the sensuous consciousness. In order to accept himself, Whitman, as we have seen, simply abandons moral standards altogether. But in Kierkegaard's view, a man can choose himself only when he faces and accepts his responsibilities as a moral agent. The name which Kierkegaard gives to the inner act of self-realization is repentance. The man who has chosen himself "repents himself back into himself, back into the family, back into the race, until he finds himself in God."[34] According to Kierkegaard, "only when I choose myself as guilty do I choose myself absolutely, if my absolute choice of myself is to be made in such a way that it is not identical with creating myself."[35] For Whitman the path to self-acceptance is easier; he simply asserts his freedom of any need to repent.

Kierkegaard regards the individual's place in human history as a moral dilemma. If he is to free himself from the necessity imposed upon him by history, the individual must accept responsibility for more than his own guilt. "Though it were the iniquity of the father which passed by inheritance to the son, he repents of this as well, for only thus can he choose himself . . . His self is, as it were, outside of him, and it has to be acquired, and repentance is his love for this self, because he chooses it absolutely out of the hand of the eternal God."[36] The man who has chosen himself ethically

> becomes conscious of himself as this definite individual, with these talents, these dispositions, these instincts, these passions, influenced by these definite surroundings, as this definite product of a definite environment. But being conscious of himself in this way, he assumes responsibility for all this. . . . As product he is pressed into the forms of reality, in the choice of himself he makes himself elastic, transforming all the outwardness into inwardness. He has his place in the world, with freedom he chooses his place, that is, he chooses this very place.[37]

Whitman, too, chooses and rejoices in his unique place in history, but he sees it as the result of the magnificent, amoral operation of evolutionary forces.

> Immense have been the preparations for me,
> Faithful and friendly the arms that have help'd me.
>
> Cycles ferried my cradle, rowing and rowing like cheerful
>   boatmen,
> . . . .
> Before I was born out of my mother generations guided me
> . . . .
> All forces have been steadily employ'd to complete and
>   delight me,
> Now on this spot I stand with my robust soul.
>   *("Song of Myself")*

Both Whitman and Kierkegaard were concerned with the individual and his ego, and both of them related this problem in different ways to the growing indifference to religion. But Kierkegaard, although he did not wish to put on the robes of the prophet, was trying to lead the individual back to Christianity. *"Without authority* to call attention to religion, to Christianity, is the category for my whole activity as an author," he declared.[38] The peculiar problem of the age, he believed, was how to become a Christian in Christendom. Whitman, on the other hand, regarded himself as a liberator of men, the high priest of a new Adamic religion. He thought he was leading the individual forward to a religion which lay beyond Christianity. Actually, he was leading the way back to a worship which was much older than Christianity.

The comparison with Kierkegaard helps us to realize how truly primitive Whitman's world is. The world which opens up from Kierkegaard's exploration of the self has an ethical center; from Whitman's ego flows the world of amoral nature whose center is erotic. Whitman goes back to an Arcady so real and earthy that it makes the whole romantic tradition of the pastoral with its various revivals of paganism and its nature cults look like sophisticated make-believe.

It is a mistake to pretend that Whitman was a great mystic and religious prophet, to magnify his utterances concerning the soul and immortality and to minimize his celebration of nature in all its nakedness. He is obviously not a dependable moral or spiritual guide, for in the depths of his poetry he believed in no morals at all and the soul he really believed in was the uninhibited spirit of primeval energy. It was ironical that many of his fellow romantics should turn squeamishly away from his frank erotism. The history of primitive religions would seem to show that here Whitman was consistent as his critics were not; wherever and whenever nature has been worshipped, eros has always played a prominent part. Whitman's world was a pagan Eden, complete with the phallic serpent.

It is precisely Whitman's value that he is a great primitive poet; he gives us a rich poetic sense of primitive nature in all its luxuriance, prodigality, and power. His best poetry derives its unquestioned authority from his perception that this divinely created natural life is good, so good that it promises another life still better. His zestful songs in praise of nature's life and nature's death testify to a genuine poetic, if not a high religious, inspiration.

THE LITERARY HISTORIANS

The Brahmins Contemplate the Past

MASON WADE

In the golden age of American historical literature, the middle years of the nineteenth century, history was not a closed preserve for the schoolmen and history was not written by professors chiefly for other professors to read. The first chair of history in an American college was inaugurated by Jared Sparks only in 1839; while the first volume of George Bancroft's *History of the United States* appeared in 1834, Prescott's *Ferdinand and Isabella* in 1837, his *Conquest of Mexico* in 1843, and his *Conquest of Peru* in 1847, Parkman's *Conspiracy of Pontiac* in 1851, and Motley's *Rise of the Dutch Republic* in 1856. These works and others by non-academic writers at once became immensely popular with the general reading public. Bancroft's first volume reached its tenth edition within ten years; Prescott's *Conquest of Mexico* sold 5,000 copies in four months, his *Peru* 7,500 in the same period, while both works subsequently went through edition after edition. To a lesser degree Motley and Parkman also won similar popularity at home and high reputations abroad through their books. These writers made history a force in the mainstream of American life.

No wonder that in 1871 their historical godson, Henry Adams, advised his young student Henry Cabot Lodge to follow history as a profession:

> The question is whether the historico-literary line is practically worth following, not whether it will amuse or improve you. Can you make it *pay?* either in money, reputation, or any other solid value.
> Now if you will think for a moment of the most respectable and respected products of our town of Boston, I think that you will see at once that this profession does pay. No one has done better

and won more in any business or pursuit, than has been acquired by men like Prescott, Motley, Frank Parkman, Bancroft, and so on in historical writing; none of them men of extraordinary gifts, or who would have been likely to do much in the world if they had chosen differently. What they did can be done by others.

. . . Any one who has the ability can enthrone himself here as a species of literary lion with ease, for there is no rival to contest the throne. With it, comes social dignity, European reputation, and a foreign mission to close.[1]

Such were the inducements that led some of the Boston Brahmins to adopt history as their lifework.

The flowering of the Brahmin tradition in the writing of history was a logical development of the impact of German nineteenth-century scholarship upon Boston's classical eighteenth-century English culture, and of the growth of an American sense of tradition which had been fostered by Sparks's biographical and editorial labors. Edward Everett and George Ticknor were sent abroad to Germany in 1815 to be trained in the best traditions of the new European scholarship and, after their return to Harvard, Göttingen and later Berlin became the ultimate goals of ambitious undergraduates. Everett became the most brilliant classical scholar in America; Ticknor launched the scientific study of modern languages: and two other European-trained Harvard professors, E. G. Cogswell and Longfellow, introduced modern library science and enriched a provincial literature with borrowings from abroad. George Bancroft, who was sent to Göttingen by Harvard in 1818 to pursue his theological studies by perfecting his knowledge of the ancient languages, returned after five years to become first an experimental schoolmaster and literary critic, and then to undertake his dual lifework of writing the history of the United States while taking an active part in its political and diplomatic life.

These pioneers were influential. Ticknor induced his friend Prescott to pursue a scholarly career and filled him with his own enthusiasm for Spanish studies, so that in January 1826 Prescott chose the subject of the reign of Ferdinand and Isabella, and then devoted the rest of his life to the writing of Spanish history. Motley, who had studied German under Bancroft at the latter's Round Hill school, which sought in the 1820's to introduce the methods of Fellenberg, Pestalozzi, and the Prussian *gymnasium* into the American school system, attended both Göttingen and Berlin in the early 1830's after finishing at Harvard. Then, after writing some critical articles on German literature and two romantic novels, Motley finally chose the history of Holland as his field in 1850, and divided the rest of his life between history and diplomacy as Bancroft did. Parkman's precarious health after his Oregon Trail adventure in 1846 did not permit formal study abroad, but he had others comb the French, Spanish, and British archives which the condition of his sight enabled him to investigate for himself only at rare intervals in a lifetime of invalidism. Parkman was profoundly influenced both by English and French romanticism, and the new scientific scholarship of Europe.

With the exception of Bancroft, who has justly been called a "Brahmin rebel" by his most recent biographer, R. B. Nye, these four Massachusetts historians were a remarkably homogeneous group. Bancroft, who came from a poor minister's family in Springfield, was a rebel against the political code of Boston Brahminism, as his father, the Reverend Aaron Bancroft, had been a rebel against the orthodox Congregationalism of the 1780's. Young Bancroft was a poor scholarship boy at Exeter and Harvard, who sought to rise in the world by learning; while Prescott, Motley, and Parkman were gilded youths who only had to work hard enough to get by. Bancroft was a Democrat, when all proper Bostonians were Federalists or later Whigs, and still worse a practical politician, when politics was ceasing, by Bostonian lights, to be a career for a gentleman. He paid no heed to Prescott's injunction: "Why do you coquet with such a troublesome termageant as politics, when the glorious Muse of History opens her arms to receive you?" Instead, he became the leader of the Massachusetts Democrats before abandoning his native state for good in 1845, when he went to Washington as Polk's Secretary of the Navy. In 1846 he was named Minister to England, where he served until 1849, and in 1867 Minister to Prussia, where he remained for seven years. To the end he fed upon politics as others feed upon meat and drink. As a historian, Bancroft also differed from the three greater Brahmin historians, Prescott, Motley, and Parkman. He wrote American history in the eagle-screaming tradition of countless Fourth of July orators, seeing it as "a record of events which, in their steady march from tyranny to liberty, from heterogeneity to homogeneity, from scattered colonies to federated republic, illustrated in a single sweep the inevitability of man's progress and the unity of humanity."[2] Strong in his conviction that the history of the United States was the culmination of progress since the Reformation, he was not overly concerned with the search for facts, adopting those from older authors which suited his patriotism and his politics. Many of his readers felt that the *History*, which enjoyed great esteem in Bancroft's early days but was superseded before his death, "voted for Jackson." It was essentially a political performance.

On the other hand, the true Brahmin historians, Prescott, Motley, and Parkman, were men of the study rather than of the platform, although Motley's career to some extent paralleled Bancroft's. They found a romance and a drama in the ancient annals of Spain, Holland, and France which to their minds was sadly lacking in the life of their own times and country. The three had much in common. William Hickling Prescott was born in Salem, the citadel of Federalism, in 1796, the son of one of the leading lawyers in that maritime capital and later in Boston. John Lothrop Motley was born in Dorchester in 1814, the son of a wealthy Boston merchant. Francis Parkman was born on Beacon Hill in 1823, the son of a leading Unitarian minister and the grandson of one of Boston's merchant princes. All three went to Harvard after attending the best schools of their day. They were born and bred in the inner circles of a patrician society highly conscious of its great traditions and of its dominant role in American life. They were Federalists in politics, Unitarians or agnostics in religion, and liberal conservatives in their social outlook. They were oligarchs who aped the way of life of eighteenth-century English aristocrats, while paying lip-service to the republican ideas of their forebears, whose evolution in their own time they increasingly distrusted. They were born to a life of leisure, thanks to the prosperity which Massachusetts' maritime trade had brought their families; but the still-persistent Puritan ethic forbade leisure and demanded social usefulness. The ministry, the law, politics, or medicine were the natural professions for men who looked down upon the commerce which had brought their ancestors wealth. But as the old standing order of New England crumbled under the onslaught of new ideas, the sons of the Puritans revolted against theology, found the law tedious and politics vulgar, and scorned medicine as a higher charlatanry. So all three turned to history, after dabbling in belles-lettres and the novel, since the lingering Puritan heritage made mere literature suspect, while history was a recognized form of solid endeavor, sanctioned by the great eighteenth-century precedents of Gibbon, Hume, and Robertson, and the con-

temporary examples of Sparks and Washington Irving. Both
Prescott and Parkman overcame the severe handicap of near-
blindness in accomplishing their self-appointed tasks, while Motley struggled with equal stoutheartedness against ill health and
a broken diplomatic career while completing his last book.

I

The career of Prescott, the eldest of the group, served as an
example to both Parkman and Motley, whose interest in history
was early aroused by Sparks's and Bancroft's successful labors.
Though Prescott belonged to an older generation, Parkman and
Motley were bred on almost the same intellectual diet, for their
Boston was highly traditional, despite the radical changes of
American life in the first half of the nineteenth century. They were
educated like English gentlemen of the day on the Latin and Greek
classics; on Milton, Pope, Cowper, Addison, Thomson, and Goldsmith; the rationalist historians of the eighteenth century; and
the Scottish philosophers. To varying degrees they subsequently
fell under the spell of the English Romantics, despite their classical training. Prescott early came under the influence of the
Reverend William Ellery Channing, who made Unitarianism
instead of Congregationalism the new established church of New
England and paved the way for the coming of Transcendentalism.
Prescott formally adopted the new persuasion in 1819. His credo
was a Protestantism diluted by Deism:

> To do well and act justly, to fear and to love God, and to love
> our neighbours as ourselves—in these is the essence of religion.
> For what we believe, we are not responsible. . . . For what we do
> we shall indeed be accountable. The doctrine of the Saviour
> unfolds the whole code of morals by which our conduct should be
> regulated.[3]

Prescott's notion of the end of being was that it was "best answered by a life of active usefulness, and not by one of abstract
contemplation, or selfish indulgence, or passive fortitude." In
accordance with these beliefs, he overcame the severe handicaps
of the loss of his left eye in a college prank, the subsequent almost
complete disablement of his right eye, and severe headaches and
rheumatism; and devoted his life to study and writing. He kept
private account of his habitual faults, and sought earnestly to
overcome them. Forced to abandon the law by his ailments, he

checked his natural inclination for the indolent life of a man about town by the reflection: "It is of little moment whether I succeed in this or that thing, but it is of great moment that I am habitually industrious."⁴ By struggling against his nature he acquired industrious habits, and by 1850 found it "hard work to make a *life of* pleasure,"⁵ when he permitted himself a four months' vacation in Europe, after a quarter-century of constant endeavor.

When in 1821 Prescott decided upon a literary career, he began to write critical articles for the *North American Review,* which had been founded in 1815 as an organ of American nationalism and had recently become so internationally-minded under the editorship of Edward Everett that it was nicknamed the *"North Unamerican."* Everett had made it the organ of the German-trained group which brought European influences to bear on American literature and education. Ticknor, who had studied at Göttingen when it was a center of Spanish studies, and who was to devote his life to the writing of a *History of Spanish Literature* (1849), undoubtedly led Prescott to study first French and Italian literature, and then Spanish. By 1825 Prescott was seeking a subject on which to write, and was divided between Italian literature, American history, Roman history, and biography. Again it was probably Ticknor's influence that led him early in 1826 to settle upon the reign of Ferdinand and Isabella, a topic which eventually led him into an almost complete series of studies of the rise and fall of the Spanish Empire from 1474 to 1574.⁶

The antiquarian and Gothic writers of both Britain and the United States had already begun the literary exploitation of Spanish history when Prescott formed his project. The Incas and Aztecs had already been celebrated in popular poetry, drama, and novels; and it is clear that Southey's *Madoc* influenced Prescott profoundly. The Peninsular Wars gave British writers a new interest in Spain, which was further stimulated by the Carlist risings of the 1830's. The Spanish archives were opened to scholars in 1780, and the subsequent publication of new source material made necessary the rewriting of Spanish history. A month after Prescott decided upon his subject, Washington Irving began in Madrid an adopted translation of Navarrete's book on Columbus' voyages, which he published in 1828 as the *Life and Voyages of Columbus.* The following year appeared Irving's *Conquest of Granada,* which the tyro Prescott gloomily thought "superseded all further necessity for poetry, and unfortunately for me, history."⁷ Irving's *Companions of Columbus* was published in 1831 and his *Legends of the Alhambra* in 1832. These by-products of Irving's diplomatic life, in which romantic Spain was charmingly exploited, helped to create the wide audience which unexpectedly welcomed Prescott's *Ferdinand and Isabella* in 1837.

Two years later Irving generously renounced his plan to write an account of the conquest of Mexico when he learned that Prescott was at work upon the subject. He later noted: "I doubt whether Mr. Prescott was aware [that I] gave him up my bread."[8] For Irving lived by his pen, while the wealthy Prescott was able "to make [his] books rather a source of pleasure than a business."[9] Prescott made handsome acknowledgment to Irving in his preface to *The Conquest of Mexico*, and a lasting sense of obligation and adherence to the Golden Rule probably guided him in 1848, when he in turn renounced to Motley the Dutch aspects of the reign of Philip II, and even seriously thought of offering the young and untried historian the use of his collection of source materials, unmatched in America.

Since Prescott was physically unable to use his own eyes to investigate the European archives, he did so through the eyes of others whose services were secured through his wealth and the good offices of his well-connected and well-placed friends. One of the chief duties of the American Foreign Service at this period, when it was dominated by Massachusetts men, seems to have been the collection of historical materials for American writers. Free from financial pressure, Prescott slowly digested the materials gathered abroad, which were read to him by secretaries and friends. He mentally composed as many as sixty pages before dictating them, and revised carefully and thoroughly through the many drafts of what he called his "tortoise-like progress." *Ferdinand and Isabella* was the product of ten years' intensive work; *Mexico* of six; *Peru* of four; and *Philip II* of nine. Only Parkman, suffering from similar physical difficulties and greater mental ones, was to surpass Prescott's record of dedication to a self-appointed task.

What was Prescott's conception of the historian's role? He preferred the modern rationalist historians to the Greeks and Romans, though he admired the imaginativeness, the elegance of form, and the narrative power of Herodotus and Livy. He had high regard for Voltaire, Sismondi, and Augustin Thierry, but his great idol was Gibbon, whom he daily read before beginning to write. He was much influenced by the Abbé Gabriel de Mably, whose *De l'étude de l'histoire* (1778) was his professional handbook, and also by the Baron de Barante, the contemporary historian of the Dukes of Burgundy, whose use of the old chroniclers to give the reader a sense of participation in the past he adopted for his own works.

Prescott distrusted Gibbon's skepticism, while sharing his rationalism and his belief in progress. He prefered Christianity to paganism or Mohammedanism, and Protestant Christianity to Catholicism. He took the usual disparaging Anglo-Saxon view of feudalism and the Middle Ages, and saw the Reformation as freeing men's minds from the "influence of a tyrannical priesthood."[10] To him American Protestantism was the fine flower of the Reformation, for here was "no feudal tyrant to grind the poor man to the dirt on which he toiled, no Inquisition to pierce the thought, and to make thought a crime." He assigned the Anglo-Saxon conquest of America to love of freedom rather than to the love of gain or "the more specious pretext of proselytism" which had animated the Spaniards. To him the Portuguese and Spanish colonies, "shooting up into the endless splendors of a tropical vegetable, exhibited, even in their prime, the sure symptoms of decay."

But this Anglo-Saxonism, with its derogatory view of the Latin and Catholic peoples (which Motley and Parkman shared to varying degrees) did not prevent Prescott from thinking it fortunate that the Western Hemisphere was discovered by the "two races best fitted to conquer and colonize it." His fair-mindedness, despite his prejudices, led Archbishop Hughes of New York to commend his treatment of Catholics and the *Dublin Review* to call him unbiased, although Archbishop Spaulding of Baltimore accused him of hating the religion of the Conquerors and a Baltimore Catholic journal called him a Deist. Protestant critics found him unbiased, while foreign Catholics were inclined to accuse him of prejudice. John Quincy Adams thought it difficult to tell whether Prescott were a Protestant or a Catholic, a monarchist or a republican; Guizot found him unbiased; while his Mexican translator detected "something of the old Puritan acid in [his] anti-Catholic strictures," and his Spanish one condemned his hostility to the Inquisition.[11]

Prescott himself, writing to a Spanish correspondent of the differences raised by Señor Sabau, the translator of *Ferdinand and Isabella*, found them natural enough: "For am I not the child of democracy? Yet no bigoted one, I assure you. I am no friend to bigotry in politics or religion, and I believe that forms are not so important as the manner in which they are administered."[12] This self-criticism appears on the whole to have been just, for Prescott was pleased that Archbishop Hughes had thanked him for the "liberality I had shown in my treatment of the Catholics,"[13] and he never let his distaste for the "dirty trade of politics" or his Federalist dislike for the Democrats to interfere with his friendship for George Bancroft, and his publicly expressed admiration for the latter's *History*.

The truth seems to be that Prescott was a conservative republican who disliked Jacksonian democracy, a Hamiltonian who called himself a Whig, but who found that "a log cabin and hard cider are indifferent qualifications for the presidency."[14] He believed in liberty and freedom of conscience but disliked enthusiasm in either politics or religion. He approved of the Reformation and the American Revolution, but opposed both the philosophy and the results of the French Revolution. He was an Anglophile and something of an Anglo-Saxon racist, who thought Britain and the United States "the only two great nations where constitutional liberty exists."[15] When the revolutions of 1848 swept Europe, he noted: "Liberty and equality seem to be too great stimulants for some constitutions. They suit the Anglo-Saxon better than any."[16] He held England in high regard, but preferred his "own dear wild America." Bred on English Protestant literature of the Puritan period and the eighteenth century, he had an emotional hatred of Spanish cruelty and Spanish despotism, whether political or ecclesiastical. But his suppressed romanticism reveled in the color and pageantry of the Spanish Empire in its great days, and the military code which he had inherited from a grandfather who fought at Bunker Hill made him admire the grim courage of the Spaniards who conquered the New World in the name of a Faith which was abhorrent to him.

Basically Prescott was far more a romantic storyteller than a rationalistic or moralistic historian. As he remarked of Walter Scott, he himself had "a natural relish for gunpowder; and his mettle roused, like that of the war-horse, at the sound of the trumpet."[17] Edward Eggleston somewhat unreasonably accused him of belonging to the outmoded drum-and-trumpet school of history, when his subject was essentially military history; while Theodore Parker more justly objected to his lack of attention to the people and to prosaic developments, in his preoccupation with great men and great events. In his last work, *Philip II*, Prescott did pay more attention to political, constitutional, and diplomatic history, but these themes dear to von Ranke and the new German historians were not his forte. His concept of history was graphic and dramatic; like Carlyle he prefered the biographical and the pictorial to the impersonal. In *Ferdinand and Isabella* and in *The Conquest of Mexico* he combined scholarly research, classical devotion to form, and dramatic power to make these books classics of our literature. Historians are once more beginning to appreciate the merit of these works, which in the pendulum fashion of historical reputation are coming back into the esteem which they enjoyed in Prescott's lifetime, now that the "scientific" historians and archeologists of a later day have in turn had their own reputations exploded as they exploded Prescott's, and readers are once more insisting that history be written for the many rather than the few.

II

Motley might have been a son of Prescott, representing the same tradition with the differences of a younger generation. While Prescott, playing as a boy in the Athenaeum, had donned helmet and breastplate from an old suit of armor, Motley and his playfellows acted Byronic melodramas clad in doublet and cloak. Thanks to his Round Hill training in German, Motley early became interested in Goethe, reading a paper on the poet at his Harvard senior exhibition and translating *Faust* during his Göttingen and Berlin days, when he became a close friend of the young Bismarck. The Puritan patrician and the Prussian *Junker* had enough in common for the friendship to be lifelong. Clever, supercilious, high-spirited, and fickle, the young Motley, who reminded Lady Byron of her husband, seemed to be cut out for anything rather than a scholar's life.

When he returned to Boston in 1855 from his *Wanderjahre* on the Continent and in England, Motley studied law, but was too full of German Romanticism to settle down in that profession. Encouraged in his literary leanings by Dr. Holmes and Longfellow, he wrote essays on German literature for the *New York Review*, and tried his hand at a novel, *Morton's Hope* (1839), which was aptly described as a "compound of Byronism, Bulwerism, and Vivian Greyism."[18] This autobiographical novel, which mixed scenes of German university life and of the American frontier during the French and Indian Wars, was unsuccessful. It was weak in plot and characterization, and written in a bombastic mishmash of imitations of Motley's favorite Romantic authors. A second novel, *Merry-Mount,* published ten years later, was not much more successful as such, but displayed increased narrative, pictorial, characterization powers, for here Motley was working with historical materials rather than relying on his own creative ability. After having had "two novels killed under me," Motley realized that "my place was among the sappers and pioneers and not the lancers"[19] of literature.

In 1845, a year before writing his second novel, Motley had already begun the traditional apprenticeship of the Brahmin historians by publishing an article on Peter the Great in the *North American Review.* The subject was probably suggested by several months spent as secretary of legation in St. Petersburg in 1841-1842. This lively sketch of the great Russian ruler's career was well received, and led Motley's friends to advise him to write history or biography rather than fiction. In another *North American* article of 1849 on "Polity of the Puritans," Motley used a review of a German work on the colonization of New England to challenge Bancroft's democratic interpretation of that period. In the gradual evolution of freedom and self-government Motley finally found his lifelong theme, for in the following year he began work on the early history of the Dutch provinces, in whose struggle to liberate themselves from Spain he found a parallel to the American Revolution. To him William the Silent was an earlier George Washington, for both had led small Protestant and democratic peoples in the struggle for independence against the tyrannical rulers of great empires. To him the rise of Protestantism and of political freedom in northern Europe were parts of the pattern of progress which spiraled upwards to the climax of American democracy.

A late Federalist who found the democracy of his own day far from perfect, Motley was nonetheless a liberal who believed that "politically and philosophically the foundation of government is by popular consent."[20] But though he accepted the doctrine of sovereignty of the people, he was less enthusiastic about *"liberté, égalité, et fraternité"* in the French interpretation. Like a true Federalist, he believed that the best government was government by the best, among whom he classed himself. Though his political career in Massachusetts was nipped in the bud after one term in the state legislature in 1849, and his two diplomatic missions abroad, won through the influence of Charles Sumner, were summarily ended by the earthy politics of post-Civil War Washington,

Motley remained a fervent believer in American democracy. By temperament and taste, however, as well as a result of his residence abroad after 1851, Motley was as out of tune with the new American order as Charles Francis Adams and his son Henry, with whom he returned from Europe in 1867. Henry Adams noted: "Had they been Tyrian traders of the year b.c. 1000, landing from a galley fresh from Gibraltar, they could hardly have been stranger on the shore of a world, so changed from what it had been ten years before."[21] They were, indeed, "survivals from the forties—bric-à-brac from the time of Louis-Philippe; stylists; doctrinaires; ornaments that had been more or less suited to the colonial architecture, but which had never had much value in Desbrosses Street or Fifth Avenue." It was not surprising that Motley welcomed appointment as Minister to Britain in 1869, and spent the rest of his life abroad.

But in addition to being ornamental, Motley was also industrious and dedicated to his chosen historical task, as well as to his diplomatic duties. After dividing the field with Prescott, he had gone to Europe in 1851 to study in the libraries and archives of Dresden, Brussels, the Hague, Paris, and London, which he frequented until his nomination as Minister to Austria in 1861. He was able to use Latin, French, German, Spanish, Dutch, and Italian as working tools. In his first historial work, the three-volume *Rise of the Dutch Republic* (1856), he relied largely on the printed collections of source materials which had been appearing during the last quarter-century, and on the standard Dutch authorities for the period. The few manuscript sources which he cited were probably already prepared for publication when he saw them. He made constant and somewhat uncritical use of a few secondary sources. In his second work, the four-volume *History of the United Netherlands* (1860-1867), he increased his use of manuscript materials, and in the third and last, the two-volume *Life and Death of John of Barnevald* (1874), he based his work chiefly on archival material. In the latter two works he was less successful in composing a unified and dramatic narrative than in his first major historical effort; and one reason why these works have not enjoyed the same popularity as *The Dutch Republic* is that they are too full of undigested documentation, like Bancroft's later volumes, and too exclusively devoted to political history.

For though Motley had read the new German historians, von Ranke, Sybel, and Niebuhr, his work revealed little of their influence. Like Carlyle, he was fascinated by the glitter of great men and great events, and the sturdy gray threads which make up the woof of history did not interest him. His dramatic instincts were stronger than his historical ones. He surpasses both Prescott and Parkman in the vivid presentation of key scenes; he is a master of the set piece. But he ranks far below them in the objective presentation of facts after exhaustive investigation and in fair-minded effort to understand the past in its own terms. Motley, for all his delving into the archives, remained a frustrated novelist; and since his intent was didactic, he never tried to be objective: "If ten people in the world hate despotism a little more and love civil and religious liberty a little better in consequence of what I have written, I shall be satisfied."[22] He measured the men and events he depicted with great literary skill by his own liberal Protestant democratic principles. He frankly espoused the cause of those who fought, as he saw it, on behalf of Protestantism and democracy:

> For the history of the United Provinces is not at all a provincial history. It is the history of European liberty. Without the struggle of Holland and England against Spain, all Europe might have been Catholic, and Spanish. It was Holland that saved England in the sixteenth century, and, by so doing, secured the triumph of the Reformation, and placed the independence of the various states of Europe upon a sure foundation.[23]

His Dutch and English Protestant heroes were all white, and his Spanish Catholic villains all black. He judged the events of the sixteenth century by the standards and prejudices of a New Englander of the mid-nineteenth. Because of his fervent partisanship, inadequate research, and preoccupation with the pictorial, his works have been outmoded by those of later writers who strove more soberly to reconstruct the past without bias, and to achieve a more comprehensive if less dramatic view. For all Motley's eloquence and narrative power, he is no longer read except as literature.

III

Francis Parkman was the climax of the great Boston historical school, though Bancroft's *History of the United States,* Prescott's *Conquest of Mexico,* and Motley's *Dutch Republic* received far more attention in their day than did his epic of *France and*

England in North America. Though Parkman was almost an exact contemporary of Motley, his major work was published after rather than before the Civil War, in the seven books which appeared from 1865 to 1892. These reflected the influence of the new school of scientific history, although Parkman himself belonged to the world of Prescott and Motley, and followed a similar literary apprenticeship, writing critical articles for the *North American* and *Christian Examiner* and sketches of the French and Indian wars for the *Knickerbocker Magazine,* which also published his account of his Oregon Trail trip before it appeared in book form in 1849. Neither *The Oregon Trail* nor his first serious historical effort, *The Conspiracy of Pontiac* (1851), which is really an epilog to his lifework, enjoyed any such vogue as Bancroft, Prescott, and Motley achieved with their first books.

American interest in American history had been largely sated by Sparks, Irving, and Bancroft; the American of the middle years of the nineteenth century looked across the Atlantic, if he were of historical or literary turn of mind, and his taste was for works that made him more familiar with the European tradition which had once more become influential on American life, though through German and other Continental channels rather than the older English ones. Parkman was the first to see that the obscure frontier skirmishes which had been chronicled by the earlier New England historians were not mere backwoods squabbles of purely sectional interest, but conflicts of more than local importance which had influenced the course of European events. Since he was the first to write the history of the French in North America in English, Parkman had to create his public, rather than to write for one which stood waiting, as Bancroft, Prescott, and Motley did.

Though he was the youngest of them, Parkman better represented the old New England order and was a truer Brahmin of the Brahmins than any of the historical writers who are usually grouped with him. Isolated by precarious health and private means from the new influences which remade New England in his lifetime, he carried on in the old tradition, devoting himself to a self-imposed task with a single-mindedness which surpassed even Prescott's. Though he cordially detested Puritanism, he had the Puritan's pride of learning and ascetic devotion to scholarship. He spared neither himself nor others in the pursuit of historical truth, despite near-blindness, crippling rheumatism, and a mental disorder which often made it impossible for him to work for long periods. Unlike the others, he was a born historian, though at the outbreak of the Civil War he regretted that he had to hold "the pen with the hand that should have grasped the sword." Even in his schooldays he had become preoccupied with the American past; he devoted his college vacations to expeditions to the scenes of the wilderness epic he already planned to write, and to experiencing at first hand the conditions under which his heroes had lived. A lover of action and the strenuous life, he was condemned to semi-invalidism while still a young man, probably because of the harshness with which he drove himself. Even the resources of his own mind, which was well stocked by wide reading in preparation for his lifework, were threatened by the nervous disorder which he called "The Enemy." For many years it allowed him to work only five minutes at a time and for but two hours a day at best. Historical work was often impossible, and it was then that he wrote a romantic novel, *Vassall Morton* (1856), which, like Motley's, is only of autobiographical interest. Yet he never gave in to invalidism, and finally completed the historical epic which he had outlined in his youth. His great history covers the story of the French in North America from the age of discovery to the end of New France in 1763.

Parkman had a great contempt for what he called "emasculate scholarship," the moralizing, dogma-ridden tradition of the New England past, which Motley in some measure carried on. He prepared himself for his chosen task by not only studying every printed and manuscript record on which he could lay his hands—like Prescott he employed agents to copy materials in the European archives—but also by familiarizing himself at first hand with every scene about which he wrote. Despite his strong Protestant and democratic principles, he was incapable of shaping his work to a predetermined view; he would not write a page until he had mastered all the sources; and he was highly scrupulous in the use of the materials he collected at great trouble and expense. In addition to his thorough research and distrust of secondary sources, he was a great narrative writer who could reduce the result of years of study to clear and vigorous writing. Since he was a pioneer in his chosen field, he had to combine the roles of researcher, monographer, compiler, and popularizer. And this he did with a skill that has not since been matched. His books are still more widely read than those of any other American historian of his era; and the value of his work has been little diminished by a half-century of intensive research in the field which he opened up. But he finished his lifework just as the new "scientific" historians became dominant; and shortly after his death his achievement was disparaged, along with the lesser work of the other romantic and rhetorical writers of his day. But Parkman's books have refused to die; and contemporary historians are now willing to pay tribute to their scholarly merits, as well as to a standard of writing which his successors have not been able to attain.

Parkman is notable for his detachment among the school to which he belonged, but he would hardly be considered a model of detachment today. His New England heritage irrevocably marked his ways of thought and his opinions. He began his lifework in the belief that the story of New France demonstrated the innate superiority of the civilization of Protestant England over that of Catholic France, and such remained his conclusion at the end. He saw the great colonial struggle in America as one between liberty and absolutism, democracy and feudalism, and he hated either political or ecclesiastical tyranny with the fervor of his Puritan forbears. But by taste and temperament, for his own ideal was "a little medieval," he was drawn to the Jesuit missionaries whose theology he deplored but whose heroism he warmly admired; to the French soldiers and seigneurs who displayed gallantry so lavishly; and to the humble *coureurs-de-bois* and *voyageurs* whose devoted loyalty he had experienced at first hand on his own great youthful adventure in the savage West. Conscious supporter that he was of the doctrine of Anglo-Saxonism, of the innate superiority of the plain man of English blood and Protestant faith to men of another race and creed, he was temperamentally sympathetic with those who displayed the aristocratic virtues of an older order and who represented a mature European culture rather than a rude and raw American one, for all their Latin blood and their Catholicism.

Despite his prejudices against what New France stood for, he fell in love with his subject, which is probably the most colorful and romantic of all historical periods. Among the French Canadians he made many friends, chief of whom, despite Parkman's anti-clericalism, was the Abbé Henri-Raymond Casgrain, who shared his passion for the history of New France. The efforts of his friends at Laval University to award him an honorary degree for his work, which they admired, though they differed from some of his conclusions, were frustrated by the intransigent ultramontanes of the day in Quebec, who caused a weary Roman Cardinal to remark that French Canada made more trouble for the Sacred

Congregations than the rest of Christendom together. The Laval incident undoubtedly strengthened Parkman's anti-clerical bias and his anti-Catholic feelings, but did not prevent him from being just by his lights.

Unlike Bancroft, whose later volumes reflect a flagging of interest and devotion to his task, and unlike Prescott and Motley, whose later works are inferior to their first and who never completed the tasks they had set for themselves, Parkman rounded out his lifework with virtually unfailing vigor and mastery. His cousin Henry Adams greeted the completion of the epic with the observation:

> You have had the singular good fortune to complete successfully a great work which puts you at the head of our living historians; and I leave the dead ones out of account only because we cold-blooded Yanks detest the appearance of exaggeration so much more than we love what the French call *mesure*. Let the dead rest in peace. . . .[24]

Despite his uncanny intuitions of the future, Adams was probably unaware that his graceful compliment was to prove so accurate. But the fact is that Bancroft, Prescott, Motley, and Adams' own historical works slumber on the shelves, while Parkman is read in part if not as a whole, and remains a model for young historians who want to be read by others than their colleagues. Parkman inspired the historical novelists and popular historians who have revived the general reader's interest in history. Thanks to his own achievement and to his wide influence, he may be considered not only the greatest of the mid-nineteenth-century literary historians, but also the greatest American historian.

The four great Brahmin historians strengthened the Protestant tradition of American historiography, which derived from English, French, and German writers of the eighteenth and early nineteenth centuries. Though they were all affected to various degrees by the splintering of New England Puritanism under the impact of nineteenth-century rationalism, they preserved the Christian code of ethics and behavior which they had inherited from more pious forebears, while their religious convictions lapsed into Deism or agnosticism. Two of them were minister's sons, and all were affected by the anti-clericalism of their intellectual world. Their Protestant bias was emotional rather than rational, and all were sometimes attracted by the color, pageantry, esthetic richness, and heroism of the French and Spanish Catholic traditions.

But intellectually, to them Catholicism was medieval superstition, a religion whose adherents consisted mostly of the ignorant immigrants who poured into New England in their lifetimes, led, in their view, by scheming priests whose dominant motives were not spiritual. Parkman was deeply concerned that New England might be taken by the flood of French-Canadian immigration after the Civil War. The others doubtless looked down upon the Know-Nothings and their cry of "Rum, Romanism, and Rebellion," but shared to varying degrees the anti-Catholic prejudices of the Old Yankee demagogs who led that movement. To a surprising degree all four wrote in the spirit of the Protestant Reformation in England, still waging a long-ended battle, which was revived by the appearance of the *Syllabus of Errors* of Pius IX and the promulgation of the dogma of the infallibility of the Pope. In their work there is virtually no recognition of the new scientific Catholic historians who escaped from the old apologetic and hotly partisan tradition of the Counter Reformation. Catholic readers will always have reserves about the works of the Brahmin historians, which contain passages highly offensive to Catholics, but that fact should not interfere with recognition of great achievements in historical writing which as yet have not been equaled by American Catholics.

APPENDIX I

THE ERA OF THE HALF-GODS IN AMERICAN LITERATURE

NOTES

I

1. Boston, 1956. 2. *Speculations,* New York, 1926. 3. Feidelson, Charles, *Symbolism and American Literature,* Chicago, 1953, p. 43. 4. *Times Literary Supplement* (London), Aug. 17, 1956. Emphasis added. 5. *Literary History of the United States,* ed. by R. E. Spiller and others, 3 vols., New York, 1948, Vol. I, p. 365. 6. Mersch, Émile, S. J., *The Theology of the Mystical Body,* trans. Cyril Vollert, S. J., St. Louis, 1952, pp. 118-19. The whole of Chapter 5, "The Teaching of Philosophy on Man and His Unity," is a wonderfully suggestive chapter not only for the student of theology and philosophy, but for the student of literature. It can be said, I believe, to outline the basis for a "theology of literature." It certainly contains a myriad pregnant hints on the teleology of literature—what the inner bent of the creative process is, as the writer ponders the "mystery of man." Consider these phrases, culled at random from the preceding pages of the chapter: "In accordance with the principle *operari sequitur esse,* a being that is only itself and is absolutely nothing else but itself, cannot know anything else but itself. To be able to know and will others, one must be these others to a certain degree: to the precise degree in which they are truly to be known and willed." "In order that the human form [the soul] may be free from limitations, it must, in the words of the ancient phrase, be *aliquo modo omnia;* in a sense it must become the whole human universe, and must possess and express that universe as it actually exists." "Man does not know himself unless he knows the universe of man and humanity. This explains the interest man takes in other men and in material phenomena. They truly concern him; they make up his completeness." "If we take man's spiritual soul into account, we cannot say simply and purely that he is less than the whole of humanity. In his own way he has all of humanity within him." 7. The statements of Emerson are quoted in John Jay Chapman's famous essay which is conveniently available in Edmund Wilson's *The Shock of Recognition.* New York, 1955, pp. 595-658. 8. Compare here Mersch., *op. cit.,* p.102: "To render full account of his moral attitude, man has need of the universe. . . . God has placed [the human soul] in the midst of matter to perceive the moral significance of material phenomena, and thus to assimilate the universe into the spirit. . . . Therefore man must come to love and will these laws of the world which are also his own laws. . . . Thus he will discharge one of his noblest functions: that of transforming the entire material order into the life of the spirit and into moral activity, and of making, along with the whole human race, an immense act of love of the good and of God." 9. Cf. Parrington, Vernon L., *Main Currents in American Thought,* 3 vols., New York, 1927-1930, Vol. II, p. 382: "The Unitarians had pronounced [as against the Calvinists' 'dogma' of inherent depravity and of election and reprobation] human nature to be excellent; the transcendentalists pronounced it divine. They made it . . . the dwelling place of the Most High; discovered the secret voice of God in the buried life that men call instinct; refused to heed any other command save this inner voice of God." This somewhat glamorized account by Parrington of the genesis and development of Transcendentalism is, in general, the summary that most critics give. It is quite at variance with Brownson's appreciation of Transcendentalism in his later

years. Then he conceded that the movement had been concerned, at least as
it was carried on by such men as Emerson, much more with combatting Calvinism than with inculcating any "pantheism." 10. Brownson, who knew the
Transcendentalist movement from the inside, stated that the steady decline of
dogma within Protestantism could lead only to Transcendentalism. 11. Parrington, *op. cit.*, p. 380. 12. *Ibid.*, p. 381. 13. 2 Peter 1/4. 14. Parrington, *op. cit.*,
p. 382. 15. Wilson, Edmund, *op. cit.*, p. 638. 16. *Ibid.*, p. 631. 17. *Ibid.*, p. 630.
It seems a little hard to reconcile the two criticisms of Chapman. If Emerson
believed in the complete "self-sufficiency" of the individual, how could his
concept of the Moral Law constitute a "crucifixion" of the individual conscience? Perhaps the explanation Chapman would give lies in his earlier estimate in the same essay: "From the point of view of Emerson, there is no
such thing as inconsistency. Every man is each day a new man. Let him be
today what he is today. It is immaterial and a waste of time to consider what
once he was or what he may be." This judgment contrasts oddly with the
pattern of Emerson's leading thoughts, as traced in the study in this symposium.
18. It may seem that an insistence on the influence of Transcendentalism is to
attribute too much to a doctrine that men like Poe, for example, expressly
repudiated. But the movement was such—if, indeed, it was homogeneous enough
to be called a movement—that no one in the intellectual currents of the time
could escape it. Cooper was too early for it and the "literary historians"
were laboring in a field that might be little touched by it, but all the other
authors considered in these studies felt its impact. Feidelson remarks (*op. cit.*,
p. 104), in his discussion of the Transcendentalists' concept of symbolism:
"To say, as Alcott did, that 'the world is but the symbol of mind, and speech
a mythology woven of both,' was not to reduce truth and fact to a barren
subjectivity, but to give all the shapes of language an objectivity . . .
'Transcendentalism' in this sense would not be escaped by writers like Melville,
Hawthorne and Poe, who were hostile to its superficial features." 19. Curti,
Merle, *The Growth of American Thought*, 2nd ed., New York, 1951, p. 69.
20. Parrington, *op. cit.*, p. 443. 21. *Ibid.*, p. 402 sq. 22. New York, 1927, pp.
37-77. 23. I am indebted to Sister Mary Teresita, O.S.B., librarian at Villa
Madonna College, Covington, Kentucky, for calling my attention to an unpublished thesis, submitted in 1940 by Charles C. Charvat to the College of
the State University of Iowa in partial fulfillment of the requirements for
the degree of Doctor of Philosophy. The subject of the thesis was "Emerson and
Catholicism," and the author's conclusions, I am informed, state that "Emerson
was not indifferent to Catholicism. . . . At times he rejected its influence. . . .
He made no considered attempts to abjure Catholic tenets; and he recommended
the reading of Pascal and Fénélon, not to mention St. Augustine and Thomas
à Kempis. . . . Non-partisan investigation can and ought, therefore, to clarify
appreciably the relation of Emerson and Catholicism, or at least to engender
discussion in which '*du choc des idées jaillit la lumière.*'" The thesis carries
an acknowledgement of assistance given by the Rev. Francis J. Yealy, S.J., of
the Creighton University, Omaha, Nebraska. 24. This thought was to be
restated long after by T. S. Eliot, who doubts "Whether belief proper enters
into the activity of a great poet *qua* poet. That is, Dante, *qua* poet, did not
believe or disbelieve the Thomist cosmology or theory of the soul; he merely
made use of it, or a fusion took place between his initial emotional impulses
and a theory—for the purpose of making poetry." ("Shakespeare and the
Stoicism of Seneca," in *Selected Essays, 1919-1932*, New York, 1932, p. 118).
The same observation obtains in these studies; it is not a question whether any
one of the authors *believed*, say, in the fullness of the Creed, but whether
whatever knowledge he had of that fullness fused with his impulses to color his
work. 25. Machen, Arthur, *Hieroglyphics*, New York, 1913, pp. 195 sq.

EMERSON: *The Single Vision*
NOTES

I

1. Whicher, Stephen E., *Freedom and Fate*, Philadelphia, 1953, p. 173. 2. *Ibid.*
3. Hopkins, Vivian C., *Spirals of Form*, Cambridge, Mass., 1951, p. 225. 4. *Ibid.*
5. Feidelson, Charles, Jr., *Symbolism and American Literature*, Chicago, 1953,
p. 123. 6. Rusk, Ralph L., *The Life of Ralph Waldo Emerson*, New York, 1949,
p. 103. 7. Gray, Henry David, *Emerson: A Statement of New England Transcendentalism as Expressed in the Philosophy of its Chief Exponent*, Stanford
Univ., Calif., 1917, p. 103. 8. Feidelson, *op. cit.*, p. 158. 9. "Natural History of
Intellect," *Works*, Vol. XII, p. 11. 10. "Experience," *Works*, Vol. III, p. 49.
11. *Ibid.* 12. Cf. Chap. 1 of *Emerson's Angle of Vision*, by Sherman Paul, Cambridge, Mass., 1952. 13. "Nature," *Works*, Vol. I, p. 65. 14. *Ibid.*, p. 74. 15.
Ibid., p. 66. 16. *Ibid.*, p. 65. 17. *Ibid.*, p. 62. 18. *Ibid.*, p. 74. 19. Noyes, Al-
fred, *Some Aspects of Modern Poetry*, London, n.d., p. 59. 20. "Fate," *Works*,
Vol. VI, p. 22. 21. Noyes, *op. cit.*, p. 63. 22. "Nature," (Second Series), *Works*,
Vol. III, p. 180. 23. "The Poet," *Works*, Vol. III, p. 5. 24. *Ibid.*, p. 6. 25.
"Nature," *Works*, Vol. I, pp. 36-37. 26. *Ibid.*, p. 8. 27. "The American Scholar,"
Works, Vol. I, p. 87. 28. *Journals*, Vol. II, p. 223. 29. "Self-Reliance," *Works*,
Vol. II, p. 68. 30. "Nature," *Works*, Vol. I, p. 64. 31. "The American Scholar,"
Works, Vol. I, p. 87. 32. "The Over-Soul," *Works*, Vol. II, p. 287. 33. "Nature,"
(Second Series), *Works*, Vol. III, p. 178.

II

1. Fairchild, Hoxie, *Religious Trends in English Poetry* (New York, Vol. I, 1939;
Vol. II, 1942; Vol. III, 1949), Vol. III, p. 8. 2. Caponigri, A. Robert, "Brownson
and Emerson: Nature and History," *New England Quarterly*, Vol. XVIII (Sept.
1945), p. 377. 3. Feidelson, *op. cit.*, p. 124. 4. The Divinity School "Address,"
Works, Vol. I, p. 123. 5. "The Over-Soul," *Works*, Vol. II, p. 269. 6. "Self-
Reliance," *Works*, Vol. II, p. 70. 7. "The Method of Nature," *Works*, Vol. I,
p. 199. 8. "Nature," *Works*, Vol. I, p. 62. 9. *Ibid.*, pp. 62, 63. 10. *Ibid.*, p. 63.
11. "Nature" (Second Series), *Works*, Vol. III, p. 171. 12. "Experience,"
Works, Vol. III, p. 54. 13. "The Over-Soul," *Works*, Vol. II, p. 280. 14.
"Intellect," *Works*, Vol. II, p. 328. 15. "Self-Reliance," *Works*, Vol. II, p.
64. 16. "Experience," *Works*, Vol. III, p. 54. 17. "Literature," *Works*, Vol. V,
p. 254. 18. "Self-Reliance," *Works*, Vol. II, p. 63. 19. "Experience," *Works*,
Vol. III, p. 53. 20. "Nature" (Second Series), *Works*, Vol. III, p. 170. 21. The
Divinity School "Address," *Works*, Vol. I, p. 123. 22. *Ibid.*, p. 124. 23.
"Literary Ethics," *Works*, Vol. I, p. 185. 24. The Divinity School "Address,"
Works, Vol. I, p. 129. 25. "Nature," *Works*, Vol. I, p. 13. 26. The Divinity
School "Address," *Works*, Vol. I, p. 137. 27. "Nature," *Works*, Vol. I, p. 73.
28. The Divinity School "Address," *Works*, Vol. I, p. 146-47. 29. "The Method
of Nature," *Works*, Vol. I, p. 216. 30. Rusk, *op. cit.*, p. 368.

III

1. "Plato: New Readings," *Works*, Vol. IV, p. 81. 2. *Ibid.*, p. 82. 3. Carpenter,
F. I., *Emerson and Asia*, Cambridge, 1930. 4. Santayana, George, *Interpretations of Poetry and Religion*, New York, 1900, p. 233. 5. "Plato; Or, The
Philosopher," *Works*, Vol. IV, p. 52. 6. "Worship," *Works*, Vol. VI, p. 219.
7. "Fate," *Works*, Vol. VI, p. 49. 8. Feidelson, *op. cit.*, p. 126. 9. *Ibid.*, p. 127.
10. *Ibid.*, p. 124. 11. *Ibid.*, p. 123. 12. "Education," *Works*, Vol. X, p. 147.
13. *Ibid.* 14. *Journals*, Vol. IV, pp. 435-36. 15. *Ibid.*, p. 248. 16. "Experience,"
Works, Vol. III, p. 74. 17. "Considerations by the Way," *Works*, Vol. VI, p.

254. 18. *Journals*, Vol. IV, p. 249. 19. "Nature," *Works*, Vol. I, p. 44. 20. "The American Scholar," *Works*, Vol. I, p. 85. 21. *Ibid.* 22. "Nature" (Second Series), *Works*, Vol. III, pp. 182-83. 23. *Ibid.*, p. 170. 24. "Self-Reliance," *Works*, Vol. II, p. 70. 25. "The American Scholar," *Works*, Vol. I, p. 98. 26. "Experience," *Works*, Vol. III, p. 68. 27. "Fate," *Works*, Vol. VI, p. 36. 28. "The Over-Soul," *Works*, Vol. II, p. 297.

IV

1. "Education," *Works*, Vol. X, p. 128. 2. "Fate," *Works*, Vol. VI, p. 31. 3. "The American Scholar," *Works*, Vol. I, p. 85. 4. "Nature," *Works*, Vol. I, p. 24. 5. "Beauty," *Works*, Vol. VI, p. 303. 6. "Nature," *Works*, Vol. I, p. 43. 7. "History," *Works*, Vol. II, p. 36. 8. "Fate," *Works*, Vol. VI, p. 36. 9. *Ibid.*, p. 48. 10. Paul, *op. cit.*, p. 171. 11. "History," *Works*, Vol. II, p. 3. 12. "Quotation and Originality," *Works*, Vol. VIII, p. 200. 13. *Ibid.*, p. 178. 14. "New England Reformers," *Works*, Vol. III, pp. 266-67. 15. "The American Scholar," *Works*, Vol. I, p. 83. 16. "Self-Reliance," *Works*, Vol. II, pp. 46-47. 17. "The American Scholar," *Works*, Vol. I, pp. 115, 116. 18. "The Over-Soul," *Works*, Vol. II, p. 297. 19. "The American Scholar," *Works*, Vol. I, p. 105. 20. "Self-Reliance," *Works*, Vol. II, p. 47. 21. The Divinity School "Address," *Works*, Vol. I, p. 144. 22. "Self-Reliance," *Works*, Vol. II, p. 67. 23. Quoted by Paul, *op. cit.*, p. 170. 24. "Compensation," *Works*, Vol. II, p. 97. 25. *Ibid.*, p. 101. 26. *Ibid.*, p. 102. 27. *Ibid.*, p. 101. 28. "Quotation and Originality," *Works*, Vol. VIII, p. 201. 29. "Compensation," *Works*, Vol. II, p. 110. 30. *Ibid.*, pp. 104-05. 31. "Spiritual Laws," *Works*, Vol. II, p. 144. 32. "History," *Works*, Vol. II, p. 10. 33. *Ibid.*, p. 4. 34. Cf. *Richard Philip Garrold, S.J.*, C. C. Martindale, S. J., London, 1921, pp. 94-95. Speaking of Emerson's "Essay on History," Father Garrold says, "Every teacher of history should read it slowly, and digest it." And again, with reference to this same essay, he says, Emerson "is engagingly rhetorical and sometimes a little vague, but he delivers the goods." 35. "Intellect," *Works*, Vol. II, p. 330. 36. "Education," *Works*, Vol. X, p. 137. 37. James, William, *The Varieties of Religious Experience*, New York, 1902, p. 489. 38. "The American Scholar," *Works*, Vol. I, p. 103. 39. *Ibid.*, p. 115. 40. "Nature" (Second Series), *Works*, Vol. III, p. 185.

V

1. "Education," *Works*, Vol. X, p. 132. 2. *Ibid.* 3. "The Poet," *Works*, Vol. III, p. 4. 4. *Ibid.*, p. 16. 5. *Ibid.*, p. 26. 6. "Nature," *Works*, Vol. I, p. 45. 7. Santayana, *op. cit.*, p. 217. 8. "The Poet." *Works*, Vol. III, p. 13. 9. *Ibid.*, p. 30. 10. "Nature," *Works*, Vol. I, p. 30. 11. *Journals*, Vol. VIII, p. 100. 12. "Quotation and Originality," *Works*, Vol. VIII, p. 199. 13. "The Poet," *Works*, Vol. III, p. 22. 14. *Ibid.*, p. 34. 15. "Circles," *Works*, Vol. II, pp. 304-05; and "Natural History of the Intellect," *Works*, Vol. XII, p. 58. 16. Thompson, Francis, *The Works of Francis Thompson*, London, 1913, Vol. II, p. 232. 17. *Ibid.*, p. 235. 18. *Ibid.*, p. 234. 19. "Plato; Or, The Philosopher," *Works*, Vol. IV, p. 55. 20. *Journals*, Vol. I, p. 334. 21. "Nature" (Second Series), *Works*, Vol. III, p. 190. 22. "Nature," *Works*, Vol. I, p. 27. 23. "The Poet," *Works*, Vol. III, p. 26. 24. Hopkins, *op. cit.*, p. 133. 25. *Ibid.*, p. 131. 26. *Ibid.* 27. "The Poet," *Works*, Vol. III, pp. 9-10. 28. *Ibid.*, pp. 37-38.

VI

1. Fairchild, *op. cit.*, Vol. III, p. 511. 2. New York, 1939, p. 124. 3. P. 409. 4. Wilder, Amos N., *Modern Poetry and the Christian Tradition*, New York, 1952, p. 41. 5. *Ibid.*, p. 42. 6. *Ibid.*, pp. 36-37. 7. *Ibid.*, p. 37. 8. "The Sovereignty of Ethics," *Works*, Vol. X, pp. 203-04. 9. *Journals*, Vol. IV, p. 31.

10. "Boston," *Works*, Vol. XII, p. 193. 11. "The Method of Nature," *Works*, Vol. I, p. 220. 12. "The Over-Soul," *Works*, Vol. II, p. 272. 13. Murdock, Kenneth B., *Literature and Theology in Colonial New England*, Cambridge, 1939, p. 20. 14. "Fate," *Works*, Vol. VI, p. 5. 15. *Ibid.* 16. "Education," *Works*, Vol. X, p. 131.

VII

1. Hopkins, *op. cit.*, p. 228. 2. Edwards, Jonathan, *Images or Shadows of Divine Things*, ed. by Perry Miller, New Haven, 1948. Cf. Perry Miller, "Jonathan Edwards to Emerson," *New England Quarterly*, Vol. XIII (Dec. 1940), pp. 589-617. 3. *Collected Papers of Charles Sanders Peirce*, ed. by Charles Hartshorne and Paul Weiss, Cambridge, 1931-35: 5.77n., 1.560. Cf. James Feibleman, *An Introduction to Peirce's Philosophy*, New York and London, 1946. Cf. also F. I. Carpenter, "C. S. Peirce: Pragmatic Transcendentalist," *New England Quarterly*, Vol. XIV (March, 1941), pp. 34-48. 4. Caponigri, *op. cit.*, p. 375. 5. Paul, *op. cit.*, p. 9. 6. *Ibid.*, p. 25. 7. Du Bos, Charles, *What Is Literature?* London, 1940, pp. 24, 25. 8. "The American Scholar," *Works*, Vol. I, p. 111. 9. *Journals*, Vol. IV, p. 242. 10. The Divinity School "Address," *Works*, Vol. I, p. 142. 11. "Education," *Works*, Vol. X, p. 133. 12. "Self-Reliance," *Works*, Vol. II, p. 65. 13. "Experience," *Works*, Vol. III, p. 53. 14. "Literary Ethics," *Works*, Vol. I, p. 186. 15. *Ibid.* 16. "The American Scholar," *Works*, Vol. I, p. 94. 17. "The Method of Nature," *Works*, Vol. I, pp. 208-09. 18. "Experience," *Works*, Vol. III, pp. 50-51. 19. James, Henry, "Emerson," in *The Art of Fiction*, New York, 1948, p. 221. 20. *Ibid.*, p. 239. 21. *Ibid.*, pp. 238-39. 22. *Ibid.*, p. 239.

SELECTED BIBLIOGRAPHY

PRIMARY

The Complete Works of Ralph Waldo Emerson, ed. by Edward Waldo Emerson, Centenary Edition, 12 vols. Boston, 1903-04.
The Journals of Ralph Waldo Emerson, ed. by Edward Waldo Emerson and Waldo Emerson Forbes, 10 vols., Boston, 1909-14.
The Letters of Ralph Waldo Emerson, ed. by Ralph L. Rusk, 6 vols., New York, 1939.

SECONDARY

Arnold, Matthew, "Emerson," in *Discourses in America*, New York, 1924, pp. 138-207.
Beach, Joseph W., "Coleridge, Emerson, and Naturalism" and "Emerson's Nature-Poetry," in *The Concept of Nature in Nineteenth-Century English Poetry*, New York, 1936, pp. 318-69.
Brooks, Van Wyck, *Emerson and Others*, New York, 1927.
Cabot, James Elliot, *A Memoir of Ralph Waldo Emerson*, Boston, 1887.
Cameron, Kenneth W., *Emerson the Essayist*, 2 vols., Raleigh, N. C., 1945.
Caponigri, A. Robert, "Brownson and Emerson: Nature and History," *New England Quarterly*, Vol. XVIII (Sept. 1945), pp. 368-90.
Carpenter, Frederic I., *Emerson Handbook*, New York, 1953.
———, *Emerson and Asia*, Cambridge, Mass., 1930.
Chapman, John Jay, "Emerson," in *Emerson and Other Essays*, New York, 1909, pp. 3-108.
Dewey, John, "Ralph Waldo Emerson," in *Characters and Events*, New York, 1929, Vol. I, pp. 69-77.
Feidelson, Charles, Jr., *Symbolism and American Literature*, Chicago, 1953.

Foerster, Norman, "Emerson," in *American Criticism*, Boston, 1928, pp. 52-111.
———, "Emerson," in *Nature in American Literature*, Boston and New York, 1928, pp. 37-68.
Gray, Henry David, *Emerson: A Statement of New England Transcendentalism as Expressed in the Philosophy of its Chief Exponent*, Stanford, Calif., 1917.
Harrison, John S., *The Teachers of Emerson*, New York, 1910.
Holmes, Oliver Wendell, *Ralph Waldo Emerson*, Boston, 1885.
Hopkins, Vivian C., *Spires of Form: A Study of Emerson's Aesthetic Theory*, Cambridge, Mass., 1951.
James, Henry, "Emerson," in *Partial Portraits*, London, 1905, pp. 1-33. Also in *The Art of Fiction and Other Essays*, with an introduction by Morris Roberts, New York, 1948, pp. 220-40.
Matthiessen, Francis O., *American Renaissance: Art and Expression in the Age of Emerson and Whitman*, New York, 1941.
Metzger, Charles R., *Emerson and Greenough: Transcendental Pioneers of an American Esthetic*, Berkeley and Los Angeles, 1954.
Miller, Perry, "Jonathan Edwards to Emerson," *New England Quarterly*, Vol. XIII (Dec. 1940), pp. 589-617.
———, *The New England Mind: The Seventeenth Century*, New York, 1939.
———, *The Transcendentalists: An Anthology*, Cambridge, Mass., 1950.
More, Paul Elmer, "Emerson," in *Cambridge History of American Literature*, New York, 1947, Vol. I, pp. 349-62.
Mumford, Lewis, *The Golden Day*, New York, 1926, pp. 94-106.
Noyes, Alfred, "The Poetry of Emerson," in *Some Aspects of Modern Poetry*, London, n.d., pp. 55-68.
Parrington, Vernon L., "Ralph Waldo Emerson: Transcendental Critic," in *Main Currents of American Thought*, 3 vols., New York, 1927-1930, Vol. II, pp. 386-99.
Paul, Sherman, *Emerson's Angle of Vision: Man and Nature in American Experience*, Cambridge, Mass., 1952.
Perry, Bliss, *Emerson Today*, Princeton, 1931.
Pritchard, John Paul, "Ralph Waldo Emerson," in *Return to the Fountains*, Durham, N. C., 1942, pp. 44-60.
Rusk, Ralph L., *The Life of Ralph Waldo Emerson*, New York, 1949.
Santayana, George, "Emerson," in *Interpretations of Poetry and Religion*, New York, 1900, pp. 217-33.
———, "The Genteel Tradition in American Philosophy," in *Winds of Doctrine*, New York, 1913, pp. 186-215.
Sherman, Stuart P., "The Emersonian Liberation," in *Americans*, New York, 1922, pp. 62-121.
[Spiller, Robert E.] "Ralph Waldo Emerson," in *Literary History of the United States*, 3 vols., ed. by R. E. Spiller and others, New York, 1948, Vol. I, pp. 358-87. Bibliography in Vol. III, pp. 492-501.

Cooper: *Myth-Maker and Christian Romancer*

NOTES

1. Bewley, Marius, *The Complex Fate: Hawthorne, Henry James and Some Other American Writers*, with an Introduction and Two Interpolations by F. R. Leavis, London, 1952, pp. 1, 2. 2. Cooper, James Fenimore, "A Journal Kept by James Fenimore-Cooper, January–May, 1948," in *Correspondence of James Fenimore Cooper*, New Haven, 1922, Vol. II, p. 752. 3. Cooper, James Fenimore, *The Chainbearer*, New York, 1895-1900, p. 162. 4. Hemingway, Ernest, *Green Hills of Africa*, New York, 1935, p. 22. 5. Conrad, Joseph, "Tales of the Sea," in *Notes on Life and Letters*, New York, 1925, pp. 55-56. 6. Cooper,

James Fenimore, *The Wept of Wish-ton-Wish*, New York, 1895-1900, pp. 402-03.
7. *The Chainbearer*, p. 101. 8. Cooper, James Fenimore, preface to *The Ways of the Hour*, New York, 1895-1900, p. v. 9. Parrington, Vernon L., *Main Currents in American Thought*, 3 vols., New York, 1927-1930, Vol. II, p. 231.
10. Cooper, James Fenimore, *The Pioneers*, New York, 1895-1900, p. 405. 11. *The Pioneers*, p. 477. 12. Cooper, James Fenimore, *The Pathfinder*, New York, 1895-1900, pp. 462-63.

BIBLIOGRAPHY

Balzac, Honoré de, "Fenimore Cooper et Walter Scott," in *Oeuvres Complètes*, Vol. XXIII, Paris, 1879.
Brooks, Van Wyck, *The World of Washington Irving*, New York, 1944.
Brownell, William C., *American Prose Masters*, New York, 1909. Somewhat old-fashioned, but very sound.
Boynton, Henry Walcott, *James Fenimore Cooper*, New York, 1931.
Bryant, William Cullen. His eloquent *Discourse* has been reprinted in *Orations and Addresses*, New York, 1873.
Conrad, Joseph, *Notes on Life and Letters*, New York, 1921.
Cooper, James Fenimore, ed., *Correspondence of James Fenimore Cooper*, 2 vols., New Haven, 1922.
Grossman, James, *James Fenimore Cooper*, American Men of Letters Series, New York, 1949. This is probably the most generally satisfactory biography of Cooper.
Lawrence, D. H., *Studies in Classic American Literature*, New York, 1953. Idiosyncratic and inaccurate, but on occasion brilliantly perceptive.
Lounsbury, Thomas R., ed., *James Fenimore Cooper*, Boston, 1882.
Melville, Herman, review of *The Sea Lions*, in *The Literary World*, April 28, 1849.
Nevins, Allan, introduction to *The Leatherstocking Saga*, New York, 1954.
Outland, Ethel R., *The "Effingham" Libels on Cooper*, Madison, University of Wisconsin Studies in Language and Literature, No. 28, 1929.
Poe, Edgar Allan, review of *Wyandotté*, *Graham's Magazine*, November, 1843.
Ross, John F., *The Social Criticism of Fenimore Cooper*, Berkeley, Calif., 1933.
Smith, Henry Nash, introduction to *The Prairie*, New York, 1950.
Spiller, Robert E., *Fenimore Cooper, Critic of His Times*, New York, 1931. Professor Spiller accents the political and social aspects of the novels.
——, *James Fenimore Cooper: Representative Selections, with Introduction, Bibliography, and Notes*, New York, 1936.
——, and Philip C. Blackburn, *A Descriptive Bibliography of the Writings of James Fenimore Cooper*, New York, 1934.
Twain, Mark, "Fenimore Cooper's Literary Offenses." This most celebrated of the many Cooper parodies is most easily accessible nowadays in *The Shock of Recognition*, edited by Edmund Wilson, New York, 1955; or in *A Subtreasury of American Humor*, edited by E. B. White and Katharine S. White, New York, 1941. Thackeray is responsible for an equally excellent lampoon on the Cooper of the sea romances.
Van Doren, Carl, *The American Novel*, New York, 1921.
Waples, Dorothy, *The Whig Myth of Fenimore Cooper*, New Haven, 1938.
Winters, Yvor, *In Defense of Reason*, Denver, 1947.

EDITIONS:

There is no collected edition of Cooper in print. The reader must rely upon such separate editions as the *Scribner Illustrated Classics* edition of *The Deerslayer* and *The Last of the Mohicans;* the Heritage Press edition of *The Last of the Mohicans;* the Dodd, Mead edition of *Afloat and Ashore;* the Rinehart edition of *The Prairie;* the Knopf Vintage Book edition of *The American Democrat.* Luckily, all five Leatherstocking volumes are generally available in one form or another; as is *The Spy.*

BROWNSON: *The Critique of Transcendentalism*

NOTES

A word is called for on footnote references. For Brownson's early essays I have referred to the *Boston Quarterly Review* only when the quotation is neither in his collected *Works*, nor in Miller's *The Transcendentalists*, nor in my *Brownson Reader*. The latter two anthologies have been referred to where possible as being the most readily available.

1. Schlesinger, Arthur M., Jr., *Orestes A. Brownson, A Pilgrim's Progress*, Boston, 1939, p. 286.   2. *The Works of Orestes A. Brownson*, Detroit, 1882-87, Vol. V, p. 43. Henceforth this twenty-volume edition will be referred to as *Works*. 3. *Works*, Vol. V, p. 39.   4. It did not appear in print, however, until Perry Miller included it in his anthology, *The Transcendentalists*, Cambridge, Mass., 1950, pp. 284-93. In Miller's words: "From then [1834] until his resignation Ripley frequently repeated it; it was regarded as one of the finest expressions of the new doctrine."   5. Miller, *The Transcendentalists*, pp. 290-91.   6. *Ibid.*, p. 85.   7. *Ibid.*, p. 86.   8. *Ibid.*, p. 88.   9. *Works*, Vol. IV, p. 28; also in my edition of the *Brownson Reader*, New York, 1955, p. 327.   10. Miller, *op. cit.*, p. 99.   11. *Ibid.*, p. 107.   12. *Ibid.*, p. 113.   13. *Boston Quarterly Review*, Vol. I (1838), p. 501.   14. *Ibid.*, p. 502.   15. *Ibid.*, p. 504.   16. *Ibid.*, p. 505. 17. *Ibid.*, p. 506.   18. *Ibid.*, p. 508.   19. *Ibid.*, pp. 510-11.   20. *Ibid.*, p. 512. 21. *Ibid.*, p. 514.   22. Miller, *op. cit.*, p. 206.   23. *Ibid.*, p. 208.   24. *Works*, Vol. XX, p. 262; see also *Brownson Reader*, p. 341.   25. Miller, *op. cit.*, pp. 211-12.   26. *Ibid.*, p. 226.   27. *Ibid.*, p. 240.   28. *Ibid.*, p. 242; in *Boston Quarterly Review*, Vol. III (1840), p. 270.   29. Miller, *op. cit.*, p. 245; in *Boston Quarterly Review*, Vol. III (1840), p. 278.   30. *Boston Quarterly Review*, Vol. III (1840), p. 384.   31. Miller, *op. cit.*, p. 272.   32. *Boston Quarterly Review*, Vol. IV (Oct. 1841), p. 436-74.   33. *Ibid.*, p. 441.   34. *Works*, Vol. V, p. 151. 35. *Ibid.*, Vol. IV, p. 65.   36. *Ibid.*, p. 97.   37. *Ibid.*, p. 95.   38. *Ibid.*, p. 333. 39. *Ibid.*, p. 361.   40. *Ibid.*, p. 147; also in *Brownson Reader*, p. 266.   41. *Works*, Vol. IV, p. 151; *Brownson Reader*, p. 268.   42. *Works*, Vol. IV, p. 157; *Brownson Reader*, p. 269.   43. *Works*, Vol. IV, p. 157; *Brownson Reader*, p. 269.   44. In a letter to Elizabeth Peabody, *Letters*, ed. by Ralph L. Rusk, New York, 1939, Vol. III, pp. 63-64.   45. *Works*, Vol. V, p. 128.   46. *Ibid.*, Vol. IV, p. 119.   47. *Ibid.*, Vol. V, p. 134.   48. *Ibid.*, Vol. IV, p. 399; *Brownson Reader*, p. 194.   49. *Works*, Vol. V, p. 140.   50. See Wellek, René, "The Minor Transcendentalists and German Philosophy," *New England Quarterly*, Vol. XV (1942), pp. 652-80.   51. *Works*, Vol. IV, p. 519.   52. *Ibid.*, Vol. VI, p. 83.   53. *Ibid.*, pp. 84-85.   54. *Ibid.*, p. 4.   55. *Ibid.*, Vol. XIV, p. 544.   56. *Ibid.*, p. 544.   57. *Basic Writings of St. Thomas Aquinas*, ed. by Anton C. Pegis, New York, 1945, Vol. II, p. 750.   58. *Works*, Vol. XIV, p. 557.   59. *Ibid.*, p. 14; *Brownson Reader*, pp. 277-78.   60. *Boston Quarterly Review*, Vol. IV (1841), pp. 438, 440.   61. *Works*, Vol. XIV, p. 5; *Brownson Reader*, p. 275.   62. Benard, Edmond D., *A Preface to Newman's Theology*, St. Louis, 1945, p. 114. See especially pp. 92-105 on Brownson's criticism of Newman's development theory. 63. *Works*, Vol. X, p. 112.   64. *Ibid.*, p. 113.   65. *Boston Quarterly Review*, Vol. III (1840), p. 322.

SELECTED BIBLIOGRAPHY

Benard, Edmond D., *A Preface to Newman's Theology*, St. Louis, 1945.
The Boston Quarterly Review, 5 vols., Boston, 1838-1842.
Brownson, Henry F., *Orestes A. Brownson's Early Life: From 1803 to 1844*, Detroit, 1898.

——, *Orestes A. Brownson's Middle Life: From 1845 to 1855,* Detroit, 1899.
——, *Orestes A. Brownson's Latter Life: From 1855 to 1876,* Detroit, 1900.
The Works of Orestes A. Brownson, collected and arranged by Henry F. Brownson, 20 vols., Detroit, 1882-1887.
Caponigri, A. Robert, "Brownson and Emerson: Nature and History," *New England Quarterly,* Vol. XVIII (1945), pp. 368-90.
Commager, Henry Steele, *Theodore Parker,* Boston, 1936.
The Complete Works of Ralph Waldo Emerson, ed. by Edward Waldo Emerson, 12 vols., Boston, 1903-1904.
Faust, Clarence H., "The Background of the Unitarian Opposition to Transcendentalism," *Modern Philology,* Vol. XXXV (1938), pp. 297-324.
Frothingham, Octavius B., *Transcendentalism in New England: A History,* New York, 1876.
Goddard, Harold C., *Studies in New England Transcendentalism,* New York, 1908.
Gohdes, Clarence L. F., *The Periodicals of American Transcendentalism,* Durham, N. C., 1931.
[Hecker, Isaac T.], "The Transcendental Movement in New England," *Catholic World,* Vol. XXIII (1876), pp. 528-37.
——, "Dr. Brownson's Road to the Church," *Catholic World,* Vol. XLVI (1887), pp. 1-11.
——, "Dr. Brownson and Catholicity," *Catholic World,* Vol. XLVI (1887), pp. 222-35.
Ladu, Arthur I., "Channing and Transcendentalism," *American Literature,* Vol. XI (1939), pp. 129-37.
Matthiessen, F. O., *American Renaissance,* New York, 1941.
Maynard, Theodore, *Orestes Brownson: Yankee Radical, Catholic,* New York, 1943.
Miller, Perry, ed., *The Transcendentalists: An Anthology,* Cambridge, Mass., 1950.
Newman, John Henry, *An Essay on the Development of Christian Doctrine,* New York, 1949.
The Works of Theodore Parker, 15 vols., Boston, 1907-1913.
Parrington, Vernon L., *Main Currents in American Thought,* 3 vols., New York, 1927-1930. (Vol. II: 1800-1860, *The Romantic Revolution in America.*)
[Ripley, George], "Brownson's Writings," *Dial,* Vol. I (1840), pp. 22-46.
Ryan, Alvan S., ed., *The Brownson Reader,* New York, 1955.
Schlesinger, Arthur M., Jr., *Orestes A. Brownson, A Pilgrim's Progress,* Boston, 1939.
[Ward, William George], "Mr. Brownson on Developments," *Dublin Review,* Vol. XXIII (1847), pp. 373-405.
Wellek, René, "The Minor Transcendentalists and German Philosophy," *New England Quarterly,* Vol. XV (1942), pp. 652-80.

HAWTHORNE: *God and Man in New England*

NOTES

1. Alexander Cowie and Austin Warren feel that Hawthorne accepted the Calvinistic doctrine of predestination as a convenient explanation for man's inability to cope with the world. See Cowie, *The Rise of the American Novel,* New York, 1948, p. 356, and Warren, *Nathaniel Hawthorne,* New York, 1934, p. xxi. Yvor Winters and Carl Van Doren agree that Hawthorne turned his back upon the conceptions of his Puritan ancestors. See Winters, *In Defense of Reason,* New York, 1947, p. 174, and Van Doren, *What Is American Literature?,* New York, 1945, p. 590. 2. The *Dial* (1840-1844), a "modest quarterly journal" published in Concord by Margaret Fuller and Ralph Waldo Emerson, was the chief organ of the Transcendental movement. 3. One might mention Cowie

and Warren again as well as Mark Van Doren, *The Best of Hawthorne,* New York, 1951, p. 11, and Arlin Turner, "Hawthorne and Reform," *New England Quarterly,* Vol. XV (1942), p. 708. Even Randall Stewart, who spends much time insisting that Hawthorne is much more of an extrovert than ordinarily believed, feels that he accepted some form of belief in depravity and predestination. See *Nathaniel Hawthorne: A Biography,* New Haven, 1948, pp. 244ff. Richard Fogle straddles the fence with his point that "ambiguity" solves most of the problems concerned with evaluating the philosophy of Hawthorne's fiction. See *Hawthorne's Fiction: The Light and the Dark,* Norman, Okla., 1952, pp. 3-14, *et passim.* 4. Quoted by Robert Cantwell in *Nathaniel Hawthorne: The American Years,* New York, 1948, p. 89. 5. *The Complete Writings of Nathaniel Hawthorne,* The Old Manse edition, ed. by H. E. Scudder, 22 vols., Boston, 1900, Vol. IV, p. 277. Unless otherwise noted, all subsequent citations will be to this edition. When the specific name of the work does not appear in the text, it will be mentioned in the footnote. 6. "The Great Stone Face," Vol. III, p. 55. 7. *Works,* Vol. V, p. 10. 8. "Night Sketches," Vol. II, p. 275. 9. "The Procession of Life," Vol. IV, p. 311. 10. The sermon for "The Feast of S. Martin" describes the virtues of a saint. Rev. M. C. D'Arcy, S.J., selects it as an introduction to St. Thomas himself for the Everyman edition of *Thomas Aquinas: Selected Writings,* New York, 1946, pp. 1-11. 11. *The American Notebooks of Nathaniel Hawthorne,* ed. by Randall Stewart, New Haven, 1932, pp. 97-98. 12. "Night Sketches," Vol. II, p. 271. 13. *Septimus Felton,* Vol. XIV, p. 83. 14. *Notes of Travel,* Vol. XXI, p. 342. 15. *House of the Seven Gables,* Vol. VII, p. 56. 16. Introduction, Stewart's edition of *The American Notebooks,* p. lxxii. 17. Quoted in Turner, Arlin, *Hawthorne as Editor,* Louisiana State University Studies, 42, University, La., 1940, pp. 209-10. 18. Stewart's edition of *The American Notebooks,* p. 98. 19. *The American Notebooks,* Vol. XVIII, p. 143. 20. *Ibid.,* p. 249. 21. Stewart, *Nathaniel Hawthorne: A Biography,* pp. 264-65. 22. "The Artist of the Beautiful," Vol. V, p. 330.

BIBLIOGRAPHY

Arvin, Newton, *Hawthorne,* Boston, 1929.
Bridge, Horatio, *Personal Recollections of Nathaniel Hawthorne,* New York, 1893.
Brownell, W. C., "Hawthorne," in *American Prose Masters,* New York, 1909.
Cantwell, Robert, *Nathaniel Hawthorne: The American Years,* New York, 1948.
Cargill, Oscar, "Nemesis and Nathaniel Hawthorne," in *Publications of the Modern Language Association,* Vol. LII (Sept. 1937), pp. 848-62.
Cowie, Alexander, *The Rise of the American Novel,* New York, 1948.
Davidson, Edward H., *Hawthorne's Last Phase,* New Haven, 1949.
Hall, Lawrence S., *Hawthorne, Critic of Society,* New Haven, 1944.
Haroutunian, Joseph, *Piety Versus Moralism,* New York, 1932.
Hawthorne, Julian, *Hawthorne and His Circle,* New York, 1903.
——, *Hawthorne Reading,* Cleveland, 1902.
——, *Nathaniel Hawthorne and His Wife,* 2 vols., Boston, 1884.
Hawthorne, Nathaniel, *The Complete Writings of Nathaniel Hawthorne,* The Old Manse Edition, ed. by H. E. Scudder, 22 vols., Boston, 1900.
——, *The American Notebooks,* ed. by Randall Stewart, New Haven, 1932.
——, *The English Notebooks,* ed. by Randall Stewart, New York, 1941.
James, Henry, *Hawthorne,* English Men of Letters Series, New York, 1879.
Lathrop, George P., *A Study of Hawthorne,* Boston, 1876.
Lathrop, Rose H., *Memories of Hawthorne,* Boston, 1879.
Loggins, Vernon, *The Hawthornes,* New York, 1951.
Morris, Lloyd, *The Rebellious Puritan: Portrait of Mr. Hawthorne,* New York, 1927.
Schneider, Herbert W., *The Puritan Mind,* New York, 1939.

Stewart, Randall, "Melville and Hawthorne," *South Atlantic Quarterly,* Vol. LI (July 1952), pp. 436-46.

——, *Nathaniel Hawthorne: A Biography,* New Haven, 1948.

Turner, Arlin, "Hawthorne and Reform," *New England Quarterly,* Vol. XV (1942), p. 708.

Van Doren, Carl, *The American Novel,* New York, 1921.

Van Doren, Mark, *Nathaniel Hawthorne,* American Men of Letters Series, New York, 1949.

Waggoner, H. H., *Hawthorne,* Cambridge, 1955.

Warren, Austin, ed., *Nathaniel Hawthorne: Representative Selections,* New York, 1934.

Winters, Yvor, *In Defense of Reason,* New York, 1947.

Woodberry, George E., *Nathaniel Hawthorne,* Boston, 1902.

LONGFELLOW: *Poet of the Feeling Heart*

NOTES

With the exceptions noted below, all quotations from Longfellow's poetry and prose are taken from the Standard Library Edition, edited by Horace E. Scudder: *The Works of Henry Wadsworth Longfellow,* Boston, 1886-1891, 14 vols. This edition includes the *Life of Henry Wadsworth Longfellow* by Samuel Longfellow. Volumes I, II, and III of the *Life* form Volumes XII, XIII, and XIV of the *Works.*

George Thomas Little, *Longfellow's Boyhood Poems,* edited by Ray W. Pettengill, Saratoga Springs, New York, 1925, gives the following poems not included in the Standard Library Edition: "Winter," "There's Not A Cloud," "The Poor Student . . . A Dramatic Sketch," "To the Novice Of The Convent Of The Visitation," "Jepthah's Daughter," "Old Parish Church," "Night-Fall In November," "A Winter's Night," "Valentine," "On A Lock Of Hair," "Youthful Years."

Boston Prize Poems, and Other Specimens of Dramatic Poetry, Boston, Joseph T. Buckingham, at the Office of the New England Galaxy, 1824, contains Longfellow's untitled Shakespearean poem.

Andrew Hilen, *Longfellow and Scandinavia,* Yale Studies in English, Vol. 107, New Haven, 1947, contains Longfellow's untitled poem on death transcribed in his Scandinavian Journal (June 16 to September 24, 1835).

1. Thompson, Lawrance, *Young Longfellow (1807-1843),* New York, 1938, p. 86. 2. *Ibid.,* p. 359. The same quotation in slightly different form is given in Godwin, Parke, *A Biography of William Cullen Bryant,* 2 vols., New York, 1883, Vol. I, p. 193. 3. Little, *op. cit.,* p. 51. 4. *Ibid.,* pp. 25, 26, 32, 35, 36, 35. 5. *Works,* Vol. XIV, p. 411. 6. *Ibid.,* Vol. XII, p. 168. 7. *Ibid.,* Vol. VII, p. 20. 8. *Ibid.,* Vol. IV, p. 19. 9. *Ibid.,* Vol. XII, p. 53. 10. Carman, Bliss, "Longfellow," in *The Poetry of Life,* Boston, 1905, p. 140. 11. Whitman, Iris Lilian, *Longfellow and Spain,* New York 1927, p. 86. 12. Long, Orie William, *Literary Pioneers: Early American Explorers of European Culture,* Cambridge, Mass., 1935, p. 170. 13. Thompson, *op. cit.,* p. 223. Cf. p. 395, note 25. 14. Hilen, *op. cit.,* p. 16 and p. 126, footnote 5. 15. *Works,* Vol. XII, p. 225. 16. Hatfield, James Taft, *Four Lectures Given at German Universities in February 1936,* Evanston, Ill., 1936. 17. *Ibid.,* p. 102. 18. See *Voices of the Night,* in *Works,* Vol. I, especially pp. 20, 22, 23, 25. 19. *Works,* Vol. VIII, p. 275. 20. *Dictionary of American Biography,* Vol. XI, p. 385. 21. Ferguson, John De Lancey, *American Literature in Spain,* New York, 1916, p. 126. Ferguson is quoting the critic Victor Suarez Capalleja. 22. See "The Cross of Snow" by Longfellow. 23. Harriet Monroe in *Poetry,* Vol. XXIX (Feb.

1927), pp. 266-74. 24. See Hawthorne's review of *Evangeline* in the *Salem Advertiser* of Nov. 13, 1847, as quoted by Randall Stewart in "Hawthorne's Contributions to the Salem Advertiser," *American Literature,* Vol. V (Jan. 1934), pp. 327-41. 25. Hawthorne, Manning, and Henry Wadsworth Longfellow Dana, *The Origin and Development of Longfellow's "Evangeline,"* Portland, Maine, 1947, pp. 40-41. 26. *Works,* Vol. VIII, p. 288, and Vol. XIII, p. 135. 27. *Ibid.,* Vol. XIII, p. 151. 28. *Ibid.,* p. 152. 29. "Longfellow's Golden Legend," in *Blackwood's Edinburgh Magazine,* Vol. LXXXI, No. CCCCXXXVI (Feb. 1852), pp. 212-25. 30. Saintsbury, George, "Longfellow's Poems," in *Prefaces and Essays,* London, 1933, p. 332; and Ruskin, John, *Modern Painters,* New York, 1890, Vol. V, p. 367. 31. Carman, Bliss, *op. cit.,* p. 145. 32. Whitman, Walt, "Death of Longfellow," in *The Complete Poetry and Prose of Walt Whitman,* New York, 1948, Vol. II, p. 191. 33. A phrase used by Longfellow in a letter of Dec. 10, 1837, cited by O. W. Long in "Goethe and Longfellow," *Germanic Review,* Vol. VII (April 1932), pp. 145-75. 34. *Works,* Vol. XIV, p. 246. 35. *Ibid.,* Vol. XIII, p. 123. 36. *Ibid.* 37. Rev. I. T. Hecker, "Doctor Brownson and Catholicity," in *The Catholic World,* Vol. XLVI (1887), pp. 222-35. 38. *Works,* Vol. XII, p. 55. 39. *Ibid.* Vol. VII, pp. 220-21. 40. *Ibid.,* Vol. XII, p. 250. 41. *Ibid.,* p. 251. 42. *Ibid.,* Vol. XIII, p. 244. 43. *Ibid.,* p. 125. 44. *Ibid.,* p. 124. 45. *Journal of a Visit to London and the Continent by Herman Melville: 1849-1850,* edited by Eleanor Melville Metcalf, Cambridge, Mass., 1948, p. 62. 46. *Works,* Vol. XIII, p. 400. 47. *Ibid.,* p. 28. 48. *Ibid.,* p. 269. 49. *Ibid.,* p. 405, and cf. Vol. XIV, p. 19. 50. *Ibid.,* Vol. XIII, p. 211. 51. *Ibid.,* p. 277. 52. Strong, Augustus Hopkins, *American Poets and Their Theology,* Philadelphia, 1916, p. 236. 53. *Ibid.,* p. 223. 54. *Works,* Vol. V, p. 124. 55. *Ibid.,* Vol. XIII, p. 218. 56. W. D. Howells, "The Art of Longfellow," *North American Review,* Vol. DCX (March 1, 1907), pp. 472-85. 57. *The Athenaeum,* London, April 1, 1882, p. 412. 58. "The Builders." 59. "A Day of Sunshine." 60. "Pegasus in Pound." 61. "Travels by the Fireside." 62. "The Occultation of Orion." 63. "Palingenesis." 64. *The Golden Legend,* Part IV, "The Cloisters." 65. "The Evening Star." 66. "The Golden Mile-Stone." 67. "Autumn" (1824). 68. "Autumn" (1845). 69. "The Birds of Killingworth." 70. *Works,* Vol. XIII, p. 348. 71. For the expression "the primary facts" I am indebted to H. E. Scudder's excellent article "Longfellow's Art," in *The Atlantic Monthly,* Vol. LIX (March 1887), pp. 398-409. In it he speaks of Longfellow's mind which "by natural disposition busied itself with the secondary rather than the primary facts of nature and society."

SELECTED BIBLIOGRAPHY

BIOGRAPHY

Longfellow, Samuel, *The Life of Henry Wadsworth Longfellow,* 3 vols., Boston, 1891.
Thompson, Lawrance, *Young Longfellow* (1807-1843), New York, 1938.
Wagenknecht, Edward, *Longfellow: A Full-Length Portrait,* New York, 1955.

LONGFELLOW AND OTHER CULTURES

De Armond, Anna Janney, "Longfellow and Germany," *Delaware Notes,* Series 25, Newark, 1952, pp. 15-33.
Goggio, Emilio, "Italian Influences on Longfellow's Works," *The Romanic Review,* Vol. XVI (July-Sept. 1925), pp. 208-22.
Gohdes, Clarence, "Longfellow," in *American Literature in Nineteenth-Century England,* New York, 1944, pp. 99ff.
Hatfield, James Taft, *New Light on Longfellow,* Boston, 1933.
Hecht, David, "Longfellow in Russia," *New England Quarterly,* Vol. XIX (Dec. 1946), pp. 531-34.

Hickey, Richard P., *Catholic Influence on Longfellow*, Kirkwood, Mo., 1928.
Hilen, Andrew, *Longfellow and Scandinavia*, New Haven, 1947.
Johnson, Carl Leonard, *Longfellow and France*, Harvard University, Graduate School of Arts and Sciences, *Summaries of Theses, 1933*, Cambridge, Mass., 1934, pp. 311-12.
La Piana, Angelina, "Henry Wadsworth Longfellow," in *Dante's American Pilgrimage, A Historical Survey of Dante Studies in the United States 1800-1944*, New Haven, 1948.
Long, Orie William, "Henry Wadsworth Longfellow," in *Literary Pioneers*, Cambridge, Mass., 1935, pp. 159ff.
Prichard, John Paul, "The Horatian Influence upon Longfellow," *American Literature* (March 1932), pp. 22-38.
Williams, Stanley T., "Henry Wadsworth Longfellow," in *The Spanish Background of American Literature*, 2 vols., New Haven, 1955, Vol. II, pp. 152ff.

LONGFELLOW AS AN ARTIST

Allen, Gay Wilson, "Henry Wadsworth Longfellow," in *American Prosody*, New York, 1935, pp. 154ff.
Arms, George, "Longfellow," in *The Fields Were Green*, Stanford, 1953, pp. 204ff.
Colton, Arthur, "Longfellow: An Essay in Reputations," *The Bookman*, Vol. LXXVI (Feb. 1933). pp. 128-33.
Elliott, G. R., "Gentle Shades of Longfellow," in *The Cycle of Modern Poetry*, Princeton, 1929, pp. 64ff.
Hearn, Lafcadio, "On a Proper Estimate of Longfellow," in *Interpretations of Literature*, New York, 1917, Vol. II, pp. 167ff.
Howells, William Dean, "The Art of Longfellow," *North American Review*, Vol. DCX (March 1, 1907), pp. 472-85.
Jones, Howard Mumford, "Longfellow," in *American Writers on American Literature*, ed. by John Macy, New York, 1931, pp. 105ff.
More, Paul Elmer, "The Centenary of Longfellow," in *Shelburne Essays*, Fifth Series, Boston, 1908, pp. 132ff.
Noyes, Alfred, "Longfellow and Modern Critics," in *Some Aspects of Modern Poetry*, New York, 1924, pp. 245ff.
Perry, Bliss, "The Centenary of Longfellow," in *Park Street Papers*, Boston, 1908, pp. 105ff.
Pearson, Norman Holmes, "Both Longfellows," *The University of Kansas City Review*, Vol. XVI (Summer 1950), pp. 245-53.
Quinn, Arthur Hobson, "Widening Horizons in Poetry," in *The Literature of the American People*, ed. by Arthur Hobson Quinn, New York, 1951, pp. 322ff.
Scudder, H. E., "Longfellow's Art," *The Atlantic Monthly*, Vol. LIX (March 1887), pp. 398-409.
Shepard, Odell, *Henry Wadsworth Longfellow: Representative Selections*, American Writers Series, New York, 1934, Introduction, pp. xi ff.
Stedman, Edmund Clarence, "Henry Wadsworth Longfellow," in *Poets of America*, Boston, 1885, pp. 180ff.

POE: *The Incorporate Silence and the Heart Divine*

NOTES

1. See Stewart, Randall, and Dorothy Bethurum, *Classic American Fiction*, Chicago, 1954, pp. 8-9. 2. Harrison, James A., ed., *The Complete Works of Edgar Allan Poe*, 17 vols., New York, 1902. This is generally regarded as the most scholarly edition of Poe to date, but because it is difficult to obtain, all direct quotations in this article will be taken from more readily available sources.

3. Woodberry, George E., *The Life of Edgar Allan Poe, Personal and Literary with his Chief Correspondence with Men of Letters.* 2 vols., Boston, 1909. 4. Campbell, Killis, *The Mind of Poe and Other Studies,* Cambridge, Mass., 1933. 5. Quinn, Arthur Hobson, *Edgar Allan Poe: A Critical Biography,* New York, 1941. 6. Brownell, W. C., *American Prose Masters,* Sec. IV, "Poe," New York, 1909. 7. Foerster, Norman, *American Criticism,* Boston, 1928, pp. 1-51. 8. Eliot, T. S., "From Poe to Valery," in *Hudson Review,* Vol. II (1948-9), pp. 327-42. 9. Wilson, Edmund, *Axel's Castle,* New York, 1931. 10. Tate, Allen, *The Forlorn Demon,* Chicago, 1953, pp. 56-95. 11. Cowley, Malcolm, "Aidgarpo," in *The New Republic,* Nov. 5, 1945, pp. 607-10. 12. Winters, Yvor, *Maule's Curse,* Norfolk, Conn., 1938, pp. 121-22. 13. Fagin, N. Bryllion, *The Histrionic Mr. Poe,* Baltimore, 1949, pp. 4-7. 14. Allen, Hervey, *Israfel: The Life and Times of Edgar Allan Poe,* 2 vols., New York, 1926. 15. *Op cit.,* pp. 63-98. 16. Krutch, Joseph Wood, *Edgar Allan Poe: A Study in Genius,* New York, 1926. 17. An excellent recent account of the facts and of the genesis of the legends may be found in Haldeen Braddy's *Glorious Incense,* Washington, D. C., 1953, pp. 150-85. 18. Quoted in Allen, *op. cit.,* Vol. I, p. 203. 19. Quinn, *op. cit.,* p. 129. 20. Campbell, Killis, *The Poems of Edgar Allan Poe,* Toronto, 1917. 21. Jones, J. J., "Poe's 'Nicean Barks,'" *American Literature,* Vol. II (1931), pp. 433-38. 22. *The Works of Edgar Allan Poe,* newly collected and edited, with a Memoir, Critical Introductions, and Notes by Edmund Clarence Stedman and George Edward Woodberry, 10 vols., Chicago, 1894-95, Vol. I, p. 97. This edition was reissued from the same plates by Charles Scribner's Sons, New York, 1914, hereinafter indicated as *Works.* This edition is not complete, but it is available in most libraries. 23. *Works,* Vol. VII, p. 31. 24. "From Poe to Valery," *Hudson Review,* Vol. II (1948-9), p. 327. 25. Alterton, Margaret, *Origins of Poe's Critical Theory,* Ames, Iowa, 1925. 26. Quoted in Hibbard, Addison, *The Book of Poe,* introduction by Hervey Allen, New York, 1929, pp. 154-55. 27. Parrington, Vernon L., *The Romantic Revolution in America,* New York, 1927, pp. 57-59. 28. Williams, William Carlos, *In the American Grain,* New York, 1925, pp. 216-33. 29. *Op. cit.,* p. 225. 30. *Op. cit.,* p. 216. 31. *Works,* Vol. VII, p. 141. 32. Note Francis O. Matthiessen's wise observations on the "Marginalia," in *The Literary History of the United States,* ed. by R. E. Spiller and others, 3 vols., New York, 1948, Vol. I, p. 337. 33. Alterton, Margaret, and Hardin Craig, *Edgar Allan Poe,* American Writers Series, New York, 1935, pp. xxxv-xlii. 34. See Quinn, *op. cit.,* pp. 547-56. 35. *Works,* Vol. IX, p. 82. 36. *Ibid.,* p. 20. 37. Alterton, Margaret, and Hardin Craig, *op. cit., passim,* pp. 437-73. 38. *Works,* Vol. IX, p. 134. 39. Braddy, Haldeen, *op. cit.,* p. 95. 40. Eliot, T. S., *Selected Essays, 1917-1932,* New York, 1932, p. 342. 41. *Op. cit.,* pp. 344-45. 42. Lawrence, D. H., *Studies in Classic American Literature,* New York, 1930, p. 120. 43. *Works,* Vol. IX, p. 115. 44. See Strong, Augustus Hopkins, *American Poets and Their Theology,* Philadelphia. 1916, pp. 161-206.

BIBLIOGRAPHY

Allen, Hervey, *Israfel: The Life and Times of Edgar Allan Poe,* 2 vols., New York, 1926.
Alterton, Margaret, *Origins of Poe's Critical Theory,* Ames, Iowa, 1925.
———, and Hardin Craig, *Edgar Allan Poe,* American Writers Series, New York, 1935.
Auden, W. H., ed., *Edgar Allan Poe, Selected Prose and Poetry,* rev. ed., New York, 1956.
Braddy, Haldeen, *Glorious Incense,* Washington, D. C., 1953.
Brooks, Van Wyck, *The World of Washington Irving,* New York, 1944.
Brownell, W. C., *American Prose Masters,* New York, 1909.
Campbell, Killis, *The Mind of Poe and Other Studies,* Cambridge, Mass., 1933.
Cowley, Malcolm, "Aidgarpo," in *The New Republic,* Nov. 5, 1945.

Eliot, T. S., "From Poe to Valery," in *Hudson Review,* Vol. II (1948-9), pp. 327-42.

———, *Selected Essays, 1917-1932,* New York, 1932.

Fagin, N. Bryllion, *The Histrionic Mr. Poe,* Baltimore, 1949.

Foerster, Norman, *American Criticism,* Boston, 1928.

Harrison, James A., ed., *The Complete Works of Edgar Allan Poe,* 17 vols., New York, 1902.

Hibbard, Addison, *The Book of Poe,* introduction by Hervey Allen, New York, 1929.

Krutch, Joseph Wood, *Edgar Allan Poe: A Study in Genius,* New York, 1926.

Lawrence, D. H., *Studies in Classic American Literature,* New York, 1930.

Matthiessen, F. O., "Edgar Allan Poe," in *Literary History of the United States,* ed. by R. E. Spiller and others, 3 vols., New York, 1948, Vol. I.

Parrington, Vernon L., *Main Currents in American Thought,* 3 vols., New York, 1927-1930, Vol. II.

Quinn, Arthur Hobson, *Edgar Allan Poe: A Critical Biography,* New York, 1941.

———, and E. H. O'Neill, eds., *The Complete Poems and Short Stories of Edgar Allan Poe,* 2 vols., New York, 1946.

Stedman, Clarence, and George Edward Woodberry, eds., *The Works of Edgar Allan Poe,* 10 vols., Chicago, 1894-95.

Stewart, Randall, and Dorothy Bethurum, *Classic American Fiction,* Chicago, 1954.

Strong, Augustus Hopkins, *American Poets and Their Theology,* Philadelphia, 1916.

Tate, Allen, *The Forlorn Demon,* Chicago, 1953.

Williams, William Carlos, *In the American Grain,* Norfolk, Conn., 1939.

Wilson, Edmund, *Axel's Castle,* New York, 1931.

Winters, Yvor, *Maule's Curse,* New York, 1938.

Woodberry, George E., *The Life of Edgar Allan Poe, Personal and Literary with His Chief Correspondence with Men of Letters,* 2 vols., Boston, 1909.

Thoreau: *Christian Malgré Lui*

NOTES

1. Cf. Vernon L. Parrington: "Walden is the handbook of an economy that endeavors to refute Adam Smith and transform the round of daily life into something more than a mean gospel of plus and minus." *Main Currents in American Thought,* 3 vols., New York, 1927-1930, Vol. II, p. 400. 2. Cf. Spiller, R. E., and others, eds., *Literary History of the United States,* 3 vols., New York, 1948, Vol. I, p. 401. 3. Cf. Krutch, Joseph Wood, *Henry David Thoreau,* New York, 1948, p. 93. 4. Introduction, *Metaphysical Lyrics and Poems of the Seventeenth Century, Donne to Butler,* New York, 1921, pp. xiii-xiv. 5. *Thoreau,* Boston, 1938, p. 90. 6. *Ibid.,* p. 97. 7. Thoreau, *Writings,* Walden Edition, Boston, 1916, Vol. VI, p. 175. 8. *Walden,* Walden Edition, Vol. II, p. 8. 9. *Ibid.,* p. 23. 10. *Ibid.,* pp. 123-24. 11. *Ibid.,* pp. 107-08. 12. *Ibid.,* p. 90. 13. *Ibid.,* p. 92. 14. *Writings,* Vol. IV, p. 368. 15. *Walden,* Walden Edition, Vol. II, pp. 100-01. 16. *Ibid.,* pp. 5-6. 17. *Writings,* Vol. IV, p. 461. 18. *Ibid.,* pp. 459-60. 19. *Walden,* Walden Edition, Vol. II, p. 241. 20. *Ibid.,* p. 243. 21. *Thoreau,* p. 272. 22. *American Renaissance,* New York, 1941, pp. 166-75. 23. Cf. Wellek, René, "The Concept of Baroque in Literary Scholarship," *Journal of Aesthetics and Art Criticism,* Vol. V (1946), pp. 77-109. An attempt has recently been made to give greater specificity to the meaning of "baroque" by transferring a part of its burden to another term, "mannerist," also borrowed from the vocabulary of art criticism. But perhaps this involves more difficulties than advantages. Cf. Sypher, Wylie, *Four Stages of Renaissance Style,* New York, 1955.

BIBLIOGRAPHY

Allen, Francis, *Bibliography of Thoreau,* Boston, 1908.

Brooks, Van Wyck, *The Flowering of New England,* New York, 1936, pp. 286-302, 359-73, 422-42, *et passim.*

Buckley, Frank, "Thoreau and the Irish," *New England Quarterly,* Vol. XIII (1940), pp. 389-400.

Cameron, K. W., "Emerson, Thoreau and the Society of Natural History," *American Literature,* Vol. XXIV (1953), pp. 21-30.

Canby, Henry Seidel, *Thoreau,* Boston, 1939.

Collins, Thomas L., "Thoreau's Coming of Age," *Sewanee Review,* Vol. XLIX (1941), pp. 57-66.

Dabbs, James McBride, "Thoreau—The Adventure As Economist," *Yale Review,* Vol. XXXVI (1947), pp. 666-72.

Emerson, R. W., "Biographical Sketch," prefixed to Vol. I of Walden edition of Thoreau, Boston, 1916.

Gruber, Christian P., "The Education of Henry Thoreau, Harvard 1833-37," *Dissertation Abstracts,* Vol. XIV, p. 972. (Abstract of Princeton University dissertation.)

Harding, Walter, *A Centennial Check-List of the Editions of Henry Thoreau's Walden,* Charlottesville, Va., 1954.

Hicks, Granville, *The Great Tradition,* New York, 1933, pp. 9-10, *et passim.*

Kwiat, Joseph J., "Thoreau's Philosophical Apprenticeship," *New England Quarterly,* Vol. XVIII (1945), pp. 51-69.

Lorch, Fred W., "Thoreau and the Organic Principle of Poetry," *Publications of the Modern Language Association,* Vol. LIII (1938), pp. 286-302.

Lowell, J. R., "Thoreau," in *My Study Windows,* New York, 1899.

Ludlow, Robert, "Thoreau and the State," *Commonweal,* Vol. L (1949), pp. 581-82.

Manning, Clarence A., "Thoreau and Tolstoi," *New England Quarterly,* Vol. XVI (1943), pp. 234-43.

Matthiessen, F. O., *American Renaissance,* New York, 1941, pp. 76-119, 166-75.

More, Paul Elmer, "A Hermit's Notes on Thoreau," *Shelburne Essays,* Vol. I, New York, 1907.

———, "Thoreau's Journal," *Shelburne Essays,* Vol. V, Boston, 1908.

Parrington, Vernon L., *Main Currents in American Thought,* 3 vols., New York, 1927-1930, Vol. II.

Seybold, Ethel, *Thoreau: The Quest and the Classics,* New Haven, 1951.

Shanley, James Lyndon, "A Study of the Making of Walden," *Harvard Literary Quarterly,* Vol. XIV (1951), pp. 147-170.

Spiller, R. E., and others, eds., *Literary History of the United States,* 3 vols., New York, 1948.

Stevenson, R. L., "Henry David Thoreau: His Character and Opinions," *Familiar Studies of Men and Books,* New York, 1924, pp. 120 sq.

Stewart, Charles D., "A Word for Thoreau," *Atlantic Monthly,* Vol. CLVI (1935), pp. 110-16.

Thoreau, Henry David, Walden Edition, 20 vols., Boston, 1916. Other authorized editions which are without the complete *Journal* are the Riverside Edition, 11 vols., Boston, 1894, and the Riverside Pocket Edition, 11 vols., Boston, 1915.

Van Doren, Mark, *Henry David Thoreau: A Critical Study,* 1916.

Whicher, George Frisbie, *Walden Revisited,* Chicago, 1945.

White, William, *A Henry David Thoreau Bibliography 1908-1937,* Boston, 1939. Originally published in *Bulletin of Bibliography,* Vol. XVI, 1936-1939.

MELVILLE: *Loyalty to the Heart*

NOTES

1. Melville, Herman, "Hawthorne and His Mosses," in *The Shock of Recognition,* ed. by Edmund Wilson, New York, 1955, p. 193. 2. Weaver, Raymond M., *Herman Melville: Mariner and Mystic,* New York, 1921. 3. *Moby-Dick,* New York, 1931, pp. 144-45. 4. I speak only of personal involvement so far as it affects the novels. If we wish to make biographical inferences, we can note that *Mardi* ends wearily and that *Moby-Dick* is unflagging throughout. "I have written a wicked book," said Melville of the latter, "and feel spotless as a lamb." 5. Melville, *Journal of a Visit to Europe and the Levant, Oct. 11, 1856—May 6, 1857,* edited by Howard C. Horsford, Princeton, 1955, p. 118. 6. *Ibid.,* pp. 123-24. 7. Melville, *Clarel: A Poem and Pilgrimage in The Holy Land,* London, 1924, Vol. I, p. 121. 8. *Ibid.,* Vol. I, p. 116. 9. *Ibid.,* Vol. II, pp. 242-43. 10. *Ibid.,* Vol. I, p. 51.

SELECTED BIBLIOGRAPHY

A complete and definitive edition of Melville's works does not yet exist, but one is in course of publication by Hendricks House, Putney, Vermont, of which the following volumes, with informative introductions and all the appurtenances of modern scholarship, have so far appeared:

Collected Poems, ed. by Howard P. Vincent, 1946.
The Confidence-Man, ed. by Elizabeth S. Foster, 1954.
Moby-Dick or *The Whale,* ed. by Luther S. Mansfield and Howard P. Vincent, 1952.
The Piazza Tales, ed. by Egbert S. Oliver, 1948.
Pierre or *The Ambiguities,* ed. by Henry A. Murray, 1949.

The following two projected volumes in this series will be published in 1957:
Clarel, ed. by Walter Bezanson.
Melville Handbook, by Harrison Hayford.

Probably all of Melville's surviving letters are to be found in Jay Leyda's two-volume documentary collection, *The Melville Log,* New York, 1951. Among other biographies and/or studies of Melville's work, in general or in particular aspects, are:

Arvin, Newton, *Herman Melville,* American Men of Letters, New York, 1950.
Braswell, William, *Melville's Religious Thought,* Durham, N. C., 1943.
Davis, Morrell R., *Melville's Mardi,* New Haven, 1952.
Geist, Stanley, *Herman Melville: The Tragic Vision and the Heroic Ideal,* Cambridge, Mass., 1939.
Gilman, William H., *Melville's Early Life and Redburn,* New York, 1951.
Howard, Leon, *Herman Melville: A Biography,* Berkeley and Los Angeles, 1951.
Mason, Ronald, *The Spirit above the Dust,* London, 1951.
Metcalf, Eleanor Melville, *Herman Melville: Cycle and Epicycle,* Cambridge, Mass., 1953.
Pommer, Henry F., *Milton and Melville,* Pittsburgh, 1950.
Percival, M. O., *A Reading of Moby-Dick,* Chicago, 1950.
Rosenberry, Edward H., *Melville and the Comic Spirit,* Cambridge, Mass., 1955.
Sedgwick, William Ellery, *Herman Melville: The Tragedy of Mind,* Cambridge, Mass., 1945.
Stone, Geoffrey, *Melville,* New York, 1949.

Thompson, Lawrance, *Melville's Quarrel with God*, Princeton, 1952.
Vincent, Howard P., *The Trying-Out of Moby-Dick*, Boston, 1949.
Wright, Nathalia, *Melville's Use of the Bible*, Durham, N. C., 1949.

Considerations of Melville, or material concerning him, occur in the following books and periodicals:
Auden, W. H., *The Enchafèd Flood*, New York, 1950.
Belgion, Montgomery, Introduction to *Moby-Dick*, London, 1946.
Beverly, Gordon, "Herman Melville's Confidence," *Times Literary Supplement* (London), Nov. 11, 1949.
Brooks, Van Wyck, *The Times of Melville and Whitman*, New York, 1947.
Blackmur, R. P., *The Expense of Greatness*, New York, 1940.
Curl, Vega, *Pasteboard Masks*, Cambridge, Mass., 1931.
Eliot, Alexander, "Melville and Bartleby," *Furioso*, Fall 1947.
Feidelson, Charles, *Symbolism and American Literature*, Chicago, 1953.
Forster, E. M., *Aspects of the Novel*, New York, 1927.
Forsythe, Robert S., Introduction to *Pierre*, New York, 1930.
Hillway, Tyrus, "Taji's Abdication in Herman Melville's *Mardi*," *American Literature*, November 1944.
Lawrence, D. O., *Studies in Classic American Literature*, New York, 1922.
Matthiessen, F. O., *American Renaissance*, New York, 1941.
Thorp, Willard, Introduction to *Moby-Dick*, New York, 1947.
Tomlinson, H. M., Preface to *Pierre*, New York, 1929.
Winters, Yvor, *Maule's Curse*, Norfolk, Conn., 1938.

WHITMAN: *Ego in New Eden*

NOTES

1. Holloway, Emory, *The Uncollected Poetry and Prose of Walt Whitman*, New York, 1921, Vol. II, p. 66.   2. Whitman seems to have anticipated the twentieth-century Personalist Movement not only in being the first to use the term "Personalism" but in his concept of the self. He did not, of course, make the elaborate and careful distinctions between the individual and the person which Maritain and Mounier have made, but in certain passages he made it clear enough that the real self was not to be identified with accidental and material accessories. (See Section 4, "Song of Myself.") Also the self, in his view, though inviolate and distinctive, was drawn naturally toward and not away from the human community.   3. Wilson, Edmund, ed., *The Shock of Recognition*, New York, 1947, p. 297.   4. Traubel, H. L.; R. M. Bucke; and T. B. Harned, eds., *In Re Walt Whitman*, Philadelphia, 1893, p. 13. Also in Untermeyer, Louis, ed., *The Poetry and Prose of Walt Whitman*, New York, 1949, p. 531.   5. Rourke, Constance, *American Humor: A Study of the National Character*, New York, 1953, p. 65.   6. *Ibid.*, pp. 40, 44, 45.   7. Traubel, *et al., op. cit.*, pp. 19-20.   8. For these lines and for the three preceding quotations from the first edition, see *Leaves of Grass*, 1955, pp. 13, 14, 29, 30, respectively.   9. "Some Lines from Whitman," in *Poetry and the Age*, New York, p. 106.   10. *Leaves*, 1855, pp. 14, 25, 26.   11. Holloway, *op. cit.*, Vol. II, p. 68.   12. *Ibid.*, p. 71.   13. *Leaves*, 1855, pp. 27, 28.   14. Title changed to "Starting from Paumanok" in 1867.   15. *Leaves*, 1855, p. iii.   16. Holloway, *op. cit.*, Vol. II, p. 63.   17. Bucke, R. M., ed., *The Wound Dresser*, Boston, 1898, reissued, 1949, p. 32 (in 1949 edition).   18. *Ibid.*, p. 116.   19. *Ibid.*, pp. 128-29.   20. *Leaves*, 1855, pp. 44, 45, 56.   21. *Leaves*, 1855, pp. 15-16.   22. Furness, C. J., ed., *Walt Whitman's Workshop*, Cambridge, 1928, p. 136.   23. Rougemont, Denis de, *Passion and Society*, trans. by M. Belgion, London, 1940, p. 74. The original was published in Paris under the title *L'Amour et l'Occident*, 1939. The American title of the same English

translation is *Love in the Western World*. 24. Furness, *op. cit.*, p. 49. 25. Traubel, H. L., *With Walt Whitman in Camden* (March 28–July 14, 1888), Boston, 1906, p. 110. 26. *Leaves*, 1855, p. 51. 27. Kierkegaard, Sören, *Either/ Or*, trans. by Walter Lowrie, Princeton, 1944, Vol. II, p. 178. 28. *Ibid.*, p. 177. 29. *Ibid.*, p. 216. 30. *Ibid.*, pp. 216-17. 31. *Ibid.*, p. 214. 32. *Ibid.*, p. 277. 33. *Ibid.*, pp. 181-82. 34. *Ibid.*, p. 182. 35. *Ibid.*, p. 182. 36. *Ibid.*, p. 210. 37. Kierkegaard, Sören, *The Point of View*, trans. by Walter Lowrie, London, 1939, p. 155.

BIBLIOGRAPHY

EDITIONS OF WALT WHITMAN'S WRITINGS

Only the editions which are of most interest to the nonspecialist student of Whitman are listed here. For a complete bibliography and description of all editions of Whitman's writings, see G. W. Allen's *Walt Whitman Handbook*, Chap. II, pp. 104-235.

Leaves of Grass. By Walt Whitman. Reproduced from the First Edition (1855), with an Introduction by Clifton Joseph Furness. Published for the Facsimile Text Society. New York, 1939.
Leaves of Grass. Philadelphia, 1891-92.
[This ninth edition of Leaves, commonly referred to as the "deathbed" edition, was the last to be supervised by Whitman himself. As the final authorized text it is the basis of all later editions. A notice by Whitman reads, in part: "As there are now several editions of L. of G., different texts and different dates, I wish to say that I prefer and recommend this present one, complete, for future printing, if there should be any . . ."]
The Complete Writings of Walt Whitman. Issued under the editorial supervision of the Literary Executors, Richard Maurice Bucke, Thomas B. Harned, and Horace L. Traubel, with additional bibliographical and critical material by Oscar Lovell Triggs, Ph. D. 10 vols. New York and London, 1902.
[Besides Whitman's *Leaves* and collected prose, this edition contains a long biographical introduction by the editors, Whitman's letters to his mother (Vol. VIII), and *Notes and Fragments* (Vol. IX) edited by R. M. Bucke for publication in 1899.]
Leaves of Grass. Ed. Emory Holloway. Inclusive edition. Garden City, 1926. (Many reprints.)
[The standard modern text. In addition to the authorized text of *Leaves of Grass*, it contains a section of "Rejected Poems" (earlier poems rejected by Whitman in later editions and in the authorized final edition of *Leaves*) (pp. 465-87), the Prefaces (pp. 488-539), and Variorum Readings (pp. 541-709).]
The Complete Poetry and Prose of Walt Whitman. As Prepared by Him for the Deathbed Edition. With an Introduction by Malcolm Cowley. In two vols. New York, 1948.
[Combines the ninth edition of *Leaves of Grass* and *Complete Prose Works* (1892). Provides the student with the authorized complete works in a compact, attractive form.]
The Poetry and Prose of Walt Whitman. Ed. Louis Untermeyer. The Inner Sanctum Edition. New York, 1949.
[A useful volume for the Whitman student. It contains the authorized text of *Leaves*, selected prose, a selection of letters, a selection of critical commentary chronologically arranged from Emerson to Matthiessen, and a bibliography.]
There are several good, inexpensive texts of *Leaves* which usually include a selection of prose writings as well. Among the best of the paperback editions are:

Walt Whitman: "Leaves of Grass" and Selected Prose. Ed. with an Introduction
    by Sculley Bradley. Rinehart Editions, No. 28. New York, 1949.
"Leaves of Grass" and Selected Prose. Ed. with an Introduction by John Kou-
    wenhoven. Modern Library College Editions, No. T40. New York, 1950.
On December 1, 1955, the New York University Press announced a projected
edition of *The Writings of Walt Whitman* in 12 vols. under the general editorship of Gay Wilson Allen. This edition, as planned, will include a variorum
edition of *Leaves,* early poems, essays, short stories, *Franklin Evans* (Whitman's
temperance novel), newspaper editorials and articles, note books, diaries, letters,
and an extensive bibliography. According to the announcement, "The first two
volumes will be published in the spring of 1957. It is expected that the entire
edition will be available within five or six years." This edition ought to fill a
long-felt need and will probably be regarded as the standard text for our time.

THE UNCOLLECTED WRITINGS

Several volumes of uncollected materials have been published since Whitman's
death. Among the most illuminating for the student of *Leaves* are the following:
The Wound Dresser. A Series of Letters Written from the Hospitals in Washing-
    ton during the War of Rebellion by Walt Whitman. Ed. Richard Maurice
    Bucke, M.D. Boston, 1898. Reissued, with an Introduction by Oscar Cargill.
    The Bodley Press, 1949.
    [These letters reveal why Whitman's hospital experience during the Civil
    War had such a decisive effect in confirming his faith in his countrymen,
    in himself and in his poetry.]
The Uncollected Poetry and Prose of Walt Whitman. Ed. Emory Holloway. 2
    vols. New York, 1921. Reprinted, New York, 1932.
    [The richest and most rewarding of all the compilations of uncollected
    materials that have been made. Especially interesting are the notebooks
    with their early drafts of certain poems in *Leaves.*]
Walt Whitman's Workshop. Ed. Clifton Joseph Furness. Cambridge, 1928.
    [A valuable collection of unpublished prefaces, speeches, notes for projected
    lectures, etc.]
*Faint Clews and Indirections: The Manuscripts of Walt Whitman and His
    Family.* Ed. Clarence Gohdes and Rollo G. Silver. Durham, 1949.
    [This book provides an intimate view of Whitman's family which is quite
    different from the impression that Whitman himself created even among
    his friends and disciples.]

BIOGRAPHY AND CRITICISM

From the vast literature of Whitman biography, scholarship, and criticism
which exists only a few books and articles are listed here. An attempt has
been made to select those works which have contributed most significantly to
the present generally accepted informed view of Whitman as a person and as a
poet.
Allen, Gay Wilson, *Walt Whitman Handbook,* Chicago, 1946.
    [An account of the growth of the Whitman canon and a critical digest of
    Whitman scholarship and criticism from the beginning to the date of
    publication. An indispensable aid to any serious study of Whitman.]
———, *The Solitary Singer: A Critical Biography of Walt Whitman,* New York,
    1955.
    [The definitive biography for our day with critical analyses of many of
    the poems.]
———, ed., *Walt Whitman Abroad: Foreign Criticism in Translation,* Syracuse,
    1955.
Arvin, Newton, *Whitman,* New York, 1938.
    [Emphasizes Whitman's social and political thought.]

Asselineau, Roger, *L'Evolution de Walt Whitman: après la première edition des Feuilles d'Herbe*, Paris, 1954.
[Using the poems as autobiographical data, the author traces the influence of Whitman's homosexual impulses upon his career as a poet.]

Canby, Henry Seidel, *Walt Whitman: An American*, Boston, 1943.
[Based on the thesis that "the clues to the so-called mystery of Walt Whitman are not to be found in unrevealed scraps of personal experience, but in the unique history of the electric America in which he matured . . . and in his inner life, as conditioned by his youth in that America."]

Catel, Jean, *Walt Whitman: la naissance du poète*, Paris, 1929.
[A psychological study and one of the first biographies to bring Whitman into the perspective in which he is generally seen today.]

Chase, Richard, *Walt Whitman Reconsidered*, New York, 1955.

Cowley, Malcolm, "Whitman: The Poet and the Mask," Introduction to *The Complete Poetry and Prose of Walt Whitman*, New York, 1948.
[A persuasive plea for a radical revision of the conventional picture of Whitman and a preliminary sketch of the new portrait which is to be painted. "What we have to rediscover is the Whitman who wasn't acting, who spoke from the depths of his nature and wrote the greatest poems of his time. We have to rescue him from the pundits and politicians and give his work back to poetry."]

Fausset, Hugh l'Anson, *Walt Whitman: Poet of Democracy*, New Haven, 1942.
[Whitman is seen here as a man in whom the receptive feminine sensibility and the masculine will to act were imperfectly balanced.]

Hindus, Maurice, ed., *Leaves of Grass One Hundred Years After*, Stanford, 1955.
[Essays by William Carlos Williams, David Daiches, Richard Chase, Leslie Fiedler, Kenneth Burke, and John Middleton Murry.]

Holloway, Emory, *Whitman: An Interpretation in Narrative*, New York, 1926.
[An important biography by one of the most eminent of Whitman scholars.]

Jarrell, Randall, "Some Lines from Whitman," in *Poetry and the Age*, New York, 1953.
[Brings out the poetic precision of word and phrase as well as the unique personal quality in many of Whitman's lines.]

Matthiessen, F. O., "Whitman," in *American Renaissance*, New York, 1941, pp. 516-656.
[One of the best critical studies of Whitman's poetic art, seen in relation to the intellectual and cultural milieu.]

Perry, Bliss, *Walt Whitman: His Life and Work*, New York, 1906.
[The first biography to be written from a detached, scholarly point of view and still regarded as a classic in Whitman scholarship.]

Schyberg, Frederik, *Walt Whitman*, translated from the Danish by Evie Allison Allen, with an Introduction by Gay Wilson Allen, New York, 1951.
[Schyberg was the first to study the biographical implications of the revisions made in different editions of *Leaves* and to see the critical importance of the 1860 edition. In a final chapter he tries to place Whitman in the context of world literature.]

Van Doren, Mark, "Walt Whitman, Stranger," in *The Private Reader*, New York, 1942.
[A not unsympathetic yet a steady and unillusioned look at the strange, lonely man whom informed readers in the middle of the twentieth century have come to recognize as the real Walt Whitman.]

Wilson, Edmund, ed., "Emerson and Whitman," in *The Shock of Recognition: The Development of Literature in the United States Recorded by the Men Who Made It*, New York, 1947.
[A fully documented account of the relationship between these two writers, one of the most interesting of such relationships in American literary history.]

BIBLIOGRAPHICAL AND OTHER STUDY AIDS

Allen, Gay Wilson, *Walt Whitman Handbook,* Chicago, 1946.
    [Contains the most extensive bibliographies to date as well as excellent
    critical summaries of Whitman biography and criticism.]
Eby, Edwin Harold, *A Concordance of Walt Whitman's LEAVES OF GRASS
    and Selected Prose Writings,* Including Democratic Vistas; A Backward
    Glance O'er Travel'd Roads; Preface to the 1855 Edition; Preface, 1872;
    Preface, 1876; and Preface Note to 2nd Annex. In five fascicles. Seattle,
    1949-1955.
Wells, Carolyn, and Alfred F. Goldsmith, *A Concise Bibliography of the Works
    of Walt Whitman with a Supplement of Fifty Books about Whitman,*
    Boston and New York, 1922.

WADE: *The Brahmins Contemplate the Past*

NOTES

1. Ford, W. C., ed., *Letters of Henry Adams, 1858-1891,* Boston, 1930, p. 228.   2.
Nye, Russell B., *George Bancroft,* New York, 1944, p. 102.   3. Ticknor, George,
Life of William Hickling Prescott, Boston, 1860, p. 164.   4. *Ibid.,* p. 141.   5. *Ibid.,*
p. 305.   6. *A History of the Reign of Ferdinand and Isabella, the Catholic*
(1474-1517), *A History of the Conquest of Mexico* (1519-1521), *A History of
the Conquest of Peru* (1524-1550), and *A History of the Reign of Philip the
Second* (1556-1574). He also wrote "The Life of Charles V after His Abdication"
(1556-1588) as a new conclusion to William Robertson's *The History of the
Reign of Charles V* for the Boston edition of 1857, declining to prepare an
entirely new account of the period to replace a work he much admired.   7.
Ferdinand and Isabella, Vol. II, p. 109.   8. Hellman, G. S., *Washington Irving,
Esquire,* New York, 1925, p. 236.   9. Wolcott, R., ed., *The Correspondence of
W. H. Prescott,* Boston, 1925, p. 54.   10. Prescott, W. H., *Biographical and Critical
Miscellanies,* New York, 1850, p. 298-99.   11. Ticknor, *op. cit.,* p. 217.   12. *Ibid.,*
p. 251.   13. *Ibid.,* p. 217.   14. Wolcott, *op. cit.,* p. 178.   15. *Ticknor, op. cit.,* p.
353.   16. Penney, C. L., ed., *Prescott, Unpublished Letters to Gayangos,* New
York, 1927, p. 372.   17. Prescott, *Miscellanies,* p. 284.   18. Whipple, E. P.,
Recollections of Eminent Men, Boston, 1887, p. 164.   19. Curtis, G. W., ed.,
Correspondence of J. L. Motley, New York, 1889, Vol. I, p. 368.   20. "Policy
of the Puritans," *North American Review,* Vol. LXIX (October 1849), p. 477.
21. Adams, Henry, *The Education of Henry Adams,* New York, 1933, p. 237.
22. *Dutch Republic,* Vol. I, p. iv.   23. Holmes, O. W., *J. L. Motley, A Memoir,*
Boston, 1878, p. 394.   24. M. Wade, *Francis Parkman: Heroic Historian,* New
York, 1942, p. 441.

SELECTED BIBLIOGRAPHY

George Bancroft, by Russell B. Nye, New York, 1944, is a scholarly critical
    biography, which should be used with the Centenary Edition of Bancroft.
Lothrop Motley, by Chester Penn Higby and B. T. Schantz, New York, 1939.
Francis Parkman, by Wilbur L. Schramm, New York, 1938.
William Hickling Prescott, by Michael Kraus and William Charvat, New York,
    1943.
These last three volumes are in the American Writers Series and contain
representative selections and valuable introductions, bibliographies and notes to
which I am indebted.

APPENDIX II

NOTES ON CONTRIBUTORS

ROBERT C. POLLOCK

ROBERT C. POLLOCK received his B.S. and M.A. degrees from Harvard University and his Ph.D. from the University of Toronto. He was instructor and then assistant professor at the University of Notre Dame from 1932 to 1936. He is now professor of philosophy at Fordham University's Graduate School, where he has been since 1936. He collaborated in Don Luigi Sturzo's *Del Metodo Sociologico* (1950), is editor of *The Mind of Pius XII* (1955), and contributes to several scholarly journals. His essay on William James appeared in the fourth volume of *The Great Books: A Christian Appraisal* (1951).

CHARLES A. BRADY

CHARLES A. BRADY attended Canisius High School and College and Harvard University. He has been professor of English and head of the department at Canisius College since 1938 and from 1938 to 1940 he was director of graduate studies in English. A book columnist on the *Buffalo Evening News* since 1945, Charles Brady has himself published the *First Book of Canisius Verse* (1932), *Wings over Patmos* (1951), *Cat Royal* (1947), *A Catholic Reader* (1947), *Reclaim Imagination* (1953), *Stage of Fools* (1953), and *Viking Summer* (1956). He is a member of the Harvard Club and St. Ansgar's Scandinavian Catholic League.

ALVAN S. RYAN

DR. RYAN did his undergraduate studies at the University of Massachusetts. He received his M.A. in English philology from Harvard and his doctorate in English from the State University of Iowa. He has been on the English faculties of the University of Massachusetts and of Wellesley College and is at present associate professor of English at the University of Notre Dame. During 1955-56 he was Visiting Fellow in English and Faculty Fellowship from The Fund for the Advancement of Education, Princeton University. He is a member of the Modern Language Association and of the American Association of University Professors. He is author of *Newman's Conception of Literature* (The State University of Iowa, 1942), *The Brownson Reader* (1955), and has contributed essays to *La Civilisation Américaine* (edited by Yves Simon, 1950) and to *A Newman Symposium* (edited by Victor Yanitelli, S.J., 1952). His essays and reviews have appeared in *America, Mercure de France, Modern Language Quarterly, Review of Politics, Thought, The Yale Review,* and other periodicals, chiefly on nineteenth-century and contemporary English and American literature.

JOSEPH SCHWARTZ

Born in Milwaukee in 1925 and a student in private schools in Wisconsin before entering college, Joseph Schwartz received the Bachelor's degree in 1946 and Master's in 1947 from Marquette University. He was awarded the Doctor of

Philosophy degree by the University of Wisconsin in 1952. From 1946 to 1948
he taught at Marquette University and from 1948 to 1950 he was on the faculty
of the University of Wisconsin. He is presently assistant professor in the
Department of English and chairman of Freshman English at Marquette.
Articles and reviews by Dr. Schwartz have appeared in *Modern Language Notes,
Speech Activities, La Croix,* and *America.* His television program, "The
American Idea," regularly deals with the formers of the American mind in an
attempt to discover the roots of our national culture.

REV. JOSEPH E. O'NEILL, S.J.

FATHER O'NEILL made his theological studies at Louvain, Belgium, being
ordained there in 1940. He received the degree of M.A. from Fordham University in 1946 and his Ph.D. from Columbia University in 1955 in the field of
American literature, his thesis being devoted to Longfellow. He is associate
professor of English at Fordham, his courses concentrating on American literature. In 1956 he was appointed editor-in-chief of *Thought,* the scholarly quarterly published by the University.

JEREMIAH K. DURICK

JEREMIAH K. DURICK received his A.B. degree from St. Michael's College, after
which he studied at Notre Dame, Fordham, and Harvard Universities. He was
granted an M. A. degree from St. Michael's, a Ph.D. from Ottawa University.
Dr. Durick taught at Fair Haven High School, where he also served as assistant
principal, and then joined the St. Michael's College faculty where he is now
chairman of the English Department and director of the Summer Session. His
publications include *The Catholic Church in Vermont—A Centenary History*
(1953), "Newman as a Man of Letters" (in *A Newman Symposium,* 1953), and
contributions to *Commonweal, College English, English Journal, The Critic,
Catholic Educational Review, Vermont History, Spirit, The Carillon, Contemporary Verse,* and *NCEA Newsletter.* He is a member of the Modern
Language Association, the Vermont Historical Society, and the Vermont Poetry
Society.

MICHAEL F. MOLONEY

MICHAEL F. MOLONEY is at present professor of English at Marquette University.
A graduate of Notre Dame University, he holds an M. A. from Georgetown
University and a Ph.D. from the University of Illinois. He has contributed to
*Publications of the Modern Language Association, Journal of English and
Germanic Philology, Modern Language Quarterly, Notes and Queries,* and is
the author of *John Donne: His Flight From Mediaevalism,* University of
Illinois Studies in Language and Literature.

GEOFFREY STONE

MR. STONE has been an editorial assistant on *The Bookman* and an associate
editor of the *American Review.* He is the author of *Herman Melville: A Critical
Biography* (Sheed and Ward, 1949) and has edited, in collaboration with Erik
von Kuehnelt-Leddihn, an international collection of intellectual autobiographies,
The Return to Principle, to be published by the Henry Regnery Company. His
articles have appeared in *Thought, Blackfriars,* and other journals.

ERNEST SANDEEN

DR. SANDEEN is a graduate of Knox College, Galesburg, Ill., where he taught from 1935 to 1937. He received the degree of B. Litt. from Oxford University and his doctorate from the State University of Iowa, where he taught from 1937 to 1943. He is at present professor of English at the University of Notre Dame. His critical articles, appearing in such journals as *America*, the *Review of Politics*, *PMLA*, etc., have concentrated on studies in James, Faulkner, and Emerson. His poems have appeared in the *New Yorker, Poetry* (Chicago), the *Yale Review, Contemporary Poetry*, and *Commonweal*. A volume of his poems, *Antennas of Silence*, has been published by Contemporary Poetry (Baltimore, 1953).

MASON WADE

MASON WADE is Director of Canadian Studies and associate professor of history at the University of Rochester. He is the author of *Margaret Fuller* (Viking: New York, 1940), *Francis Parkman* (Viking: New York, 1942); *The French-Canadian Outlook* (Viking: New York, 1946), and *The French Canadians, 1760-1945* (Macmillan: New York, 1955); and editor of *The Selected Writings of Margaret Fuller* (Viking: New York, 1941); *The Oregon Trail* (Limited Editions Club: New York, 1943); *The Journals of Francis Parkman* (Harper, New York, 1948). He is a frequent contributor to *Commonweal*, the *New York Times Book Review*, the *New York Herald-Tribune Books*, and the *Canadian Historical Review*.

REV. HAROLD C. GARDINER, S.J.

ORDAINED in 1935, Father Gardiner received a Ph.D. in English literature from Cambridge University, England. He was appointed Literary Editor of *America*, National Catholic weekly review, in 1940. In addition to regular articles and reviews in that journal, he is author of *Mysteries' End* (1942), *Tenets for Readers and Reviewers* (1945), *Norms for the Novel* (1953), *Edmund Campion: Hero of God's Underground* (1957) and *Catholic Viewpoint on Censorship* (1958). He has edited *The Great Books: a Christian Appraisal* (4 vols, 1948-1952), *Fifty Years of the American Novel* (1951) and a modernized version of *The Imitation of Christ* (1956).